CAMBRIDGE TEXTS IN THE
HISTORY OF POLITICAL THOUGHT

———

ROUSSEAU
The Social Contract and other later
political writings

CAMBRIDGE TEXTS IN THE HISTORY OF POLITICAL THOUGHT

Series editors

RAYMOND GEUSS
Reader in Philosophy, University of Cambridge

QUENTIN SKINNER
Regius Professor of Modern History in the University of Cambridge

Cambridge Texts in the History of Political Thought is now firmly established as the major student textbook series in political theory. It aims to make available to students all the most important texts in the history of western political thought, from ancient Greece to the early twentieth century. All the familiar classic texts will be included, but the series does at the same time seek to enlarge the conventional canon by incorporating an extensive range of less well-known works, many of them never before available in a modern English edition. Wherever possible, texts are published in complete and unabridged form, and translations are specially commissioned for the series. Each volume contains a critical introduction together with chronologies, biographical sketches, a guide to further reading and any necessary glossaries and textual apparatus. When completed, the series will aim to offer an outline of the entire evolution of western political thought.

For a list of titles published in the series, please see end of book.

ROUSSEAU

The Social Contract and other later political writings

EDITED AND TRANSLATED BY
VICTOR GOUREVITCH
Wesleyan University

CAMBRIDGE
UNIVERSITY PRESS

PUBLISHED BY THE PRESS SYNDICATE OF THE UNIVERSITY OF CAMBRIDGE
The Pitt Building, Trumpington Street, Cambridge, United Kingdom

CAMBRIDGE UNIVERSITY PRESS
The Edinburgh Building, Cambridge CB2 2RU, UK
40 West 20th Street, New York, NY 10011–4211, USA
477 Williamstown Road, Port Melbourne, VIC 3207, Australia
Ruiz de Alarcón 13, 28014 Madrid, Spain
Dock House, The Waterfront, Cape Town 8001, South Africa

http://www.cambridge.org

First published 1997
Fourth printing 2004

Printed in the United Kingdom at the University Press, Cambridge

Typeset in Ehrhardt 9.5/12

A catalogue record for this book is available from the British Library

Library of Congress Cataloguing in Publication data
Rousseau, Jean-Jacques, 1712–1778
[Selections. English. 1977]
The social contract and other later political writings/Rousseau;
edited by Victor Gourevitch.
p.   cm. – (Cambridge texts in the history of political thought)
includes bibliographical references and index.
ISBN 0 521 41382 6. – ISBN 0 521 42446 1 (pbk.)
1. Political science.   2. Social contract.   I. Gourevitch,
Victor.   II. Title.   III. Series.
JC179.R7 1997
320.1′1 – dc20   96–38953 CIP

ISBN 0 521 41382 6 hardback
ISBN 0 521 42446 1 paperback

Contents

Preface

I am grateful to the many colleagues and friends from whom I have learned about Rousseau, or who have called my attention to infelicities or occasional mistakes in the translations and in the Editorial Notes, among them Steven Angle, Joshua Cohen, Maurice Cranston, Lydia Goehr, Wolfgang Iser, Leon Kass, Sam Kerstein, Ralph Leigh, Mark Lilla, John McCarthy, Terence Marshall, Heinrich Meier, Donald J. Moon, Robert D. Richardson Jr., Charles Sherover, Karl Heinz Stierle, William Trousdale, Robert Wokler. Professor Raymond Geuss has been unstinting in his advice regarding the content and the form of the Introductions.

Annotating texts as varied and as rich in references of every kind as these is a cumulative task. No single editor is so learned as to pick up and identify every one of Rousseau's sources and allusions. All students of these rich and rewarding texts are in the debt of the learned editors who have come before us, and we can only hope to repay a part of that debt by doing our share in helping those who will come after us. After a time some references become common property. I have named the sources and editions I have consulted in acknowledgment of such general debts. In the cases where I am aware of owing information to a particular editor, or an accurate or felicitous rendering to a particular translator, I have indicated that fact. In some cases I mention differences with a given edition; it should be clear that by doing so, I also indicate my esteem for that edition: it is the one worth taking seriously. I have recorded specific help in making sense of a particular passage or in tracking down an obscure quotation in the corresponding Editorial Note.

I am indebted to Joy Johannessen, Revan Schendler and Mark Lilla for their care in going over some of the new translations.

Virginia Catmur has been the most vigilant and tactful copy-editor, and I am most grateful to her for catching embarrassingly many errors and correcting numerous infelicities.

I did some of the research for these volumes during a year's fellowship at the Wissenschaftskolleg zu Berlin. The Kolleg, its Director, Professor Wolf Lepenies, and its staff have created a uniquely congenial setting for productive scholarship. I welcome this opportunity to thank them publicly.

I wish also to acknowledge research assistance from Wesleyan University over a period of years.

I am most grateful to the reference staff of Wesleyan University's Olin Library, and especially to the late Steven D. Lebergott, for their assistance.

I wish most particularly to thank Mary Kelly for her many years of generous and patient help in transforming often untidy manuscripts into legible texts.

My greatest debt is to my wife, Jacqueline, who has again sustained and inspired me far beyond anything I could hope adequately to acknowledge.

I dedicate these volumes to the memory of my father.

Introduction

I

The *Discourse on Political Economy*, *Of the Social Contract*, and the *Considerations on the Government of Poland* are Rousseau's major constructive political writings, the works in which he seeks to redeem the promise and, as far as possible, to reduce the "inconveniences" of politics. Perhaps no modern writer and certainly no modern thinker has celebrated the nobility of political life as vividly as has he. Yet it was only in his very last political writing, the *Considerations on the Government of Poland*, that he depicted the life of the citizen or patriot in anything like the concrete detail in which he had depicted the conjectural savages of the pure state of nature, the domestic education of Emile, or the domestic economy of Clarens, the country estate of the *Nouvelle Héloïse*. As has often been noted, the *Political Economy* and, in particular, the *Social Contract* are more concerned with the structure of the legitimate city, than they are with the particulars of its citizens' lives.

He wrote, or at least he finished, the *Political Economy* in 1755–1756, immediately after the *Second Discourse*. He published the two works which he called "treatises," the *Social Contract* and *Emile*, in 1762. He must have been at work concurrently on at least parts of them. Both works were condemned by the civil as well as by the ecclesiastical authorities in France and in Geneva. Both were publicly burned. Warrants were issued for their author's arrest. He was forced to flee, and spent much of the next decade on the run or living under an assumed name. It was during those years that he began writing some of the autobiographical works for which he is also remembered. His specifically political writings during this period are the *Letters Written from the Mountain* (1764), the *Project of a Constitution for Corsica* (1765) and the *Considerations on the Government of Poland*. They differ from his earlier political writings in that they directly address current political situations.

Rousseau explored a variety of ways of life. The fact that he does not consistently hold up one way of life as the standard by which to gauge all others, but calls attention to the merits and the limitations of each of the alternatives he considers, has left some readers under the impression that he was not a coherent thinker. Much of the most valuable twentieth-century Rousseau scholarship has shown that, on the contrary, his thought is remarkably coherent. One cannot help occasionally wondering whether it has not gone too far, and sought to reconcile alternatives which he thought were largely irreconcilable. He did not think it possible to combine all human goods and avoid all "inconveniences" in some one comprehensive way of life, and each one of the major works explores a distinctive way of viewing and resolving the human problem. The most general organizing principle of these explorations is the alternative man/citizen. For all intents and purposes, this alternative corresponds to the alternative ethics/politics or, more formally, natural right/political right.

Natural right and natural law traditionally refer to what, in accordance with human nature, is always and everywhere right, and therefore in some sense of the term "obligatory." "Right," in the expression "natural right," is, for the most part, synonymous with "justice" in the sense of "what is just"; as such, it may subsume right*s*, but is not itself *a* right.

Natural right and natural law are traditionally contrasted with positive right and positive law(s), the particular rules and laws which, at a given time and under given circumstances, specify what is morally and/or politically right and/or obligatory.

Treating equals equally would be a rule of natural right or a precept of natural law; driving on this side of the road or that is a matter of positive law.

Rousseau's fullest discussion of natural right and law was prompted by the Academy question whether inequality is authorized by the natural law. He begins with a distinction between two natural law traditions: that of the Roman jurists, and that of the modern philosophers (*Ineq.* P [6]–[8]). According to the Roman jurists "natural law" is the name for "the general relations established by nature between all animate beings for their common preservation." It is natural in the sense that the beings conform to it by nature. It states the minimum conditions for common existence. It is strictly descriptive. The Roman jurists' natural law is a law of nature. According to the modern philosophers, by contrast, "natural law" is the name for the rules about which it would be appropriate for free and rational, that is to say human, beings to agree for the sake of the common utility. It is natural in the sense of specifying natural ends, namely the optimum conditions for common existence. It is strictly prescriptive.

Rousseau concludes that *if* there is a natural law, it would have to satisfy both the ancient jurists' and the modern philosophers' criteria: it would have to speak immediately with the voice of nature, and the will of him whom it obligates would have to be able to submit to it knowingly; it would have to be both *natural* and *law.* He rejects this possibility. Men do not by (their) nature – by immediate, spontaneous inclinations, dispositions or impulsions – act *for the sake of* their common utility. However, they do, in his view, initially – by (their) nature – act *in conformity with* their common utility. He is reluctant to speak of this as natural *law.* He prefers to speak of it, instead, as natural *right.* When, subsequently, men take cognizance of the ends in conformity with which they had acted by nature, and come to act for the sake of them – "submit to it knowingly" – the law they follow is not, properly speaking, *natural.* He therefore sometimes speaks of it, instead, as the law of reason (*Geneva ms.* I 2 [8]; *SC* II 4 [4], cp. IV 8 [31]). In sum, when he speaks in his own name or about his own views, Rousseau for the most part speaks about natural right. He does so for two reasons among others: right, in contrast to law, states principles which may be realized in different ways in different circumstances, for example, one way "initially," another "subsequently"; law, in contrast to right, is generally understood as the rule by a superior of an inferior, hence as involving (moral) inequality and obedience; yet on Rousseau's view, "initially" men could not even have made sense of what it might mean to obey (*Ineq.* E [5], N IX [14]), and especially to obey another human being (*SC* IV 8 [1]). Law, like political society, would be a late development. Right, by contrast, could be pre- or trans-social or political. When he does use the expression "natural law," Rousseau is, for the most part, not speaking in his own terms about his own views, but in the language of his times about the doctrines of the authoritative "modern philosophers."

Natural right is, then, "natural" inasmuch as it conforms to human nature. Rousseau believes he discerns in human nature two principles prior to reason and independent of sociability: self-preservation and pity. The immediate, spontaneous impulsions which they prompt make for behavior in accordance with natural right (*Ineq.* P [10]). So that, independently of the status of reason and of sociability, men could, by the law(s) of (their) nature, live in accordance with at least the minimum requirements of natural right on a world-wide scale: pity, the spontaneous – natural – disinclination to hurt or harm others makes for conformity with the primary rule of natural right, to harm no one (*Ineq.* P [10]; *On War* [17]; *Emile* II, *OC* IV, 340, tr. 104); and self-preservation – each doing his own good – naturally and spontaneously makes for conformity with the "fundamental and universal Law of the greatest good of all" (*Geneva ms.* II 4 [17]; cp. *SC* II 7 [1]).

Self-sufficient men can act in accordance with natural right, without acting because or for the sake of it. As soon as they become materially and psychologically dependent on one another, they cease spontaneously – "naturally" – to conform to the duties of natural right; the workings of the law(s) of (human) nature cease to secure the rule of natural right. Rousseau's central thesis is that once men are irreversibly dependent on one another, the spontaneous – "natural" – and universal conformity to natural right cannot be preserved or restored on a world-wide scale.

In the *Political Economy*, but especially in the early draft of the *Social Contract* known as the *Geneva ms.*, Rousseau reviews and rejects two representative versions – Pufendorf's and Diderot's – of the view that the world-wide rule of natural right endures. Pufendorf assumes that our natural sociability, our common needs and our common humanity unite the whole of mankind, and instill the precepts of natural right in each one of us. Rousseau denies the premise as well as the conclusion. There is no evidence for a natural "great" or "general society of mankind" (*Geneva ms.* I 2 [2], [4], [8], [15], [18]; *Pol. Ec.* [19]; *Emile* I, *OC* IV, 248f.; tr. 39), and even if there were something like a "universal sociability," it would be exceedingly watery. Most souls are simply not sufficiently capacious to take an active interest in the lives of far-away people, or to feel a sincere sympathy for them (*Pol. Ec.* [30]). Diderot goes so far as to speak of a "general will" embracing the whole of mankind, and he bases natural right on a "pure act of the understanding, reasoning in the silence of the passions" (*Natural Right* ix, 2) about what, in the light of this general will, are our duties and rights as "man, citizen, subject, father, child" (*ib.* vii). Again, Rousseau denies the premise that there is a general will of mankind as a whole, and the conclusion that knowing what natural right requires will cause men to heed it. Indeed, the urgent question, in his view, is not so much the question which Diderot asks, "what is the just thing to do?", as it is the question which Diderot fails to ask, "how will men be moved to do the just thing?" Diderot's "reasoning in the silence of the passions" cannot be trusted to do so.

Rousseau consistently distinguishes two senses or uses of reason, ruling or regulative reason, and calculative or instrumental reason, and the two fundamentally different kinds of right or justice that correspond to them.

> What is good and conformable to order is so by the nature of things and independently of human conventions. All justice comes from God, he alone is its source; but if we were capable of receiving it from so high, we would need neither government nor laws. No doubt there is a universal justice emanated from reason alone; but this justice, to be admitted among us, has to be reciprocal. Considering things in human terms, the laws of justice are vain among men for want of natural sanctions; they only bring good to the wicked and evil to the just when he observes them toward everyone while no one observes them toward him. Conventions and laws are therefore necessary to combine rights with duties and to bring justice back to its object. (*SC* II 6 [2]; cp. *Ineq.* I [23] and *Geneva ms.* I 2 [3])

Rousseau leaves open the question whether the goodness of the natural order and the justice of which he is here speaking refer to our world and to ourselves only, or to the universe as a whole, including the inhabitants of Saturn and Sirius (*To Philopolis* [12], *To Voltaire* [21]). He also leaves open the question of whether the justice he says comes from God is the same as the universal justice he says emanates from reason alone. However, he leaves no doubt whatsoever about the difference between justice in either of these senses, and the justice which might be "admitted among us" because it is reciprocal, has sanctions attached to it, requires conventions, and makes governments necessary. He leaves no doubt whatsoever about the fact that justice, in order to be "admitted among us," must be diluted. If we could live by the first, non-reciprocal and sanction-less justice emanating from reason alone, we would have no need of government, but could quite literally live "without civil society," that is to say in a state of nature. However, "considering things in human terms," most of us will not live by justice emanating from reason alone. Justice emanating from reason alone may guide the wise (*Ineq.* I [38], *Geneva ms.* I 2 [11], *Emile* II, *OC* IV, 320 and V, *OC* IV, 857) and, under exceptional circumstances like those Rousseau describes in the *Emile* and in the *Nouvelle Héloïse*, it may guide some few people who happen to be ruled by the wise. Rousseau is mindful of the wise, but he speaks of them sparingly and, when he does, he does so from the moral/political perspective of most men most of the time (*To Franquières* [9]). Most men, "men as they are," will not heed disinterested and dispassionate reason.

Human contrivance, art or reason, must therefore repair or complete nature, and devise a justice of reciprocity and sanctions which "will be admitted among us." Now, reciprocity with sanctions enforceable on a world-wide scale would be difficult if not impossible to achieve for the very same reasons that sociality does not embrace the whole of mankind: most souls are not sufficiently capacious, and there is no reason to believe that they could be made to experience anything like a lively fellow feeling for the whole of mankind. There is therefore also no reason to believe that it is possible – and hence that it is desirable – to try to fashion a general political society embracing the whole of mankind.

> We conceive of the general society in terms of our particular societies, the establishment of small Republics leads us to think of the large one, and we do not properly begin to become men until after having been Citizens. (*Geneva ms.* I 2 [15])

One important reason for regarding Rousseau as preeminently a political thinker is precisely this central tenet of his moral psychology, that we are moral agents by virtue of being citizens, or at least members of political societies; we are not moral agents first who then may or may not become political agents.

It follows that the most reasonable way to deal with the breakdown of independence and of the world-wide rule of natural right is to institute particular, local, "municipal" political societies subject to political right.

II

Rousseau presents the principles of political right in his "small treatise" *Of the Social Contract.* It is the most systematic of his works, the one which most consistently proceeds in the form of a sustained, rigorous argument. It is therefore also in many respects the most difficult. Yet even this austere treatise begins with "I" and ends with "myself."

The title continues to make for some misunderstanding. In all likelihood he settled on "social contract" because, like "state of nature," "civil state," "natural right," "natural law" and so many other more or less technical locutions, it had become a term of art in the political vocabulary of the mid-eighteenth century. It stood not so much for the view that civil or political societies normally come into being by a formal, explicit contract between independent individuals, as for the view that legitimate political rule is not based directly on either a divine or a natural title to rule, but must be ratified – "authorized" – by the consent of the ruled. The expression which Rousseau adopts as his subtitle, and which he uses on a number of other occasions – *Principles of Political Right* – from the very first alerts the reader to a distinction between political and natural right.

Rousseau reserves the expression "natural right" to refer to the principles or rules of conduct between individual human beings *qua* human beings – "man *qua* man" – either prior to or independently of positive laws and of political societies. "Political right," by contrast, refers primarily to the principles or rules for what he often calls "well-constituted" states (*Narcissus* [19], *SC* II 10 [5], III 4 [6], III 15 [3], IV 3 [8], IV 8 [13]), their institution and end; sovereignty, its legitimate bases and scope; government, its major structures, its forms, and which government is best; and, most particularly, the principles and rules that specify the relations between political rulers and ruled or between being a citizen and being a subject; in short, issues most of which would now be considered under the heading "constitutional law."

The featured place which Rousseau assigns to the expression "political right" and the distinction between natural and political right which it implies underscores his view that political society and rule are not, strictly speaking, "natural": men may by their nature be sociable or at least made to become sociable (*Emile* IV (Vicar), *OC* IV, 600, tr. 290; *Languages* 9 [23]), but they are not by their nature unqualifiedly inclined to form political societies or to participate in them; political life is not unqualifiedly the best life; we may therefore not be under an unqualified, "natural," obligation to strive for full membership in political society. Rousseau's rejection of the view that political society is natural goes hand in hand with his rejection of the view that political rule is natural. Since political society and rule are not natural, the modern philosophers were wrong to call "natural law" "the rules about which it would be appropriate for men to agree among themselves for the sake of the common utility" (*Ineq.* P [7]). They should have called these rules "the law of reason" (*Geneva ms.* I 2 [8]; *SC* II 4 [4], cp. IV 8 [31]). Political society is a being of reason (*SC* I 7 [7]) guided by the law of reason (*SC* II 4 [4]; cp. I 4 [10]).

Since political society and rule are not "natural," they require conventions, or are "conventional." They have to be authorized by the consent of their members (*Ineq.* E [2]; *SC* I 1 [2]); indeed, they *are* by virtue of their members' consent or agreement.

The aim therefore is, as Rousseau announces in the very first sentence of the *Social Contract*,

> ... to inquire whether in the civil order there can be some legitimate and sure rule of administration, taking men as they are, and the laws as they can be: In this inquiry I shall try always to combine what right permits with what interest prescribes, so that justice and utility may not be disjoined. (*SC* I [1], consider IV, 9)

Whereas the principles of natural right are derived from "the nature of man" (*Ineq.* P [5]), the principles of political right are derived from "men as they are," here and now, and whose amour propre, individual interests and common utility or common good have to be taken into account. Political right is, then, as Rousseau explicitly announces from the first, not right as such, but right diluted by the interests and utility of men as they are. Up to a point, right or justice "permits" the dilution which interests and utility "prescribe." Political right so diluted constitutes "legitimacy." Rousseau expands on his concern with legitimacy in the first chapter. "Man is born free, and everywhere he is in chains . . . What can make . . . [this] legitimate? I believe I can solve this question." The basic condition, our everywhere being in chains, that is to say in political society, is irreversible. It may also be perfectly legitimate.

Rousseau's most general statement of what constitutes a legitimate civil order is well known:

> . . . a form of association that will defend and protect the person and goods of each associate with the full common force, and by means of which each, uniting with all, nevertheless obey[s] only himself and remain[s] as free as before. (*SC* I 6 [4])

The associates constitute a civil or political society by pooling all of their resources, their forces, capacities, goods and rights. In short, they give up each being judge in his own case. Instead, they place the society – and hence themselves – under the guidance of its – and hence their – "general will." Rousseau sometimes also calls a society so constituted a "people." The society or people so constituted is sovereign (*SC* I 6 [6]–[10]). Popular sovereignty so understood is the defining feature of what Rousseau calls "political right" or "legitimacy." Thus republican or popular rule is legitimate (*SC*, II 6 [9]; cp. *Pol. Ec.* [19], [47], [59]); tyranny and despotism are illegitimate (*SC* III 10 [10]).

The most distinctive feature of the social contract and, more generally, of the social state as Rousseau conceives of it is the moral and psychological change each one of us undergoes as we come to conceive of ourselves as members of our political community. To say that the parties to the social contract pool their resources is, first and foremost, to describe a change in our relation to ourselves (*SC* I 7 [1]). Rousseau consistently stresses how difficult it is for us to learn to be – and to perceive ourselves as – a part of the corporate whole to which we belong and from which we draw so much of our sustenance (*SC* I 6 [10]). In the *Social Contract* he describes this task of civic education as, "so to speak, changing human nature" or "denaturing" us (*SC* II 7 [3]; cp. *Geneva ms.* II 2 [3], *OC* III, 313; *Emile* I, *OC* IV, 250; tr. 40; and consider *Pol. Ec.* [47]). Becoming a party to the social contract is, then, not so much some historical event in the more or less distant past, as it is our constantly renewed recognition of ourselves as members of a common political or civil society (*SC* IV 1 [1]), and of how intimately intertwined our own good is with the common good. To become a party to it is to become *civil*-ized in the original sense of the term (*SC* I 8).

Perhaps the most conspicuous mark of the differences between natural and political right is that pity, which occupies such a featured place in the moral psychology of the pre-political condition of the *Second Discourse* and of the *Essay on the Origin of Languages*, and in the "domestic education" of the *Emile*, plays no role whatsoever in the moral–political psychology of the *Social Contract*, and is never so much as mentioned in it or in any of Rousseau's other finished writings primarily devoted to political right. It is not surprising that it should not be. Pity, especially pity in the sense of not harming anyone, can be the guiding principle of action and conduct only for solitaries.

> The precept never to harm another person entails that of being attached as little as possible to human society; for in the social state one person's good necessarily makes for the other's evil. (*Emile* II, *OC* IV, 340*, tr. 105* and context; cp. *Rêveries* VI [21], *OC* I, 1059, tr. 84)

Pity, especially pity in the original sense Rousseau attaches to the term, can, therefore, simply not be the guiding principle of men in the civil state, let alone of citizens. In political right, amour propre and reciprocity take the place which pity occupies in natural right.

In the legitimate political society, political right or justice is reciprocal.

> The commitments which bind us to the social body are obligatory only because they are mutual, and their nature is such that in fulfilling them one cannot work for others without also working for oneself . . . Why do all consistently will each one's happiness, if not because there is no one who does not appropriate the word *each* to himself, and think of himself as he votes

for all. Which proves that the equality of right and the notion of justice which it produces follows from everyone's preference for himself and hence from the nature of man ... (*SC* II 4 [5]; cp. [8], II. 6 [2])

This "notion of justice" based on reciprocity – "do unto others as you would have them do unto you" (*Ineq.* I [38]) – requires equality. Only equals will treat others as they would be treated by them. Since men are not equal by nature (*Ineq.* E [2], *SC* I 9 [7], I I [1], IV 2 [5]), they have to be made equal by convention. Nothing short of their pooling all of their resources will reduce them to total equality (*SC* I 6 [6]).

Equality is not an end in itself for Rousseau. It is the means to secure political freedom. The aim of the conventional equality established by all of the parties pooling all of their resources is to render all unearned inequalities irrelevant before the law. However, nothing prevents equals from instituting laws that recognize inequalities earned by contributions to the public good. Conventional equality, precisely because it is no more than conventional, is inherently unstable: men's natural inequalities will repeatedly reassert themselves (*SC* II 11 [3]; *Emile* III, IV, *OC* IV, 461, 524f.). Conventional equality therefore has to be repeatedly restored. Membership in the community constituted by the pooling of its members' resources provides a close civil counterpart to the natural freedom and equality of Rousseau's pre-civil state of nature: in the pre-civil state of nature, men are equal because they are free; their natural inequalities make no significant difference because they are not dependent on one another; in the civil state they would be free because equal (*SC* II 11 [1]). Civic freedom and equality provide the conditions for popular sovereignty, and hence for public happiness and for moral and political excellence (*SC* I 8). However, excellence is not the primary aim; freedom is.

Rousseau holds that what he formally characterizes as the total alienation of each member's total resources to the community does not pose a threat of what has come to be called "totalitarianism." The sovereign imposes the laws. Since the sovereign is the people assembled, the laws are self-imposed. Since they are reciprocal, no one is outside or above them. It therefore stands to reason that the sovereign will not impose any unnecessarily burdensome or restrictive laws: "It cannot even will to do so: for under the law of reason nothing is done without cause, any more than under the law of nature" (*SC* II 4 [4]; cp. I 4 [10]). The contract, far from depriving the parties to it of anything, on the contrary restores to them all the resources they had pooled, only now their claim to them is also guaranteed by the common force (cp. *SC* I 6 [4] with II 4 [10]).

Rousseau calls the guiding principle of the sovereign body established by the social contract the general will. The general will wills the general good. It is the will of the members *qua* citizens, their concern with the general conditions of their communal life which they can affect by their actions. Each one of us cares about the well-being of the society to which we belong, and within the context of which we pursue our private interests (*SC* II 1 [1]). Each one of us more or less adequately perceives and more or less adequately wills whatever contributes to the common utility. At the same time, each one of us has experienced tensions between whatever we may happen to perceive as our private interest and what we perceive to be in the common interest, or the general will; and each one of us has had the experience of subordinating our particular to our general will. This is as true in our relations within our families and in the innumerable more or less tight-knit associations to which we belong at work and at play as it is of ourselves as citizens. Rousseau therefore sometimes speaks of our having several general wills (*Pol. Ec.* [15], *SC* III 2 [5]). Like all political thinkers, he worries lest the general wills of factions, parties, and especially of what he calls the government, become independent of the comprehensive general will of the political society as a whole and, as a result, distort it.

The general will is "general" because it attends to general objects, kinds or types of cases, and the comprehensive framework within which each one of us pursues his own private ends or goods. Accordingly, its pronouncements are couched in the form of laws: general propositions about general matters. The defining feature of Rousseau's political teaching is freedom under self-imposed law: by being a party to the social contract, each one of us is a member of the sovereign; the sovereign's will is the general will; the general will declares itself through laws; to obey the law is, therefore, only to obey oneself; and "obedience to the law one has prescribed to oneself is freedom" (*SC* I 8 [3]). Law liberates from that greatest and most galling evil, dependence on the will of another, by substituting for it dependence on impersonal necessity. That is why "the worst of laws is still preferable to the best master . . ." (*LM* VIII, *OC* III, 842f.). On one occasion, Rousseau makes the point in a particularly dramatic way:

> . . . whoever refuses to obey the general will shall be con-
> strained to do so by the entire body: which means nothing other
> than that he shall be forced to be free; for this is the condition
> which, by giving each Citizen to the Fatherland, guarantees
> him against all personal dependence . . . (*SC* I 7 [8])

The formula is so arresting that its point is sometimes missed: even those who do not themselves obey the laws are protected by them.

Since the general will wills the common good, it may be said to be invariably upright (*droit*) (*SC* II 3 [1], II 4 [5], II 6 [10]). Is it also invariably right? In one important respect the question simply does not make sense: the common quest for the common good is not guided by some independent pattern or "idea," nor is it accountable to any standard other than itself. Rather, it is what, after a suitably free and public debate, a majority of informed and public-spirited citizens declares it to be; and what they declare it to be cannot be "right" or "wrong," "true" or "false," for the simple reason that it is not true to some standard that is in any sense independent of what a self-legislating citizenry declares it to be. If there were such a standard, the case for self-legislation would, to say the least, be significantly weakened.

Still, there clearly is a sense in which the question whether the general will is right does make perfectly good sense: the people may will the common good, and yet not know how to attain it (*SC* II 12 [2]).

The great problem for the doctrine of popular sovereignty is that achieving the willed good requires wisdom (*SC* II 6 [10]). Rousseau fully acknowledges how difficult if not impossible it is to reconcile popular sovereignty and wisdom. He explores various ways to resolve the difficulty throughout much of his work: in his studies of "morals" (*moeurs*), patriotism and civil religion; in how he conceives of the Lawgiver (*SC* II 7); by arguing that the best government is elective aristocracy (*SC* III 5 [4], cp. *Ineq.* II [48]); and by considering various voting procedures (*SC* IV 2–4).

The justice based on reciprocity between "men as they are" may unite their powers, but leave their wills divided. To unite wills, morals (*moeurs*) must complement what the laws dictate. In his classification of laws, Rousseau therefore assigns pride of place to morals, the beliefs, habits and practices which characterize and continually re-enforce a people's distinctive way of life, what it does and what it prizes and honors, its attitudes toward freedom, equality, citizen responsibility: in short, the dispositions which energize and direct the general will (*SC* II 12 [5]). To unite wills, the passion to be counted on is love, specifically the form of love which Rousseau calls amour propre, suitably generalized to make the common good and hence the general will an object of true attachment by becoming patriotism. Patriotism, "enlightened patriotism" (*Poland* 9 [4]), is the most immediate, accessible form of public-spirited devotion to the common good. It is the passional surrogate of practical wisdom. It is what most immediately makes the difference between the self-seeking calculations which hold even a band of robbers together, and the politics of citizenship (*Pol. Ec.* [30], cp. *Fragments politiques, OC* III, 536, and *Poland, passim*). By taking us outside and beyond narrow self-absorption, and helping us to see ourselves as parts of a larger whole, it ennobles political life (*SC* I 8 [1], *Poland* 2 [5], 3 [6]). "The soul insensibly proportions itself to the objects that occupy it" (*First Discourse* [59]). From the *First Discourse* through the *Considerations on the Government of Poland*, Rousseau not only speaks vigorously and sometimes eloquently about patriotism, he also casts himself in the role of a patriot who signs his most explicitly political writings "Citizen of Geneva," takes the highly unusual step of dedicating one of his writings to his native city, and justifies writing the *Social Contract* on the grounds that the right to vote imposes on him the duty to learn about public affairs (*SC* [3]).

Rousseau's discussion of the Lawgiver is one of the high points – and one of the stumbling blocks – of his political teaching. The Lawgiver must know what to do and how to do it. Rousseau repeatedly speaks of the Lawgiver's wisdom. He must persuade the people to give up the rewards they know for the sake of the greater rewards they are only promised. He cannot do so by arguments. They would be too abstruse. Besides, reason rarely moves to action. He must therefore "persuade without convincing" (*SC* II 7 [9], *To Voltaire* [30], and Introduction to *Discourses* tr., p. xxix): he has to place the conclusions reached by his "sublime reason which rises beyond the reach of vulgar men . . . in the mouth of the immortals, in order to rally by divine authority those whom human prudence could not move." "This," he goes on, "has at all times forced the fathers of nations to resort to the intervention of heaven and to honor the Gods with their own wisdom" (*SC* II 7 [11], [10]); and, lest careless readers mistake his meaning, he adds, ". . . it is not up to just anyone to make the Gods speak or to have them believe him when he proclaims himself their interpreter . . ." (*SC* II 7 [11]). The remark goes some way toward resolving the question he had left open earlier, whether the justice he said comes from God is the same as the universal justice emanating from reason alone (*SC* II 6 [2]). By concentrating on the people's religion, its morals, its distinctive way of life (*SC* II 12 [5], *Poland* 2), the Lawgiver seeks to embed as deeply as possible habits, tastes, dispositions for what the community esteems, so that they might become, as it were, its "fundamental laws."

It is sometimes said that the importance Rousseau attaches to founders, as had Machiavelli before him, mistakenly attributes to some legendary figure of heroic proportions the often quite fortuitous effect of long-range trends which no one controls. In part he speaks about such traditional, larger-than-life figures – Lycurgus, Romulus and Numa, Moses, Muhammad – for transparent prudential reasons: they are in a safe because distant past. In part he does so because founders do deserve special honor. At the same time, he is well aware that there are many other ways of being a Lawgiver than to craft constitutions or to mold a people's morals. He clearly conceives of the task of the Lawgiver as being carried on by thoughtful and public-spirited citizens throughout the life of a political society. Just as "contract" in part stands for the ongoing *civilizing* process in which all of us are in varying degrees involved throughout our lives, as were our forebears, and as our descendants will be, so "Lawgiver" in part stands for the activities of every generation of public-spirited citizens (cp. *Poland* 7 [3], [10], [12]).

The theme of the *Social Contract* is popular sovereignty, and every issue and argument which Rousseau takes up in the course of the work seeks either to strengthen the case for it, or to ward off possible challenges to it. This is particularly true of the sharp distinction which he draws half-way through the work between sovereign on the one hand, and government or Prince on the other.

The distinction is central to his conception of political right, and of legitimacy. The sovereign people promulgates or ratifies the laws. It cannot and it ought not to implement them. It cannot implement them because it is simply too unwieldy for the people assembled to do so. It ought not to implement them because the exercise of sovereignty consists in attending to the general will, that is to say to general concerns, whereas implementing the law is necessarily a matter of particulars (*Ineq.* ED [10], II [36]; *SC* II 4 [6], II 1 [3], III 4 [2]). To assign implementation to some part of the sovereign would divide it, and to divide the sovereign would be to annihilate it. Sovereignty is indivisible and inalienable. The sovereign people must therefore delegate the responsibility and the power to implement the laws to a body of magistrates or government in the strict sense Rousseau attaches to this term (*SC* III 1). Now, if, as Rousseau holds, government is merely the minister of the sovereign people, it clearly follows that every government is provisional, and that the sovereign people may, and, Rousseau argues, should regularly call it to accounts and renew its mandate (*SC* III 13, 18). It is easy to see how this doctrine more than any other caused the *Social Contract* to be condemned by the Genevan as well as by the French political authorities.

Two dangers threaten Rousseau's separation of sovereign and government: the sovereign may usurp the role of government by retaining executive and administrative functions; alternatively, the government may encroach upon the sovereignty and gradually usurp it (*Ineq.* ED [5], II [36]; *SC* II 4 [6]; III 16 [5]). The first is characteristic of pure or direct democracy, the second of absolute monarchy. Rousseau therefore rejects both forms of government. As for the third traditional form of government, aristocracy, he distinguishes between natural, elective and hereditary aristocracy. He sets aside natural aristocracy as suited only to primitive peoples (or to such sub-political communities as that described in the *Nouvelle Héloïse*), and rejects hereditary aristocracy as the worst form of government. Elective aristocracy, by contrast, is the best form of government (*SC* III 5; cp. *Ineq.* II [48]). What he here calls elective aristocracy is for all intents and purposes what elsewhere he calls democratic government wisely tempered (*Ineq.* ED [3]; cp. *SC* III 10 [3]* ¶ 4, and III 7 [5]). Elective aristocracy or wisely tempered democracy is best because it combines the strictest requirement of legitimate political rule, election, with the most natural claim to rule, wisdom in the service of the common good (*SC* III 5 [7]). The *Considerations on the Government of Poland* explores in some detail how a hereditary aristocracy might be transformed into an elective aristocracy without a revolution. As in his discussion of the Lawgiver, so, in his discussion of elective aristocracy or democracy wisely tempered, Rousseau seeks to combine and reconcile popular sovereignty with wisdom (see also Introduction to *Discourses* tr., p. xxv).

The extended discussion, through much of Book IV, of the divisions of the Roman people – "that model of all free Peoples" (*Ineq.* ED [6]) – into tribes and comitia, of their complex voting procedures, of the Tribunes, the Censors, and the other institutions designed to maintain a proper balance between the various sectors of the sovereign people and the various "intermediate forces" (*SC* III 1 [8]) or branches of government, considers exemplary ways of forestalling and delaying as much as possible the imbalances between sovereign and government which in the long run inevitably lead to the decline and fall of even the best political societies (*SC* III 11 [1] *et seq.*, *Poland* 7 [39], *LM* VI [31], *OC* III, 809).

So, in large measure, does the famous chapter on civil religion (*SC* IV 8). Rousseau's preoccupation with the relations between religion and society can be traced through all of his writings. In the chapter on civil religion he enlarges upon the reflections about this problem which he had begun to develop in the chapter on the Lawgiver (*SC* II 7). Religion is a branch of what Rousseau calls "political right" because the parties to the social contract will not regard as binding an apparently foundation-less, self-validating pact: "no State has ever been founded without Religion serving as its base" (*SC* IV 8 [14], cp. *Ineq.* II [46]); and because the problem therefore arises of how to reconcile the claims of popular sovereignty with the claims of religion, or, as Rousseau puts it, how to reunite the two heads of the eagle (*SC* IV 8 [13]). Initially they were united. At first all political societies were ruled each by its own gods. All polities were theocracies, all religions national and, so to speak, citizen religions: patriotism ennobled and hallowed by divine sanction (consider *SC* I 1 [2]). Jesus introduced a radically new alternative: a religion not of citizen but of man, a religion embracing the whole of mankind. By driving a wedge between the citizens' allegiance to the political realm and their allegiance to the spiritual realm, he radically disjoined being a citizen and being a man. Christianity became the vehicle for disseminating all over the world "the healthy ideas of natural right and of the common brotherhood [*fraternité*] of all men" (*Geneva ms.* I 2 [16], *SC* IV 8 [20], cp. *Languages* 9 [1]). It seeks to universalize a trait which Rousseau attributes to but a few "Cosmopolitan Souls" (*Ineq.* II [33] and Editorial Note) and which, he says, will "always escape the multitude" (*Geneva ms.* I 2 [11]). In the process of getting universalized and transformed into a religion for the multitude, "the purely internal cult of the Supreme God" therefore inevitably changes in character. Before long, the Christians' "supposedly otherworldly kingdom" became "the most violent despotism in this world" (*SC* IV 8 [9]). In becoming an earthly Principality, it drove the fatal wedge into the bodies politic by now dividing sovereignty as well (*SC* IV 8 [12]). As a result sound polity became impossible in Christian States (*SC* IV 8 [10]). It is a constant of Rousseau's thought that Christianity tends radically to subvert political life (*SC* IV 8 [8], [10], [16], [17] [21]–[30]; *To Usteri* [2]–[8]; *LM* I, *OC* III, 704f.). In his *Letter to Voltaire* he had gone so far as to say that any religion that attacks the foundations of society ought to be exterminated ([34]). In the *Social Contract* he leaves it at proposing a reinterpreted Christianity which might be compatible with sound politics. Specifically, his bold proposal is to combine a stripped Christianity – "the purely internal cult of the Supreme God and the eternal duties of morality", or "divine natural right" (*SC* IV 8 [15] and the Editorial Note) – and a civil religion with a civil profession of faith fostering sentiments of sociability or citizenship – or "divine civil or positive right." The positive dogmas of this civil religion would be few and simple: the existence of the powerful, intelligent, beneficent, prescient, and provident Divinity, the life to come, the happiness of the just, the punishment of the wicked, the sanctity of the social contract and the laws; its one negative dogma is the prohibition of intolerance. While Christians and, possibly, Jews and Muslims as well, should have no objections to the bulk of the positive dogmas, they do go far beyond anything Rousseau himself was publicly on record as finding persuasive, let alone convincing (*To Voltaire* [29], and Introduction to *Discourses* tr., pp. xxvii–xxx). Once again he solves this problem by drawing a sharp distinction between beliefs and conduct. The sole admissible gauge of beliefs is how one acts; and only actions are subject to right strictly and properly so called (*Ineq.* N XIX, *Geneva ms.* I 6 [5], II 4 [14], *To d'Alembert*, *OC* V, 61; tr. 66), that is to say to scrutiny and enforcement by the laws (*SC* IV 8 [31], cp. II 4 [3]; *To Voltaire* [32]; *Ineq.* N XIX). It is true that anyone who does not *believe* the articles of the purely civil profession of faith may be banished, but as Rousseau makes clear in the context, the only evidence of one's not believing them, is one's failure publicly to acknowledge them, in other words, once again how one *acts* (*NH* V 5, *OC* II, 592f.). The last two dogmas of the civil profession of faith are the most radical. They proclaim the sanctity of the social contract and the laws, hence the civil society's indivisible and inalienable sovereignty, and hence that no Church has a legitimate rival claim to authority in the state's affairs (*SC* I 7 [3]; *Ineq.* ED [5]).

Rousseau's discussion of Christianity in the chapter on civil religion is more explicit than anything he ever said on the subject either in print or in private correspondence, and it contributed significantly to the condemnation of the *Social Contract*.

Like most political philosophers, Rousseau attends to domestic policy far more exhaustively than he does to foreign policy. In the brief concluding chapter of the *Social Contract*, he lists – but does no more than list – the major branches of what he calls the right of nations and we would call international law: (1) international commerce, (2) war, and (3) public right or alliances, negotiations and treaties. The existing laws of the right of nations are nothing but "chimeras": sovereign states are in a state of nature with one another, and the few more or less tacit conventions between them cannot be enforced for want of sanctions (*Ineq.* II [33] *et seq.*; *War* [6]). Yet his own proposals for a federation of European states and for a sound right of war remain fragmentary. The major reform he proposes is that war be recognized as a state between civil societies, that is to say between "moral" entities, and not between individual, "physical" human beings; and that, accordingly, its rightful aim be recognized to consist in breaking the common or general will holding the enemy society together. It is not rightful to kill the enemy's population, let alone to enslave them in exchange for sparing their lives (*War* [34]–[57], *SC* I 4 [7]–[12]).

III

In Rousseau's judgment, political right, citizenship in a well-constituted, legitimate political society, which is self-contained, self-sufficient and patriotic, provides the best or most satisfactory collective solution possible for "men as they are." It does not provide the best or most satisfactory solution simply to the human problem. He does not think that this problem admits of a single best solution. He indicates this most clearly by refusing to ignore or even to minimize the tension between natural right and political right, between the claims of cosmopolitanism and humanity on the one hand, and the claims of citizenship and patriotism on the other. As noted earlier, one illustration of this tension is that he does not so much as mention pity in the works devoted primarily to political – in contrast to natural – right. In civil society, Rousseau explicitly subordinates pity to justice, and "there are a thousand cases where it is an Act of justice to hurt one's neighbor," as Brutus's just condemnation of his sons to death so dramatically illustrates (*Geneva ms.* II 4 [17], cp. *Pol. Ec.* [28], *Emile* I, *OC* IV, 248f., tr. 39 and IV, *OC* IV, 548, tr. 253; *Last Reply* [5]*, [54]–[56]; *Franquières* [20]).

The subordination of pity to justice in civil life is but one consequence of Rousseau's dictum that we are citizens of our country or fatherland first, and citizens of the world or men second. For even those who, as he says, only have a country (*pays*) and not a fatherland (*patrie*) (*Emile* V, *OC* IV, 858, cp. *NH* VI 5, *OC* II, 657) learn about justice from the laws of the country in and by which they are raised. Admittedly, these laws are not always based on justice, but even bad and unjust laws maintain a pretense of the form of justice (*Geneva ms.* II 4 [15], *Emile* V, *OC* IV 858, tr. 473), and thus point to what law could and should be – just as the initial contract may have been flawed, but at least was in the form of a contract (see Introduction to *Discourses* tr., p. xxiii).

Civil society and the laws provide the shield behind which "natural right" is restored. This restored natural right assumes two forms: civility and beneficence in our relations with our fellow-citizens (*Geneva ms.* II 4 [13]), and reasoned or systematic natural right (*droit naturel raisonné*) in our relations with strangers (*Geneva ms.* II 4 [14]).

> Extend this maxim [of the greatest good or utility of a given
> civil society] to the general society of which the State gives us
> the idea, protected by the society of which we are members,
> or by that in which we live, the natural revulsion to do evil no
> longer being offset by the fear of having evil done to us, we
> are inclined at once by nature, by habit, by reason, to deal with
> other men more or less as [we do] with our fellow-citizens, and
> this disposition reduced to actions gives rise to the rules of
> reasoned [or: systematic] natural right [*droit naturel raisonné*],
> different from natural right properly so called, which is
> founded on nothing but a true but very vague sentiment often
> stifled by the love of ourselves. (*Geneva ms.* II 4 [14])

The province of civility and of reasoned or systematic natural
right, like that of natural right properly so called, is the conduct of
individuals with one another. Natural right cannot replace political
right. It cannot regulate the conduct of domestic or of foreign
policy.

> Patriotism and humanity ... are incompatible virtues in their
> very thrust [*énergie*], especially so in an entire people. The
> Lawgiver who strives for them both will achieve neither: such
> a combination has never been seen; it will never be seen,
> because it is against nature, and it is impossible to assign two
> objects to one and the same passion. (*LM* I, *OC* III, 706*; *Pol.
> Ec.* [30])

Entire peoples simply cannot wholeheartedly devote their best energies both to the greatest good of their own country and to the greatest good of mankind as a whole.

Being a citizen and being a man, guiding one's life by political
right and guiding it by natural right, make for fundamentally different economies of the soul, and fundamentally different ways of life.
One way in which Rousseau illustrates this difference is that in the
education of man, he has instruction in natural religion precede
instruction in citizenship; Emile is taught the Savoyard Vicar's
natural religion before he is taught a summary of the *Social Contract*, and the summary of it which he is taught makes no mention
of the civil religion; man is brought up to conceive of his political
place in the light of his place in the whole. The citizen, by contrast,
would appear to be brought up to conceive of his place in the whole
in the light of his membership in his political society, and the

religion he is taught is the civil religion. The competing claims of the two ways of life and the tensions between them is the central theme of Rousseau's work, and it is the organizing principle of his writings. He states it most succinctly and dramatically in the contrast he draws between Cato, the model citizen, and Socrates, the model philosopher or, more precisely, between the best and most responsible of those who seek and find their happiness in the happiness of their city, and the best and most responsible of those who seek and find their happiness in self-sufficiency. He assigns pride of place to the model citizen because, as he says, citizenship is concerned with the happiness accessible to the greater number (*Pol. Ec.* [30]; cp. *To Usteri* [8], ed. note). This is why, for the most part, he proceeds on the principle that among men he who makes himself most useful to others should be the foremost (*Hero* [7]) and that "in politics, as in ethics, not to do good is a great evil, and every useless citizen may be looked upon as a pernicious man" (*First Discourse* [39]; cp. *Rêveries* VI [12], *OC* I, 1056, tr. 80). He even goes so far as to imply that if Socrates could have entered political life, he would have done so: "Athens was already lost, and Socrates no longer had any other fatherland than the whole world" (*Pol. Ec.* [30], *Hero* [5]; however, *Narcissus* [25]). He explicitly says that Jesus began as a citizen intent, like Moses, on leading his people out of political bondage, and that he directed his efforts at revolutionizing the world only once his efforts to revolutionize his own people had failed (*To Franquières* [24]). In other words, he fully recognizes that citizenship is not always an option. At the same time, the way of Socrates, to say nothing of the way of Jesus, is accessible only to the few. He therefore explores or, more precisely, he constructs ways of life accessible to at least some ordinary people who are *in* political societies without being *of* them: the domestic – in contrast to the political – economy of the Wolmar household in the *Nouvelle Héloïse*, and the life of Emile and of his Sophie. While theirs is not a life of citizenship in the strong sense of the term, it is dependent on their country for the security and the moral education which allows them to lead lives of civility and of reasoned natural right (*SC* II 5 [2]; *Emile* III, *OC* IV, 470, tr. 195), and they are under obligation to repay this debt.

IV

Rousseau's political thought is sometimes said to be "utopian." The reason for saying that it is, is that the three basic principles of his politics, that man is by nature good, that political society corrupts him, and that everything is radically dependent on politics, are taken to entail the conclusion that the human problem could be fully and satisfactorily solved by the right political arrangements, or by sloughing off the political condition, either by returning to a pre-political state, or by progressing to a trans-political state. There is no denying that some of his statements appear to invite such a reading: "There is not a single wicked man [*méchant*] who could not be made good for something" (*SC* II 5 [6]). However Rousseau categorically denies that any political solution can transform "men as they are" into "men as they ought to be." He holds out no prospect whatsoever of an end to politics, be it by men's rationally choosing what is in their enlightened self-interest, or by their becoming "moralized," or by the "withering away of the state." There is no alternative to politics. No political solution can be definitive. "If Sparta and Rome perished, what State can hope to last forever?" (*SC* III 9 [1], cp. III 13 [10]). He rejects from first to last the suggestion that progress can eliminate political problems (*SC* II 8 [1], *To Mirabeau* [1]). The attempt to eliminate need by providing ever greater plenty merely exacerbates need. Only the utmost austerity might succeed in containing political problems (*Last Reply* [72], *To Mirabeau* [4]–[6]). The attempt to substitute culture for public-spiritedness is a threat to moral and political freedom. At every level there is, at the very least, a tension between the good of the whole and the good of its parts, and even the most satisfactory resolutions of these tensions are fragile.

Chronology of Jean-Jacques Rousseau

1712   28 June, born in Geneva; the second son of the watchmaker Isaac Rousseau and his wife Suzanne Bernard; both parents are "citizens" of Geneva; on 7 July his mother dies.

1722–1728   Isaac Rousseau flees Geneva after a quarrel; his sons, who had received no formal education, were apprenticed. Jean-Jacques worked briefly as a notary's clerk, and then (1725–1728) as apprentice to an engraver.

1728–1740   One night in March 1728, Rousseau finds himself locked out of Geneva, and decides to seek his fortune elsewhere; goes to Annency in the Savoy, where he meets Mme. de Warens. She sends him to Turin, where he renounces Calvinism and converts to Roman Catholicism (briefly attending a seminary for priests, then a choir school). Works intermittently as a lackey, an engraver, and a music teacher. Becomes Mme. de Warens's lover (1733–1740) and begins to write while living with her.

1740–1741   Tutor in the house of M. de Mably, in Lyon, where he also makes the acquaintance of de Mably's two elder brothers, Etienne Bonnot, who comes to be known as the Abbé de Condillac, and the Abbé de Mably.

1742–1749   Arrives in Paris with a scheme of musical notation, a comedy, an opera, and a collection of poems. During these years Rousseau made a precarious living tutoring, writing, and arranging music. For a time (1743–1744) he is secretary to the Comte de Montaigu, France's ambassador to Venice. Befriends Diderot, who commissions him to write the articles on music for the *Encyclopedia*; meets Thérèse Levasseur, who becomes his life-long companion.

1750　Wins the prize from the Academy of Dijon for his so-called *First Discourse (Discours sur les sciences et les arts)*, published in January 1751, and an immediate, resounding success throughout Europe.

1752　His short opera, *Le Devin du village (The Village Soothsayer)*, is performed at Court; a comedy, *Narcisse*, performed at the Théâtre Français; refuses a royal pension.

1753　*Lettre sur la musique française (Letter about French Music)*, expressing a strong preference for Italian over French music.

1754–1755　The so-called *Second Discourse (Discours sur l'origine et les fondements de l'inégalité parmi les hommes)* completed in May 1754. On 1 June, Rousseau leaves Paris for a visit to Geneva, where he returns to Protestantism; his rights as citizen of Geneva are restored. Back in Paris in October. The *Discourse* is published in May 1755. In November the *Political Economy* appears in volume v of Diderot and d'Alembert's *Encyclopedia*.

1756　Leaves Paris, and settles in a cottage, The Hermitage, on the estate of Mme. d'Epinay. Begins writing his novel *Julie*.

1758　*Letter to M. d'Alembert (Lettre sur les spectacles)* critical of d'Alembert's article on Geneva in the *Encyclopedia*, and in particular of his proposal to open a theater in Geneva. The publication of the *Letter* made final his break with most of the *philosophes*.

1761　Publication of the epistolary novel *Julie, ou la nouvelle Héloïse*, which becomes a runaway best-seller.

1762　Publication of *Du contrat social* (15 May) as well as of *Emile* (22 May). Both are condemned and ordered to be publicly burned in Geneva as well as in France;

	the French government orders Rousseau's arrest; he flees to Neuchâtel, then governed by Prussia.
1763–1765	While in Neuchâtel, Rousseau renounces his Genevan citizenship. He writes a draft of a constitution for Corsica; is fiercely attacked by Voltaire in an anonymous pamphlet, and decides to write his autobiography, the *Confessions*.
1765	Spends some weeks of intense happiness on the island of Saint Pierre in the Lac de Bienne.
1765–1767	Under increasing attack wherever he seeks refuge, he accepts David Hume's offer of help to settle in England. (Falsely) suspecting Hume of having had a hand in writing an anonymous pamphlet ridiculing him, he quarrels with him and returns to France (although the order for his arrest had not been rescinded).
1768	While living under an assumed name, Renou, he marries his long-time companion Thérèse Levasseur, by whom he had had five children, all of whom he had left at a home for foundlings.
1772	He writes the *Considérations sur le gouvernement de Pologne*, and *Dialogues: Rousseau juge de Jean-Jacques*, neither of which gets published at this time.
1777	Writes the *Rêveries du promeneur solitaire*.
1778	Dies quite suddenly on 2 July.
1782	Publication of the Du Peyrou-Moultou edition of the *Works* which incorporates many of Rousseau's additions and corrections, and makes public for the first time his autobiographical writings, a number of his later political writings, as well as many shorter works, fragments and letters.
1794	Rousseau's ashes are transferred to the Panthéon.

A brief guide to further reading

The elegant five volumes of the Pléiade Jean-Jacques Rousseau, *Oeuvres complètes* (or *OC*; for details, see A Note on the Texts, p. xliii), make available in a convenient and compact format the most complete collection of Rousseau's published and unpublished writings. The different texts were assigned to different editors, and accordingly the extensive critical apparatus and annotations vary in usefulness. Also, unfortunately not all the texts are entirely reliable: aside from inevitable typographical errors, some of which remain uncorrected in printing after printing, not all – not even all important – variants are recorded; capitalization is not consistently faithful to Rousseau's original, or modernized uniformly throughout the edition. Close readers will therefore also have to consult the most authoritative editions of individual works: George R. Havens's critical edition of the *First Discourse*, Heinrich Meier's critical edition of the *Second Discourse*, and the various classical critical editions of the *Social Contract*. For full details about these editions, see the beginning of the Editorial Notes for each work. The most complete guide to Rousseau editions, printings, and translations up to 1950 is Jean Sénelier's *Bibliographie générale des oeuvres de J.-J. Rousseau* (PUF, Paris, 1950).

Ralph A. Leigh's critical apparatus and annotations in his magisterial *Correspondance complète* (for details, see A Note on the Texts, p. xliii) make his edition a doubly invaluable source.

References to standard translations of most of Rousseau's more important works are included in the Editorial Notes. Most of Rousseau's major political writings not included in the present volume will be found in Jean-Jacques Rousseau, *The 'Discourses' and Other Early Political Writings*, translated, with an Introduction and Notes, by Victor Gourevitch (Cambridge Texts in the History of Political Thought, Cambridge, 1997).

The *Annales de la Société Jean-Jacques Rousseau* (1905–) publish articles, reviews and notices of particular interest to Rousseau scholars; so, frequently, do *Studies on Voltaire and the Eighteenth Century* (1955–).

The North American Association for the Study of Jean-Jacques Rousseau publishes a Bulletin and holds Symposia, the Proceedings of which are published under the title *Pensée libre*.

The secondary literature about Rousseau's life and works is enormous. The following list is no more than a highly selective, preliminary guide to further reading. It concentrates on – but is not limited to – works about Rousseau's political philosophy; and it concentrates on – but is not limited to – works in English. Numerous other, often more specialized references, will be found in the Editorial Notes. The bibliographies in the works listed here and in those Notes will guide the interested reader further, as will Peter Gay's "Reading about Rousseau: A Survey of the Literature," in his *The Party of Humanity* (Knopf, New York, 1964), pp. 211–238.

Although, or perhaps because, he wrote several autobiographies, of which the *Confessions* is the best known and most complete, Rousseau has been a favorite subject of biographers. Two biographies stand out for their balance: Jean Guéhenno's *Jean-Jacques Rousseau* (Gallimard, Paris, 1962; translated by John and Doreen Weightman, Routledge & Kegan Paul, London, 1966), and the two volumes which Maurice Cranston lived to complete, *Jean-Jacques, The Early Life and Work of Jean-Jacques Rousseau, 1712–1754* (Allen Lane, London, 1983) and *The Noble Savage, Jean-Jacques Rousseau, 1754–1762* (Viking/Penguin, London and University of Chicago Press, Chicago, 1991). Sir Gaven de Beer's *Jean-Jacques Rousseau and his World* (Putnam's, New York and Thames & Hudson, London, 1972) may be consulted for its numerous, mostly eighteenth-century images of persons, places and memorabilia associated with Rousseau. Jean Starobinski's *J.-J. Rousseau, La Transparence et l'obstacle* (Plon, Paris, 1957, second, expanded edition, Gallimard, Paris, 1971), translated as *Jean-Jacques Rousseau: Transparency and Obstruction* (University of Chicago Press, Chicago, 1988), is the best, and the best-known, attempt to understand Rousseau's writings in the light of the kind of person he is supposed to have been, and to construct the kind of person he is supposed to have been on the basis of his writings; it focuses on the "images, obsessional desires, nostalgias, that dominate Jean Jacques' conduct and almost permanently guide his actions"; it does not attend to his thought as such. By contrast, Christopher Kelly's *Rousseau's Exemplary Life, the "Confessions" as Political Philosophy* (Cornell Univerity Press, Ithaca, 1987) reads Rousseau's account of his life in the light of his thought.

The most reliable and accessible accounts in English of Rousseau's thought as a whole are Charles W. Hendels's *Jean-Jacques Rousseau: Moralist* (2 vols., Oxford Univerity Press, London and New York, 1934; second edition, Library of Liberal Arts, New York, 1962); and Robert Wokler's *Rousseau*, in the Past Masters series (OUP, Oxford, 1995), a lively, succinct distillation of the author's extensive acquaintance with the texts, the secondary literature and the period. Two French studies of Rousseau's work as a whole belong on even a short list of books about Rousseau: Pierre Burgelin's massive *La Philosophie de l'existence de J.-J. Rousseau* (PUF, Paris, 1952), and Tzvetan Todorov's compact *Frêle bonheur, essai sur Rousseau* (Hachette, Paris, 1985); so do two general studies in German: Martin Rang, *Rousseaus Lehre vom Menschen* (Vandenhoek & Ruprecht, Göttingen, 1959), which surveys the entire *oeuvre* from the perspective of the *Emile*, and Iring Fetscher's illuminating and reliable *Rousseaus politische Philosophie* (Hermann Luchterhand Verlag, Neuwied, 1960), which called attention to the difficulties raised by Rousseau's apparently inconsistent accounts of "pity" in the *Second Discourse* and in the *Essay on the Origin of Languages* long before this became an issue in the French-language debates.

The most influential modern study of Rousseau's political philosophy is Robert Derathé's *Jean-Jacques Rousseau et la science politique de son temps* (Vrin, Paris, 1970). One of the strengths of this study and of Derathé's numerous other contributions to Rousseau scholarship is his consistent attention to the coherence and the cogency of Rousseau's thought. Among earlier discussions in English of Rousseau's political philosophy, much can be learned from T. H. Green's *Lectures on the Principles of Political Obligation* (first delivered in 1879, and first published posthumously in R. L. Nettle-ship's edition of Green's *Works* [OUP, London and New York, 1886], vol. II, pp. 307–553; paperback reprint, University of Michigan Press, Ann Arbor, 1967), Bernard Bosanquet's *Philosophical Theory of the State* (Macmillan, London, 1899), and C. E. Vaughan's "Introduction" to his *Jean-Jacques Rousseau: The Political Writings* (CUP, Cambridge, 1915, reprint Basil Blackwell, Oxford, 1962, vol. I, pp. 1–117). Judith N. Shklar's *Men and Citizens* (CUP, Cambridge, 1969) seeks to capture and convey the tenor of what her sub-title calls Rousseau's "social theory." Roger Masters, *The Political Philosophy of Rousseau* (Princeton University Press, Princeton, 1968), provides detailed analyses of each of the major works. John C. Hall's concise and lucid *Rousseau; An Introduction to his Political Philosophy* (Schenkman, Cambridge, MA and Macmillan, London, 1972) concludes with a brief but helpful discussion of "Some Modern Applications"; A. M. Melzer's *The Natural Goodness of Man* (University of Chicago Press, Chicago, 1990) explores Rousseau's political philosophy thoroughly and thoughtfully; Zev M. Trachtenberg, *Making Citizens* (Routledge, London and New York, 1993) pays special attention to the role Rousseau attaches to morals (*moeurs*), and reviews the claims that the "general will" is best understood in the light of theories of "rational choice"; Tracy B. Strong, *Jean-Jacques Rousseau, The Politics of the Ordinary* (Sage, London, 1994) is an eclectic, wide-ranging, and spirited exploration of the work by perhaps the only scholar who proclaims himself a "Rousseauian."

Kant acknowledged how indebted his moral thought was to Rousseau. This has unfortunately misled some academics to portray him as a lisping Kant. In an influential article, Eric Weil even went so far as to claim that "it took Kant to *think Rousseau's thoughts*" ("J.-J. Rousseau et sa politique," *Critique* [January 1952], 56:3-28, reprinted in *Essais et Conférences* [Plon, Paris, 1971], vol. II, pp. 115–148). The best-known summaries of the influence of Rousseau on Kant's moral thought are Ernst Cassirer's balanced *The Question of Jean-Jacques Rousseau* (originally published in 1932; translated by Peter Gay, Indiana University Press, Bloomington, 1963) and "Kant and Rousseau," in *Rousseau, Kant, Goethe* (Princeton University Press, Princeton, 1945). It remained for Richard L. Velkley's original, learned and absorbing *Freedom and the End of Reason*

(Chicago University Press, Chicago, 1989) to show Rousseau's profound and pervasive influence on Kant's critical philosophy as a whole. Andrew Levine's thoughtful *The Politics of Autonomy: A Kantian Reading of Rousseau's Social Contract* (University of Massachusetts Press, Amherst, 1976) is mindful of the differences between Rousseau and Kant; however his Kant is, as the author announces from the first, Marxicized by way of Althusser; see also his recent *The General Will: Rousseau, Marx, Communism* (CUP, Cambridge, 1993); Louis Althusser's analytic-Marxist reading, "Sur le Contrat Social (Les décalages)," *Cahiers pour l'analyse* (1970), 8:5-42), translated by B. Brewster, is included in his *Montesquieu, Rousseau, Marx: Politics and History* (Verso, London, 1982); Michel Launay, *Jean-Jacques Rousseau écrivain politique* (CEL/ACER, Grenoble, 1972) views Rousseau's political writings from what might, by contrast, be called an historical-Marxist perspective, in the light of a very detailed account of the political circumstances in which they were composed.

The debate about whether Rousseau's legitimate, well-constituted State is what is now often called totalitarian goes at least as far back as the debates about the relation between his thought and the French Revolution and especially the Terror. The most conspicuous attacks on him on this score are Edmund Burke's, particularly in his *Reflections on the Revolution in France* (1790), in which Burke did, however, also recognize that Rousseau himself "would be shocked at the practical frenzy of his scholars"; and by Benjamin Constant, especially in his *Principles of Politics* (1815) and his *Liberty of the Ancients as compared with that of the Moderns* (1819), both translated by B. Fontana in *Constant, Political Writings* (Cambridge Texts in the History of Political Thought, Cambridge, 1988); for a review of the debate, see J. W. Chapman, *Rousseau: Totalitarian or Liberal?* (AMS Press, New York, 1968); a widely influential argument for the view that Rousseau laid the foundation for "totalitarian democracy" is made by J. L. Talmon, *The Origins of Totalitarian Democracy* (Secker & Warburg, London, 1952; paperback reprint, Praeger, New York, 1960); however, the most tenacious contemporary critic of Rousseau's presumably totalitarian teaching and personality is Lester G. Crocker, for example in his *Rousseau's Social Contract, An Interpretive Essay* (Case Western Reserve Press, Cleveland, 1968); Richard Fralin, *Rousseau and*

Representation (Columbia University Press, New York, 1978) examines one of the central problems in this all-too-often highly polemical debate with scrupulous care.

For the study of Rousseau's thoughts about foreign policy, J. L. Windenberger, *Essai sur la politique étrangère de J.-J. Rousseau* (Picard et Fils, Paris, 1900) remains valuable; see also Grace G. Roosevelt, *Reading Rousseau in the Nuclear Age* (Philadelphia, Temple University Press, 1990); and the "Introduction" by Stanley Hoffmann and David P. Fidler to their anthology of Rousseau writings, *Rousseau on International Relations* (Clarendon, Oxford, 1991).

Among the works devoted to individual texts, Leo Strauss's study of the *First Discourse*: "On the Intention of Rousseau," *Social Research* (1947), 14:455-487, reprinted in Maurice Cranston and Richard S. Peters, eds., *Hobbes and Rousseau* (Doubleday, New York, 1972), pp. 254–290, stands out; John Hope Mason has written a "Reading Rousseau's First Discourse," *Studies on Voltaire and the Eighteenth Century* (1987), 249:251–266; Patrick Coleman's *Rousseau's Political Imagination: Rule and Representation in the 'Lettre à d'Alembert'* (Droz, Geneva, 1984) should be mentioned in this context; my own "Rousseau on the Arts and Sciences," *The Journal of Philosophy* (1972), 69:737–754 develops and documents in detail some of the points I make in the Introduction to *Discourses* tr. Among the works devoted to the *Second Discourse*, Arthur O. Lovejoy's "The Supposed Primitivism of Rousseau's *Discourse on Inequality*" (1923), in *Essays in the History of Ideas* (Johns Hopkins University Press, Baltimore, 1948) did much to alert readers to the distinction Rousseau draws between different stages of the state of nature; Victor Goldschmidt's *Anthropologie et politique: Les Principes du système de Rousseau* (Vrin, Paris, 1974) provides the most detailed commentary on this *Discourse*; I have discussed some of the difficulties in interpreting the *Second Discourse* in "Rousseau's 'Pure' State of Nature," *Interpretation* (1988), 16:23-59. The single most sustained interpretation of the *Essay on the Origin of Languages* is Jacques Derrida's often insightful and just as often willful reading of that text: *De la grammatologie* (Editions de Minuit, Paris, 1967), translated by Gayatri C. Spivak as *Of Grammatology* (Johns Hopkins University Press, Baltimore and London, 1976); Robert Wokler's *Rousseau on Society, Politics, Music and Language* (Garland, New York, 1987) is valuable; I have discussed the *Essay* in " 'The First

Times' in Rousseau's *Essay on the Origin of Languages*," *Graduate Faculty Philosophy Journal* (1986), 11:123 146, and in "The Political Argument of Rousseau's *Essay on the Origin of Languages*," in *Pursuits of Reason, Essays in Honor of Stanley Cavell* (Texas Tech. University Press, Lubbock, 1993), pp. 21–36. Two very different commentaries on the *Social Contract* are particularly helpful: Maurice Halbwachs's *Rousseau, Du contrat social* (Aubier, Paris, 1943), and Hilail Gildin's *Rousseau's Social Contract: The Design of the Argument* (University of Chicago Press, Chicago, 1983).

A note on the texts

The present collection brings together most of Rousseau's most important "political" writings, as well as some briefer polemical writings, and a few fragments and letters which shed light on the more formal, finished texts. By and large they appear here and in the companion volume, *The "Discourses" and other early political writings*, in the order in which they were written or published.

Some of the material included in this collection was not originally published by Rousseau himself, and it is not in all cases clear that he intended it to appear in print. Its inclusion therefore calls for at least a brief comment. We simply can no longer read and try to understand Rousseau exactly as he himself chose to present his thought and his person, and as his contemporaries came to know them. Many important drafts and fragments which he discarded or suppressed have been discovered in the course of the past two centuries. In addition, some fifty massive volumes of his correspondence have been published. Purists may regret the incorporation into his *oeuvre* of this material. Yet no conscientious student of Rousseau can simply ignore it, if only because much of it develops or illumines what he did publish or intend for publication. At the same time, conscientious scholars will take into account whether – and why – he may or may not have intended a given passage or text to be made public. Many of his better-known letters are short essays about important aspects of his thought. That is why they are well known. He fully expected that they would be made public, either by their addressees – a number of whom did, in fact, circulate and publish letters they had received from the by now famous Rousseau – or by himself. He certainly did not write the few letters included in this collection to unburden himself or to confide his inmost thoughts. He wrote them, as he repeatedly points out, in order to fulfill a moral obligation, to help or to benefit his addressees. They are as carefully crafted as his explicitly public writings. They, too, are politic.

The present standard edition of Rousseau's works is the five-volume Jean-Jacques Rousseau, *Oeuvres complètes*, edited by B. Gagnebin and M. Raymond (Paris, Pléiade, 1959–1995). In order to make it easier for readers to check the translation against the original, I introduced the practice of providing volume and page references to this edition: for example, *OC* III, 202–204, refers to pages 202–204 of volume III in the Pléiade *Oeuvres complètes*; [*202*] in the body of a translation indicates that what follows corresponds to page 202 of that volume of the Pléiade edition. A number of other translators have since felt free also to adopt this practice. In order further to facilitate cross-references, I have numbered Rousseau's paragraphs: *SC* III 2 [1] refers to the first paragraph in the second chapter of the third book of the *Social Contract*.

The present standard edition of Rousseau's correspondence is Jean-Jacques Rousseau, *Correspondance complète*, collected, edited, and annotated by R. A. Leigh (Institut et Musée Voltaire, Geneva and The Voltaire Foundation at the Taylor Institution, Oxford, 1965–1989); all references to this remarkable work are abbreviated *CC*, followed by the Roman numeral indicating the volume, and the Arabic numeral(s) indicating the page(s).

A note on the translations

Rousseau is a writer of uncommon range and power. Kant, the sober Kant, said that his writing so swept him away that he could not attend to his argument upon a first reading. No translation can hope to do justice to his original. My aim has therefore been no more than to render what he said and how he said it as faithfully and as unobtrusively as possible.

He was aware that understanding his writings may require effort. He repeatedly calls for attentive readers (e.g. *Ineq.* I [53]; *SC* III I [1]), and on at least one occasion he expressly invites us to re-read him with care (*Poland* 14 [3]; see also *Ineq.*, Notice about the Notes). In a letter to Mme. d'Epinay he tells her that she will have to "learn my 'dictionary'" because "my terms rarely have their usual meaning" (March 1756, *CC* III, 296). All of his readers have to learn his "dictionary." The following brief remarks are no more than preliminary notes for it.

Art, "art": see *First Discourse* [5], Editorial Note.

Bon (adj.), *bonté* (n.), *bien* (n., adv.), "good," "goodness," "good(s)" and "well," together with their antonyms, are key terms for Rousseau. For a brief comment about translating them, see the Editorial Note to *Letter to Voltaire* [3].

For the most part, I have translated *liberté* as "freedom," but *affranchir*, *affranchissement*, as "emancipation."

Morale (n.) means ethics; *moralité* (n.), "morality"; and, much of the time, *moral* (adj.), "moral," simply means what we mean by that term, namely whatever pertains to what is morally right or wrong. However, often Rousseau also uses "moral" in contrast to

xliv

"physical." We still do so as well, when we say that we have a moral certainty, to indicate that we believe something to be the case although we have no "physical" evidence to support that belief (cp. *Voltaire* [38]). More generally, Rousseau follows Pufendorf in speaking of "moral persons," associations, institutions, corporations which have no physical existence properly so called, but owe their existence to agreements, covenants, contracts, or to shared beliefs, opinions, attitudes, to *moeurs*, "morals]' or ways of life; such "moral persons" may perfectly intelligibly be said to pursue corporate ends or goods, and to possess a corporate will. *Moral* and *moeurs* are closely related: Pufendorf derives *moeurs* from *moral*; Burlamaqui derives *moral* from *moeurs*. *Moeurs* is notoriously difficult to translate. No single English word consistently means "shared public morality." "Manners" might seem plausible, but the burden of Rousseau's numerous discussions of *moeurs* is the discrepancy between manners and morals. From the *First Discourse* onwards, his constant concern is with this moral core of *moeurs*: he understands the Dijon Academy's Question about the impact of the arts and sciences on *moeurs* as a question about their impact on the moral tastes, dispositions, judgments, conduct, characteristic of a community's way of life. That is one reason why I have almost always translated *moeurs* as "morals." Admittedly, *moeurs* can also mean "customs" or "ways," as does its Latin root, *mores*. However, Rousseau distinguishes between *moeurs* and customs (e.g. in *Narcissus* [15]*; *SC* II 12 [5]). In a few rare cases – as when Le Roy speaks of the mating *moeurs* of partridges, deer and wolves (in the last line of his remarks about the *Second Discourse*); and when Rousseau speaks of the savages' ferocious *moeurs* (*Languages* 9 [5]) – I have translated *moeurs* as "ways." Although on one occasion Rousseau speaks of *moeurs* as one kind of law (*SC* II 12 [5]), he consistently adheres to the traditional distinction between *moeurs* and laws. Pre-political – barbarous and savage – peoples live by *moeurs* alone, whereas *civil*-ized peoples live also according to law strictly and properly so called (*Ineq.* II [15], [20]; *Languages* 5 [5]). Indeed, law more than anything else defines civil society, and hence being *civil*-ized. At the same time, Rousseau would fully agree with Montesquieu that ". . . a people invariably knows, loves, and defends its morals more than its laws" (*Spirit of the Laws* X 11). One more important reason for translating *moeurs* as "morals" is that what

Rousseau calls *moeurs* is very precisely what Kant calls *Sitten*, and Kant's *Sitten* is traditionally, and rightly, translated "morals" (as, for example, in *Groundwork of the Metaphysics of Morals*).

Patrie is now most commonly translated by "country," as in "my country." Yet "country" will not do, because Rousseau contrasts *patrie* and *pays*, "fatherland" and "country," and those who have a country (pays), even if they cannot be said to have a fatherland (*patrie*) (*Emile* v, *OC* iv 858; cp. *NH* vi 5, *OC* ii, 657). I have therefore consistently rendered *patrie* as "fatherland." "Fatherland" also preserves the traditional suggestion that citizenship bears a certain similarity to a filial relationship – filial, not necessarily paternal: in spite of its etymology, it is feminine (*la patrie*); and Rousseau does not hesitate to speak of the *mère patrie*, the mother fatherland (*Pol. Ec.* [34]; *Poland* 3 [8]). Unfortunately "fatherland" does not capture the echo of *patrie* which Rousseau also wants his reader to hear in "patriotism." No English word does.

Science: see *First Discourse* [5], Editorial Note.

In a number of cases I have tried to preserve some of the associations of the original: *force* (n.) means "strength" as well as "force." I have tried to render it as consistently as possible by "force." In part I have done so simply to keep before the reader's eyes how very frequently Rousseau uses "force" and cognates; in part I have done so in order to convey as faithfully as possible Rousseau's repeated inquiries into possible parallels and contrasts between physical and moral or psychological "force" – as when he characterizes the contract as a pooling of forces, or when, in a famous and ambiguous phrase, he speaks of men's being "forced to be free" (*SC* i 7 [8]), or when he derives "virtue" from "force" (*Emile* v, *OC* iv, 817; *Franquières* [21]; cp. *SC* iv 4 [1]*) and defines it as "the strength [*force*] and vigor of the soul" (*First Discourse* [11]; *Hero* [33] and Editorial Note). These inquiries are best seen as so many case studies of his constant, comprehensive examination of the relations between the law(s) of nature and the natural law(s). Unfortunately it is not always possible to convey this point as clearly in the translation as Rousseau made it in the original: when, in the brief paragraph introducing the *Social Contract*, Rousseau says he had overestimated his *forces*, it seems forced to avoid "strength;" and "The most inviolable law of nature is the law *du plus fort*" has to be "of the stronger" (*Poland* 13 [3]). *Fort* (n., adj.), "strong," clearly has the same root as *force* and *forcer*, and its occurrence therefore reinforces the associations with these words, whereas "strong" of course does not immediately evoke an association with "force." That association grows still weaker when it comes to *à force de* (see, in particular, *SC* II 9 [1]), which means "by dint of," and will evoke "force" only to the etymologically schooled reader; it cannot be rendered at all for *force de* (as in *Poland* 3 [2]), meaning "many," and suggesting that there is force in numbers. (See also the Introduction, p. xxi above, and the Introduction to *Discourses* tr., p. xxiii.)

In some cases I have tried to preserve associations with the writings of other authors. To take but one example: *inconvénient* (n., adj.) is commonly rendered "drawback" or "disadvantage." I have tried consistently to render it as "inconvenience" and "inconvenient," because that is the term Machiavelli uses quite routinely, as when he remarks that against the *inconvinienti* facing a newly established free State there is "no remedy more powerful, more valid, more secure, or more necessary than the killing of the sons of Brutus . . ." (*Discourses* I 16, with which cp. Rousseau's *Last Reply* [54]–[56]); it is the term Grotius uses in a crucial passage in which he also notes that ". . . you can frame no Form of Government in your Mind, which will be without Inconveniences [*incommodis*] and Dangers . . ." (*Right of War and Peace* I, 3, § viii); it is the term Hobbes uses: e.g. "The condition of man in this life shall never be without Inconveniences . . ." (*Leviathan* ch. XX, last para.; cp. ". . . the estate of Man can never be without some incommodity or other": *Leviathan* ch. XVIII, and *De cive*, ch. X, *passim*), which Sorbière, in whose translation Rousseau read Hobbes, sometimes renders *inconvénients* and sometimes *incommodités*; it is also the term Locke uses: ". . . *Civil Government* is the proper Remedy for the Inconveniences of the State of Nature, which must certainly be Great, where Men may be Judges in their own Case . . ." (*Second Treatise*, ch. II, § xiii; cp. *ib.*, ch. VII, §§ 90, 91; ch. VIII, § 101; ch. XI, §§ 127, 136), which the contemporary French translations render *inconvénients*; cp. *SC* III 15 [10]. What Rousseau calls "inconvenience(s)" in some contexts is what in other contexts he calls "evil(s)."

In a few cases I took advantage of the fact that some French words and expressions have become part of English by leaving them untranslated: "entre nous," "corvée," "amour propre." "Amour propre," one of the key terms of Rousseau's moral psychology, is a traditional stumbling-block for translators. Hume had already complained about the difficulties of finding a suitable English equivalent for it.

> It seems, indeed, certain that the *sentiment* of conscious worth, the self-satisfaction proceeding from a review of a man's own conduct and character – it seems certain, I say, that this sentiment which, though the most common of all sentiments, has no proper name in our language ... The term pride is commonly taken in a bad sense; but this sentiment seems indifferent ... The French express this sentiment by the term *amour-propre*; but as they also express self-love as well as vanity by the same term, there arises a great confusion ... *An Inquiry concerning the Principles of Morals*, Appendix IV: "Of Some Verbal Disputes," § 3 and note.

The obvious candidates for Rousseau's *amour propre* are "vanity," "vainglory" and "pride," especially since he introduces *amour propre* as a technical term in the context of his criticism of Hobbes's understanding of "vanity" or "vainglory." Yet none of these three English terms will do, if only because he also uses *vanité, orgueil* and *fierté*, and he contrasts them in the *Project for a Constitution for Corsica*, *OC* III, 937f. Fortunately, "amour propre" has found its way into Webster's *Dictionary* as well as into the *OED*. I therefore felt free to let it stand as is.

Sauvage (n., adj.) is consistently rendered "savage"; it is helpful to keep in mind that in French the word also means "wild" in contrast to "cultivated" and "domesticated," as in "wild flowers" or "wildlife;" for example, *Ineq.* I [11], and see *To Franquières* [9].

Sense (v., n.), in French as in English and in so many other languages, refers to physical as well as to moral and intellectual apprehension. Hence the distinction between being "sentient" or "sensitive" (*sensible*) and being "sensible" (*sensitif*). One prominent form the mid-eighteenth-century debate about materialism took was a debate about whether matter is or could be sentient or sensitive (see Editorial Note to *Letter to Voltaire* [8]). Rousseau explores the relations between "physical" sense and "moral" sense in all of his major writings, but perhaps most searchingly in the *Essay on the Origin of Languages* (especially in chapters 13 and 15); and at one time he considered writing a *morale sensitive*, an ethics based on sentience or sensibility, which he also thought of as *le matérialisme du Sage*, "the wise man's materialism" (*Conf.* IX, *OC* I, 409). His most sustained discussions of the virtues related to the senses, temperance, moderation, sobriety, are found at the end of Book IV of the *Emile* and in the second *Dialogue*, *OC* I, 804ff. William Empson has devoted four classical studies to the changing fortunes of this family of terms, in *The Structure of Complex Words*; Jane Austen explored it beautifully in *Sense and Sensibility*; and John Austin explored it ingeniously in *Sense and Sensibilia*. The secondary literature on "sensibility" is enormous. To my knowledge, the best history of the medical background remains Oswei Temkin's classical "Studien zum 'Sinn'-Begriff in der Medizin," *Kyklos* (1929), 2:21–105. I am not aware of a comparable study of the French background, but rich materials for one can be found in Jacques Roger's classical *Les Sciences de la vie dans la pensée du* XVIII*è* siècle (Armand Colin, Paris, 1963). Anyone interested in studying Rousseau's usage in detail will want to consult *Le Vocabulaire du sentiment dans l'oeuvre de J.-J. Rousseau*, compiled under the direction of Michel Gilot and Jean Sgard at the Centre d'Etude des Sensibilités de l'Université de Grenoble (Editions Slatkine, Geneva and Paris, 1970), and J. J. Spink, "Rousseau et la morale du sentiment (lexicologie, idéologie)," in *Rousseau after 200 Years*, edited by R. A. Leigh (CUP, Cambridge, 1982), pp. 239–250. Questions surrounding "sense" are further complicated by questions about *sentiment* or "sentiment." Rousseau reserves the term for the inmost stratum of our being and experience, what he came to call "the sentiment of one's own existence" (references in the Editorial Notes to *Second Discourse* I [21]). More generally, both "sense" and "sentiment" come to be seen as less rigorous but deeper, more rooted than reason or "mere ratiocination," and both French and English come increasingly to use "sentiment" in place of opinion, or judgment, or even thought – as Hume does in the passage about *amour propre* quoted above. Rousseau himself remains ever mindful of the difference between sentiment and thought, and he draws a sharp distinction between "proof by sentiment" and rational proof, a distinction which very strictly corresponds to the important distinction he frequently draws between persuasion and conviction (e.g. Voltaire [30]; *Franquières* [II], *To Mirabeau* 14]). For these reasons among others, it is preferable, whenever possible, to render *sentir* with "to sense" or "to be sensible to," rather than with the more usual "to feel." *Sentimental* ("sentimental") enters the language in the mid-eighteenth century, but plays no role in Rousseau's vocabulary; how much it, too, becomes saturated with the ambiguities of its root term is nicely conveyed by Flaubert's title *Education sentimentale*, "Sentimental Education."

Whenever Rousseau qualifies something as *véritable*, "genuine," he is explicitly or implicitly contrasting it with what he regards as a spurious alternative; *vrai*, "true" does not imply such a contrast.

Although he is remarkably consistent in the use of his technical vocabulary, Rousseau expressly calls attention to the fact that he finds it impossible to be invariably so (*Emile* II, *OC* IV, 345*); and that it sometimes suits his purposes not to be so (*SC* I 6 [10] near the end), in other words that it sometimes suits his purposes to be deliberately ambiguous in the use of his political language. Thus, for example, he will occasionally use the language of natural law, although he rejects the idea or concept of natural law. At times it suits him to use "government" to refer to what most of us would most of the time call either "government" or "the state" – as he does in the title of his work on *Poland* – although for precise, technical purposes, he restricts "government" to strictly subordinate administrative and executive functions (he reviews the various senses of "government" in *Lettres de la montagne* V, *OC* III, 770f. and *ib.*, VI, *OC* III, 808f.; also see *Emile* V, *OC* IV, 844–848, tr. Bloom 463–466). "Government," as he defines it, is not sovereign (*SC* III 1 [3]–[5]). The people is. In Rousseau's technical vocabulary, *peuple* or "people" corresponds to what we would now refer to either as "a people" or a "nation": as, for example, in "the French people or nation" (*SC* I 6 [10]); ". . . the act by which a people is a people . . . is the true foundation of society" (*SC* I 5 [2]). Like "nation," "people" can be used both in the singular – e.g. "the people is sovereign"; "it can be misled" – and in the plural – e.g. "there are no more peoples being formed" (*SC* IV 4 [1]). Rousseau also uses "people" to refer to the many, those who labor and are poor – e.g. "It is the people that makes up mankind; what is not people is so slight a thing as not to be worth taking into account" (*Emile* IV, *OC* IV, 509, tr. Bloom 225) – and whenever he uses "people" in his more technical sense, he wants his reader to have the association

1

with *peuple* in this more common sense of the term. Rousseau's use of *peuple(s)* significantly influenced later uses – and conceptions – of "folk," especially in the German sense of *Volk*.

Police means "political organization" or "administration" (*SC* III 15 [12], IV 1 [3]; *Poland* 7 [24]). *Policé* literally means "politicized" in contrast to being in the state preceding political society; the Latinized version of the word, "civilized," fails to do justice to the French word because it no longer has a primarily political connotation; also, Rousseau sometimes uses "civilize," and when he does, he uses it as we would use it now. Where possible I have therefore translated it "politically organized." I am not aware of a single occurrence of *civilization* in Rousseau; its first recorded use in French (in 1757) is by Rousseau's correspondent, Mirabeau ("Civilization: Contribution à l'histoire du mot," E. Benveniste, *Problèmes de linguistique générale* [Gallimard, Paris, 1966], pp. 336–345). *Politesse* is "politeness" in the sense of "urbanity" in contrast to "rusticity" or even to "boorishness" (see especially *First Discourse* [10], [14]); whereas "civility" consists in acting in conformity with natural right toward fellow-citizens, in contrast to "humanity," which consists in acting in conformity with it toward strangers. The contrast literally corresponds to the contrast citizen/man: see pp. x–xxx above. On *politic* (adj.) or "political" right and laws, see, again, the Introduction to *SC* tr. *Politique(s)* (n.) is now commonly translated "political theorist(s)," which suggests departments of political science, and has little to do with Rousseau's meaning. The true *politique*, he tells the Archbishop of Paris, seeks to render peoples happy and good by striving for the harmony between the private and the public good (*To Beaumont*, *OC* IV, 937). Bacon sometimes simply kept the French term – ". . . it is as hard and severe a thing to be a true politique, as to be truly moral" (*Advancement of Learning* II) – and sometimes used "politic men." I have somewhat reluctantly translated it as "politician(s)." The *politiques* were also the party of those who, like Bodin, sought political solutions to religious conflicts, and the term long had the same associations in its English use.

Such examples could be multiplied almost at will. An adequate discussion of any one of the more important terms in Rousseau's vocabulary would require a full essay. Every now and then I have flagged some of these terms in the Editorial Notes. In the

Introduction (pp. x–xxx above), I have sketched the broad outlines of what a fuller survey of his use of the key term "right" might look like.

While Rousseau is not perfectly consistent in his use of capitalization, certain words clearly mean one thing when he capitalizes them, and another when he does not. A few examples will, again, have to suffice. For the most part he uses *Cité*, "City," as a technical term roughly equivalent to the Latin *civitas*; it is, of course, the root of "Citizen," a term to which he did so much to restore its distinctive resonance. By contrast, *ville*, "city," means just what we mean when we speak about a city or a town; occasionally it is spelled *Ville*, and "City" then does not mean anything like *civitas*, but simply refers to a specific city, e.g. Lisbon. These differences should always be clear enough from the context.

Etat, "state," refers to (1) any more or less stable, lasting condition, as in "the state of her health" or in "state of affairs" and, of course, in "state of nature" or "civil state"; this is the meaning of "state" that informs Hume's criticism of Hobbes's state of nature: "Whether such a condition of human nature could ever exist, or if it did, could continue so long as to merit the appellation of a *state*, may justly be doubted" (*Concerning the Principles of Morals* 1, 3). (2) It refers to "estate" (German: *Stand*) as in "the third estate," as well as "rank" or "station" as in "my station and its duties." However, (3) *état* in this sense must sometimes be translated by "position," as in "being in a position to . . ." (4) Finally, Rousseau writes *état* in referring to any particular given political state, e.g. "the French state," whereas in reference to the political state in general he writes "State" (*Etat*): The ". . . public person . . . formed by the union of all the others, formerly assumed the name *City*, and now assumes that of *Republic* or of *body politic*, which is called by its members *State* when it is passive, *Sovereign* when active . . ." (*SC*, 1 7 [10]).

Gouvernement, "Government," is the institution of government; *gouvernement*, "government," refers to any given government, the government of this State or that, or of this or that province, municipality or other sub-division of the State.

The modern reader cannot help being struck by the fact that Rousseau does not capitalize certain words which contemporary writers would regard it as irreverent or inconsiderate not to capitalize.

Punctuation is almost as much a problem in rendering a text from one language into another as is vocabulary. Decisions about punctuation are decisions about respecting the meaning, but also the rhythm and flow of the text, and hence of the thought. Rarely is anything gained by breaking up a competent writer's sentences, and almost always something is lost in the process.

A note on the editorial notes and the index

The Editorial Notes have been relegated to the end in order to keep them from intruding between text and reader. They identify persons, events, texts or passages, and sometimes doctrines which Rousseau mentions or alludes to. Very occasionally they call attention to parallels with what he says in other writings. They remain at or near the surface of the texts. They do not analyze or interpret.

The Index is designed to be of help even to close readers of these texts.

The Social Contract
and other later political writings

DISCOURSE ON POLITICAL ECONOMY

[1] Economy (*Ethics and Politics*), the word is derived from οἰκός, house, and νομός, *law*, and originally merely means the wise and legitimate government of the household, for the common good of the entire family. The meaning of the term was subsequently extended to the government of the large family which is the state. In order to distinguish the two usages, it is called *general* or *political* economy in the latter case, and in the former, *domestic* or *private economy*. This article deals only with the first. Regarding domestic economy, see FATHER OF THE FAMILY.

[2] Even if there were a relation between the state and the family as close as a number of authors claim, it would still not follow that the rules of conduct appropriate to one of these two societies are suited to the other: they differ too much in size to admit of being administered in the same way, and there will always be a very great difference between domestic government, where the father can see everything for himself, and civil government, where the chief sees almost nothing but through someone else's eyes. For things to become equal in this respect, the father's talents, force, and all of his faculties would have to increase in proportion to the size of the family, and the soul of a powerful monarch would have to be in proportion to an ordinary man's soul as the extent of his empire is to a private person's inheritance.

[3] But how could the government of the state be like that of the family, when its foundation is so different? The father being physically stronger than his children, paternal power is rightly taken to be established by nature so long as they require his assistance. In the large family all of whose members are naturally equal, political authority, which is purely arbitrary in its institution, can be founded only on conventions, and the ma[*242*]gistrate can command others only by virtue of the laws. The father's duties are dictated to him by natural sentiments, and in a tone that rarely allows him to disobey. Chiefs have no comparable rule, and are really bound to the people only for what they have promised it they would do, and which it has a right to demand they perform. Another even more important difference is that since children have nothing but what they receive from the father, it is obvious that all the rights of

property belong to him, or emanate from him; the very opposite is the case in the large family, where the general administration is established solely to insure private property, which is prior to it. The primary aim of the entire household's labors is to preserve and to increase the father's patrimony, so that he might some day divide it among his children without impoverishing them; whereas the treasury's wealth is but a means, often poorly understood, of maintaining private persons in peace and plenty. In a word, the small family is destined to die out, and to break up some day into a number of other similar families; but since the large family is made to last forever in the same state, the first has to increase in order to multiply [into a number of other similar families]: whereas not only does it suffice for the other to preserve itself, but it can easily be proved that any increase is more prejudicial than useful to it.

[4] For various reasons derived from the nature of the matter, the father ought to command in the family. In the first place, the authority of the father and of the mother ought not to be equal; rather, there has to be a single government, and when opinions are divided there has to be one predominant voice that decides. In the second place, regardless of how slight the incapacities specific to women may be thought to be; since they invariably impose intervals of inaction on her, this is a sufficient reason to exclude her from this primacy: for when the balance is perfectly equal, a straw is enough to tip it. Moreover, the husband has to be able to review his wife's conduct: for it matters to him that the children he is forced to recognize and to raise belong to none other than himself. The wife, who has nothing comparable to fear, has not the same right over the husband. In the third place, the children ought to obey the father, initially out of necessity, then out of grati[*243*]tude; after having their needs attended to by him for the first half of their life, they should devote the second half to providing for his needs. In the fourth place, as regards servants, they also owe him their services in exchange for his providing their subsistence; unless they break the bargain when it no longer suits them. I say nothing about slavery; because it is contrary to nature, and no right can authorize it.

[5] None of this obtains in political society. Far from the chief's having a natural interest in the happiness of private individuals, it is not uncommon for him to seek his own happiness in their misery.

When magistrature is hereditary, a child often commands men: when it is elective, a thousand inconveniences attend elections, and in either case all the advantages of paternity are lost. If you have but a single chief, you are at the discretion of a master who has no reason to love you; if you have several, you have to bear both their tyranny and their dissentions. In a word, abuses are inevitable and their consequences fatal in any society, where the public interest and the laws have no natural force whatsoever, and are constantly under attack from the personal interest and the passions of the chief as well as of the members.

[6] Although the functions of the father of a family and of the foremost magistrate should aim at the same goal, they do so in such different ways; their duty and rights are so distinct that it is impossible to equate them without forming false ideas about the fundamental laws of society, and committing errors fatal to humankind. Indeed, while the voice of nature is the best counsel a good father should heed in order to fulfill his duties well, it is for the magistrate nothing but a false guide which constantly tends to distance him from his duties, and sooner or later drags him to his own and to the state's ruin unless he is restrained by the most sublime virtue. The only precaution the father of the family needs is to guard against depravation and to keep his natural inclinations from growing corrupt; but it is these very inclinations that corrupt the magistrate. To do well, the first need only consult his heart; the other becomes a traitor the moment he heeds his: he should be wary even of his reason, and follow no other rule than the public reason, which is the law. Indeed, nature has made many [*244*] good fathers of families; but it is doubtful that since the beginning of the world human wisdom made even ten men capable of governing their fellow-men.

[7] From everything I have just set forth, it follows that *public economy* has rightly been distinguished from *private economy*, and that since the family and the state have nothing in common but their chiefs' obligation to make each happy, the same rules of conduct could not apply to both. It seemed to me that these few lines would suffice to overthrow the odious system which Sir Filmer tried to establish in a work entitled *Patriarcha*, and to which two illustrious men did too much honor by writing books to refute it: besides, this error is very old, since even Aristotle saw fit to combat

it with arguments that can be found in the first book of his *Politics*.

[8] I invite my readers also clearly to distinguish *public economy*, which is my topic, and which I call *government*, from the supreme authority, which I call *sovereignty*; a distinction which consists in this, that the one has the legislative right and in some cases obligates the very body of the nation, whereas the other has only the executive power, and can only obligate individuals. *See* POLITICS and SOVEREIGNTY.

[9] Allow me to use for a moment a common and in many respects imprecise comparison, but one suited to making myself better understood.

[10] The body politic, taken by itself, can be looked upon as an organized body, alive, and similar to a man's. The sovereign power represents the head; the laws and customs are the brain, the principle of the nerves and the seat of the understanding, of the will, and of the senses, of which the judges and magistrates are the organs; commerce, industry, and agriculture are the mouth and stomach which prepare the common subsistence; public finances are the blood which a wise *economy*, performing the functions of the heart, sends out to distribute nourishment and life throughout the entire body; the citizens are the body and the members that make the machine move, live, and work, and no part of which can be hurt without the painful impression of it being straightaway conveyed to the brain, if the animal is in a state of health.

[*245*] [11] The life of the one as well of the other is the *self* common to the whole, the reciprocal sensitivity and the internal correspondence of all the parts. What if this communication should cease, the formal unity vanish, and the contiguous parts no longer belong together except by being next to one another? the man is dead, or the state is dissolved.

[12] The body politic is, then, also a moral being that has a will; and this general will, which always tends to the preservation and the well-being of the whole and of each part, and which is the source of the laws, is, for all the members of the state, in relation to one another and to it, the rule of what is just and what unjust; a truth which, incidentally, shows with how little sense so many writers have treated as theft the cunning prescribed to Lacedaemonian children to earn their frugal meal, as if anything the law com-

mands could fail to be legitimate. *See under* RIGHT the source of this great and luminous principle, which that article develops.

[13] It is important to note that this rule of justice, dependable with respect to all citizens, can be false with respect to strangers; and the reason for this is clear: that in that case the will of the state, although general with respect to its members, is no longer so with respect to the other states and their members, but becomes for them a particular and individual will that has its rule of justice in the law of nature, which is equally consistent with the principle established: for in that case the great city of the world becomes the body politic of which the law of nature is always the general will, and of which the various states and peoples are merely individual members.

[14] From these same distinctions applied to every political society and its members flow the most universal and dependable rules by which to judge a good or a bad government and, in general, the morality of all human actions.

[15] Every political society is made up of other, smaller societies of different kinds, each one of which has its interests and maxims; but these societies, which everyone perceives because they have an external and authorized form, are not the only ones that really exist in the state; all private individuals who are united by a common interest make up as many other, permanent or transient [societies] whose force is no less real for being [*246*] less apparent, and whose various relations, well observed, constitute the genuine knowledge of morals. It is all these tacit or formal associations which in so many ways modify the appearance of the public will by the influence of their own. The will of these particular societies always has two relations; for the member of the association, it is a general will; for the large society, it is a particular will, which very often proves to be upright in the first respect, and vicious in the second. A given person may be a devout priest, or a courageous soldier, or a zealous lawyer, and a bad citizen. A given deliberation may be advantageous to the small community, and most pernicious to the large one. It is true that since particular societies are always subordinate to those that contain them, one ought to obey the latter in preference to the former, that the duties of the citizen take precedence over those of the senator, and those of man over those of the citizen: but

unfortunately personal interest is always inversely proportional to duty, and increases in direct proportion as the association grows narrower and the commitment less sacred; invincible proof that the most general will is also the most just, and that the voice of the people is indeed the voice of God.

[16] It does not follow, however, that public deliberations are always equitable; they may not be so regarding foreign affairs; I have stated the reason why this is so. Thus it is not impossible that a well-governed republic might wage an unjust war. Nor is it impossible that the council of a democracy pass bad decrees or condemn the innocent: but none of this will ever happen unless the people is seduced by private interests which some few skillful men succeed by their reputation and eloquence to substitute for the people's own interest. Then the public deliberation will be one thing, and the general will another thing entirely. Do not, therefore, raise the democracy of Athens as an objection to me, because Athens was in fact not a democracy, but a most tyrannical aristocracy governed by learned men and orators. Attend carefully to what happens in any deliberation, and you will see that the general will is always for the common good; but very often some secret division develops, some tacit alliance which causes the assembly's natural disposition to be eluded in favor of private views. [247] Then the social body really divides into other bodies whose members adopt a general will, good and just with regard to these new bodies, unjust and bad with regard to the whole from which each of them dismembers itself.

[17] It is evident how easy it is, by means of these principles, to explain the apparent contradictions found in the conduct of so many men who are full of scruples and honor in some respects, deceitful and knavish in others, who trample underfoot the most sacred duties, yet are faithful to the death to commitments that are often illegitimate. Thus do the most corrupt men invariably render some sort of homage to the public faith; this (as was pointed out in the *article* RIGHT) is how even brigands, the enemies of virtue in the large society, worship its semblance in their dens.

[18] In establishing the general will as the first principle of public *economy* and the fundamental rule of government, I did not believe it necessary to inquire seriously whether the magistrates belong to the people or the people to the magistrates, and whether in public affairs it is the good of the state or the good of the chiefs that

should be consulted. The question has long since been settled one way by practice, and another by reason; and in general it would be a great folly to hope that those who are masters in fact would prefer some other interest to their own. Public *economy* should therefore be further subdivided into popular and tyrannical. The first is that of any state where there is unity of interest and will between the people and the chiefs; the other will necessarily exist wherever the government and the people have different interests, and hence opposing wills. Its maxims are recorded throughout the annals of history and the satires of Machiavelli. The others are found only in the writings of the philosophers who dare to call for the rights of humanity.

[19] I. The first and the most important maxim of legitimate or popular government, that is to say of government that has the good of the people as its object, is then, as I have said, in all things to follow the general will; but in order to follow it, one has to know it, and above all clearly to distin[*248*]guish it from the particular will beginning with oneself; a distinction it is always very difficult to draw and on which only the most sublime virtue can shed adequate light. Since one has to be free in order to will, another, no lesser, difficulty is to secure both public freedom and governmental authority. Inquire into the motives that have led men united by their mutual needs in the great society to unite more closely by means of civil societies; you will find none other than that of securing the goods, the life, and the freedom of each member through the protection of all: but how can men be forced to defend the freedom of one of them without infringing on the freedom of the others? and how can the public needs be met without disturbing the particular [or private] property of those who are forced to contribute to them? Regardless of the sophisms by which all this may get colored, certain it is that if someone can compel my will, I am no longer free, and that I am no longer master of my goods if someone else can interfere with them. This difficulty, which must have seemed insurmountable, was resolved together with the first difficulty by the most sublime of all human institutions, or rather by a celestial inspiration that taught man to imitate here below the immutable decrees of the divinity. By what inconceivable art were the means found to subjugate men in order to make them free? to use the goods, the labor and even the life of all of its members in

the service of the state, without compelling and consulting them? to shackle their will by their own agreement? to have their consent prevail over their refusal, and to force them to punish themselves when they do what they did not want? How can it be that they obey and no one commands, that they serve yet have no master; all the freer in fact than in apparent subjection, no one loses any more of his own freedom than might harm someone else's? These marvels are the work of law. It is to law alone that men owe justice and freedom. It is this salutary organ of the will of all that restores in [the realm of] right the natural equality among men. It is this celestial voice that dictates the precepts of public reason to every citizen, and teaches him to act in conformity with the maxims of his own judgment, and not to be in contradiction with himself. [*249*] It alone is also what the chiefs should cause to speak when they command; for as soon as one man lays claim to subjecting another to his private will independently of the laws, he instantly leaves the civil state and places himself in relation to him in the pure state of nature where obedience is never prescribed except by necessity.

[20] The chief's most urgent interest, as well as his most indispensable duty is therefore to see to it that the laws of which he is the minister and on which his entire authority is founded are observed. His having to make others observe them is all the more reason for himself, who enjoys all of their benefits, to observe them. For his example carries such force that even if the people were willing for him to cast off the yoke of the law, he should refrain from taking advantage of such a dangerous prerogative, which others would soon seek to usurp in turn, often to his prejudice. In the final analysis, since all of society's commitments are by their [very] nature reciprocal, it is not possible to place oneself above the law without renouncing its advantages, and no one owes anything to anyone who claims not to owe anyone anything. For the same reason, in a well-regulated government no exemption from the law will ever be granted on any grounds whatsoever. Even the citizens who have deserved well of the fatherland should be rewarded with honors and never with privileges: for the republic is on the brink of ruin as soon as one can think it a fine thing not to obey the laws. But if ever the nobility, or the military, or any other order in the

state were to adopt such a maxim, everything would be irremediably lost.

[21] The power of the laws depends even more on their own wisdom than on their ministers' severity, and the public will derives its greatest influence from the reason that dictated it: this is why Plato considers it a most important precaution always to place at the head of edicts a reasoned preamble which shows their justice and utility. Indeed, the first of all laws is to respect the laws: harshness of punishments is nothing but a vain expedient thought up by small minds to substitute terror for this respect which they are unable to achieve. It has always been noted that the countries where punishments are most terrible are also the countries where they [250] are most frequent; so that the cruelty of penalties shows nothing more than the large number of people breaking the law, and that by punishing everything equally severely, the guilty are forced to commit crimes in order to escape punishment for their failings.

[22] But although the government is not the master of the law, it is a considerable thing to be its guarantor and to dispose of a thousand ways of making it beloved. This is all that the talent for ruling consists in. With force in hand, there is no art to making everyone tremble, and not even much to winning men's hearts; for experience long ago taught the people to give its chiefs much credit for all the harm they do not inflict on it, and to adore them when they do not hate it. An imbecile who is obeyed can punish transgressions just like anyone else: the genuine statesman knows how to prevent them; he exercises his respectable dominion over wills even more than over actions. If he could bring it about that everyone did well, he himself would have nothing left to do, and the masterpiece of his labors would be to be able to remain idle. At least this much is certain, that the greatest talent of chiefs consists in disguising their power in order to render it less odious, and to lead the state so peacefully that it appears not to need leaders.

[23] I therefore conclude that just as the first duty of the lawgiver is to conform the laws to the general will, the first rule of public *economy* is that the administration conform to the laws. This much will even suffice for the state not to be badly governed, provided the lawgiver has attended as he should to everything required by

the location, the climate, the soil, the morals, the neighbors, and all the particular relations of the people that it was his task to institute. Not that an infinite number of details of policy and of *economy* is not left to the wisdom of the government: but it always has two infallible rules for acting well on such occasions: one is the spirit of the law, which should help decide the cases it could not anticipate; the other is the general will, the source and supplement of all the laws, and which should always be consulted in their absence. How, I shall be asked, can the general will be known in the cases in which it has not declared itself? Will the entire nation have to be assembled at each unanticipated event? It will be all the less [*251*] necessary to assemble it, as it is not certain that its decision would be the expression of the general will; as this method is impractical with a large people, and is rarely necessary when the government is well intentioned: for the chiefs know well enough that the general will is always on the side most favorable to the public interest, that is to say, the most equitable; so that one need only be just in order to be sure of following the general will. Often, when it is too flagrantly crossed, it allows itself to be perceived in spite of the dreadful curb [on it] by the public authority. I look as close by as I can for examples to follow in such a case. In China, the prince's constant maxim is to find his officers in the wrong in all disputes that arise between them and the people. Is bread expensive in some province? the commissioner is put in jail: does a riot break out in another? the governor is demoted and every mandarin is answerable with his life for all the evil that occurs in his department. Not that the affair is not subsequently examined in a regular trial: but this is the verdict anticipated on the basis of long experience. It rarely makes for an injustice that requires redress; and the emperor, persuaded that public clamor never arises without cause, always discovers among the seditious cries which he punishes some just grievances which he corrects.

|24| It is a considerable accomplishment to have brought the rule of order and peace to all parts of the republic; it is a considerable accomplishment to have the state tranquil and law respected; but if one does no more than this, it will all be more appearance than reality, and if the government limits itself to obedience it will find it difficult to get itself obeyed. While it is good to know how to use men as they are, it is much better still to make them what one

needs them to be; the most absolute authority is that which penetrates to man's inmost being, and affects his will no less than it does his actions. Certain it is that in the long run peoples are what government makes them be. Warriors, citizens, men, when it wants; mob and rabble when it pleases: and every prince who despises his subjects dishonors himself by showing that he did not know how to make them worthy of esteem. Therefore, form men if you want to command men: if you would have the laws obeyed, see to it [*252*] that they are loved, and that in order to do what one ought, it suffices to think that one ought to do it. That was the great art of ancient governments in those remote times when philosophers gave laws to peoples, and only used their authority to make them wise and happy. Hence the many sumptuary laws, the many regulations regarding morals, the many public maxims that were adopted or rejected with the utmost care. Even tyrants did not ignore this important part of administration, and they attended to the corruption of their slaves' morals as carefully as the magistrates did to the improvement of their fellow-citizens' morals. But our modern governments which believe that they have done everything when they have extracted money do not even imagine that it is necessary or possible to go that far.

[25] II. Second essential rule of public *economy*, no less important than the first. Do you wish the general will carried out? See to it that all particular wills take their bearings by it; and since virtue is nothing but this conformity of the particular will to the general will, to say the same thing in a word, make virtue reign.

[26] If politicians were less blinded by their ambition, they would see how impossible it is for any establishment whatsoever to function in conformity with the spirit of its institution, if it is not guided by the law of duty; they would sense that the mainspring of public authority is in the hearts of the citizens, and that nothing can replace morals in sustaining government. Not only are none but good people capable of administrating the laws, but basically none but honest people are capable of obeying them. Anyone who manages to withstand remorse will soon manage to withstand corporal punishment; a less harsh, less constant punishment, and one from which there is at least some hope of escaping; and regardless of the precautions that may be taken, those who are only waiting for impunity to do evil will scarcely lack means of eluding the law or

escaping the penalty. Then, once all particular interests unite against the general interest which is no longer that of anyone, public vices have greater force to enervate the laws than the laws have to repress the vices; and the corruption of the people and the chiefs finally spreads to the government, how[*253*]ever wise it may be: the worst of all abuses is to obey the laws in appearance only to break them safely in fact. Soon the best laws become the most harmful: it would be a hundred times better if they did not exist; it would be one resource remaining when no others are left. In such circumstances it is useless to add edicts upon edicts, regulations upon regulations. All this does is to introduce new abuses without correcting the earlier ones. The more you multiply laws, the more you cause them to be despised: and all the overseers you institute are nothing but new lawbreakers bound either to share [their bounty] with the old ones, or to do their plundering on their own. Soon the prize of virtue is awarded to brigandage: the vilest men enjoy the most credit; the greater they are, the more contemptible they are; their infamy bursts forth in their dignities, and they are dishonored by their honors. If they buy the votes of the chiefs or the protection of women, it is so that they might sell justice, duty, and the state in turn; and the people which does not see that its vices are the first cause of its misfortunes grumbles and, moaning, cries out, "All my evils come only from those I pay to protect me against them."

[27] At such times, in place of the voice of duty which no longer speaks in men's hearts, the chiefs are forced to substitute the cry of terror or the lure of some apparent interest by which they deceive their creatures. At such times one has to have recourse to all the petty and contemptible ruses they call *maxims of state* and *secrets of the cabinet*. All the vigor the government has left is used by its members to ruin and supplant one another while [the public] business is left unattended or gets attended to only as personal interest requires and directs. In the end all of these great politicians' skill consists in so dazzling those they need that each believes he is working for his own interest while working for *theirs*; I say theirs, as if it were indeed the case that the chiefs' genuine interest consisted in annihilating peoples in order to subjugate them, and in ruining their own good in order to secure its possession.

[28] But when the citizens love their duty, and the trustees of the public authority sincerely try to foster this love by their example and their [254] efforts, then all difficulties vanish, administration becomes so easy that it can do without that shady art which is secret only because it is so sinister. Those large spirits, so dangerous and so admired, all those great ministers whose glory is associated with the people's misery, are no longer missed; public morals take the place of the chiefs' genius; and the more virtue reigns, the less the need for talents. Even ambition is better served by duty than by usurpation: the people, convinced that its chiefs labor solely to make for its happiness, spares them, by its deference, from having to work at consolidating their power; and history shows us in a thousand places that the authority the people grants to those it loves and is loved by is a hundred times more absolute than all the tyranny of usurpers. This does not mean that the government should be afraid of using its power, but that it ought to use it only in a legitimate manner. History provides a thousand examples of ambitious or pusillanimous chiefs who have been undone by laxness or vanity, none [of a chief] who fared badly for being only equitable. But negligence should not be mistaken for moderation, nor gentleness for weakness. To be just, one has to be severe: to tolerate the wickedness one has the right and the power to repress is to be wicked oneself.

[29] It is not enough to tell the citizens, be good; they have to be taught to be so; and example itself, which in this respect is the first lesson, is not the only means that should be used: love of fatherland is the most effective; for as I have already said, every man is virtuous when his particular will conforms in all things to the general will, and we readily want [or will] what the people we love want [or will].

[30] It would seem that the sentiment of humanity dissipates and weakens as it spreads to the whole earth, and that we cannot be as touched by the calamities of Tartary or Japan as we are by those of a European people. Interest and commiseration must in some way be constricted and compressed in order to be activated. Now since this inclination in us can be useful only to those with whom we have to live, it is good that [the sentiment of] humanity, concentrated among fellow-citizens, acquire in them added force through

the habit of seeing one another, and the common interest [255] that unites them. Certain it is that the greatest marvels of virtue have been produced by love of fatherland: this gentle and lively sentiment which combines the force of amour propre with all the beauty of virtue, endows it with an energy which, without disfiguring it, makes it into the most heroic of all the passions. It is patriotism that produced the many immortal actions whose brilliance dazzles our weak eyes, and the many great men whose antique virtues are treated as fables ever since patriotism has been turned into derision. That should not surprise us; the transports of tender hearts look like so many chimeras to anyone who has not felt them; love of fatherland, a hundred times more lively and delightful than the love of a mistress, can also be conceived only by experiencing it: but it is easy to recognize in all the hearts it excites, in all the actions it inspires, this seething and sublime ardor which even the purest virtue does not radiate when separated from love of fatherland. Let us dare to contrast Socrates himself with Cato: the one was more a philosopher, the other more a citizen. Athens was already lost, and Socrates no longer had any other fatherland than the whole world: Cato always carried his fatherland within his heart; he lived for it alone, and could not outlive it. Socrates's virtue is that of the wisest of men: but compared to Caesar and Pompey, Cato seems like a god among mortals. The one teaches some few private individuals, fights the sophists, and dies for the truth: the other defends the state, freedom, the laws against the conquerors of the world, and finally leaves the earth when he no longer finds on it a fatherland to serve. A worthy disciple of Socrates would be the most virtuous of his contemporaries; a worthy imitator of Cato would be the greatest of his contemporaries. The virtue of the first would make for his own happiness, the second would seek his happiness in that of all. We would be taught by the one and led by the other, and this alone would determine the preference between them: for no one has ever made a people of wise men, but it is not impossible to make a people happy.

[31] Do we want peoples to be virtuous? Let us then begin by making them love their fatherland: but how will they love it if the fatherland is nothing more to them than it is to foreigners, and grants them only what it cannot refuse to anyone? It would be much worse if they did not even enjoy civil security in it, [256] and their

goods, their life or their freedom were at the discretion of powerful men, without their being able or permitted to dare invoke the laws. Then, subject to the duties of the civil state without enjoying even the rights of the state of nature and without being able to use their force to defend themselves, they would therefore be in the worst condition in which free men can find themselves, and the word *fatherland* could only have an odious or a ridiculous meaning for them. It is not believable that an arm can be injured or cut off and the pain of it not be conveyed to the head; it is no more believable that the general will would agree to have any member of the State, regardless of who he may be, injure or destroy another, than that the fingers of a man in possession of his reason gouge out his eyes. Private safety is so closely bound up with the public confederation that, if it were not for the concessions that have to be made to human weakness, this convention would by right be dissolved if a single citizen in the state perished who could have been saved; if a single one were wrongfully kept in jail, and if a single lawsuit were lost through a manifest injustice: for once the fundamental conventions have been violated, it is no longer clear what right or interest could maintain the people in the social union, lest it be retained in it by sheer force, which makes for the dissolution of the civil state.

[32] Indeed, is not the body of the nation committed to provide as conscientiously for the preservation of the least of its members as for that of all the others? and is the safety of a single citizen any less the common cause than the safety of the entire state? If we are told that it is good that a single person perish for all, I will admire this statement from the mouth of a worthy and virtuous patriot who voluntarily and out of duty consecrates himself to die for his country's safety: but if what is meant is that the government is permitted to sacrifice one innocent person for the safety of the many, I hold this to be one of the most execrable maxims that tyranny ever invented, the most false that might be advanced, the most dangerous that might be accepted, and the most directly contrary to the fundamental laws of society. Far from a single person having to perish for the sake of all, all have pledged their goods and their lives to the defense of each one of them, to the end that individual weakness might always be protected by [257] the public force, and each member by the whole state. Assume cutting off one person after another from the people, and then press the partisans

of this maxim to explain more fully what they understand by *the body of the state*, and you will see that they will finally reduce it to a small number of men who are not the people but the people's officers and who, having obligated themselves by personal oath to perish for its safety, claim that this proves that it is up to the people to perish for theirs.

[33] If one wants to find examples of the protection the state owes its members, and of the respect it owes their persons, one should look for them exclusively among the most illustrious and the most courageous nations on earth, and it is almost only among free peoples that they know what a man is worth. Everyone knows how perplexed the entire republic was when the question of punishing a guilty citizen arose in Sparta. In Macedonia a man's life was a matter of such importance that for all of his greatness, Alexander, that powerful monarch, would not have dared to have a criminal Macedonian put to death in cold blood, without having had the accused appear and defend himself before his fellow-citizens, and been condemned by them. But the Romans distinguished themselves above all peoples on earth by the government's regard for private individuals, and its scrupulous care to respect the inviolable rights of all members of the state. Nothing was as sacred as the life of simple citizens; it required no less than the assembly of the entire people to condemn one of them: neither the senate itself nor the consuls in all their majesty had this right, and among the most powerful people on earth, the crime and the punishment of a citizen was a public calamity; indeed it seemed so harsh to shed a citizen's blood for any crime whatsoever, that by the *lex Porcia* the death penalty was commuted to exile for all those who might wish to survive the loss of so sweet a fatherland. Everything in Rome and in the armies breathed the citizens' love for one another, and the respect for the name Roman which roused the courage and animated the virtue of anyone who had the honor to bear it. The hat of a citizen freed from slavery, the civic crown of the one who had saved another's life, were what people looked upon with the greatest pleasure in victory parades; and it should be no[258]ted that of the crowns with which fine actions were honored in wartime, only the civic and the victors' crown were made of grass and leaves; all the others were merely gold. This is how Rome was virtuous and became mistress of the world. Ambitious chiefs! A shepherd gov-

erns his dogs and his flocks, and is but the least of men. If it is fine to command, it is so when those who obey us can do us honor: therefore, respect your fellow-citizens, and you will render yourselves respectable; respect freedom and your power will increase daily: never exceed your rights and soon they will be boundless.

[34] Let the fatherland then prove to be the common mother of the citizens, let the advantages they enjoy in their country endear it to them, let the government leave them a large enough share of the public administration to feel they are at home, and let the laws be in their eyes nothing but the guarantors of the common freedom. These rights, fine as they are, belong to all men; but without appearing to attack them directly, the ill will of the chiefs easily reduces their effect to naught. Law that is abused serves the powerful both as an offensive weapon and as a shield against the weak, and the pretext of the public good is always the people's most dangerous scourge. What is most needful and perhaps most difficult in government is a strict integrity to render justice to all, and above all to protect the poor against the tyranny of the rich. The greatest evil has already been done where there are poor people to defend and rich people to restrain. The full force of the laws is effective only in the middle range; they are equally powerless against the rich man's treasures and the poor man's misery; the first eludes them, the second escapes them; the one tears the web, the other slips through it.

[35] It is, therefore, one of the most important tasks of government to prevent extreme inequality of fortunes, not by taking their treasures away from those who possess them, but by depriving everyone of the means to accumulate treasures, nor by building poorhouses, but by shielding citizens from becoming poor. Men unevenly distributed across the territory and crowded in one place while others get depopulated; the arts of pleasure and of pure skill favored at the expense of the useful and the [259] arduous trades; agriculture sacrificed to commerce; the tax-farmer made necessary by the bad administration of the state's finances; finally, venality pushed to such excess that reputation is reckoned in cash, and the virtues themselves are sold for money: such are the most perceptible causes of opulence and of misery, of private interest replacing the public interest, of the citizens' hatred of one another, of their indifference to the common cause, of the corruption of the people, and

of the weakening of all the springs of government. These are therefore evils difficult to cure by the time they make themselves felt,
but which a wise administration must prevent in order to maintain,
by means of good morals, respect for the laws, love of fatherland,
and the vigor of the general will.

[36] But all of these precautions will be insufficient if one does
not go about it at an ever deeper level. I conclude this part of
public *economy* where I should have begun it. The fatherland cannot
endure without freedom, nor freedom without virtue, nor virtue
without citizens; you will have everything if you form citizens; if
you do not, you will have nothing but nasty slaves, beginning with
the chiefs of the state. Now to form citizens is not the business of
a single day; and to have them be citizens when they are grown,
they have to be taught when they are children. I may be told that
anyone who has to govern men should not look for a perfection
beyond their nature of which they are not capable; that he must
not seek to destroy their passions, and that carrying out such a
project would be no more desirable than it would be possible. I will
grant all this all the more readily as a man devoid of all passions
would certainly be a very bad citizen: but it must also be granted
that while men cannot be taught not to love anything, it is not
impossible to teach them to love one object rather than another,
and to love what is genuinely fine rather than what is malformed.
If, for example, they are taught from sufficiently early on never to
look upon their individual [self] except in its relations with the body
of the state, and to perceive their own existence as, so to speak,
only a part of its existence, they will at last succeed in somehow
identifying with this larger whole, to feel themselves members of
the fatherland, to love it with that exquisite sentiment which any
isolated man has only for himself, to raise [260] their soul perpetu-
ally to this great object, and thus to transform into a sublime virtue
the dangerous disposition that gives rise to all of our vices. Not
only does Philosophy demonstrate the possibility of these new
directions, but History provides a thousand striking examples of it:
the reason they are so rare among us is that no one cares whether
there are citizens and still less does it occur to anyone to go about
forming them early enough. It is too late to change our natural
inclinations once they are set in their course, and habit has joined

amour propre; it is too late to draw us out of ourselves once the *human self*, concentrated within our hearts, has there become actively engaged in the contemptible concerns that do away with all virtue and make up the life of petty souls. How could the love of fatherland arise in the midst of so many other passions that stifle it? and what is left for fellow-citizens of a heart already divided between greed, a mistress, and vanity?

[37] It is from the first moment of life that one must learn to deserve to live; and since one shares in the rights of citizens from birth, the instant of our birth ought to be when we begin to practice our duties. Since there are laws for maturity, there should be laws for childhood that teach obedience to others; and as each man's own reason is not allowed to be the sole judge of his duties, the education of their children ought even less to be abandoned to their fathers' lights and prejudices, since it matters to the state even more than it does to the fathers; for in the course of nature the father's death often deprives him of the last fruits of that education, but the fatherland feels its effects sooner or later; the state endures and the family dissolves. If, by taking the fathers' place and assuming this important function, the public authority acquires their rights by fulfilling their duties, they have all the less reason to complain of it, as, strictly speaking, they do no more in this respect than change names, and under the name "citizen" they will have in common the same authority over their children which they exercised separately under the name *fathers*, and they will be no less obeyed by them when they speak in the name of law, than they were when they spoke in the name of nature. Public education under rules prescribed by the government, and under magistrates established by the sovereign is, then, [261] one of the fundamental maxims of popular or legitimate government. If children are raised in common in the midst of equality, if they are imbued with the laws of the state and the maxims of the general will, if they are taught to respect them above all things, if they are surrounded by examples and objects that constantly speak to them of the tender mother that nurtures them, of her love for them, of the invaluable goods she bestows on them, and of what they owe her in return, let us not doubt that this way they will learn to cherish one another as brothers, never to want anything but what the society wants, to

substitute the deeds of men and citizens for the sterile and vain babble of sophists, and one day to become the defenders and fathers of the fatherland whose children they will have been for so long.

[38] I shall say nothing of the magistrates destined to preside over this education, which is surely the most important business of the state. Clearly if such marks of public trust were granted lightly, if this sublime office were not the reward for their labors of those who had worthily discharged all the other offices, the honorable and sweet repose of their old age, and the culmination of all their honors, then the entire enterprise would be useless, and the education unsuccessful; for wherever the lesson is not backed by authority and the precept by example, instruction remains fruitless, and virtue itself is discredited in the mouth of one who does not practice it. But let illustrious warriors, bent under the weight of their laurels, preach courage; let upright magistrates grown grey in high office and on the bench teach justice; they will, in doing so, form virtuous successors, and transmit from age to age unto succeeding generations the experience and the talents of chiefs, the courage and the virtue of citizens, and the emulation common to all of them to live and to die for the fatherland.

[39] I know of only three peoples that engaged in public education in former times; namely, the Cretans, the Lacedaemonians, and the ancient Persians: it was a very great success among all three, and among the last two it achieved wonders. Once the world was divided into nations too large to be well governed, public education was no longer practicable; and other reasons which [262] are readily evident to the reader further prevented its being tried among any modern people. It is most remarkable that the Romans were able to do without it; but Rome was for five hundred years one continual miracle which the world should not hope to see again. The Romans' virtue, born of the horror of tyranny and the crimes of tyrants, and by the innate love of the fatherland, turned all their homes into so many schools of citizens; and the fathers' unlimited power over their children made for such severity in private governance that the father, more feared than the magistrate, was the censor of morals and the avenger of the laws in his domestic tribunal.

[40] This is how an alert and well-intentioned government, constantly vigilant to maintain or restore love of fatherland and good morals among the people, forestalls from afar the evils that sooner

or later result from the citizens' indifference to the fate of the republic, and contains within narrow bounds the personal interest which so isolates individuals that the state is weakened by their power and has nothing to hope for from their good will. Wherever the people loves its country, respects its laws, and lives simply, there is little left to be done to make it happy; and in public administration, where fortune plays less of a role than it does in the fate of individuals, wisdom is so close to happiness that the two merge.

[41] III. It is not enough to have citizens and to protect them; it is also necessary to give thought to their subsistence; and to provide for the public needs is a clear consequence of the general will, and the third essential duty of government. It should be evident that this duty consists not in filling the granaries of individuals and exempting them from work, but in keeping plenty so within their reach that, in order to acquire it, work is always necessary and never useless. It also extends to all operations involved in managing the public treasury and the expenses of public administration. Thus, having spoken about general *economy* in relation to the government of persons, it remains for us to consider it in relation to the administration of goods.

[42] This part offers no fewer difficulties to resolve or contradictions to remove than the preceding one. It is cer[*263*]tain that the right of property is the most sacred of all the rights of citizens, and more important in some respects than freedom itself; either because it bears more directly on the preservation of life; or because goods being easier to usurp and more difficult to defend than persons, greater respect ought to be accorded to what can more easily be seized; or, finally, because property is the true foundation of civil society, and the true guarantee of the citizens' commitments: for if persons were not answerable with their goods, nothing would be so easy as to elude one's duties and scoff at the laws. On the other hand, it is no less certain that the maintenance of the state and the government involves costs and expenditures; and since anyone who grants the end cannot refuse the means, it follows that the members of the society must contribute to its upkeep with their goods. What is more, it is difficult to protect the property of individuals on one side without attacking it on another, and the regulations regarding inheritances, wills and contracts cannot possibly avoid constraining citizens to some extent in disposing of their own goods and hence in their right of property.

[43] But besides what I have said above about the conformity between the authority of the law and the freedom of the citizen, one important observation about the disposition of goods overcomes a good many difficulties. Namely, that, as Pufendorf has shown, the right of property does not, by its nature, extend beyond the life of the proprietor, and the moment a man is dead, his goods no longer belong to him. To prescribe to him the conditions under which he may dispose of them is, therefore, at bottom, not so much seemingly to abridge the right of property, as to expand it in fact.

[44] In general, although the institution of the laws that regulate the power individuals have to dispose of their goods belongs exclusively to the sovereign, the spirit of these laws which the government should heed in implementing them is that from father to son and from kin to kin the family's goods leave it or are alienated as little as possible. There is a sensible reason for this as regards children, for whom the right of property would be quite useless if the father left them nothing, and who, moreover, since they have often contributed by their labor to the acquisition of [264] the father's goods, participate in this right on their own. But another, more remote but no less important, reason for it is that nothing is more fatal to morals and to the republic than continual changes of station and fortune among the citizens; changes that are both the proof and the source of a thousand disorders, that overwhelm and confuse everything, and as a result of which, since those who were brought up for one position now find themselves destined for another, neither those who rise nor those who fall can adopt the maxims or the enlightenment suited to their new station, much less fulfill its duties. I turn to the topic of public finances.

[45] If the people governed itself, and there were no intermediary between the administration of the state and the citizens, they would simply have to assess themselves as the occasion required, in proportion to public needs and individual resources; and since no one would ever lose sight of how monies are collected or used, neither fraud nor abuse could insinuate itself into how they are managed: the state would never be hobbled by debts, nor the people overwhelmed by taxes, or it would at least be consoled for the harshness of the levy by feeling confident about the use of these taxes. But things cannot possibly work this way; and however limited a state may be, its civil society is always too numerous to allow it to be

governed by all of its members. Public monies must necessarily pass through the hands of the chiefs who, in addition to the state's interest, all have their own private interest, which is not heeded last. The people, for its part, more alert to the chiefs' greed and mad expenditures than to the public needs, grumbles at seeing itself despoiled of necessities in order to contribute to the superfluities of others; and once these machinations have to a certain extent embittered it, even an administration of the utmost integrity will not succeed in restoring confidence. So that if the contributions are voluntary, they yield nothing; if they are forced, they are illegitimate; and the difficulty of a just and wise *economy* consists in this cruel alternative of either allowing the state to perish or attacking the sacred right of property which is its support.

[46] The first thing the founder of a republic must do after establishing the laws is to find funds sufficient for the upkeep of the magistrates [*265*] and other officers, and for all public expenditures. This fund is called *aerarium* or *public treasury* if it is in money; *public domain* if in land, and this latter is far preferable to the other for obvious reasons. Anyone who has given this matter sufficient thought could hardly reach a different conclusion about it than Bodin, who regards the public domain as the most honest and most secure of all means to provide for the state's needs; and it is worth noting that the first thing Romulus did in dividing the land was to set aside a third of it for this use. I recognize that it is not impossible for the yield from a badly administered domain to be reduced to nothing; but it is not of the essence of the domain to be badly administered.

[47] Before any use is made of this fund, it should be assigned or accepted by the assembly of the people or of the estates of the country, which should then determine its use. After this solemnity, which renders such funds inalienable, they so to speak change in nature, and their proceeds become so sacred that to divert the least portion to the detriment of their intended purpose is not only the most infamous of all thefts, but a crime of Lese-Majesty. It is a great dishonor for Rome that the integrity of the quaestor Cato should have aroused notice, and that an emperor rewarding a singer's talents with a few coins had to add that this money came from his family's goods, and not from the state's. But if there are few Galbas, where shall we look for Catos? and once vice no longer

dishonors, what chiefs will be sufficiently scrupulous as to refrain from touching the public revenues left to their discretion, and as not promptly to deceive even themselves, by pretending to confound their vain and scandalous dissipations with the glory of the state, and the means of extending their authority with those of increasing its power? In this delicate part of the administration above all, the only effective instrument is virtue, and the magistrate's integrity is the only curb capable of restraining his greed. The books and all of the managers' accounts serve less to lay bare their breaches of trust than to cover them up; and prudence is never as prompt to think up new precautions as knavery is to elude them. Therefore, leave be registers and [266] papers, and return the finances to trustworthy hands; it is the only way to have them managed in a trustworthy fashion.

[48] Once the public funds are established, the chiefs of the state are its rightful administrators; for this administration makes up one part of government, always essential, though not always equally so; its influence increases as that of the others decreases; and a government may be said to have reached its ultimate degree of corruption when it has no other sinews left but money: now, since all government continually tends to slacken, this reason alone shows why no state can subsist unless its revenues continually increase.

[49] The first hint that such an increase is needed is also the first sign of internal disorder in the state: and the wise administrator, while thinking about how to find money to attend to the present need, does not neglect inquiring into the remote cause of this new need: just as a sailor, seeing water flood his vessel, does not forget, as he gets the pumps working, also to locate and plug the leak.

[50] From this rule flows the most important maxim for the administration of finances, which is to concentrate much more carefully on preventing needs than on increasing revenues; however diligent one might be, help that comes only after the harm, and more slowly, invariably leaves the state on sufferance: as one tries to remedy one inconvenience, another is already making itself felt, and the very correctives produce new inconveniences; so that in the end the nation goes into debt, the people is downtrodden, the government loses all its vigor, and does but little with much money. I believe that from this great maxim, well established, flowed the wonders of ancient governments, which did more with their parsi-

mony than ours do with all their treasures; and this is perhaps the derivation of the meaning of the word *economy*, understood as the wise management of what one has rather than as the means of acquiring what one has not.

[51] Independently of the public domain, which yields to the state in proportion to the probity of those who manage it, anyone adequately acquainted with the full force of the general administration, especially when it is limited to legitimate means, [267] would be astounded at the resources chiefs have to anticipate all public needs, without touching the goods of individuals. Since they are the masters of all of the state's commerce, nothing is as easy for them as to direct it in a manner that provides for everything, often without their appearing to be involved. The true secret of finances and the source of their increase is to distribute food, money, and commodities in just proportions, according to times and places, provided that those who administer it are capable of looking far enough ahead, and of occasionally taking an apparent and immediate loss for the sake of a huge real gain in the long run. One has to have seen with one's own eyes a government subsidize, instead of taxing, the export of grain in years of plenty, and its import in years of scarcity, to believe it, and one would treat such facts as fictions if they had occurred in the distant past. Let us suppose it were suggested that in order to prevent scarcity in bad years, public granaries be established, would not the upkeep of such a useful establishment serve as the pretext for new taxes in any number of countries? In Geneva such granaries, established and maintained by a wise administration, are the public resource in bad years, and the principal state revenue at all times. *It nourishes and enriches* is the fine and just inscription one reads on the façade of the building. In order to present here the economic system of a good government, I have often turned my eyes toward that of this republic: happy thus to find in my fatherland the example of the wisdom and happiness I would like to see reign in all countries.

[52] If one inquires into how the needs of a state grow, one will discover that often they grow rather as do the needs of individuals, less out of genuine need than by a growth of useless desires, and that frequently expenditures are increased only to provide a pretext to increase income; so that it would sometimes benefit the state to forgo being rich, and this apparent wealth is basically a greater

burden to it than would be poverty itself. True, one might hope to keep peoples more tightly dependent by giving them with one hand what one has taken from them with the other, [*268*] and this was the policy Joseph followed with the Egyptians; but this vain sophism is all the more fatal to the state, as the money no longer returns to the same hands as those it left, and as with such maxims one only enriches lazy folk at the expense of useful men.

[53] An appetite for conquests is one of the most perceptible and dangerous causes for such an increase [in public needs and expenditures]. This appetite, often engendered by another kind of ambition than the one it seems to announce, is not always what it appears to be, and its genuine motive is not so much the apparent desire to aggrandize the nation as the hidden desire to increase the chiefs' domestic authority with the help of an increase in troops and under cover of the distraction which the objects of war cause in the minds of citizens.

[54] This much, at least, is most certain, that nothing is as downtrodden or as miserable as conquering peoples, and that their very successes only increase their miseries: even if this were not the lesson of history, reason alone would prove to us that the larger a state is, the more massive and burdensome do its expenditures become; for all the provinces have to contribute their share to the cost of the general administration, and in addition each province has to spend as much for its own particular administration as if it were independent. Add to this that all fortunes are made in one place and spent in another; which soon upsets the balance between production and consumption, and impoverishes much of the countryside to enrich a single town.

[55] Another source of the increase of public needs, related to the preceding one [, is this]. A time may come when the citizens, no longer regarding themselves interested in the common cause, would cease being the defenders of the fatherland, and the magistrates would rather command mercenaries than free men, if only in order sometime, somewhere, to use the first the better to subjugate the others. Such was the state of Rome at the end of the republic and under the emperors; for all the victories of the first Romans, like those of Alexander, had been won by courageous citizens who were ready to shed their blood for the fatherland when necessary, but who never sold it. Marius was the first who, in the war against Jugurtha, dishonored the [*269*] legions by introducing freedmen,

vagabonds, and other mercenaries into them. The tyrants, having become the enemies of the peoples they had assumed the responsibility of making happy, established standing armies, in appearance to contain foreigners, and in fact to oppress the local population. In order to raise these armies, tillers had to be taken off the land, the shortage of them lowered the quality of the produce, and their upkeep introduced taxes which raised its price. This first disorder caused peoples to grumble: in order to repress them, the number of troops had to be increased, and hence so had the misery; and the more despair increased, the greater the compulsion to increase it still more in order to avoid its consequences. On the other hand, these mercenaries, whose worth could be judged by the price at which they sold themselves, proud of their debasement, despising the laws that protected them and their brothers whose bread they ate, believed it brought them more honor to be the henchmen of Caesar than the defenders of Rome; and dedicated to blind obedience, they by their station held the dagger raised over their fellow-citizens, ready to slaughter all at the first signal. It would not be difficult to show that this was one of the principal causes of the ruin of the Roman empire.

[56] In our times the invention of artillery and of fortresses has forced the sovereigns of Europe to introduce the use of standing armies to defend their fortifications; but while the motives may be more legitimate, there is cause to fear that the effect may be equally fatal. It will be no less necessary to depopulate the countryside in order to form armies and garrisons; in order to maintain them, it will be no less necessary to oppress peoples; and of late these dangerous establishments have been growing so rapidly everywhere in our part of the world, that one can only anticipate the early depopulation of Europe, and sooner or later the ruin of the peoples that inhabit it.

[57] Be that as it may, it must be evident that such institutions necessarily subvert the true economic system which derives the state's principal revenues from the public domain, and leave only the deplorable resource of subsidies and imposts, which it remains for me to discuss.

[58] It should be recalled in this connection that the foundation of the social pact is property, and its first condition that everyone be maintained in the peaceful enjoyment of what [270] belongs to

him. It is true that by the same treaty everyone obligates himself, at least tacitly, to contribute toward the public needs; but since this commitment may not violate the fundamental law, and assumes that the contributors recognize the evidence of need, it is plain that in order to be legitimate, this contribution has to be voluntary, not by [each] individual will, as if it were necessary to have each citizen's consent, and he had to provide only what he pleases, which would go directly counter to the spirit of the confederation, but by a general will, with a majority vote, and in accordance with proportional rates that eliminate all arbitrariness from the imposition [of taxes].

[59] This truth, that taxes can be established legitimately only by the consent of the people or its representatives, has been generally recognized by all philosophers and jurisconsults who have achieved any reputation in matters of political right, not excepting Bodin himself. While some few have established apparently contrary maxims; besides its being easy to see the personal motives that led them to do so, they hedge them with so many conditions and restrictions that at bottom it comes to exactly the same thing: for whether the people can refuse or the sovereign ought not to exact, as regards right, it is a matter of indifference; and if it is only a question of force, then it is utterly useless to inquire what is and what is not legitimate.

[60] The contributions levied on the people are of two kinds: some real, which are levied on things [i.e. property]; the others personal, which are paid by the head. Both are called either *imposts* or *subsidies*: when the people fixes the sum it grants, it is called a *subsidy*; when it grants the full proceeds of a tax, it is an *impost*. In the book on the *Spirit of the Laws* one finds that the head tax is more in keeping with servitude, and the real tax more conformable with freedom. This would unquestionably be so if the shares paid per head were equal; for nothing would be more disproportionate than such a tax, and it is above all in strictly observed proportions that the spirit of freedom consists. But if taxation by head is strictly proportioned to individuals' means, as what in France is called *capitation* could be, and is thus both real and personal; then it is the most [271] equitable and hence the most conformable to free men. At first these proportions appear quite easy to observe because they are relative to a person's station in the world, and the marks of

one's station are always public; but quite aside from the fact that greed, influence, and fraud find ways to elude even such [public] evidence, it is rare that all the elements that should be included in these calculations are taken into account. First, the relation of quantities should be considered, according to which, all other things being equal, someone who has ten times more goods than another ought to pay ten times more. Second, the relation of uses, that is to say, the distinction between the necessary and the superfluous. Someone who has only the bare necessities should not pay anything at all; taxation of someone who has superflux may, if need be, go up to the full amount that exceeds his necessities. To which he will answer, in view of his rank, what would be superfluous for an inferior person is necessary for him; but this is a lie: for the Great have two legs, just as cowherds do, and like them they have but one stomach. Besides, these supposed necessities are so little necessary to his rank that if he could bring himself to give them up for some praiseworthy cause, he would be all the more respected for doing so. The people would prostrate themselves before a minister who would go to the council on foot because he had sold his carriages when the state was in dire need. Finally, the law does not prescribe magnificence to anyone, and propriety is never an argument against right.

[61] A third relation that is never taken into account, and yet should always count first, is the utility each person derives from the social confederation, which strongly protects the immense possessions of the rich and scarcely lets a wretch enjoy the hut he built with his own hands. Are not all the advantages of society on the side of the powerful and the rich? are not all the lucrative posts filled by them alone? are not all exceptions, all exemptions reserved for them? and is not all public authority to their advantage? Let a man of standing rob his creditors or commit other mischief, is he not always certain of impunity? Are not the canings he inflicts, the acts of violence he commits, even the murders and assassinations of which he is guilty, affairs that are hushed up, and within six months [272] no longer mentioned? Let the same man be robbed, the entire police is immediately astir, and woe to the innocents he suspects. Is he traveling in a dangerous place? there is the escort taking the field: does the axle of his carriage break? everyone flies to his aid: is there noise at his gate? he says a word, and all falls

silent: does the crowd bother him? he gives a sign, and all falls into place: is a cart-driver in his way? his people are ready to beat him up; and fifty honest pedestrians going about their business would be crushed to death rather than have one idle fop delayed in his coach. All these attentions cost him not a penny; they are the rich man's right, and not the price of riches. How different is the picture of the poor man! the more humanity owes him, the more society denies him: all doors are closed to him, even when he has the right to have them opened; and if sometimes he obtains justice, it is with greater difficulty than another would obtain a pardon; if there are corvées to be done, a militia to be raised, he is the first to be called up; in addition to his own burden, he always bears the burden from which his richer neighbor has the influence to get himself exempted; at the least accident that befalls him, everyone avoids him: if his poor cart tips over, far from being helped by anyone, I consider him fortunate if in making his way he escapes being battered by some young duke's ruffians; in a word, all free assistance flees him when he needs it, precisely because he lacks the means to pay for it; but I regard him a lost man if he has the misfortune to have an honest soul, an attractive daughter, and a powerful neighbor.

[62] Another, no less important point to note is that the losses of the poor are far more difficult to make up for than those of the rich, and that the difficulty of acquiring always grows in proportion to need. Nothing is made out of nothing; that is as true in business as in Physics: money is the seed of money, and the first ten francs are sometimes harder to earn than the second million. There is still more: that everything the poor man pays is forever lost to him, and remains in the hands of the rich or returns to them; and since the proceeds of taxes sooner or later go only to those who have a share in government or are close to it, they have a clear interest in raising taxes even as they pay their share.

[*273*] [63] Let us summarize in a few words the social pact of the two estates: *You need me because I am rich and you are poor; let us therefore enter into an agreement with one another: I will allow you the honor of serving me, provided you give me the little you have left for the trouble I shall take to command you.*

[64] When all these things are carefully put together, the conclusion will be that in order to distribute taxation in an equitable

and truly proportional fashion it should be imposed not solely in proportion to the taxpayers' goods, but in a proportion that takes account of the difference in their stations as well as of how much of their goods is superfluous. A most important and most difficult calculation which is performed daily by a host of clerks who are decent folk and know arithmetic, but which a Plato or a Montesquieu would have dared to undertake only with trembling and calling on heaven for enlightenment and integrity.

[65] Another inconvenience of the personal tax is that it is felt too directly and collected too harshly, which does not prevent its being evaded in many ways because it is easier to hide one's head than one's possessions from the tax-rolls and from prosecution.

[66] Of all the other kinds of assessment, quitrent on land or the tax on real estate [*taille réelle*] has always been considered the most advantageous in countries where they care more about how much and how reliably revenue is collected than they do about causing the people less distress. Some have even dared to say that the peasant has to be burdened in order to rouse him from his laziness, and that he would do nothing if he had nothing to pay. But the experience of all peoples belies this ridiculous maxim: it is in Holland, in England where the grower pays very little, and above all in China where he pays nothing, that the land is best cultivated. By contrast, wherever he is assessed in proportion to the yield from his land, he lets it lie fallow or produces only just what he needs to live. For to him who loses the fruit of his labor, to do nothing is to profit; and to place a fine on work is rather an odd way to get rid of laziness.

[67] Taxation on land or grain, especially when excessive, results in two inconveniences so terrible that in the long run they must depopulate and ruin all countries where it is established.

[*274*] [68] The first arises from the lack of circulation of specie because commerce and industry draw all the money from the countryside into the capitals: and since the tax destroys any proportion that might still have obtained between the grower's needs and the price of his grain, money constantly leaves and never returns; the richer the town, the more miserable the countryside. The proceeds from the land-taxes [*taille*] pass from the hands of the prince or the financier into the hands of artists and merchants; and the grower who never receives but the smallest share of these

proceeds finally wears himself out by forever paying the same and forever receiving less. How can a man be expected to live if he had only veins and no arteries, or if his arteries carried blood only to within four inches of his heart? Chardin says that in Persia the king's duties on commodities are also paid in commodities; this practice, which Herodotus reports to have formerly prevailed in that country up to the time of Darius, might prevent the evil of which I have been speaking. But unless in Persia intendants, directors, clerks, and warehouse guardians are a different kind of folk from anywhere else, I find it hard to believe that the least part of all this produce ever reaches the king, that the grain does not spoil in all those granaries, and that fire does not consume most of the warehouses.

[69] The second inconvenience arises from an apparent advantage, which lets evils get worse before they are noticed. Grain is a commodity whose price is not raised by taxes in the region that produces it, and in spite of its being absolutely necessary its supply decreases without its price increasing, which is why many people die of hunger even though grain continues to be cheap, and why the grower alone bears the burden of a tax he could not pass on in his selling price. It should be noted that one must not think about the real estate tax [*taille réelle*] in the same way one thinks about [sales taxes or] duties that raise the price of the merchandise on which they are imposed, and are thus paid not so much by the sellers as by the buyers. For these duties, however heavy they may be, are nevertheless voluntary, and are paid by the seller only in proportion to the quantity he buys; and since he buys only in proportion to his sales, he lays down the law to individuals. But the grower, who is compelled to pay at specified times for the land he cultivates, regardless of whether he sells or not, is not [275] free to wait until his produce commands the price he wants for it; and even if he were not to sell it to support himself, he would be forced to sell it to pay the land tax, so that sometimes it is the enormity of the assessment that keeps the commodity at a low price.

[70] Note, further, that the resources of commerce and industry, far from making the land tax [*taille*] more bearable because of an abundance of money, only make it more burdensome. I will not dwell on an obvious point, namely that although a greater or lesser quantity of money in a state may give it more or less credit abroad,

it in no way changes the real wealth of the citizens, and does not cause them to be better or worse off. But I will make the following two important remarks: the first, that unless the state has a food surplus and the abundance of money comes from selling it abroad, only trading towns are sensible of that abundance, while the peasant only grows relatively poorer because of it: the second, that since the price of everything rises with an increase in the money supply, taxes also have to rise proportionately, so that the grower finds himself more burdened without having more resources.

[71] It should be evident that the tax [*taille*] on land is actually a tax on its produce. Yet everyone agrees that nothing is so dangerous as a tax on grain paid by the buyer: how can they fail to see that the evil is a hundred times worse when this tax is paid by the grower himself? Is this not to attack the state's subsistence at its very source? Is it not also to work as directly as possible at depopulating the country; and hence at ruining it in the long run? For there is no worse scarcity for a nation than a scarcity of men.

[72] Only the genuine statesman raises his sights higher than the financial objective in setting tax rates, transforms burdensome obligations into useful ways of regulating policy, and causes the people to wonder whether the aim of such establishments might not have been the good of the nation rather than tax receipts.

[73] Duties on the import of foreign merchandise which the population craves but the country does not need, on the export of domestic merchandise of which the country has no excess and which foreigners cannot [*276*] do without, on the productions of the useless and excessively lucrative arts, municipal duties on pure amenities, and in general on all luxury items, will achieve this two-fold objective fully. Taxes such as these, which relieve poverty and burden riches, are the way to forestall the ever-widening inequality of fortunes, the subjection to the rich of a multitude of workers and of useless servants, the increase of idle people in cities, and the desertion of the countryside.

[74] It is important to set a proportion between the price of things and the duties imposed on them such that individuals' greed not be too tempted by the magnitude of the profits to commit fraud. Contraband should also be made less easy by favoring merchandise that is least easy to hide. Finally, the tax should be paid by the user of the taxed item rather than by the seller who would be exposed to

more temptations and means to commit fraud by the many duties with which he would be burdened. Such is the consistent practice in China, the country in the world with the highest and the best collected taxes: the merchant pays nothing; the buyer alone pays the duty, without its giving rise to grumbling or sedition; for, since the commodities necessary for life, such as rice and grain, are completely tax-exempt, the people are not oppressed, and the tax falls only on the well-to-do. In any event, all these precautions should be dictated not so much by the fear of contraband as by the care the government should exercise to protect individuals from being seduced by illegitimate profits which, after having turned them into bad citizens, would soon turn them into dishonest folk.

[75] Let heavy taxes be imposed on liveries, carriages, mirrors, chandeliers, and fancy furniture, fabrics and gilding, town-house courtyards and gardens, theatrical performances of every kind, the idle professions: such as buffoons, singers, actors, and, in a word, on the host of objects of luxury, diversion and idleness that strike all eyes, and are all the more difficult to hide as their sole use is show, and they would be useless if they were not seen. There is no reason to fear that the proceeds from such taxes would be haphazard because they are only based on things that are not absolutely necessary: it shows a very poor knowledge of men to believe [277] that once they have let themselves be seduced by luxury they can ever renounce it; they would a hundred times sooner renounce necessities and even rather die of hunger than of shame. The increased expense will be just one more reason to sustain it, when the vanity of showing that one is opulent finds its reward in the price of the object and the cost of the tax. As long as there are rich people, they will want to distinguish themselves from the poor, and the state cannot possibly devise a less burdensome or a more secure revenue than one based on this distinction.

[76] For the same reason industry would not in the least suffer from an economic order that enriched public Finances, revived Agriculture by relieving the grower, and insensibly brought all fortunes closer to that moderate condition which makes for a state's genuine force. I admit that some fashions might disappear more rapidly as a result of taxes; but only to be replaced by others from which the worker would gain, without the Treasury's suffering any loss. In a word, if we assume that the spirit of the government is

consistently to raise all taxes from the superflux of riches, then one of two things will happen: either the rich will renounce their superfluous expenditures in favor of exclusively useful ones which will redound to the profit of the state; in that case the tax rate will have brought about the same result as the best sumptuary laws; the expenditures of the state will necessarily have been reduced along with those of individuals; and the Treasury would take in less this way only if it had to pay out much less: or, if the rich do not in any way reduce their excesses, the Treasury will collect in tax proceeds the resources it was seeking in order to provide for the state's real needs. In the first place the Treasury is richer by all the expenditures it does not have to make; in the second, it is also richer by the useless expenditures of individuals.

[77] Let us add to all this an important distinction in the matter of political right, and to which governments intent on doing everything by themselves should pay close attention. I said that since personal taxes and imposts on things that are absolutely necessary directly attack the right of property, and hence the true foundation of political society, they are always liable to dangerous consequences, unless they are [*278*] established with the express consent of the people or of its representatives. This is not so regarding duties on things the use of which one can deny oneself; for since in that case the individual is not absolutely constrained to pay, his contribution may be taken to be voluntary; so that the individual consent of each of the contributors takes the place of the general consent, and in a way even presupposes it: for why would the people oppose any assessment that affects only those who are willing to pay it? It seems to me certain that whatever is neither proscribed by the laws nor contrary to morals, and the government may forbid, it may permit subject to a duty. If, for example, the government may prohibit the use of carriages, it may with all the more reason impose a tax on carriages, a wise and useful way to censure their use without putting a halt to it. Taxation may then be looked upon as a kind of fine, the amount of which compensates for the infraction it punishes.

[78] It might be objected that since those whom Bodin calls *imposteurs*, that is to say those who impose or think up taxes, belong to the class of the rich, they will not take pains to spare others at their own expense, and burden themselves in order to relieve the

poor. But such ideas must be rejected. If in every nation those to whom the sovereign commits the government of peoples were by their very station the peoples' enemies, it would not be worth the trouble to inquire what they must do to make the people happy.

Of
the Social Contract

or

Principles
of Political Right

by

Jean Jacques Rousseau
Citizen of Geneva

– foederis aequas
Dicamus leges

Aeneid, xi

NOTICE

This small treatise is drawn from a larger work, undertaken many years ago without consulting my strength and long since abandoned. Of the various sections that could be extracted from what did get done, this is the most considerable, and the one that has seemed to me the least unworthy of being submitted to the public. The rest no longer exists.

BOOK I

[1] I want to inquire whether in the civil order there can be some legitimate and sure rule of administration, taking men as they are, and the laws as they can be: In this inquiry I shall try always to combine what right permits with what interest prescribes, so that justice and utility may not be disjoined.

[2] I begin without proving the importance of my subject. I shall be asked whether I am a prince or a lawgiver that I write on Politics? I reply that I am not, and that that is why I write on Politics. If I were a prince or a legislator, I would not waste my time saying what needs doing; I would do it, or keep silent.

[3] Born a citizen of a free State, and a member of the sovereign, the right to vote in it is enough to impose on me the duty to learn about public affairs, regardless of how weak might be the influence of my voice on them. Happy, whenever I meditate about Governments, always to find in my inquiries new reasons for loving that of my country!

CHAPTER ONE
SUBJECT OF THIS FIRST BOOK

[1] Man is born free, and everywhere he is in chains. One believes himself the others' master, and yet is more a slave than they. How did this change come about? I do not know. What can make it legitimate? I believe I can solve this question.

[2] If I considered only force, and the effect that follows from it, [*352*] I would say; as long as a People is compelled to obey and does obey, it does well; as soon as it can shake off the yoke and does shake it off, it does even better; for in recovering its freedom by the same right as the right by which it was robbed of it, either the people is well founded to take it back, or it was deprived of it without foundation. But the social order is a sacred right, which provides the basis for all the others. Yet this right does not come from nature; it is therefore founded on conventions. The problem is to know what these conventions are. Before coming to that, I must establish what I have just set forth.

CHAPTER TWO
OF THE FIRST SOCIETIES

[1] The most ancient of all societies and the only natural one is that of the family. Even so children remain bound to the father only as long as they need him for their preservation. As soon as that need ceases, the natural bond dissolves. The children, exempt from the obedience they owe the father, the father exempt from the cares he owed the children, all equally return to independence. If they remain united, they are no longer so naturally but voluntarily, and even the family maintains itself only by convention.

[2] This common freedom is a consequence of man's nature. His first law is to attend to his own preservation, his first cares are those he owes himself, and since, as soon as he has reached the age of reason, he is sole judge of the means proper to preserve himself, he becomes his own master.

[3] The family is, then, if you will, the first model of political societies; the chief is the image of the father, the people are the image of the children, and all, being born equal and free, alienate their freedom only for the sake of their utility. The only difference is that in the family the father's love for his children repays him for the cares he bestows on them, and that in the State the pleasure of commanding takes the place of the chief's lack of love for his peoples.

[4] Grotius denies that all human power is established for [*353*] the sake of the governed: he gives slavery as an example. His most frequent mode of argument is always to establish right by fact.* One could use a more consistent method, but not one more favorable to Tyrants.

[5] So that, according to Grotius, it is an open question whether humankind belongs to a hundred men, or whether those hundred men belong to humankind, and throughout his book he appears to incline to the first opinion: that is also Hobbes's sentiment. Here,

---

* "Learned investigations of public right are often nothing but the history of ancient abuses, and it was a misplaced single-mindedness to have taken the trouble to study them too closely." *Ms Treatise on the Interests of France in Relation to Her Neighbors; by M. L[e] M[arquis] d'A[rgenson].* This is precisely what Grotius did.

then, is humankind, divided into herds of cattle, each with its chief who tends it to devour it.

[6] As a shepherd is of a nature superior to his flock's, so too are the shepherds of men, who are their chiefs, of a nature superior to their peoples'. This is how, according to Philo, the Emperor Caligula reasoned; concluding rather well from this analogy that kings were Gods, or that peoples were beasts.

[7] Caligula's reasoning amounts to that of Hobbes and of Grotius. Aristotle before all of them had also said that men are not naturally equal, but that some were born for slavery and others for domination.

[8] Aristotle was right, but he mistook the effect for the cause. Any man born in slavery is born for slavery, nothing could be more certain. Slaves lose everything in their chains, even the desire to be rid of them; they love their servitude, as the companions of Ulysses loved their brutishness.* Hence, if there are slaves by nature, it is because there were slaves contrary to nature. Force made the first slaves, their cowardice perpetuated them.

[9] I have said nothing about King Adam, or about emperor Noah, father of three great monarchs who among themselves divided the uni[*354*]verse, as did the children of Saturn, whom some believed they recognized in them. I hope my moderation will be appreciated; for since I am a direct descendant from one of these Princes, and perhaps from the elder branch, for all I know, I might, upon verification of titles, find I am the legitimate King of humankind. Be that as it may, it cannot be denied that Adam was Sovereign of the world as Robinson was of his island, as long as he was its sole inhabitant; and what made this empire convenient was that the monarch, secure on his throne, had neither rebellions, nor wars, nor conspirators to fear.

CHAPTER THREE
THE RIGHT OF THE STRONGER

[1] The stronger is never strong enough to be forever master, unless he transforms his force into right, and obedience into duty. Hence

---

* See a small treatise by Plutarch entitled: *That Beasts Use Reason.*

the right of the stronger; a right which is apparently understood ironically, and in principle really established: But will no one ever explain this word to us? Force is a physical power; I fail to see what morality can result from its effects. To yield to force is an act of necessity, not of will; at most it is an act of prudence. In what sense can it become a duty?

[2] Let us assume this alleged right for a moment. I say that it can only result in an unintelligible muddle. For once force makes right, the effect changes together with the cause; every force that overcomes the first, inherits its right. Once one can disobey with impunity, one can do so legitimately, and since the stronger is always right, one need only make sure to be the stronger. But what is a right that perishes when force ceases? If one has to obey by force, one need not obey by duty, and if one is no longer forced to obey, one is no longer obliged to do so. Clearly, then, this word "right" adds nothing to force; it means nothing at all here.

[3] Obey the powers that be. If this means yield to force, the precept is good but superfluous, I warrant that it [*355*] will never be violated. All power comes from God, I admit it; but so does all illness. Does this mean it is forbidden to call the doctor? A brigand takes me by surprise at the edge of a woods: am I not only forced to hand over my purse, but also obliged in conscience to hand it over even if I could withhold it? For the pistol he holds is, after all, also a power.

[4] Let us agree, then, that force does not make right, and that one is only obliged to obey legitimate powers. Thus my original question keeps coming back.

Chapter Four
Of Slavery

[1] Since no man has a natural authority over his fellow-man, and since force produces no right, conventions remain as the basis of all legitimate authority among men.

[2] If, says Grotius, an individual can alienate his freedom, and enslave himself to a master, why could not a whole people alienate its freedom and subject itself to a king? There are quite a few ambiguous words here which call for explanation, but let us confine

ourselves to the word *alienate*. To alienate is to give or to sell. Now, a man who enslaves himself to another does not give himself, he sells himself, at the very least for his subsistence: but a people, what does it sell itself for? A king, far from furnishing his subjects' subsistence, takes his own entirely from them, and according to Rabelais a king does not live modestly. Do the subjects then give their persons on condition that their goods will be taken as well? I do not see what they have left to preserve.

[3] The despot, it will be said, guarantees civil tranquility for his subjects. All right; but what does it profit them if the wars his ambition brings on them, if his insatiable greed, the harassment by his administration cause them more distress than their own dissension would have done? What does it profit them if this very tranquility is one of their miseries? Life is also tranquil in dungeons; is that enough to feel well in them? The Greeks imprisoned in the Cyclops's cave lived there [*356*] tranquilly, while awaiting their turn to be devoured.

[4] To say a man gives himself gratuitously is to say something absurd and inconceivable; such an act is illegitimate and null, for the simple reason that whoever does so is not in his right mind. To say the same of a whole people is to assume a people of madmen; madness does not make right.

[5] Even if everyone could alienate himself, he could not alienate his children; they are born men and free; their freedom belongs to them, no one but they themselves has the right to dispose of it. Before they have reached the age of reason, their father may in their name stipulate conditions for their preservation, for their well-being; but he cannot give them away irrevocably and unconditionally; for such a gift is contrary to the ends of nature and exceeds the rights of paternity. Hence, for an arbitrary government to be legitimate, the people would, in each generation, have to be master of accepting or rejecting it, but in that case the government would no longer be arbitrary.

[6] To renounce one's freedom is to renounce one's quality as man, the rights of humanity, and even its duties. There can be no possible compensation for someone who renounces everything. Such a renunciation is incompatible with the nature of man, and to deprive one's will of all freedom is to deprive one's actions of all morality. Finally, a convention that stipulates absolute authority

on one side, and unlimited obedience on the other, is vain and contradictory. Is it not clear that one is under no obligation toward a person from whom one has the right to demand everything, and does not this condition alone, without equivalent and without exchange, nullify the act? For what right can my slave have against me, since everything he has belongs to me, and his right being mine, this right of mine against myself is an utterly meaningless expression?

[7] Grotius and the rest derive from war another origin of the alleged right of slavery. Since, according to them, the victor has the right to kill the vanquished, the latter can buy back his life at the cost of his freedom; a convention they regard as all the more legitimate because it proves profitable to both parties. But it is clear that this alleged right to kill the vanquished in no way results from the state of war. Men are not naturally enemies, if only because when they live in their primitive independence [*357*] the relation among them is not sufficiently stable to constitute either a state of peace or a state of war. It is the relation between things and not between men that constitutes war, and since the state of war cannot arise from simple personal relations but only from property relations, private war or war between one man and another can exist neither in the state of nature, where there is no stable property, nor in the social state, where everything is under the authority of the laws.

[8] Individual fights, duels, skirmishes, are acts that do not constitute a state; and as for the private wars authorized by the ordinances of King Louis IX of France and suspended by the peace of God, they are abuses of feudal government, an absurd system if ever there was one, contrary both to the principles of natural right and to all good polity.

[9] War is then not a relationship between one man and another, but a relationship between one State and another, in which individuals are enemies only by accident, not as men, nor even as citizens,*

---

* The Romans who understood and respected the right of war better than any nation in the world were so scrupulous in this regard that a citizen was not allowed to serve as a volunteer without having enlisted specifically against the enemy, and one designated as such by name. When a Legion in which the Younger Cato fought his first campaign under Popilius was reorganized, the Elder Cato wrote to Popilius that if he was willing to have his son continue to serve under him, he would have to have him take a new military oath because, the first oath having

but as soldiers; not as members of the fatherland, but as its defenders. Finally, any State can only have other States, and not men, as enemies, inasmuch as it is impossible to fix a true relation between things of different natures.

[10] This principle even conforms to the established maxims of all ages and to the constant practice of all civilized peoples. Declarations of war are warnings not so much to the powers as to their subjects. The foreigner, whether he be a king, a private individual, or a people, who robs, kills, or detains subjects without declaring war on their prince, is not an enemy, he is a brigand. Even in the midst of war, a just prince may well seize everything in enemy territory that belongs to the public, but he respects the person and the goods of private individuals; he respects rights on which his own are founded. Since the aim of war is the destruction of the enemy State, one has the right to kill its defenders as long as they bear arms; but as soon as they lay down their arms and surrender they cease to be enemies or the enemy's instruments, and become simply men once more, and one no longer has a right over their life. It is sometimes possible to kill the State without killing a single one of its members: and [*358*] war confers no right that is not necessary to its end. These principles are not those of Grotius; they are not founded on the authority of poets, but follow from the nature of things, and are founded on reason.

[11] As regards the right of conquest, it has no other foundation than the law of the stronger. If war does not give the victor the right to massacre vanquished peoples, then this right which he does not have cannot be the foundation of the right to enslave them. One has the right to kill the enemy only when one cannot make him a slave. Hence the right to make him a slave does not derive from the right to kill him: it is therefore an iniquitous exchange to make him buy his life, over which one has no right whatsoever, at the cost of his freedom. Is it not clear that by establishing the right of life and death by the right of slavery, and the right of slavery by the right of life and death, one falls into a vicious circle?

been vacated, he could no longer bear arms against the enemy. And the same Cato wrote to his son to be careful not to appear in battle without having taken this new oath. I know that the siege of Clusium and other individual facts can be urged against me, but I cite laws, practices. The Romans are the people who least frequently transgressed their laws, and they are the only ones to have had such fine ones. [1782 edn.]

[12] Even assuming this terrible right to kill all, I say that a slave made in war or a conquered people is not bound to anything at all toward their master, except to obey him as long as they are forced to do so. In taking an equivalent of his life, the victor did not spare it: instead of killing him unprofitably, he killed him usefully. So far, then, is he from having acquired over him any authority associated with his force, that they continue in a state of war as before; their relation itself is its effect, and the exercise of the right of war presupposes the absence of a peace treaty. They have made a convention; very well: but that convention, far from destroying the state of war, presupposes its continuation.

[13] Thus, from whatever angle one looks at things, the right to slavery is null, not only because it is illegitimate, but because it is absurd and meaningless. These words *slavery* and *right* are contradictory; they are mutually exclusive. Either between one man and another, or between a man and a people, the following speech will always be equally absurd. *I make a convention with you which is entirely at your expense and entirely to my profit, which I shall observe as long as I please, and which you shall observe as long as I please.*

[359]

Chapter Five
That One Always Has to Go back to a First Convention

[1] Even if I were to grant everything I have thus far refuted, the abettors of despotism would be no better off. There will always be a great difference between subjugating a multitude and ruling a society. When scattered men, regardless of their number, are successively enslaved to a single man, I see in this nothing but a master and slaves, I do not see in it a people and its chief; it is, if you will, an aggregation, but not an association; there is here neither public good, nor body politic. That man, even if he had enslaved half the world, still remains nothing but a private individual; his interest, separate from that of the others, still remains nothing but a private interest. When this same man dies, his empire is left behind scattered and without a bond, like an oak dissolves and collapses into a heap of ashes on being consumed by fire.

[2] A people, says Grotius, can give itself to a king. So that according to Grotius a people is a people before giving itself to a king. That very gift is a civil act, it presupposes a public deliberation. Hence before examining the act by which a people elects a king, it would be well to examine the act by which a people is a people. For this act, being necessarily prior to the other, is the true foundation of society.

[3] Indeed, if there were no prior convention, then, unless the election were unanimous, why would the minority be obliged to submit to the choice of the majority, and why would a hundred who want a master have the right to vote on behalf of ten who do not want one? The law of majority rule is itself something established by convention, and presupposes unanimity at least once.

[*360*]

Chapter Six
Of the Social Pact

[1] I assume men having reached the point where the obstacles that interfere with their preservation in the state of nature prevail by their resistance over the forces which each individual can muster to maintain himself in that state. Then that primitive state can no longer subsist, and humankind would perish if it did not change its way of being.

[2] Now, since men cannot engender new forces, but only unite and direct those that exist, they are left with no other means of self-preservation than to form, by aggregation, a sum of forces that might prevail over those obstacles' resistance, to set them in motion by a single impetus, and make them act in concert.

[3] This sum of forces can only arise from the cooperation of many: but since each man's force and freedom are his primary instruments of self-preservation, how can he commit them without harming himself, and without neglecting the cares he owes himself? This difficulty, in relation to my subject, can be stated in the following terms.

[4] "To find a form of association that will defend and protect the person and goods of each associate with the full common force, and by means of which each, uniting with all, nevertheless obey

49

and remain as free as before." This is the fundamental
hich the social contract provides the solution.

ses of this contract are so completely determined by
⌐₀ the act that the slightest modification would render
them null and void; so that although they may never have been
formally stated, they are everywhere the same, everywhere tacitly
admitted and recognized; until, the social compact having been violated, everyone is thereupon restored to his original rights and
resumes his natural freedom while losing the conventional freedom
for which he renounced it.

[6] These clauses, rightly understood, all come down to just one,
namely the total alienation of each associate with all of his rights
to the whole community: For, in the first place, since each gives
himself entirely, the condition is [*361*] equal for all, and since the
condition is equal for all, no one has any interest in making it burdensome to the rest.

[7] Moreover, since the alienation is made without reservation,
the union is as perfect as it can be, and no associate has anything
further to claim: For if individuals were left some rights, then,
since there would be no common superior who might adjudicate
between them and the public, each, being judge in his own case on
some issue, would soon claim to be so on all, the state of nature
would subsist and the association necessarily become tyrannical or
empty.

[8] Finally, each, by giving himself to all, gives himself to no
one, and since there is no associate over whom one does not acquire
the same right as one grants him over oneself, one gains the equivalent of all one loses, and more force to preserve what one has.

[9] If, then, one sets aside everything that is not of the essence
of the social compact, one finds that it can be reduced to the following terms: *Each of us puts his person and his full power in common
under the supreme direction of the general will; and in a body we receive
each member as an indivisible part of the whole.*

[10] At once, in place of the private person of each contracting
party, this act of association produces a moral and collective body
made up of as many members as the assembly has voices, and which
receives by this same act its unity, its common *self*, its life and its
will. The public person thus formed by the union of all the others

formerly assumed the name *City** and now assumes [*362*] that of *Republic* or of *body politic*, which its members call *State* when it is passive, *Sovereign* when active, *Power* when comparing it to similar bodies. As for the associates, they collectively assume the name *people* and individually call themselves *Citizens* as participants in the sovereign authority, and *Subjects* as subjected to the laws of the State. But these terms are often confused and mistaken for one another; it is enough to be able to distinguish them where they are used in their precise sense.

CHAPTER SEVEN
OF THE SOVEREIGN

[1] This formula shows that the act of association involves a reciprocal engagement between the public and private individuals, and that each individual, by contracting, so to speak, with himself, finds himself engaged in a two-fold relation: namely, as member of the Sovereign toward private individuals, and as a member of the State toward the Sovereign. But here the maxim of civil right, that no one is bound by engagements toward himself, does not apply; for there is a great difference between assuming an obligation toward oneself, and assuming a responsibility toward a whole of which one is a part.

[2] It should also be noted that the public deliberation which can obligate all subjects toward the Sovereign because of the two differ-

---

* The true sense of this word is almost entirely effaced among the moderns; most take a city for a City, and a bourgeois for a Citizen. They do not know that houses make the city but Citizens make the City. This same error once cost the Carthaginians dear. I have not read that the subjects of any Prince were ever given the title *Cives*, not even the Macedonians in ancient times nor, in our days, the English, although they are closer to freedom than all the others. Only the French assume the name *Citizen* casually, because they have no genuine idea of it, as can be seen in their Dictionaries; otherwise they would be committing the crime of Lese-Majesty in usurping it: for them this name expresses a virtue and not a right. When Bodin wanted to speak of our Citizens and Bourgeois, he committed a bad blunder in taking the one for the other. M. d'Alembert made no mistake about it, and in his article *Geneva* he correctly distinguished the [*362*] four orders of men (even five, if simple foreigners are included) there are in our city, and only two of which make up the Republic. No other French author has, to my knowledge, understood the true meaning of the word *Citizen*.

ent relations in terms of which each subject is viewed cannot, for the opposite reason, obligate the Sovereign toward itself, and that it is therefore contrary to the nature of the body politic for the Sovereign to impose on itself a law which it cannot break. Since the Sovereign can consider itself only in terms of one and the same relation, it is then in the same situation as a private individual contracting with himself: which shows that there is not, nor can there be, any kind of fundamental law that is obligatory for the body of the people, not even the social contract. This does not mean [*363*] that this body cannot perfectly well enter into engagements with others about anything that does not detract from this contract; for with regard to foreigners it becomes a simple being, an individual.

[3] But the body politic or Sovereign, since it owes its being solely to the sanctity of the contract, can never obligate itself, even toward another, to anything that detracts from that original act, such as to alienate any part of itself or to subject itself to another Sovereign. To violate the act by which it exists would be to annihilate itself, and what is nothing produces nothing.

[4] As soon as this multitude is thus united in one body, one cannot injure one of the members without attacking the body, and still less can one injure the body without the members being affected. Thus duty and interest alike obligate the contracting parties to help one another, and the same men must strive to combine in this two-fold relation all the advantages attendant on it.

[5] Now the Sovereign, since it is formed entirely of the individuals who make it up, has not and cannot have any interests contrary to theirs; consequently the Sovereign power has no need of a guarantor toward the subjects, because it is impossible for the body to want to harm all of its members, and we shall see later that it cannot harm any one of them in particular. The Sovereign, by the mere fact that it is, is always everything it ought to be.

[6] But this is not the case regarding the subjects' relations to the Sovereign, and notwithstanding the common interest, the Sovereign would have no guarantee of the subjects' engagements if it did not find means to ensure their fidelity.

[7] Indeed each individual may, as a man, have a particular will contrary to or different from the general will he has as a Citizen. His particular interest may speak to him quite differently from the common interest; his absolute and naturally independent existence

may lead him to look upon what he owes to the common cause as a gratuitous contribution, the loss of which will harm others less than its payment burdens him and, by considering the moral person that constitutes the State as a being of reason because it is not a man, he would enjoy the rights of a citizen without being willing to fulfill the duties of a subject; an injustice, the progress of which would cause the ruin of the body politic.

[*364*] [8] Hence for the social compact not to be an empty formula, it tacitly includes the following engagement which alone can give force to the rest, that whoever refuses to obey the general will shall be constrained to do so by the entire body: which means nothing other than that he shall be forced to be free; for this is the condition which, by giving each Citizen to the Fatherland, guarantees him against all personal dependence; the condition which is the device and makes for the operation of the political machine, and alone renders legitimate civil engagements which would otherwise be absurd, tyrannical, and liable to the most enormous abuses.

CHAPTER EIGHT
OF THE CIVIL STATE

[1] This transition from the state of nature to the civil state produces a most remarkable change in man by substituting justice for instinct in his conduct, and endowing his actions with the morality they previously lacked. Only then, when the voice of duty succeeds physical impulsion and right succeeds appetite, does man, who until then had looked only to himself, see himself forced to act on other principles, and to consult his reason before listening to his inclinations. Although in this state he deprives himself of several advantages he has from nature, he gains such great advantages in return, his faculties are exercised and developed, his ideas enlarged, his sentiments ennobled, his entire soul is elevated to such an extent, that if the abuses of this new condition did not often degrade him to beneath the condition he has left, he should ceaselessly bless the happy moment which wrested him from it forever, and out of a stupid and bounded animal made an intelligent being and a man.

[2] Let us reduce this entire balance to terms easy to compare. What man loses by the social contract is his natural freedom and

an unlimited right to everything that tempts him and he can reach; what he gains is civil freedom and property in everything he possesses. In order not to be mistaken about these compensations, one has [*365*] to distinguish clearly between natural freedom which has no other bounds than the individual's forces, and civil freedom which is limited by the general will, and between possession which is merely the effect of force or the right of the first occupant, and property which can only be founded on a positive title.

[3] To the preceding one might add to the credit of the civil state moral freedom, which alone makes man truly the master of himself; for the impulsion of mere appetite is slavery, and obedience to the law one has prescribed to oneself is freedom. But I have already said too much on this topic, and the philosophical meaning of the word *freedom* is not my subject here.

CHAPTER NINE
OF REAL PROPERTY

[1] Each member of the community gives himself to it at the moment of its formation, such as he then is, he himself with all his forces, of which the goods he possesses are a part. It is not that by this act possession changes in nature by changing hands, and becomes property in the hands of the Sovereign: But just as the City's forces are incomparably greater than a private individual's, so public possession in fact has greater force and is more irrevocable, without being any more legitimate, at least for foreigners. For with regard to its members, the State is master of all their goods by the social contract which serves as the basis of all rights within the State; but with regard to other Powers it is master of all of its members' goods only by the right of the first occupant which it derives from private individuals.

[2] The right of the first occupant, although more real than the right of the stronger, becomes a true right only after the right of property has been established. Every man naturally has the right to everything he needs; but the positive act that makes him the proprietor of some good excludes him from all the rest. Having received his share, he must be bound by it, and he has no further

right to the community [of goods]. That is why the right of the first occupant, so weak in the state of nature, is respected by everyone living in civil society. [*366*] In this right one respects not so much what is another's as what is not one's own.

[3] In general, to authorize the right of the first occupant to any piece of land, the following conditions must apply. First, that this land not yet be inhabited by anyone; second, that one occupy only as much of it as one needs to subsist: In the third place, that one take possession of it not by a vain ceremony, but by labor and cultivation, the only sign of property which others ought to respect in the absence of legal titles.

[4] Indeed, does not granting the right of the first occupant to need and to labor extend it as far as it can go? Can this right be left unbounded? Shall it suffice to set foot on a piece of common land forthwith to claim to be its master? Shall having the force to drive other men off it for a moment suffice to deprive them of the right ever to return? How can a man or a people seize an immense territory and deprive all mankind of it except by a punishable usurpation, since it deprives the rest of mankind of a place to live and of foods which nature gives to all in common? When Núñez Balboa, standing on the shore, took possession of the southern seas and of all of South America in the name of the crown of Castile, was that enough to dispossess all of its inhabitants and to exclude all the Princes of the world? If it had been, then such ceremonies were repeated quite unnecessarily, and all the catholic King had to do was from his council-chamber all at once to take possession of the entire universe; except for afterwards subtracting from his empire what the other Princes already possessed before.

[5] It is intelligible how individuals' combined and contiguous pieces of ground become the public territory, and how the right of sovereignty, extending from subjects to the land they occupy, becomes at once real and personal; which places the possessors in a position of greater dependence, and turns their very forces into the guarantors of their fidelity. This advantage seems not to have been fully appreciated by ancient monarchs who, only calling themselves Kings of the Persians, of the Scythians, of the Macedonians, seem to have looked upon themselves as chiefs of men rather than as masters of the country. Present-day monarchs [*367*] more

shrewdly call themselves Kings of France, of Spain, of England, etc. By thus holding the land, they are quite sure of holding its inhabitants.

[6] What is remarkable about this alienation is that the community, far from despoiling individuals of their goods by accepting them, only secures to them their legitimate possession, changes usurpation into a genuine right, and use into property. Thereupon the possessors, since they are considered to be the trustees of the public good, since their rights are respected by all the members of the State and preserved by all of its forces against foreigners, have, by a surrender that is advantageous to the public and even more so to themselves, so to speak acquired everything they have given. The paradox is easily explained by the distinction between the rights the Sovereign and the proprietor have to the same land, as will be seen below.

[7] It may also happen that men begin to unite before they possess anything and that, seizing a piece of land sufficient for all, they enjoy its use in common or divide it among themselves, either equally or according to proportions established by the Sovereign. Regardless of the manner of this acquisition, the right every individual has over his own land is always subordinate to the right the community has over everyone, without which there would be neither solidity in the social bond, nor real force in the exercise of Sovereignty.

[8] I shall close this chapter and this book with a comment that should serve as the basis of the entire social system; it is that the fundamental pact, rather than destroying natural equality, on the contrary substitutes a moral and legitimate equality for whatever physical inequality nature may have placed between men, and that while they may be unequal in force or in genius, they all become equal by convention and by right.*

---

* Under bad governments this equality is only apparent and illusory; it serves only to maintain the poor in his misery and the rich in his usurpation. In fact the laws are always useful to those who possess something and harmful to those who have nothing: Whence it follows that the social state is advantageous for men only insofar as all have something and none has too much of anything.

Book ii

Chapter One
That Sovereignty is Inalienable

[1] The first and the most important consequence of the principles established so far is that the general will alone can direct the forces of the State according to the end of its institution, which is the common good: for while the opposition of particular interests made the establishment of societies necessary, it is the agreement of these same interests which made it possible. What these different interests have in common is what forms the social bond, and if there were not some point on which all interests agree, no society could exist. Now it is solely in terms of this common interest that society ought to be governed.

[2] I say, then, that sovereignty, since it is nothing but the exercise of the general will, can never be alienated, and that the sovereign, which is nothing but a collective being, can only be represented by itself; power can well be transferred, but not will.

[3] Indeed, while it is not impossible that a particular will agree with the general will on some point, it is in any event impossible for this agreement to be lasting and constant; for the particular will tends, by its nature, to partiality, and the general will to equality. It is even more impossible to have a guarantee of this agreement, even if it always obtained; it would be an effect not of art, but of chance. The Sovereign may well say, I currently will what a given man wills or at least what he says he wills; but it cannot say: what this man is going to will tomorrow, I too shall will it; since it is absurd for the will to [*369*] shackle itself for the future, and since no will can consent to anything contrary to the good of the being that wills. If, then, the people promises simply to obey, it dissolves itself by this very act, it loses its quality of being a people; as soon as there is a master, there is no more sovereign, and the body politic is destroyed forthwith.

[4] This is not to say that the commands of the chiefs may not be taken for general wills as long as the sovereign is free to oppose them and does not do so. In such a case the people's consent has

to be presumed from universal silence. This will be explained more fully.

Chapter Two
That Sovereignty is Indivisible

[1] For the same reason that sovereignty is inalienable, it is indivisible. For either the will is general* or it is not; it is either the will of the body of the people, or that of only a part. In the first case, the declaration of this will is an act of sovereignty and constitutes law; in the second case it is merely a particular will, or an act of magistracy; at most it is a decree.

[2] But our politicians, unable to divide sovereignty in its principle, divide it in its object; they divide it into force and will, into legislative and executive power, into rights of taxation, justice and war, into domestic administration and the power to conduct foreign affairs: sometimes they mix up all these parts and sometimes they separate them; they turn the Sovereign into a being that is fantastical and formed of disparate pieces; it is as if they were putting together man out of several bodies one of which had eyes, another arms, another feet, and nothing else. Japanese conjurors are said to carve up a child before the spectators' eyes, then, throwing all of its members into the air one after the other, they make [*370*] the child fall back down alive and all reassembled. That is more or less what our politicians' tricks are like; having dismembered the social body by a sleight-of-hand worthy of the fairground, they put the pieces back together no one knows how.

[3] This error comes from not having framed precise notions of sovereign authority, and from having taken what were mere emanations from this authority for parts of this authority itself. Thus, for example, the act of declaring war and that of making peace have been regarded as acts of sovereignty, which they are not; for neither of these acts is a law but only an application of the law, a particular act which decides a case, as will clearly be seen once the idea that attaches to the word *law* has been fixed.

---

* For a will to be general, it is not always necessary that it be unanimous, but it is necessary that all votes be counted; any formal exclusion destroys generality.

[4] By examining the other divisions in the same way, one would discover that whenever one believes one sees sovereignty divided, one is mistaken, that the rights which one takes for parts of this sovereignty are all subordinate to it, and always presuppose supreme wills which these rights simply implement.

[5] It would be difficult to exaggerate how much this lack of precision has clouded the conclusions of writers on matters of political right when they sought to adjudicate the respective rights of kings and peoples by the principles they had established. Anyone can see in chapters three and four of the first Book of Grotius how that learned man and his translator Barbeyrac get entangled and constrained by their sophisms, fearful of saying too much or not saying enough according to their views, and of offending the interests they had to reconcile. Grotius, a refugee in France, discontented with his fatherland, and wanting to pay court to Louis XIII to whom his book is dedicated, spares nothing to despoil peoples of all their rights, and to invest kings with them as artfully as possible. This would certainly also have been to the taste of Barbeyrac, who dedicated his translation to King George I of England. But unfortunately the expulsion of James II, which he calls an abdication, forced him to be on his guard, to equivocate, to be evasive, in order not to make a usurper of William. If these two writers had adopted the true principles, all their difficulties would have been solved, and they would always have been consistent; but they would have sadly told the truth and [*371*] paid court only to the people. Now, truth does not lead to fortune, and the people confers no ambassadorships, professorships or pensions.

CHAPTER THREE
WHETHER THE GENERAL WILL CAN ERR

[1] From the preceding it follows that the general will is always upright and always tends to the public utility: but it does not follow from it that the people's deliberations are always equally upright. One always wants one's good, but one does not always see it: one can never corrupt the people, but one can often cause it to be mistaken, and only when it is, does it appear to want what is bad.

[2] There is often a considerable difference between the will of all and the general will: the latter looks only to the common interest, the former looks to private interest, and is nothing but a sum of particular wills; but if, from these same wills, one takes away the pluses and the minuses which cancel each other out,* what is left as the sum of the differences is the general will.

[3] If, when an adequately informed people deliberates, the Citizens had no communication among themselves, the general will would always result from the large number of small differences, and the deliberation would always be good. But when factions arise, small associations at the expense of the large association, the will of each one of these associations becomes general in relation to its members and particular in relation to the State; there can then no longer be said to be as many voters as [*372*] there are men, but only as many as there are associations. The differences become less numerous and yield a less general result. Finally, when one of these associations is so large that it prevails over all the rest, the result you have is no longer a sum of small differences, but one single difference; then there is no longer a general will, and the opinion that prevails is nothing but a private opinion.

[4] It is important, then, that in order to have the general will expressed well, there be no partial society in the State, and every Citizen state only his own opinion.* Such was the single sublime institution of the great Lycurgus. That if there are partial societies, their number must be multiplied, and inequality among them prevented, as was done by Solon, Numa, Servius. These are the only precautions that will ensure that the general will is always enlightened, and that the people make no mistakes.

---

* *Each interest*, says the M[arquis] d'A[rgenson], *has different principles. The agreement between two individual interests is formed by opposition to a third party's interest.* He might have added that the agreement between all interests is formed by opposition to each one's interest. If there were no different interests, the common interest would scarcely be sensible since it would never encounter obstacles: everything would run by itself, and politics would cease to be an art.

* "In truth, says Machiavelli, some divisions harm Republics, and some benefit them; harmful are those that are accompanied by factions and parties; beneficial are those that do not give rise to factions and parties. Therefore, since the founder of a Republic cannot prevent enmities, he must make the best provision possible against factions." *Hist[ory] of Floren[ce]*, Bk. VII [ch. 1].

CHAPTER FOUR
OF THE LIMITS OF SOVEREIGN POWER

[1] If the State or the City is only a moral person whose life consists in the union of its members, and if the most important of its cares is the care for its self-preservation, then it has to have some universal and coercive force to move and arrange each part in the manner most conformable to the whole. Just as nature gives each man absolute power over his members, the social pact gives the body politic absolute power over all of its members, and it is this same power which, directed by the general will, bears, as I have said, the name of sovereignty.

[*373*] [2] But in addition to the public person, we must consider the private persons who make it up, and whose life and freedom are naturally independent of it. It is therefore important to distinguish clearly between the respective rights of the Citizens and of the Sovereign,* as well as between duties which the former have to fulfill as subjects, and the natural right which they must enjoy as men.

[3] It is agreed that each man alienates by the social pact only that portion of his power, his goods, his freedom, which it is important for the community to be able to use, but it should also be agreed to that the Sovereign is alone judge of that importance.

[4] All the services a Citizen can render the State, he owes to it as soon as the Sovereign requires them; but the Sovereign, for its part, cannot burden the subjects with any shackles that are useless to the community; it cannot even will to do so: for under the law of reason nothing is done without cause, any more than under the law of nature.

[5] The commitments which bind us to the social body are obligatory only because they are mutual, and their nature is such that in fulfilling them one cannot work for others without also working for oneself. Why is the general will always upright, and why do all consistently will each one's happiness, if not because there is no one who does not appropriate the word *each* to himself, and think of himself as he votes for all? Which proves that the equality of

---

* Attentive readers, please do not rush to accuse me of contradiction. I have not been able to avoid it verbally, in view of the poverty of the language; but wait.

right and the notion of justice which it produces follows from each one's preference for himself and hence from the nature of man; that the general will, to be truly such, must be so in its object as well as in its essence, that it must issue from all in order to apply to all, and that it loses its natural rectitude when it tends toward some individual and determinate object; for then, judging what is foreign to us, we have no true principle of equity to guide us.

[6] Indeed, whenever what is at issue is a particular fact or right regarding a point not regulated by a general and prior convention, the affair grows contentious. [*374*] In such a suit, where interested private individuals are one of the parties, and the public the other, I do not see what law should be followed or what judge should pronounce judgment. It would be ridiculous, under these circumstances, to try to invoke an express decision of the general will, which can only be the decision of one of the parties, and is, therefore, as far as the other party is concerned, nothing but a foreign, particular will which on this occasion is inclined to injustice and subject to error. Thus, just as a particular will cannot represent the general will, so the general will changes in nature when it has a particular object, and it cannot, being general, pronounce judgment on a particular man or fact. For example, when the people of Athens appointed or cashiered its chiefs, bestowed honors on one, imposed penalties on another, and by a multitude of particular decrees indiscriminately performed all the acts of government, the people no longer had a general will properly so called; it no longer acted as a Sovereign but as a magistrate. This will appear contrary to the commonly held ideas, but I must be allowed the time to set forth my own.

[7] In view of this, one has to understand that what generalizes the will is not so much the number of voices, as it is the common interest which unites them: for in this institution, everyone necessarily submits to the conditions which he imposes on others; an admirable agreement between interest and justice which confers on common deliberations a character of equity that is seen to vanish in the discussion of any particular affair, for want of a common interest which unites and identifies the rule of the judge with that of the party.

[8] From whatever side one traces one's way back to the principle, one always reaches the same conclusion: namely, that the

social pact establishes among the Citizens an equality such that all commit themselves under the same conditions and must all enjoy the same rights. Thus by the nature of the pact every act of sovereignty, that is to say every genuine act of the general will, either obligates or favors all Citizens equally, so that the Sovereign knows only the body of the nation and does not single out any one of those who make it up. What, then, is, properly, an act of sovereignty? It is not a convention of the superior with the inferior, but a convention of the body with each one of its members: [*375*] A convention which is legitimate because it is based on the social contract, equitable because it is common to all, and secure because the public force and the supreme power are its guarantors. So long as subjects are subjected only to conventions such as these, they obey no one, but only their own will; and to ask how far the respective rights of Sovereign and Citizens extend is to ask how far the Citizens can commit themselves to one another, each to all, and all to each.

[9] From this it is apparent that the Sovereign power, absolute, sacred, and inviolable though it is, does not and cannot exceed the limits of the general conventions, and that everyone may fully dispose of such of his goods and freedom as are left him by these conventions: so that it is never right for the Sovereign to burden one subject more than another, because it then turns into a particular affair, and its power is no longer competent.

[10] These distinctions once admitted, it is so [evidently] false that the social contract involves any renunciation on the part of individuals, that [rather] as a result of the contract their situation really proves to be preferable to what it had been before, and that instead of an alienation they have only made an advantageous exchange of an uncertain and precarious way of being in favor of a more secure and better one, of natural independence in favor of freedom, of the power to harm others in favor of their own security, and of their force which others could overwhelm in favor of right made invincible by the social union. Their very life which they have dedicated to the State is constantly protected by it, and when they risk it for its defense, what are they doing but returning to it what they have received from it? What are they doing that they would not have done more frequently and at greater peril in the state of nature, when, waging inevitable fights, they would be defending the

means of preserving their lives by risking them? All have to fight for the fatherland if need be, it is true, but then no one ever has to fight for himself. Isn't it nevertheless a gain to risk for the sake of what gives us security just a part of what we would have to risk for our own sakes if we were deprived of this security?

CHAPTER FIVE
OF THE RIGHT OF LIFE AND DEATH

[1] It is asked how individuals who have no right to dispose of their own life can transfer to the Sovereign this same right which they do not have. The question seems difficult to resolve only because it is badly put. Everyone has the right to risk his life in order to save it. Has anyone ever said that a person who jumps out of a window to escape a fire is guilty of suicide? Has that crime even ever been imputed to a person who dies in a storm, although he was not unaware of the danger when he set out?

[2] The social treaty has the preservation of the contracting parties as its end. Whoever wills the end, also wills the means, and these means are inseparable from certain risks and even certain losses. Whoever wants to preserve his life at the expense of others ought also to give it up for them when necessary. Now, the Citizen is no longer judge of the danger the law wills him to risk, and when the Prince has said to him, it is expedient to the State that you die, he ought to die; since it is only on this condition that he has lived in security until then, and his life is no longer only a bounty of nature, but a conditional gift of the State.

[3] The death penalty imposed on criminals can be looked upon from more or less the same point of view: it is in order not to become the victim of an assassin that one consents to die if one becomes an assassin oneself. Under this treaty, far from disposing of one's own life, one only thinks of guaranteeing it, and it should not be presumed that at the time any of the contracting parties is planning to get himself hanged.

[4] Besides, every evil-doer who attacks social right becomes a rebel and a traitor to the fatherland by his crimes, by violating its laws he ceases to be a member of it, and even enters into war with it. Then the preservation of the State is incompatible with his own,

one of the two has to perish, and when the guilty man is put to death, it is less as a Citizen than as an enemy. The proceedings, the [377] judgment are the proofs and declaration that he has broken the social treaty, and consequently is no longer a member of the State. Now, since he recognized himself as one, at the very least by residence, he must be cut off from it either by exile as a violator of the treaty, or by death as a public enemy; for such an enemy is not a moral person, but a man, and in that case killing the vanquished is by right of war.

[5] But, it will be said, the condemnation of a Criminal is a particular act. Granted; and indeed such a condemnation does not belong to the Sovereign's province; it is a right the Sovereign can confer without itself being able to exercise it. My ideas all fit together, but I cannot well present them all at once.

[6] Besides, frequent harsh punishments are always a sign of weakness or laziness in the Government. There is not a single wicked man who could not be made good for something. One only has the right to put to death, even as an example, someone who cannot be preserved without danger.

[7] As for the right to pardon, or to exempt a guilty man from the penalty prescribed by law and imposed by a judge, it belongs exclusively to the one which is above judge and law; that is to say, to the Sovereign: And even the Sovereign's right in this is not altogether clear, and the occasions to exercise it are very rare. In a well-governed State there are few punishments, not because many pardons are granted, but because there are few criminals: when the State is in decline the large number of crimes ensures their impunity. Under the Roman Republic neither the Senate nor the Consuls ever attempted to grant pardons; nor did the people itself grant any, although it sometimes revoked its own verdict. Frequent pardons proclaim that crimes will soon no longer need them, and anyone can see where that leads. But I feel my heart murmur and check my pen; let us leave these questions to be discussed by the just man who has never lapsed, and never himself been in need of pardon.

CHAPTER SIX
OF LAW

[1] By the social pact we have given the body politic existence and life: the task now is to give it motion and will by legislation. For the initial act by which this body assumes form and unity still leaves entirely undetermined what it must do to preserve itself.

[2] What is good and conformable to order is so by the nature of things and independently of human conventions. All justice comes from God, he alone is its source; but if we were capable of receiving it from so high, we would need neither government nor laws. No doubt there is a universal justice emanating from reason alone; but this justice, to be admitted among us, has to be reciprocal. Considering things in human terms, the laws of justice are vain among men for want of natural sanctions; they only bring good to the wicked and evil to the just when he observes them toward everyone while no one observes them toward him. Conventions and laws are therefore necessary to combine rights with duties and to bring justice back to its object. In the state of nature, where everything is common, I owe nothing to those to whom I have promised nothing. I recognize as another's only what is of no use to myself. It is not so in the civil state where all rights are fixed by law.

[3] But what, then, finally, is a law? So long as one leaves it at attaching only metaphysical ideas to this word, one will continue reasoning without understanding one another, and even once it has been stated what a law of nature is, one will not have been brought any closer to knowing what a law of the State is.

[4] I have already said that there is no general will about a particular object. Indeed, this particular object is either within the State or outside the State. If it is outside the State, a will that is foreign is not general in relation to it; and if this object is inside the State, it is a part of it: Then a relation is formed between the whole and its part that makes them into two separate beings, of which the part is [*379*] one, and the whole, less that part, the other. But the whole less a part is not the whole, and as long as this relation persists there is no longer a whole but two unequal parts; from which it follows that neither is the will of one of these parts general in relation to the other.

[5] But when the whole people enacts statutes for the whole people it considers only itself, and if a relation is then formed, it is between the entire object from one point of view and the entire object from another point of view, with no division of the whole. Then the matter with regard to which the statute is being enacted is general, as is the enacting will. It is this act which I call law.

[6] When I say that the object of the laws is always general, I mean that the law considers the subjects in a body and their actions in the abstract, never any man as an individual or a particular action. Thus the law can very well state that there will be privileges, but it cannot confer them on any one by name; the law can create several Classes of Citizens, it can even specify the qualifications that entitle to membership in these classes, but it cannot nominate this person or that for admission to them; it can establish a royal government and hereditary succession, but it cannot elect a king or name a royal family; in a word, any function that relates to an individual does not fall within the province of the legislative power.

[7] On this idea one immediately sees that one need no longer ask whose province it is to make laws, since they are acts of the general will; nor whether the Prince is above the laws, since it is a member of the State; nor whether the law can be unjust, since no man can be unjust toward himself; nor how one is both free and subject to the laws, since they are merely records of our wills.

[8] One also sees that since the law combines the universality of the will and that of the object, what any man, regardless of who he may be, orders on his own authority is not a law; what even the Sovereign orders regarding a particular object is not a law either, but a decree, nor is it an act of sovereignty but of magistracy.

[9] I therefore call Republic any State ruled by laws, whatever may be the form of administration: for then the public interest alone governs, and the [*380*] public thing counts for something. Every legitimate Government is republican:* I shall explain in the sequel what Government is.

---

* By this word I understand not only an Aristocracy or a Democracy, but in general any government guided by the general will, which is the law. To be legitimate, the Government must not be confused with the Sovereign, but be its minister: Then monarchy itself is a republic. This will become clearer in the following book.

[10] Laws are, properly speaking, nothing but the conditions of the civil association. The People subject to the laws ought to be their author; only those who are associating may regulate the conditions of the society; but how will they regulate them? Will it be by common agreement, by a sudden inspiration? Has the body politic an organ to state its wills? Who will give it the foresight necessary to form its acts and to publish them in advance, or how will it declare them in time of need? How will a blind multitude, which often does not know what it wills because it rarely knows what is good for it, carry out an undertaking as great, as difficult as a system of legislation? By itself the people always wills the good, but by itself it does not always see it. The general will is always upright, but the judgment which guides it is not always enlightened. It must be made to see objects as they are, sometimes as they should appear to it, shown the good path which it is seeking, secured against seduction by particular wills, bring together places and times within its purview, weigh the appeal of present, perceptible advantages against the danger of remote and hidden evils. Individuals see the good they reject, the public wills the good it does not see. All are equally in need of guides: The first must be obligated to conform their wills to their reason; the other must be taught to know what it wills. Then public enlightenment results in the union of understanding and will in the social body, from this union results the smooth cooperation of the parts, and finally the greatest force of the whole. Hence arises the necessity of a Lawgiver.

[*381*]

Chapter Seven
Of the Lawgiver

[1] To discover the best rules of society suited to each Nation would require a superior intelligence who saw all of man's passions and experienced none of them, who had no relation to our nature yet knew it thoroughly, whose happiness was independent of us and who was nevertheless willing to care for ours; finally, one who, preparing his distant glory in the progress of times, could work in

one century and enjoy the reward in another.* It would require gods to give men laws.

[2] The same reasoning Caligula made as to fact, Plato made as to right in defining the civil or royal man he seeks in his book on ruling; but if it is true that a great Prince is a rare man, what of a great Lawgiver? The first need only follow the model which the other must propose. He is the mechanic who invents the machine, the first is nothing but the workman who assembles and operates it. At the birth of societies, says Montesquieu, it is the chiefs of republics who make the institution, and after that it is the institutions that form the chiefs of republics.

[3] Anyone who dares to institute a people must feel capable of, so to speak, changing human nature; of transforming each individual who by himself is a perfect and solitary whole into part of a larger whole from which that individual would as it were receive his life and his being; of weakening man's constitution in order to strengthen it; of substituting a partial and moral existence for the independent and physical existence we have all received from nature. In a word, he must take from man his own forces in order to give him forces which [*382*] are foreign to him and of which he cannot make use without the help of others. The more these natural forces are dead and destroyed, the greater and more lasting are the acquired ones, and the more solid and lasting also is the institution: So that when each Citizen is nothing and can do nothing except with all the others, and the force acquired by the whole is equal or superior to the sum of the natural forces of all the individuals, the legislation may be said to be at the highest pitch of perfection it can reach.

[4] The Lawgiver is in every respect an extraordinary man in the State. While he must be so by his genius, he is no less so by his office. It is not magistracy, it is not sovereignty. This office which gives the republic its constitution has no place in its constitution: It is a singular and superior function that has nothing in common with human empire; for just as he who has command over men ought not to have command over the laws, so neither should he who has command over the laws have command over men; otherwise the

---

* A people becomes famous only once its legislation begins to decline. No one knows how many centuries the institution of Lycurgus made for the Spartans' happiness before the rest of Greece took notice of them.

laws, as ministers to his passions, would often only perpetuate his injustices, and he could never avoid having particular views vitiate the sanctity of his work.

[5] When Lycurgus gave his fatherland laws, he began by abdicating the Kingship. It was the custom of most Greek cities to entrust the establishment of their laws to foreigners. The modern Republics of Italy often imitated this practice: the Republic of Geneva did so as well and to good effect.* Rome in its finest period witnessed the rebirth of all the crimes of Tyranny in its midst, and found itself on the verge of perishing, for having united the legislative authority and the sovereign power in the same hands.

[6] Yet the Decemvirs themselves never arrogated to themselves the right to have any law passed solely on their authority. *Nothing we propose*, they used to say to the people, *can become law without your consent. Romans, [383] be yourselves the authors of the laws that are to make for your happiness.*

[7] Thus he who drafts the laws has, then, or should have no legislative right, and the people itself cannot divest itself of this non-transferable right, even if it wanted to do so; because according to the fundamental pact only the general will obligates particulars, and there can never be any assurance that a particular will conforms to the general will until it has been submitted to the free suffrage of the people: I have said this already, but it is not useless to repeat it.

[8] So that one finds at one and the same time two apparently incompatible things in the work of legislation: an undertaking beyond human force, and to execute it an authority that is nil.

[9] A further difficulty which deserves attention. The wise who would speak to the vulgar in their own rather than in the vulgar language will not be understood by them. Yet there are a thousand kinds of ideas which it is impossible to translate into the language of the people. Views that are too general and aims that are too remote are equally beyond its reach; each individual, appreciating no other scheme of government than that which bears directly on

---

* Those who look upon Calvin as only a theologian fail to appreciate the range of his genius. The framing of our wise Edicts, in which he played a large part, does him as much honor as his institution. Whatever revolutions time may bring about in our rites as long as love of fatherland and freedom is not extinguished among us, the memory of that great man will never cease to be honored in it.

his particular interest, has difficulty perceiving the advantages he is supposed to derive from the constant privations required by good laws. For a nascent people to be capable of appreciating sound maxims of politics and of following the fundamental rules of reason of State, the effect would have to become the cause, the social spirit which is to be the work of the institution would have to preside over the institution itself, and men would have to be prior to laws what they ought to become by means of them. Thus, since the Lawgiver can use neither force nor reasoning, he must of necessity have recourse to an authority of a different order, which might be able to rally without violence and to persuade without convincing.

[10] This is what has at all times forced the fathers of nations to resort to the intervention of heaven and to honor the Gods with their own wisdom, so that peoples, subject to the laws of the State as to those of nature, and recognizing the same power in the formation of man and in that of the city, freely obey the yoke of public felicity, and bear it with docility.

[11] This sublime reason which rises beyond the reach [*384*] of vulgar men it is whose decisions the Lawgiver places in the mouth of the immortals, in order to rally by divine authority those whom human prudence could not move.* But it is not up to just anyone to make the Gods speak or to have them believe him when he proclaims himself their interpreter. The great soul of the Lawgiver is the true miracle which must prove his mission. Any man can carve tablets of stone, bribe an oracle, feign secret dealings with some divinity, train a bird to speak in his ear, or find other crude ways to impress the people. Someone who can do only that much might even by chance succeed in assembling a flock of fools, but he will never found an empire, and his extravagant work will soon perish together with him. Empty tricks form a passing bond, only wisdom can make it lasting. The Jewish law which still endures, that of Ishmael's child which has ruled half the world for ten centuries, still proclaim today the great men who dictated them; and while prideful philosophy or blind party spirit regards them as

---

* "The truth is, says Machiavelli, that there has never been in any country a lawgiver who has not invoked the deity; for otherwise his laws would not have been accepted. A wise man knows many useful truths which cannot be demonstrated in a way that will convince other people." *Discourses on Livy*, Bk. I, ch. 11.

nothing but lucky impostors, the true politician admires in their institutions the great and powerful genius which presides over enduring establishments.

[12] One should not from all this conclude with Warburton that among us politics and religion have a common object, but rather that at the origin of nations the one serves as the instrument of the other.

CHAPTER EIGHT
OF THE PEOPLE

[1] Just as an architect, before putting up a large building, observes and tests the ground to see whether it can support the weight, so the wise institutor does not begin by [*385*] drawing up laws good in themselves, but first examines whether the people for whom he intends them is fit to bear them. That is why Plato refused to give laws to the Arcadians and Cyrenians, since he knew that both peoples were rich and could not tolerate equality: that is why there were good laws and wicked men in Crete, for Minos had done no more than to discipline a vice-ridden people.

[2] A thousand nations on earth have been brilliant which could never have tolerated good laws, and even those which could have tolerated them could have done so only for a very brief period in the course of their entire lifetime. Peoples, like men, are docile only in their youth, with age they grow incorrigible; once customs are established and prejudices rooted, it is a dangerous and futile undertaking to try to reform them; the people cannot tolerate having their evils touched even if only to destroy them, like those stupid and cowardly patients who tremble at the sight of a doctor.

[3] This is not to say that, just as some illnesses overwhelm men's minds and deprive them of the memory of the past, there may not also sometimes occur periods of violence in the lifetime of States when revolutions do to peoples what certain crises do to individuals, when horror of the past takes the place of forgetting, and when the State aflame with civil wars is so to speak reborn from its ashes and recovers the vigor of youth as it escapes death's embrace. Such was Sparta at the time of Lycurgus, such was Rome after the Tarquins; and such, among us, were Holland and Switzerland after the expulsion of the Tyrants.

[4] But such events are rare; they are exceptions the reason for which is always found in the particular constitution of the State in question. They could not even happen twice with the same people, for a people can free itself as long as it is merely barbarous, but it can no longer do so once the civil mainspring is worn out. Then troubles may destroy it while revolutions may not be able to restore it, and as soon as its chains are broken, it falls apart and ceases to exist: From then on it needs a master, not a liberator. Free peoples, remember this maxim: Freedom can be gained; but it is never recovered.

[*386*] [5] For Nations as for men there is a time of maturity for which one has to wait before subjecting them to laws; but the maturity of a people is not always easy to recognize, and if one acts too soon the work is ruined. One people is amenable to discipline at birth, another is not amenable to it after ten centuries. The Russians will never be truly politically organized because they were politically organized too early. Peter's genius was imitative; he did not have true genius, the kind that creates and makes everything out of nothing. Some of the things he did were good, most were misguided. He saw that his people was barbarous, he did not see that it lacked the maturity for political order; he wanted to civilize it when all it needed was to be made warlike. He wanted from the first to make Germans, Englishmen, whereas he should have begun by making Russians; he prevented his subjects from ever becoming what they could be by persuading them that they are what they are not. In the same way a French Tutor forms his pupil for a moment's brilliance in childhood, and to be nothing after that. The Russian Empire will try to subjugate Europe, and will itself be subjugated. The Tartars, its subjects or neighbors, will become its masters and ours: This revolution seems to me inevitable. All the Kings of Europe are working in concert to hasten it.

CHAPTER NINE
CONTINUED

[1] Just as nature has set limits to the stature of a well-formed man, beyond which it makes only Giants and Dwarfs, so, too, with regard to the best constitution of a State, there are bounds to the size it

can have in order not to be either too large to be well governed, or too small to be self-sustaining. In every body politic there is a maximum of force which it cannot exceed, and from which it often strays by dint of growing too large. The more the social bond stretches, the looser it grows, and in general a small State is proportionately stronger than a large one.

[*387*] [2] A thousand reasons prove this maxim. First, administration grows more difficult at great distances just as a weight grows heavier at the end of a larger lever. It also grows more burdensome as the levels of administration multiply; for, to begin with, each city has its own [administration] for which the people pays, each district has its own for which the people again pays, then each province, then the large governments, the Satrapies, the Viceregencies, which always have to be paid more the higher up one climbs, and always at the expense of the wretched people; finally comes the supreme administration which crushes everything. All these taxes upon taxes steadily exhaust the subjects; far from being better governed by these various agencies, they are less well governed than if they had just one over them. Yet hardly any resources are left over for emergencies, and when they have to be drawn on, the State is always on the brink of ruin.

[3] Nor is this all; not only is the Government less vigorous and less prompt in enforcing the laws, preventing provocations, correcting abuses, thwarting seditious undertakings which may be getting hatched in outlying areas; but also the people has less affection for its chiefs whom it never sees, for a fatherland which in its eyes is as [big as] the world, and for its fellow-citizens most of whom are strangers to it. The same laws cannot suit such a variety of different provinces with different morals, living in widely different climates, unable to tolerate the same form of government. Different laws give rise to nothing but trouble and confusion among peoples who, living under the same chiefs and in constant contact with one another, move back and forth from their own territory to their neighbors', inter-marry, and, since they are then subject to different customs, never quite know whether their patrimony is really theirs. Talents are hidden, virtues unknown, vices unpunished in this multitude of men who do not know one another, and whom the seat of the supreme administration has brought together in one place. The Chiefs, overwhelmed by public affairs, see nothing by them-

selves, clerks govern the State. In the end the measures which have to be taken to maintain the general authority, an authority which so many distant Officials want either to elude or take advantage of, absorb all public attention, there is none left for the people's happiness, and scarcely any left for its defense in an emergency, [*388*] and that is how a body too large for its constitution collapses and perishes, crushed under its own weight.

[4] Again, a State has to provide itself with some base so as to be solid, so that it can withstand the shocks it is bound to experience and the efforts it will be compelled to make to sustain itself: for all peoples have a kind of centrifugal force by which they constantly act against one another and tend to enlarge themselves at their neighbors' expense, like Descartes's vortices. Thus the weak are in danger of being swallowed up before long, and none can preserve itself except by establishing a kind of equilibrium with all the others, which would more or less equalize the pressure all around.

[5] This shows that there are reasons to expand and reasons to contract, and it is not the least of the politician's talents to find the proportion between these two sets of reasons which most favors the preservation of the State. In general it may be said that the first, since they are merely external and relative, should be subordinated to the others, which are internal and absolute; a healthy and strong constitution is the first thing to strive for, and one should rely more on the vigor born of a good government, than on the resources provided by a large territory.

[6] Still, States have been known which were so constituted that the necessity of conquests entered into their very constitution, and which were forced constantly to expand in order to maintain themselves. They may have been very pleased by this happy necessity which, together with the limitation on their size, however, also showed them the inevitable moment of their fall.

CHAPTER TEN
CONTINUED

[1] A body politic can be measured in two ways, by the extent of its territory and by the number of its people, and an appropriate ratio has to obtain between these two measures for the State to be

given its genuine [*389*] size: The men make up the State, and the land feeds the men; thus the ratio requires that there be enough land to support its inhabitants, and as many inhabitants as the land can feed. It is in this proportion that the maximum force of a given number of people consists; for if there is too much land its defense is burdensome, its cultivation deficient, its produce superfluous; this is the proximate cause of defensive wars; if there is not enough land, the State finds itself at its neighbors' discretion for the supplement [it needs]; this is the proximate cause of offensive wars. Any people which, because of its location, has no other alternative than commerce or war is inherently weak; it is dependent on its neighbors; it is dependent on circumstances; it can never have any but a precarious and brief existence. Either it subjugates and changes its situation, or it is subjugated and is nothing. It can preserve its freedom only by being very small or very large.

[2] It is therefore impossible to calculate a fixed ratio between the amount of land and the number of men each requires; because of the differences in properties of the soil, its degrees of fertility, the nature of its products, the influence of climates, as much as because of the differences in temperaments one observes among the men who live in these different climates, some of whom consume little in a fertile country, and others who consume much with a harsh soil. One also has to take into account the greater or lesser fertility of the women, what the country may offer that is more or less favorable to the growth of population, the number of people the lawgiver can hope to contribute to the population by the institutions he establishes; so that he should not base his judgment on what he sees but on what he foresees, nor focus as much on the present state of the population as on the state it should naturally reach. Finally, there are a thousand occasions when particular accidental features of a given place require or permit taking up more land than appears needed. Thus men will spread out a good deal in a mountainous country where the natural produce, namely woods, pastures, require less work, where experience teaches that women are more fertile than in the plains, and where large stretches of sloping terrain leave only a small horizontal band which alone should be counted as land available for vegetation. By contrast, men can draw together at the edge of the sea, even among rocks and sand that are [*390*] nearly barren; because there fishing can in large

measure substitute for products of the earth, because men have to live more closely assembled to repulse pirates, and because, besides, it is easier to rid the country of its excess population by colonies.

[3] To these conditions for the institution of a people, one more has to be added which cannot replace any other, but without which all the rest are useless: the enjoyment of prosperity and peace; for when a State is being organized, like when a battalion is drawing up in formation, is the time when the body is least able to resist and easiest to destroy. One would offer better resistance at a time of absolute disorder than at a time of fermentation when everyone is preoccupied with his rank rather than with the peril. If a war, a famine, a sedition were to arise in such a time of crisis, the State will inevitably be overthrown.

[4] Not that many governments have not been established during such storms; but then it is those governments themselves that destroy the State. Usurpers invariably bring about such times of trouble or choose them and, taking advantage of the public panic, get destructive laws passed which the people would never adopt when calm. The choice of the moment of institution is one of the most reliable features by which to distinguish the work of the Law-giver from the Tyrant's.

[5] What people, then, is fit for legislation? One which, while finding itself already bound together by some union of origin, inter-est, or convention, has not yet borne the true yoke of laws; one with neither deep-rooted customs nor deep-rooted superstitions; one which is not in fear of being overrun by a sudden invasion; which without taking part in its neighbors' quarrels can resist each one of them by itself, or enlist the help of one to repulse the other; one whose every member can be known to all, and where one is not forced to charge a man with a greater burden than a man can bear; one which can do without all other peoples and without which every other people can do;* One which is neither [*391*] rich nor

---

* If one of two neighboring peoples could not do without the other, the situation would be extremely hard for the first, and extremely dangerous for the second. Any wise nation would, in such a case, try promptly to relieve the other of this dependence. The Republic of [*391*] Tlaxcala, an enclave in the Empire of Mexico, preferred doing without salt to buying it from the Mexicans, and even to accepting any free of charge. The wise Tlaxcalans saw the trap hidden in this generosity. They preserved their freedom, and in the end this small State, enclosed within that great Empire, was the instrument of its ruin.

poor, and can be self-sufficient; finally, one which combines the stability of an ancient people with the docility of a new people. What makes the work of legislation difficult is not so much what has to be established as what has to be destroyed; and what makes success so rare is the impossibility of finding the simplicity of nature linked with the needs of society. It is true that it is difficult to find all of these conditions together. This is one reason why one sees few well-constituted States.

[6] There is one country left in Europe capable of receiving legislation; it is the island of Corsica. The valor and steadfastness with which this brave people was able to recover and defend its freedom would amply deserve that some wise man teach it to preserve it. I rather suspect that this small island will one day astound Europe.

Chapter Eleven
Of the Various Systems of Legislation

[1] If one inquires into precisely what the greatest good of all consists in, which ought to be the end of every system of legislation, one will find that it comes down to these two principal objects, *freedom* and *equality*. Freedom, because any individual dependence is that much force taken away from the State; equality, because freedom cannot subsist without it.

[2] I have already said what civil freedom is; with regard to equality, this word must not be understood to mean that degrees of power and wealth should be absolutely the same, but that, as for power, it stop short of all violence and never be exercised except by virtue of rank and the laws, and that as for wealth, no citizen be so very rich that he can buy an[392]other, and none so poor that he is compelled to sell himself: Which assumes, on the part of the great, moderation in goods and influence and, on the part of the lowly, moderation in avarice and covetousness.*

---

* Do you, then, want to give the State stability? bring the extremes as close together as possible; tolerate neither very rich people nor beggars. These two states, which are naturally inseparable, are equally fatal to the common good; from one come the abettors of tyranny, and from the other tyrants; it is always between these two that there is trafficking in public freedom; one buys it, the other sells it.

[3] This equality, they say, is a chimera of speculation which cannot exist in practice: But if abuse is inevitable, does it follow that it ought not at least be regulated? It is precisely because the force of things always tends to destroy equality, that the force of legislation ought always to tend to maintain it.

[4] But these general aims of every good institution must be adapted in each country to the relations that arise as much from local conditions as from the character of the inhabitants, and it is on the basis of these relations that each people has to be assigned a particular system of institutions which is the best, not, perhaps, in itself, but for the State for which it is intended. For example, is the soil unprofitable and barren, or the country too small for its inhabitants? Turn to industry and the arts, the products of which you can trade for the foods you lack. Do you, on the contrary, occupy rich plains and fertile slopes? Have you good soil but too few inhabitants? Devote all of your efforts to agriculture, which increases the population, and drive out the arts which would only depopulate the country completely by concentrating in just a few points of its territory the few inhabitants it does have.* Do you occupy extensive and convenient shores? Cover the sea with ships, cultivate commerce and navigation; you will have a brilliant and a brief existence. Does the sea wash up against nothing but nearly inaccessible rocks along your shores? Remain barbarous and fish-eaters; you will live the more tranquil for it, perhaps the better, and certain[393]ly the happier. In a word, besides the maxims common to all, there is within each People some cause which orders these maxims in a particular manner and makes its legislation suited to itself alone. Thus formerly the Hebrews and recently the Arabs had religion as their principal object, the Athenians letters, Carthage and Tyre commerce, Rhodes seafaring, Sparta war, and Rome virtue. The Author of the *Spirit of the Laws* has shown in a great many instances the art by which the lawgiver directs the institution toward each one of these objects.

[5] What makes the constitution of a State genuinely solid and lasting is when what is appropriate is so well attended to that natural

---

* Any branch of foreign trade, says the M[arquis] d'A[rgenson], provides a kingdom in general with little more than a deceptive benefit; it may enrich a few individuals, even a few cities, but the nation as a whole gains nothing from it, and the people is no better off for it.

relations and the laws always agree on the same points, and the latter as it were only secure, accompany and rectify the former. But if the Lawgiver mistakes his object, if he adopts a principle different from that which arises from the nature of things, if one principle tends toward servitude while the other tends toward freedom, one toward wealth, the other toward population, one toward peace, the other toward conquests, then the laws will be found imperceptibly to weaken, the constitution to deteriorate, and the State will not be free of turmoil until it is either destroyed or altered, and invincible nature has resumed its empire.

CHAPTER TWELVE
CLASSIFICATION OF THE LAWS

[1] To order the whole, or to give the commonwealth the best form possible, various relations have to be considered. First, the action of the entire body acting upon itself, that is to say the relation of the whole to the whole, or of the Sovereign to the State, and this relation is made up of the relation between intermediate terms, as we shall see in the sequel.

[2] The laws which regulate this relation bear the name of political laws, and are also called fundamental laws, not altogether unreasonably if these laws are wise. For if there is but one good way of ordering any given State, the people that has found it ought to abide by it: but if the established order [*394*] is bad, why would one regard as fundamental laws which prevent it from being good? Besides, a people is in any case always master to change its laws, even the best of them; for if it pleases it to harm itself, who has the right to prevent it from doing so?

[3] The second relation is that of the members with one another or with the entire body, and this relation should be as small as possible with respect to the first, and as large as possible with respect to the second: so that every Citizen be perfectly independent of all the others, and excessively dependent on the City; which is always achieved by the same means; for it is only the State's force that makes for its members' freedom. It is from this second relation that the civil laws are born.

[4] One may consider a third sort of relation between man and the law, namely that of disobedience to penalty, and this is the

occasion for establishing criminal laws, which at bottom are not so much a particular kind of law as the sanction for all the others.

[5] To these three sorts of laws must be added a fourth, the most important of all; which is graven not in marble or in bronze, but in the hearts of the Citizens; which is the State's genuine constitution; which daily gathers new force; which, when the other laws age or die out, revives or replaces them, and imperceptibly substitutes the force of habit for that of authority. I speak of morals, customs, and above all of opinion; a part [of the laws] unknown to our politicians but on which the success of all the others depends: a part to which the great Lawgiver attends in secret, while he appears to restrict himself to particular regulations which are but the ribs of the arch of which morals, slower to arise, in the end form the immovable Keystone.

[6] Among these various Classes, political laws, which constitute the form of Government, are the only Class relevant to my subject.

BOOK III

Before speaking of the various forms of Government, let us try to fix the precise meaning of this term, which has not been adequately explained so far.

CHAPTER ONE
OF GOVERNMENT IN GENERAL

[1] I warn the reader that this chapter has to be read carefully, and that I lack the art of being clear to those who are not willing to be attentive.

[2] Every free action has two causes which concur in producing it, one moral, namely the will which determines it, the other physical, namely the power which executes it. When I walk toward an object, it is necessary, in the first place, that I will to go to it; in the second place, that my feet carry me to it. Let a paralytic will to run, let a limber man will not to do so, both stay where they are. The body politic has the same motive causes; here, too, a distinction is drawn between force and will: The latter being called *legislative power*, the former *executive power*. Nothing is or should be done in the body politic without their concurrence.

[3] We have seen that the legislative power belongs to the people, and can belong only to it. It is easy to see that, on the contrary, by the principles established above, the executive power cannot belong to the generality [of the people] in its Legislative or Sovereign capacity; for this power consists solely in particular acts which are not within the province of the law, nor, consequently, within that of the [*396*] Sovereign, since all of the Sovereign's acts can only be laws.

[4] The public force therefore has to have its own agent which unites and puts it to work in accordance with the directives of the general will, which serves as a means of communication between the State and the Sovereign, which in a sense does for the public person what the union of soul and body does in man. This is the reason why, within the State, there is Government, improperly confused with the Sovereign, of which it is merely the minister.

[5] What, then, is Government? An intermediate body established between subjects and Sovereign so that they might conform to one another, and charged with the execution of the laws and the maintenance of freedom, both civil and political.

[6] The members of this body are called magistrates or *Kings*, that is to say Governors, and the body as a whole bears the name *Prince*.* Thus those who contend that the act by which a people subjects itself to chiefs is not a contract are perfectly right. It is absolutely nothing but a commission, an office in which they, as mere officers of the Sovereign, exercise in its name the power it has vested in them, and which it can limit, modify, and resume, since alienation of such a right is incompatible with the nature of the social bond and contrary to the aim of the association.

[7] I therefore call *Government* or supreme administration the legitimate exercise of the executive power, and Prince or Magistrate the man or the body charged with that administration.

[8] It is in the Government that are located the intermediate forces whose relations constitute the relation of the whole to the whole, or of the Sovereign to the State. This last relation can be represented as the ratio between the extremes of a continued proportion of which the mean proportional is the Government. The Government receives from the Sovereign the orders which it gives the people, and for the State to be well balanced it is necessary that, all other things being equal, the product or power of the Government taken by itself be equal to the product or power of the citizens who are sovereign on the one hand, and subjects on the other.

[*397*] [9] What is more, none of these three terms could be altered without immediately destroying the proportion. If the Sovereign wants to govern, or the magistrate to give laws, or the subjects refuse to obey, disorder replaces rule, force and will no longer act in concert, and the dissolved State thus falls into despotism or anarchy. Finally, since there is only one mean proportional between each pair, there is also no more than one good government possible in any one State: But since a thousand events can change the relations of a people, not only can different governments be good

---

* Thus in Venice, the college [of Senators] is called *most serene Prince* even when the Doge is not in attendance.

for different peoples, but they can also be good for the same people at different times.

[10] To try to give some idea of the various relations which may obtain between these two extremes, I shall take as an example the number of the people, as this relation is easier to express.

[11] Let us assume that the State is composed of ten thousand Citizens. The Sovereign can only be considered collectively and in a body: But every particular person in his capacity as a subject is considered individually: Thus the Sovereign is to the subject as ten thousand is to one: That is to say that each member of the State has but a ten-thousandth of the Sovereign authority as his own share, although all of him is subject to it. Let the people be composed of a hundred thousand men, the subjects' state does not change, and each one bears the full empire of the laws equally, whereas his vote, reduced to a hundred thousandth, exercises ten times less influence in drafting the laws. Thus, since the subject always remains one, the ratio of Sovereign [to subject] increases in proportion to the number of Citizens. Whence it follows that the more the State expands, the more freedom is diminished.

[12] When I say that the ratio increases, I mean that it moves farther away from equality. Thus the greater the ratio is in the Geometer's sense of the term, the smaller it is in the ordinary sense; in the first sense, the ratio considered in terms of quantity is measured by the quotient, and in the other sense, considered in terms of identity, it is gauged by similarity.

[13] Now, the smaller the ratio of individual wills to the general will, that is to say of morals to the laws, the more does the repressive force have to increase. Hence in order to be good, the Government has to have relatively more force in proportion as the people is more numerous.

[398] [14] On the other hand, since the expansion of the State offers the trustees of the public authority more temptations and more means to misuse their power, it follows that the more force the Government has to have in order to contain the people, the more force does the Sovereign have to have in its turn in order to contain the Government. I am not here speaking about an absolute force, but about the relative force of the various parts of the State.

[15] It follows from this double ratio that the continued proportion of Sovereign, Prince and people is not an arbitrary idea but

a necessary consequence of the nature of the body politic. It further follows that since one of the extremes, namely the people as subjects, is fixed and represented by unity, every time the doubled ratio increases or decreases, the single ratio similarly increases or decreases, and the middle term is correspondingly changed. This shows that there is no unique and absolute constitution of Government but that there may be as many Governments differing in nature as there are States differing in size.

[16] If, in order to reduce this system to ridicule, it were said that, according to me, finding this mean proportional and forming the body of the Government requires no more than taking the square root of the number of the people, I would reply that I am here using this number only as an example; that the ratios about which I am speaking are measured not only by numbers of men, but more generally by the amount of activity, which is the combined result of a great many causes; that, besides, if in order to express myself in fewer words I momentarily borrow the language of geometry, I am nevertheless not unaware of the fact that geometric precision does not obtain in moral quantities.

[17] The Government is on a small scale what the body politic which contains it is on a large scale. It is a moral person endowed with certain faculties, active like the Sovereign, passive like the State, which can be analyzed into further, similar relations, from which a new proportion consequently arises, and within it yet another proportion corresponding to the judiciary, until an indivisible middle term is reached, that is to say a single chief or supreme magistrate, who might be conceived of in the middle of this progression as the unity between the series of fractions and of the series of integers.

[18] Without getting involved in this proliferation of [*399*] terms, let us leave it at considering the Government as a new body in the State, distinct from both the people and the Sovereign, and intermediate between them.

[19] The essential difference between these two bodies is that the State exists by itself, and the Government exists only by [virtue of] the Sovereign. Thus the Prince's dominant will is or should be nothing but the general will or the laws; the Prince's force is nothing but the public force concentrated in it: as soon as it wills to derive some absolute and independent act from itself, the

cohesion of the whole begins to slacken. If in the end it came to pass that the Prince had a private will more active than the Sovereign's and that in heeding that private will it used the public force in its power, so that there would be, so to speak, two Sovereigns, one by right and the other in fact; the social union would instantly vanish, and the body politic be dissolved.

[20] Yet for the body of the Government to have existence, a real life which distinguishes it from the body of the State, for all of its members to be able to act in concert and to assume responsibility for the end for which it is instituted, it has to have a particular *self*, a sensibility common to its members, a force, a will of its own that tends to its preservation. Such a particular existence presupposes assemblies, councils, power to deliberate, to decide, rights, titles, privileges which belong exclusively to the Prince and make the magistrate's position more honorable in proportion as it is more demanding. The difficulties consist in ordering this subordinate whole within the whole, so that it does not weaken the general constitution by strengthening its own, that it always keeps its particular force intended for its own preservation distinct from the public force intended for the preservation of the State, and that, in a word, it is ever ready to sacrifice the Government to the people, and not the people to the Government.

[21] However, although the artificial body of the Government is the work of another artificial body, and has, as it were, only a borrowed and subordinate life, this does not keep it from being able to act more or less vigorously or promptly, to enjoy, so to speak, a more or less robust health. Finally, without directly departing [*400*] from the goal of its institution, it may deviate from it more or less, depending on how it is constituted.

[22] It is from all of these differences that arise the various relations which ought to obtain between the Government and the body of the State, taking into account the accidental and particular relations by which that State is modified. For often the Government which is in itself the best will become the most vicious, if its relations are not adjusted to the defects of the body politic to which it belongs.

CHAPTER TWO
OF THE PRINCIPLE WHICH CONSTITUTES THE VARIOUS
FORMS OF GOVERNMENT

[1] In order to set out the general cause of these differences, it is necessary to distinguish here between the Prince and the Government, as above I distinguished between the State and the Sovereign.

[2] The body of the magistracy may be composed of a greater or lesser number of members. We have said that the ratio of Sovereign to subjects was greater in proportion as the number of the people was more numerous, and by an obvious analogy we can say the same about the Government in relation to the Magistrates.

[3] Now, since the total force of the Government is always that of the State, it never varies: from which it follows that the more of this force it uses on its own members, the less it has left to act on the whole people.

[4] Hence the more numerous the Magistrates, the weaker the Government. Since this maxim is fundamental, let us try to clarify it more fully.

[5] We can distinguish three essentially different wills in the person of the Magistrate: First, the individual's own will, which tends solely to his particular advantage; second, the common will of the Magistrates which is exclusively concerned with the advantage of the Prince, and may be called the corporate will, which is general in relation to the Government and particular in relation to the State of which the Government is a part; in the third place, the will of the people or the [*401*] sovereign will, which is general in relation both to the State considered as the whole, and to the Government considered as a part of the whole.

[6] In a perfect legislation, the particular or individual will should be null, the Government's own corporate will should be very subordinate, and consequently the general or sovereign will should always be dominant and the sole rule of all the others.

[7] According to the natural order, on the contrary, the more concentrated these different wills are, the more active they grow. Thus the general will is always the weakest, the corporate will occupies second place, and the particular will the first place of all: so that in the Government each member is first of all himself, and

then Magistrate, and then citizen. A gradation that is the direct opposite of that required by the social order.

[8] Let this be given: now assume the entire Government in the hands of a single man. The particular will and the corporate will are then perfectly united, and consequently the corporate will is at the highest degree of intensity it can attain. Now, since the use of force depends on the degree of will, and since the Government's absolute force never varies, it follows that the most active of Governments is that of a single man.

[9] On the contrary, let us combine the Government with the legislative authority; let us turn the Sovereign into the Prince and all the citizens into so many Magistrates: Then the corporate will, merged with the general will, is no more active than it, and leaves the individual will in its full force. Thus the Government, with the same absolute force, will be at its *minimum* of relative force or activity.

[10] These relations are beyond dispute, and other considerations only confirm them further. For example, it is evident that each magistrate is more active within his [corporate] body than each citizen is in his, and consequently that a particular will has far more influence in the actions of Government than it has in the actions of the Sovereign; for each magistrate is almost always responsible for some function of the Government, whereas each citizen taken by himself exercises no function of sovereignty. Besides, the more the State expands, the more its real force increases, although it does not increase in proportion to [*402*] its size: but if the State remains the same, then regardless of how much the magistrates multiply, the Government does not thereby gain greater real force, because this force is the force of the State, whose extent is still the same. Thus the relative force or activity of the Government diminishes, while its real force or activity cannot increase.

[11] Again, it is certain that business gets dispatched less expeditiously in proportion as more people are in charge of it, that by conceding too much to prudence not enough is conceded to fortune, that opportunity is allowed to escape, and that the fruits of deliberation are often lost by deliberating too much.

[12] I have just proved that the Government grows slack in proportion as magistrates multiply, and earlier I proved that the more numerous the people, the more must the repressive force increase.

From which it follows that the ratio of magistrates to Government should be the inverse of the ratio of subjects to Sovereign: That is to say that the more the State grows, the more should the Government shrink; by so much that the number of chiefs should diminish in proportion to the increase of people.

[13] However, I am here speaking only about the relative force of the Government, and not about its uprightness: For, on the contrary, the more numerous the body of the magistrates, the more closely does the corporate will approach the general will; whereas under a single magistrate this same corporate will is, as I have said, merely a particular will. Thus is lost on one side what might be gained on the other, and the art of the Lawgiver consists in knowing how to determine the point at which the force and the will of the Government, which are always inversely proportional, can be combined in the relation [or ratio] most advantageous to the State.

CHAPTER THREE
CLASSIFICATION OF GOVERNMENTS

[1] In the preceding chapter we have seen why the various kinds or forms of Government are distinguished according to the number of the members who compose them; in the present chapter it remains to be seen how this classification is made.

[*403*] [2] The Sovereign can, in the first place, entrust the charge of Government to the whole people or to the majority of the people, so that there be more citizens who are magistrates than citizens who are simple particulars. This form of Government is given the name *Democracy*.

[3] Or else it can restrict the Government into the hands of a small number, so that there be more simple Citizens than magistrates, and this form bears the name *Aristocracy*.

[4] Finally, it can concentrate the whole of Government in the hands of a single magistrate from whom all the rest derive their power. This third form is the most common, and is called *Monarchy* or royal Government.

[5] It should be noted that all of these forms, or at least the first two, admit of more or less, and they do so within a rather wide range; for Democracy can encompass the whole people or restrict

itself to as few as half. Aristocracy, in turn, can restrict itself to anywhere from half the people to the smallest number. Even Royalty admits of being shared to a certain extent. Sparta consistently had two Kings by constitution, and the Roman Empire is known to have had as many as eight Emperors at once, without its being possible to say that the Empire was divided. Thus there is a point at which each form of Government merges into the next, and it is evident that under just these three headings, Government admits of as many different forms as the State has Citizens.

[6] What is more: Since this same Government can in certain respects subdivide itself into different parts, one administered one way, the other another way, the combination of these three forms can result in a multitude of mixed forms, each of which can be multiplied by all the simple forms.

[7] There has always been much argument about the best form of Government, without considering that each one of them is the best in some cases, and the worst in others.

[8] If in each State the number of supreme magistrates should be inversely proportional to the number of Citizens, it follows that in general Democratic Government suits small States, Aristocratic Government suits [*404*] medium-sized ones, and Monarchy large ones. This rule is directly derived from the principle; but how is one to enumerate the many circumstances which can make for exceptions to the rule?

CHAPTER FOUR
OF DEMOCRACY

[1] He who makes the law knows better than anyone else how it should be executed and interpreted. It would therefore seem that there could be no better constitution than one in which the executive power is combined with the legislative: But this is precisely what makes this Government inadequate in certain respects, for things which ought to be kept distinct are not kept distinct, and the Prince and the Sovereign being nothing but the same person, form, so to speak, nothing but a Government without a Government.

[2] It is not good that he who makes the laws execute them, nor that the body of the people turn its attention away from general considerations, to devote it to particular objects. Nothing is more dangerous than the influence of private interests on public affairs, and abuse of the laws by the Government is a lesser evil than the corruption of the Lawgiver, which is the inevitable consequence of particular considerations. Then, the State being adulterated in its very substance, all reform becomes impossible. A people which would never misuse the Government would not misuse independence either; a people which would always govern well would not need to be governed.

[3] In the strict sense of the term, a genuine Democracy never has existed, and never will exist. It is against the natural order that the greater number govern and the smaller number be governed. It is unimaginable that the people remain constantly assembled to attend to public affairs, and it is readily evident that it could not establish commissions to do so without the form of the administration changing.

[4] Indeed, I believe I can posit as a principle that when the functions of Government are divided among [405] several tribunals, the least numerous sooner or later acquire the greatest authority; if only because of the ease in dispatching business, which naturally leads them to acquire it.

[5] Besides, how many things difficult to combine does not this Government presuppose? First, a very small State where the people is easily assembled, and where every citizen can easily know all the rest; second, great simplicity of morals to preclude excessive business and thorny discussions; next, much equality of ranks and fortunes, without which equality of rights and authority could not long subsist: Finally, little or no luxury; for luxury is either the effect of riches, or makes them necessary; it corrupts rich and poor alike, the one by possession, the other by covetousness; it sells out the fatherland to laxity, to vanity; it deprives the State of all its Citizens by making them slaves to one another, and all of them slaves to opinion.

[6] That is why a famous Author attributed virtue to Republics as their principle; for all these conditions could not subsist without virtue: but for want of drawing the necessary distinctions, this noble

genius often lacked in precision, sometimes in clarity, and he failed to see that since Sovereign authority is everywhere the same, the same principle must obtain in every well-constituted State, more or less, it is true, according to the form of the Government.

[7] Let us add that there is no Government as subject to civil wars and intestine turmoil as Democratic or popular Government, because there is none which tends so strongly and so constantly to change its form, nor any which requires greater vigilance and courage to maintain in its form. It is in this constitution above all that the Citizen must arm himself with force and steadfastness, and every day of his life say in the bottom of his heart what a virtuous Palatine* said in the Diet of Poland: "I prefer a perilous freedom to quiet servitude."

[*406*] [8] If there were a people of Gods, they would govern themselves democratically. So perfect a Government is not suited to men.

CHAPTER FIVE
OF ARISTOCRACY

[1] We have here two very distinct moral persons, namely the Government and the Sovereign, and consequently two general wills, one in relation to all the citizens, the other only for the members of the administration. Thus, although the Government may regulate its internal policy as it pleases, it may never speak to the people except in the name of the Sovereign, that is to say in the name of the people itself; which should never be forgotten.

[2] The first societies governed themselves aristocratically. The chiefs of families deliberated among themselves about the public business; young people readily yielded to the authority of experience. Hence the names *Priests*, *elders*, *senate*, *gerontes*. The savages of northern America still govern themselves this way in our day, and they are very well governed.

[3] But in proportion as instituted inequality prevailed over natural inequality, riches or power* was given preference over age, and

---

* The Palatine of Posnania, father of the King of Poland, Duke of Lorraine.
* It is clear that among the ancients the term *Optimates* does not mean the best, but the most powerful.

Aristocracy became elective. Finally, power bequeathed to the children together with the father's goods made families patrician, Government became hereditary, and there were twenty-year-old Senators.

[4] There are, then, three kinds of Aristocracy: natural, elective, hereditary. The first is suited only to simple peoples; the third is the worst of all Governments. The second is the best; it is Aristocracy properly so called.

[5] In addition to having the advantage of distinguishing between the two powers, Aristocracy has the advantage of choosing its members; for in [*407*] popular Government all Citizens are born magistrates, whereas this Government restricts them to a small number, and they become magistrates only by being elected;* a means by which probity, enlightenment, experience, and all the other reasons for public preferment and esteem are so many further guarantees of being well governed.

[6] Moreover, assemblies are more easily convened, business is discussed better, and dispatched in a more orderly and diligent fashion, the State's prestige is better upheld abroad by venerable senators than by an unknown and despised multitude.

[7] In a word, the best and most natural order is to have the wisest govern the multitude, so long as it is certain that they will govern it for its advantage and not for their own; institutions and procedures should not be multiplied needlessly, nor should twenty thousand men be employed to do what a hundred well chosen men can do even better. But it must be noted that here the corporate interest begins to guide the public force less in accordance with the standard of the general will, and that another inevitable decline deprives the laws of a portion of the executive power.

[8] With regard to suitable particular circumstances, the State should not be so small nor the people so simple and upright that the execution of the laws follows directly from the public will, as it does in a good Democracy. Nor should the nation be so large

---

* It is very important to regulate by laws the form of electing magistrates; because if it is left to the will of the Prince, hereditary Aristocracy is the inevitable consequence, as it was in the Republics of *Venice* and of *Berne*. Indeed, the first has long since been a dissolved State, whereas the second maintains itself through the extreme wisdom of its Senate; it is a most honorable and a most dangerous exception.

that the chiefs, scattered in order to govern it, can make decisions on behalf of the Sovereign, each in his own department, and begin by making themselves independent only to end up becoming the masters.

[9] But while Aristocracy requires somewhat fewer virtues than popular Government, it also requires others which are properly its own; such as moderation among the rich and contentment among the poor; for it seems that a rigorous equality would be out of place in Aristocracy; it was not even observed in Sparta.

[*408*] [10] Besides, while this form [of Government] involves a certain inequality of fortune, it does so primarily so that in general the administration of the public business be entrusted to those who can best devote all of their time to it, and not, as Aristotle contends, so that the rich always be preferred. On the contrary, it is important that an opposite choice should occasionally teach the people that men's merit offers more important reasons for preference than do riches.

CHAPTER SIX
OF MONARCHY

[1] So far we have considered the Prince as a moral and collective person, united by the force of laws, and the trustee of the executive power within the State. We now have to consider this power gathered in the hands of a natural person, of a real man, who alone has the right to exercise it according to the laws. He is what is called a Monarch, or a King.

[2] In direct contrast to the other administrations, in which a collective being represents an individual, in this administration an individual represents a collective being; so that the moral unity which constitutes the Prince is at the same time a physical unity in which are naturally combined all the faculties which it is so difficult for the law to combine in a collective being.

[3] Thus the will of the people, and the will of the Prince, and the public force of the State, and the particular force of the Government, everything responds to the same mover, all of the machine's levers are in the same hand, everything proceeds toward the same goal, no opposing motions cancel one another, and no kind of constitution can be imagined in which less effort would produce greater

action. Archimedes sitting quietly on the shore and effortlessly launching a large Vessel represents for me a skillful monarch governing his vast States from his study and making everything move while himself appearing to be unmoving.

[*409*] [4] But while there is no Government that is more vigorous, there is none where the particular will has greater sway and more easily dominates the other wills; everything proceeds toward the same goal, it is true, but that goal is not public felicity, and the very force of the Administration constantly works to the prejudice of the State.

[5] Kings want to be absolute, and from afar men call out to them that the best way to be so is to make themselves loved by their peoples. The maxim is very fine, and in some respects even very true. Unfortunately it will always be laughed at in Courts. The power that comes from the peoples' love is unquestionably the greatest; but it is precarious and conditional, and Princes will never be satisfied with it. The best Kings want to be able to be wicked if they please, without ceasing to be masters: A political sermonizer may well tell them that since the people's force is their force, their greatest interest is to have the people flourishing, numerous, formidable; they know perfectly well that this is not true. Their personal interest is first of all that the People be weak, wretched, and never able to resist them. I admit that, assuming always perfectly submissive subjects, it would be in the Prince's interest that the people be powerful, so that this power, being his, might render him formidable to his neighbors; but since this is only a secondary and subordinate interest, and the two assumptions are incompatible, it is natural that Princes always prefer the maxim that is most immediately useful to them. This is what Samuel forcefully represented to the Hebrews; it is what Machiavelli has conclusively shown. While pretending to teach lessons to Kings, he taught great lessons to peoples. Machiavelli's *Prince* is the book of republicans.*

---

* Machiavelli was an honest man and a good citizen: but being attached to the house of the Medici, he was forced during the oppression of his fatherland to disguise his love of freedom. The very choice of his execrable Hero suffices to exhibit his secret intention, and the contradiction between the maxims of his Book on the Prince and those of his discourses on Titus Livy and of his history of Florence proves that this profound politician has so far had only superficial or corrupt Readers. The Court of Rome has severely prohibited his book, and I should think that it would: it is the Court he depicts most clearly. [Note added in the 1782 edn.]

[6] We found on the basis of general relations [or ratios] that monarchy is suited only to large States, and we again find it to be so upon examining monarchy in itself. The more numerous the public administration, the more the ratio of Prince to subjects decreases and approaches equality, so that in Democracy this ratio is one [to one] or equality itself. This same ratio increases in proportion as the Government contracts, and it is at its maximum when the Government is in the hands of a single man. [*410*] The distance between Prince and People is then too great, and the State lacks cohesion. To form such cohesion, intermediate orders are therefore needed: to fill these, Princes, Grandees, nobility are needed. Now, none of this is suited to a small state, which all such gradations ruin.

[7] But if it is difficult for a large State to be well governed, it is much more difficult for it to be well governed by a single man, and everyone knows what happens when the King rules through proxies.

[8] One essential and inevitable defect which will always make monarchical government inferior to republican government is that in Republics the public voice almost never elevates to the highest places any but enlightened and capable men who occupy them with honor: whereas those who succeed in monarchies are most often nothing but petty bunglers, petty knaves, petty schemers whose petty talents, which at Court give access to high places, only serve to show the public their ineptitude just as soon as they have acceded to these high places. The people is much less often mistaken in this choice than the Prince, and a man of true merit in a [royal] ministry is almost as rare as a fool at the head of a republican government. Indeed, when by some happy accident one of those men who are born to govern takes the helm of affairs in a Monarchy which has been almost ruined by those crowds of fancy managers, everyone is utterly amazed at the resources he discovers, and it marks an epoch in a country['s history].

[9] For a monarchic State to be well governed, its size or extent would have to be commensurate with the faculties of the one who governs. It is easier to conquer than to rule. Given an adequate lever, a single finger can move the world, but it takes the shoulders of Hercules to hold it up. If a State is at all large, the Prince is almost always too small. On the other hand, when the State happens

to be too small for its chief, which is very rarely the case, it is still badly governed because the chief, forever pursuing his own large views, forgets the peoples' interests, and makes them no less unhappy by misusing his excess of talents, than would a stupid chief for want of the talents he lacks. A kingdom should, so to speak, expand or [*411*] contract with each reign according to the Prince's scope; by contrast, the talents of a Senate being of a more settled measure, the State can have stable boundaries and the administration run no less well.

[10] The most perceptible inconvenience of Government by a single man is the lack of that continuous succession which in the two others forms an unbroken bond. When a King dies, another is needed; elections leave dangerous intervals, they are stormy, and unless the Citizens are disinterested and upright to an extent scarcely compatible with this [form of] Government, intrigue and corruption will play their part. It is unlikely that he to whom the State has sold itself will not sell it in turn, and that he will not seek compensation at the expense of the weak for the money extorted from him by the powerful. Sooner or later everything becomes venal under such an administration, and then the peace enjoyed under Kings is worse than the disorder of interregna.

[11] What has been done to prevent these evils? Crowns have been made hereditary in certain families, and an order of Succession has been established which prevents any dispute upon the death of Kings: That is to say that, by substituting the inconvenience of regencies for that of elections, apparent tranquility has been given preference over wise administration, and the risk of having children, monsters, imbeciles for chiefs was preferred to having to dispute about the choice of good Kings; they failed to consider that by thus taking a chance on this alternative they put almost all the odds against themselves. It was a very sensible remark the Younger Dionysius made when his father, reproving him for a shameful action, said: "Did I set you such an example?" "Ah," the son replied, "your father was not a King!"

[12] Everything conspires to deprive of justice and reason a man brought up to command others. Great pains are taken, so they say, to teach young Princes the art of ruling; it does not appear that this education profits them. It would be better to begin by teaching them the art of obeying. The greatest Kings renowned in history

were not brought up to rule; it is a science one never possesses less than after having learned it to excess, and which one acquires better by obeying than by commanding. "The most practical and [*412*] shortest way to distinguish what is good and what is bad is to consider what you would or would not have wished for under another Prince."*

[13] One consequence of this lack of coherence is the instability of royal government which, following now one plan, now another, depending on the character of the ruling Prince or of those who rule for him, cannot long have a fixed objective or a consistent policy: a mutability which forever causes the State to drift from maxim to maxim, from project to project, and does not occur in the other Governments where the Prince is always the same. Thus one sees that in general, while there is more cunning at Court, there is more wisdom in a Senate, and that Republics pursue their goals in the light of views that are more steadily held and more closely adhered to, whereas every revolution in the [royal] Ministry produces a revolution in the State; for it is the common maxim of all Ministers and almost all Kings in all things to do the opposite of what their predecessors did.

[14] This same incoherence also provides the solution to a sophism common among royalist politicians; that is not only to compare civil Government to domestic Government and the Prince to the father of a family, a fallacy which has already been refuted, but also liberally to endow this magistrate with all the virtues he would need, and always to assume that the Prince is what he should be: an assumption with the help of which royal Government is evidently preferable to any other, because it is incontrovertibly the strongest, and all it lacks to be also the best is a corporate will more consonant with the general will.

[15] But if, according to Plato,* a King by nature is such a rare person, how often will nature and fortune concur to crown him, and if a royal education necessarily corrupts those who receive it, what can be expected of a succession of men brought up to rule? It is therefore deliberate self-deception to confuse royal Government with the Government of a good King. In order to see what

* Tacit[us], *Hist[ories]*, Bk. i.
* *Statesman.*

this Government is in itself, it has to be considered as it is under stupid or wicked Princes; for either that is what they will be when they accede to the throne, or it is what the throne will make them be.

[*413*] [16] Our Authors have noticed these difficulties, but they have not been disturbed by them. The remedy, they say, is to obey without a murmur. God in his wrath sends bad Kings, and they must be endured as punishments from Heaven. Such a discourse is, no doubt, edifying; but I wonder whether it would not be more appropriate in the pulpit than in a book on politics. What would one say about a Physician who promised miracles, and whose whole art consisted in exhorting his sick to be patient? Everyone knows perfectly well that when there is a bad government, it has to be put up with; the problem is to find a good one.

CHAPTER SEVEN
OF MIXED GOVERNMENTS

[1] Properly speaking, there is no simple Government. A single Chief has to have subordinate Magistrates; a popular Government has to have a Chief. Thus in the distribution of executive power there is always a gradation from the larger to the smaller number, with this difference that sometimes the larger number depends on the smaller, and sometimes the smaller depends on the larger.

[2] At times the distribution is equal; either when the constituent parts are dependent on one another, as in the Government of England; or when the authority of each part is independent but imperfect, as in Poland. This latter form is bad because the Government is without any unity, and the State lacks cohesion.

[3] Which is better, a simple or a mixed Government? The question is much debated by politicians, and it should be given the same answer I gave above about all forms of Government.

[4] In itself simple Government is best, just because it is simple. But when the executive Power is not sufficiently dependent on the legislative, that is to say when the ratio of Prince to Sovereign is greater than that of People to Prince, this lack of proportion has to be remedied [*414*] by dividing the Government; for then its several parts have no less authority over the subjects, and their division reduces their combined force against the Sovereign.

[5] The same inconvenience can also be forestalled by establishing intermediate magistrates who, leaving the Government whole, merely serve to balance the two Powers and to uphold their respective rights. Then the Government is not mixed, it is tempered.

[6] Similar means can be used to remedy the opposite inconvenience, and when the Government is too slack, Tribunals can be set up to give it concentration. This is the practice of all Democracies. In the first case the Government is divided in order to weaken it, and in the second in order to reinforce it; for the *maximum* of force and of weakness are both found in simple Governments, whereas mixed forms make for moderate force.

CHAPTER EIGHT
THAT NOT EVERY FORM OF GOVERNMENT IS SUITED TO EVERY COUNTRY

[1] Freedom, not being a fruit of every Clime, is not within the reach of every people. The more one meditates upon this principle established by Montesquieu, the more one senses its truth. The more one challenges it, the more opportunities one provides to establish it with new proofs.

[2] In all Governments of the world the public person consumes but produces nothing. Where, then, does it get the substance it consumes? From its members' labor. It is the particulars' surplus which produces the public's necessities. Whence it follows that the civil state can subsist only as long as men's labor yields in excess of their needs.

[3] Now, this overplus is not the same in every country of the world. In some it is considerable, in others moderate, in others nil, in others negative. [*415*] This relation depends on the fertility of the climate, the kind of labor the soil requires, the nature of its products, the force of its inhabitants, the greater or lesser amount they need to consume, and on various similar relations that go to make it up.

[4] On the other hand, Governments are not all of the same nature; some are more and some less rapacious, and their differences

are based on this further principle that the farther public contributions move from their source, the more burdensome they are. This burden should be measured not by the amount of taxes, but by how far they have to travel to return into the hands from which they came; when this circulation is prompt and efficient, then it does not matter whether one pays little or much; the people is always rich, and the finances always in good order. By contrast, regardless of how little the People gives, if it never gets this little back, it is soon exhausted by constantly giving; the State is never rich, and the people is always destitute.

[5] From which it follows that the greater the distance between the people and the Government grows, the more burdensome do taxes become: thus in a Democracy the people is least burdened, in an Aristocracy it is burdened more, in a Monarchy it bears the greatest weight. Hence Monarchy is suited only to opulent nations, Aristocracy to States moderate in wealth as well as in size, Democracy to small and poor States.

[6] Indeed the more one reflects on this, the greater does the difference which one finds in this respect between free and monarchical States prove to be; in the former everything is used for the public utility; in the latter, public and particular forces are reciprocal, and one increases by the other's weakening. Finally, despotism, instead of governing subjects in order to make them happy, makes them miserable in order to govern them.

[7] Here then are some natural causes in every clime by which one can determine the form of Government toward which the force of the climate directs it, and even tell what kind of inhabitants it should have. Barren and sterile places where the product is not worth the labor should be left uninhabited and deserted, or peopled only by Savages: Places where man's labor yields only the bare necessities should be inhabited by [*416*] barbarous peoples, since any polity would be impossible there: places where the excess of produce over labor is moderate suit free peoples; those where an abundant and fertile soil yields much produce in return for little labor lend themselves to being governed monarchically so that the Prince's luxury might consume the excess of the subjects' surplus; for it is better that this excess be absorbed by the government than squandered by private individuals. There are exceptions, I know;

but these very exceptions confirm the rule in that sooner or later they produce revolutions which restore things to the order of nature.

[8] Let us always distinguish between general laws and the particular causes which can modify their effect. Even if the entire south were covered with Republics and the entire north with despotic States it would be no less true that in terms of the effect of climate despotism suits warm countries, barbarism cold countries, and good polity intermediate regions. I do also see that one might grant the principle but dispute the application: one might hold that some cold countries are extremely fertile, and some warm ones extremely barren. But this is a difficulty only for those who fail to look at the matter in all of its relations. As I have already said, the relations of labor, of forces, of consumption, etc. all have to be taken into account.

[9] Let us assume that one of two equal pieces of land yields five, the other ten. If the inhabitants of the first consume four, and the second nine, the excess of the first product will be $1/5$ and that of the second $1/10$. Since, then, the ratio of these two excesses is the inverse of that of their products, the land producing only five will yield a surplus double that of the surplus yielded by the land producing ten.

[10] But there is no question of getting double the product, and I do not believe that anyone would venture to hold that the fertility of cold countries is in general even equal to that of warm countries. However, let us assume such an equality; let us equate, if you wish, England with Sicily, and Poland with Egypt. Farther south we will have Africa and the Indies, farther north we will have nothing more. For the sake of this equality of product, what a difference in cultivation. In Sicily it is enough to scratch the soil; in England what efforts it takes to till it! Now, where [*417*] more hands are needed to get the same product, the superflux must necessarily be less.

[11] Consider, further, that the same number of people consume much less in warm countries. There the climate requires that one practice moderation to stay healthy; Europeans who want to live there as they do at home all die of dysentery and indigestions: *We are,* says Chardin, *carnivorous beasts, wolves, by comparison with the Asians. There are those who attribute the Persians' moderation to the fact that their country is less cultivated; but I believe on the contrary*

that their country is less abundant in commodities because the inhabitants need fewer. If their frugality, he goes on, were an effect of the country's poverty, only the poor would eat little, whereas in general everyone does, and one would eat more or less in different provinces depending on the fertility of the land, whereas the same moderation is found throughout the Kingdom. They take great pride in their way of living, saying that one need only look at their complexion to see how much superior their way is to the Christians'! Indeed, the Persians' complexion is clear; their skin is fair, delicate, smooth, whereas the complexion of the Armenians, their subjects, who live in the European manner, is coarse, blotchy, and their bodies are fat and heavy.

[12] The closer one draws to the equator, the less do peoples live off. They eat almost no meat; rice, maize, couscous, millet, cassava, are their ordinary food. In the Indies there are millions of men whose food costs no more than a penny a day. Even in Europe we notice sensible differences in appetite between the peoples of the north and those of the south. A Spaniard will live for a week on a German's dinner. In the countries where men are more voracious objects of consumption also become objects of luxury. In England luxury appears on a table laden with meat; in Italy you are regaled with sweets and flowers.

[13] Luxury in clothing also exhibits similar differences. In climates where the seasons change rapidly and violently, clothes are better and simpler, in climates where people dress for display they strive more for effect than for utility, and the clothes themselves are a luxury. In Naples you will daily see men strolling along the Posilippo in gold-embroidered jackets and no hose. The same holds true regarding buildings; magnificence is the only consideration when there is no [*418*] damage to fear from the weather. In Paris, in London, one wants to be housed warmly and comfortably. In Madrid they have superb drawing rooms, but no windows that close, and they sleep in rat-holes.

[14] Foods are far more substantial and succulent in warm countries; this is a third difference that cannot fail to influence the second. Why do they eat so many vegetables in Italy? Because they are good, nutritious, and extremely tasty: In France, where they are fed nothing but water, they are not at all nutritious, and count for almost nothing at table. Yet they take up no less land, and are at least as much trouble to grow. It is a matter of experience that the

wheats of Barbary yield much more flour than do those of France, although they are inferior to them in other respects, and that French wheats in turn yield more than do those of the North. From which it may be inferred that a similar gradation going in the same direction generally obtains from the equator to the pole. And is it not a manifest disadvantage to get a smaller amount of nourishment from an equal amount of produce?

[15] To these various considerations I can add another which follows from them and reinforces them; it is that warm countries need inhabitants less than do cold countries, and could feed more of them; this produces a double surplus which invariably redounds to the advantage of despotism. The larger the area which a constant number of inhabitants occupy, the more difficult it is to revolt; because it is impossible to take concerted action quickly or in secret, and it is always easy for the Government to get wind of plans and to cut communications: but the closer together a numerous people draws, the less can the Government usurp from the Sovereign; chiefs deliberate as securely in their chambers as the Prince does in his council, and the crowd assembles as quickly in public squares as troops do in their barracks. In this respect great distances are therefore to a tyrannical Government's advantage. With the help of the support groups which it sets up, its force increases with distance, like that of levers.* By contrast, the people's force the acts only when concen[419]trated, it evaporates and is lost as it spreads, like the effect of gunpowder scattered on the ground and which ignites only grain by grain. The least populous countries are thus the most suited to Tyranny: wild beasts reign only in wildernesses.

Chapter Nine
Of the Signs of a Good Government

[1] Hence the question, which is absolutely the best Government,

---

* This does not contradict what I said above, Bk. II, ch. 9, about the inconveniences of large States; for there it was a question of the Government's authority over its members, and here it is a question of its force [419] against its subjects. Its scattered members serve it as fulcra for acting on the people at a distance, but it has no fulcrum for acting directly on these members themselves. Thus in the one case the length of the lever makes for its weakness, and in the other for its force.

does not admit to a solution because it is indeterminate: or, if you prefer, it has as many good solutions as there are possible combinations in the absolute and the relative positions of peoples.

[2] But if one were to ask by what sign one might tell whether a given people is well or badly governed, it would be a different matter, and the question of fact can be resolved.

[3] Yet it is left unresolved, because everyone wants to resolve it in his own way. Subjects praise public tranquility, Citizens individual freedom; one prefers security of possessions, and the other that of persons; one wants the best Government to be the most severe, the other maintains that it is the mildest; this one wants crimes to be punished, and that one wants them prevented; one thinks it a fine thing to be feared by neighbors, the other prefers to be ignored by them; one is satisfied when money circulates, the other demands that the people have bread. Even if agreement were reached on these points and others like them, would one be any better off? Since moral qualities lack a precise yardstick, even if there were agreement about the sign, how is agreement to be reached about applying it?

[4] For my own part, I am always astonished that people should fail to recognize so simple a sign, or have the bad faith not to agree on it. What is the aim of the political association? [*420*] It is the preservation and prosperity of its members. And what is the surest sign that they are preserving themselves and prospering? It is their number and their population. Look no further, then, for this much disputed sign. All other things equal, the Government under which the Citizens, without resort to external means, without naturalizations, without colonies, populate and multiply, is without fail the best: that under which a people dwindles and wastes away is the worst. Calculators, it is now up to you: count, measure, compare.*

* The same principle should be used to judge which centuries deserve preference with respect to the prosperity of humankind. People have too much admired those that have seen letters and the arts flourish, without inquiring into the secret of their cultivation, without considering their fatal effect, *such was their ignorance that they called humanity what was a beginning of servitude*. Shall we never discern in the maxims of books the coarse interest that causes the Authors to speak? No, regardless of what they may say, when for all of its brilliance a country gets depopulated, then it is not true that all is well, and one poet's having an income of a hundred thousand *livres* is not enough for his to be the best of all centuries. One should focus less on apparent repose and on the chiefs' tranquility than on the well-being of entire nations and above all of the most numerous estates. Hail

[*421*]

CHAPTER TEN
OF THE ABUSE OF GOVERNMENT AND OF ITS
TENDENCY TO DEGENERATE

[1] Just as the particular will incessantly acts against the general will, so the Government makes a constant effort against Sovereignty. The greater this effort grows, the more adulterated does the constitution get, and since there is here no other corporate will to resist the will of the Prince and so to balance it, it must sooner or later come to pass that the Prince ends up oppressing the Sovereign and breaking the Social treaty. This is the inherent and inevitable vice which relentlessly tends to destroy the body politic from the moment of its birth, just as old age and death destroy a man's body.

[2] There are two general ways in which a Government degenerates, namely when it contracts, or when the State dissolves.

[3] The Government contracts when it passes from a large to a small number, that is to say from Democracy to Aristocracy, and from Aristocracy to Kingship. This is its natural inclination.* If it

devastates a few cantons, but it rarely causes a famine. Riots, civil wars, greatly alarm chiefs, but they do not cause the true miseries of peoples, which may even experience some respite during the disputes about who will tyrannize them. Their real prosperities or calamities arise from their permanent state; it is when everything remains crushed under the yoke, that everything wastes away; when chiefs destroy them at their ease, and *where they make a desolation, they call it peace*: When the bickerings of the Great caused turmoil in the Kingdom of France, and the Cardinal Coadjutor attended Parliament with a dagger in his pocket, it did not keep the French people from living happy and numerous in honest and free well-being. Formerly Greece flourished amidst the most cruel wars; blood flowed freely, yet the entire country was full of men. It seemed, says Machiavelli, that our Republic grew all the more powerful for being in the midst of murders, proscriptions, civil wars; the virtue of its citizens, their morals, their independence, did more to reinforce it, than all its dissensions had done to weaken it. A little agitation energizes souls, and what causes the species truly to prosper is not so much peace as freedom.

* The slow formation and the progress of the Republic of Venice in its lagoons offers a notable example of this sequence: and it is rather astonishing that for more than twelve hundred years the Venetians seem still to be only at the second stage, which began with the *Serrar di Consiglio* in 1198. As for the ancient Dukes invoked in challenge to them, it has been proved that, regardless of what the *squittinio della libertà veneta* may say about them, they were not the Venetians' Sovereigns.

People will not fail to cite in objection to me the Roman Republic whose progress, they will say, followed a directly opposite course, passing from monarchy

were to retrogress from the small to [422] the large number, it might be said to slacken, but this reverse progression is impossible.

[4] Indeed, a Government never changes its form except when its worn-out mainspring leaves it too weak to preserve the form it has. Now if it were to expand, it would grow even more slack, its force would become altogether null, and it would be even less likely to subsist. What has to be done, therefore, is to rewind and tighten the spring in proportion as it gives way, otherwise the State which it upholds will fall into ruin.

[5] The dissolution of the State may come about in two ways.

[6] First when the Prince no longer administers the State according to the laws, and usurps the sovereign power. Then a remarkable change occurs; namely, it is not the Government, but the State that contracts; I mean that the large State dissolves and another is formed within it, composed solely of the members of the Government, and which is no longer anything to the rest of the People

to Aristocracy, and from Aristocracy to Democracy. I am very far from sharing this opinion.

Romulus's initial establishment was a mixed Government which promptly degenerated into Despotism. Owing to some particular causes, the State perished before its time, just as a newborn child sometimes dies before reaching manhood. The expulsion of the Tarquins was the genuine period of the Republic's birth. But it did not assume a stable form from the first, because the failure to abolish the patriciate left the work only half done. For since in [422] this way the hereditary Aristocracy, which is the worst of legitimate administrations, remained in conflict with the Democracy, the form of the Government, forever uncertain and unstable was, as Machiavelli has proved, not settled until the establishment of the Tribunes; only then was there a true Government and a genuine Democracy. Indeed, the people was then not only Sovereign, but also magistrate and judge, the Senate was no more than a subordinate tribunal to temper or to concentrate the Government, and even the Consuls, although Patricians, although the first Magistrates, although absolute Generals in war, were, in Rome, no more than the presidents of the people.

From that time on the Government was also seen to follow its natural inclination and to tend strongly toward Aristocracy. With the Patriciate abolishing itself as if on its own, the Aristocracy no longer resided in the body of Patricians as it does in Venice and in Genoa, but in the body of the Senate which was composed of both Patricians and Plebeians, and even in the body of the Tribunes once they began to usurp active power: for words do not change things, and when the people has chiefs who govern on its behalf then, regardless of the name these chiefs bear, it is still an Aristocracy.

From the abuse of the Aristocracy arose the civil wars and the Triumvirate. Sulla, Julius Caesar, Augustus became genuine Monarchs in fact, and finally under the Despotism of Tiberius the State was dissolved. Roman history thus does not belie my principle; it confirms it.

but its master and tyrant. So that the moment [*423*] the Government usurps the sovereignty, the social pact is broken, and all ordinary Citizens, restored by right to their natural freedom, are forced to obey but not obligated to do so.

[7] Dissolution of the State also comes about when the members of the Government severally usurp the power they ought to exercise only as a body; which is no less serious an infraction of the laws, and produces even greater disorder. Then there are, so to speak, as many Princes as there are Magistrates, and the State, no less divided than the Government, either perishes or changes its form.

[8] When the State dissolves, any abuse of Government whatsoever takes the general name of *anarchy*. To distinguish, *Democracy* degenerates into *Ochlocracy*, *Aristocracy* into *Oligarchy*; I would add that Kingship degenerates into *Tyranny*, but this last word is equivocal and calls for explanation.

[9] In the vulgar sense of the term, a Tyrant is a King who governs with violence and without regard for justice and the laws. In the precise sense of the term, a Tyrant is an individual who arrogates the royal authority to himself without having any right to it. That is how the Greeks understood the word Tyrant: They gave it indiscriminately to good and to bad Princes whose authority was not legitimate.* Thus *Tyrant* and *usurper* are two perfectly synonymous words.

[10] In order to give different things different names, I call *Tyrant* the usurper of the royal authority, and *Despot* the usurper of the Sovereign power. The Tyrant is one who insinuates himself contrary to the laws and governs according to the laws; the Despot is one who puts himself above the laws themselves. Thus a Tyrant may not be a Despot, but a Despot is always a Tyrant.

---

* "For all those are called and considered tyrants who exercise perpetual power in a city accustomed to freedom." Corn[elius] Nep[os], *Life of Miltiades*: It is true that Aristotle, *Nicom[achean] Eth[ics]*, Bk. VIII, ch. 10 [1060b 1-3], distinguishes between Tyrant and King in that the first governs only for his own advantage and the second solely for his subjects' advantage, but besides the fact that generally all Greek authors used the word Tyrant in a different sense, as is apparent above all from the *Hiero* of Xenophon, it would follow from Aristotle's distinction that there had never yet existed a single King since the beginning of the world.

[*424*]
CHAPTER ELEVEN
THE DEATH OF THE BODY POLITIC

[1] Such is the natural and inevitable tendency of the best constituted Governments. If Sparta and Rome perished, what State can hope to last forever? If we want to form a lasting establishment, let us therefore not dream of making it eternal. To succeed one must not attempt the impossible, nor flatter oneself that the work of men can be endowed with a solidity human things do not allow for.

[2] The body politic, just like the body of a man, begins to die as soon as it is born and carries within itself the causes of its destruction. But either body can have a constitution that is more or less robust and suited to preserve it for more or less time. The constitution of man is the work of nature, that of the State is the work of art. It is not within men's capacity to prolong their life, it is within their capacity to prolong the State's life as far as possible by giving it the best constitution it can have. Even the best constituted State will end, but later than another, if no unforeseen accident brings about its doom before its time.

[3] The principle of political life resides in the Sovereign authority. The legislative power is the heart of the State, the executive power is its brain, which gives movement to all the parts. The brain may become paralyzed and the individual still live. A man can remain imbecile and live: but as soon as the heart has stopped to function, the animal is dead.

[4] It is not by laws that the State subsists, it is by the legislative power. Yesterday's law does not obligate today, but tacit consent is presumed from silence, and the Sovereign is assumed to be constantly confirming the laws which it does not abrogate when it can do so. Everything which it has once declared it wills it continues to will, unless it revokes it.

[5] Why, then, are ancient laws accorded so much respect? For that very reason. People must believe that nothing [*425*] but the excellence of the ancient wills could have preserved them for so long; if the Sovereign had not consistently recognized them as salutary it would have revoked them a thousand times over. That is why the laws, far from growing weaker, constantly acquire new force in every well-constituted State; the prejudice in favor of

antiquity renders them daily more venerable; whereas wherever the laws grow weaker as they grow older it is proof that there is no longer any legislative power, and that the State is no longer alive.

CHAPTER TWELVE
HOW THE SOVEREIGN AUTHORITY IS MAINTAINED

[1] The Sovereign, having no other force than the legislative power, acts only by means of the laws, and the laws being nothing but authentic acts of the general will, the Sovereign can act only when the people is assembled. The people assembled, it will be said! What a chimera! It is a chimera today, but it was not so two thousand years ago: Have men changed in nature?

[2] The bounds of the possible in moral matters are less narrow than we think: It is our weaknesses, our vices, our prejudices that constrict them. Base souls do not believe in great men: vile slaves smile mockingly at the word freedom.

[3] Let us consider what can be done in the light of what has been done; I shall not speak of the ancient republics of Greece, but the Roman Republic was, it seems to me, a large State, and the city of Rome a large city. The last census showed four hundred thousand Citizens bearing arms in Rome, and the last count of the Empire more than four million Citizens, not including subjects, foreigners, women, children, slaves.

[4] What difficulty might one not imagine about frequently assembling the immense people of this capital and its environs? Yet few weeks went by when the Roman people was not assembled, and even several times. It exercised not only the rights of sove[426]reignty, but a part of those of Government as well. It dealt with some business, tried some cases, and on the public square this entire people was nearly as often magistrate as it was Citizen.

[5] If one were to go back to the earliest times of Nations, one would find that most ancient Governments, even monarchical ones like those of the Macedonians and the Franks, had similar Councils. Be that as it may, this one indisputable fact alone answers all objections: The inference from what is to what is possible seems to me sound.

CHAPTER THIRTEEN
CONTINUED

[1] It is not enough for the people assembled to have once settled the constitution of the State by giving sanction to a body of laws: it is not enough for it to have established a perpetual Government or to have provided once and for all for the election of magistrates. In addition to extraordinary assemblies which may be required by unforeseen circumstances, there must be fixed and periodic assemblies which nothing can abolish or prorogue, so that on the appointed day the people is legitimately summoned by law, without need of any further formal convocation.

[2] But except for these assemblies which are lawful by their date alone, any assembly of the People not convoked by the magistrates appointed to that end and according to the prescribed forms must be held to be illegitimate and everything done at it to be null; because the order to assemble must itself emanate from the law.

[3] As to whether legitimate assemblies should meet more or less frequently, this depends on so many considerations that it is impossible to give precise rules about it. Only it can be said in general that the more force the Government has, the more frequently ought the Sovereign show itself.

[4] I shall be told that this may be good for a single city; but what is to be done when the State includes several cities? [*427*] Is the Sovereign authority to be shared, or should it be concentrated in a single city, and all the rest be placed in subjection?

[5] I answer that neither should be done. First, the Sovereign authority is simple and single, and it cannot be divided without being destroyed. In the second place, a city can no more be legitimately subjected to another than can a Nation, because the essence of the political body consists in the concurrence of obedience and freedom, and that the words *subject* and *sovereign* are identical correlatives whose idea is combined in the single word Citizen.

[6] I answer further that it is always an evil to unite several cities into a single City, and anyone who wants to bring about such a union should not flatter himself that he can avoid its natural inconveniences. The abuse of large States should not be urged as an objection to someone who wants only small ones: but how are small States to be given enough force to resist the large ones? In the same

way that formerly the Greek cities resisted the great King, and more recently Holland and Switzerland resisted the House of Austria.

[7] However, if the State cannot be reduced to just bounds there remains one recourse; it is not to allow it a capital, to seat the Government alternately in each city, and also to assemble the country's Estates in each in turn.

[8] People the territory evenly, extend the same rights throughout it, spread abundance and life throughout it, that is how the State will at once have as much force and be as well governed as possible. Remember that the walls of cities are only built with the wreckage of farmhouses. For each Palace I see rise in the capital, I seem to see an entire countryside reduced to hovels.

CHAPTER FOURTEEN
CONTINUED

[1] The instant the People is legitimately assembled as a Sovereign body, all jurisdiction of the Government ceases, the executive power is suspended, and the [*428*] person of the last Citizen is as sacred and inviolable as that of the first Magistrate, because where the Represented is, there no longer is a Representative. Most of the commotions that arose in the comitia in Rome came from ignorance or neglect of this rule. On those occasions the Consuls were nothing but the Presidents of the People, the Tribunes were mere Speakers,* the Senate was nothing at all.

[2] These intervals of suspension [of the Government's powers] when the prince recognizes or has to recognize an actual superior have always been threatening to it, and these assemblies of the people which are the shield of the body politic and the curb of Government have at all times been the dread of chiefs: indeed they never spare cares, nor objections, nor obstacles, nor promises to turn Citizens against them. When the Citizens are greedy, cowardly, pusillanimous, more enamored of repose than of freedom, they do not long hold out against the redoubled efforts of the Government;

---

* Approximately in the sense given to this term in the English Parliament. The similarity between these functions would have brought the Consuls and the Tribunes into conflict even if all jurisdiction had been suspended.

this is how, with the opposing force constantly increasing, the Sovereign authority finally vanishes, and most Cities fall and perish before their time.

[3] But between Sovereign authority and arbitrary Government an intermediary power sometimes interposes itself which has to be discussed.

CHAPTER FIFTEEN
OF DEPUTIES OR REPRESENTATIVES

[1] As soon as public service ceases to be the Citizens' principal business, and they prefer to serve with their purse rather than with their person, the State is already close to ruin. Is there a call to battle? they pay troops and stay home; is there a summons to Council? they name Deputies and stay home. Finally, by dint of [*429*] laziness and money they have soldiers to enslave the fatherland and representatives to sell it.

[2] It is the hustle and bustle of commerce and the arts, it is the avid interest in gain, it is softness and love of comforts that change personal services into money. One gives up a portion of one's profit in order to increase it at leisure. Give money, and soon you will have chains. The word *finance* is a slave's word; it is unknown in the City. In a truly free State the citizens do everything with their hands and nothing with money: Far from paying to be exempted from their duties, they would pay to fulfill them themselves. I am very far from the commonly held ideas; I believe corvées to be less at odds with freedom than taxes.

[3] The better constituted the State, the more public business takes precedence over private business in the minds of Citizens. There even is less private business, because, since the sum of the common happiness contributes a greater share to each individual's happiness, he needs to seek less of it in his personal pursuits. In a well-conducted city everyone flies to the assemblies; under a bad Government no one likes to take a step to go to them; because no one takes an interest in what is done there, because it is predictable that the general will will not prevail in them, and finally because domestic concerns are all-absorbing. Good laws lead to making better ones, bad laws bring about worse ones. As soon as someone

says about affairs of State *What do I care?* the State has to be considered lost.

[4] The cooling of the love of fatherland, the activity of private interest, the immensity of States, conquests, the abuse of Government, have led people to imagine the expedient of Deputies or Representatives of the people in the Nation's assemblies. This is what in some countries they dare call the Third Estate. Thus the private interest of two orders is assigned first and second places, the public interest only third place.

[5] Sovereignty cannot be represented for the same reason that it cannot be alienated; it consists essentially in the general will, and the will does not admit of being represented: either it is the same or it is different; there is no middle ground. The deputies of the people therefore are not and cannot be its representatives, they are merely [*430*] its agents; they cannot conclude anything definitively. Any law which the People has not ratified in person is null; it is not a law. The English people thinks it is free; it is greatly mistaken, it is free only during the election of Members of Parliament; as soon as they are elected, it is enslaved, it is nothing. The use it makes of its freedom during the brief moments it has it fully warrants its losing it.

[6] The idea of Representatives is modern: it comes to us from feudal Government, that iniquitous and absurd Government in which the human species is degraded, and the name of man dishonored. In ancient Republics and even in monarchies, the People never had representatives; the very word was unknown. It is quite striking that in Rome, where the Tribunes were so sacred, no one ever so much as imagined that they might usurp the functions of the people, and that in the midst of such a great multitude they never attempted to pass a single Plebiscite on their own authority alone. Yet the trouble the crowd sometimes caused may be judged by what happened at the time of the Gracchi, when a portion of the Citizens cast its vote from the rooftops.

[7] Where right and freedom are everything, inconveniences are nothing. Among this wise people, everything was given its just due: it allowed its Lictors to do what its Tribunes would not have dared to do; it did not fear that its Lictors would wish to represent it.

[8] However, in order to explain how the Tribunes did sometimes represent the people, one need only consider how the Government

represents the Sovereign. Since law is nothing but the declaration of the general will, it is clear that the People cannot be represented in its Legislative power; but it can and must be represented in its executive power, which is nothing but force applied to Law. This shows that, upon closer examination, very few Nations would be found to have laws. Be that as it may, it is certain that the Tribunes, being no part of the executive power, could never represent the Roman people by the rights of their own office, but only by usurping some of the rights of the Senate.

[9] Among the Greeks, all the People had to do it did by itself; it was constantly assembled in the public square. It lived in a mild climate, it was not greedy, [*431*] slaves did its work, its chief business was its freedom. No longer having the same advantages, how are we to preserve the same rights? Your harsher climates make for more needs,* six months of the year you cannot stay out on the public square, your muted languages cannot make themselves heard in the open, you care more for your gain than for your freedom, and you fear slavery less than you fear poverty.

[10] What! Freedom can only be maintained with the help of servitude? Perhaps. The two extremes meet. Everything that is not in nature has its inconveniences, and civil society more than all the rest. In some unfortunate circumstances one can preserve one's own freedom only at the expense of someone else's, and the Citizen can be perfectly free only if the slave is utterly enslaved. Such was the situation of Sparta. As for you, modern peoples, you have no slaves, but are yourselves slaves; you pay for their freedom with your own. Well may you boast of this preference; I find in it more cowardice than humanity.

[11] I do not mean by all this that it is necessary to have slaves or that the right of slavery is legitimate, since I have proved the contrary. I simply state the reasons why modern peoples which believe themselves free have representatives, and why ancient peoples did not have them. Be that as it may, the instant a People gives itself Representatives, it ceases to be free; it ceases to be.

[12] All things considered, I do not see that among us the Sovereign can henceforth preserve the exercise of its rights unless the

---

* To adopt in cold climates the luxury and softness of Orientals is to choose to assume their chains; it is to submit to them even more inevitably than do they.

City is very small. But if it is very small, will it not be subjugated? No. I shall show below* how the external power of a great People can be combined with the simple administration and the good order of a small State.

[432]

CHAPTER SIXTEEN
THAT THE INSTITUTION OF THE GOVERNMENT IS NOT
A CONTRACT

[1] Once the legislative Power is well established, it remains likewise to establish the Executive power; for this latter, which operates only by particular acts, inasmuch as it is not of the essence of the former, is naturally separate from it. If it were possible for the Sovereign, considered as such, to have the executive power, right and fact would be so utterly confounded that one could no longer tell what is law and what is not, and the body politic thus denatured would soon fall prey to the violence against which it was instituted.

[2] The Citizens being all equal by the social contract, all may prescribe what all ought to do, but no one has the right to require that another do what he himself does not do. Now, it is specifically this right, indispensable for endowing the body politic with life and motion, that the Sovereign assigns to the Prince by instituting the Government.

[3] Some have claimed that this act of establishing Government was a contract between the People and the chiefs it gives itself; a contract stipulating for the two parties the conditions under which the one obligated itself to command, and the other to obey. Everyone will agree, I am sure, that this is an odd way of contracting! But let us see whether this opinion is tenable.

[4] First, the supreme authority can no more be modified than it can be alienated, to limit it is to destroy it. It is absurd and contradictory for the Sovereign to give itself a superior; to obligate oneself to obey a master is to return to one's full freedom.

---

* That is what I had planned to do in the sequel to this work when, in dealing with foreign relations, I would have come to confederations. The subject is entirely new and its principles have yet to be established.

[5] Moreover, it is clear that this contract of the people with specific persons would be a particular act. From which it follows that this contract could not be a law or an act of sovereignty, and that consequently it would be illegitimate.

[6] It is further evident that with respect to one another the contracting parties would be under the law of nature alone and without any guarantor [*433*] of their reciprocal engagements, which is in every way at odds with the civil state: Since whoever controls the force is invariably master of the execution, one might as well call "contract" the act of a man who said to another, "I give you all my goods on condition that you will give me back as much of it as you please."

[7] There is only one contract in the State, the contract of association; and it, by itself alone, excludes any others. It is impossible to imagine any public Contract that would not be a violation of the first.

CHAPTER SEVENTEEN
OF THE INSTITUTION OF GOVERNMENT

[1] What, then, is the idea in terms of which one should conceive of the act by which Government is instituted? I shall begin by noting that this act is complex or composed of two others, namely the establishment of law, and the execution of law.

[2] By the first, the Sovereign enacts that a body of Government of this form or that shall be established; and it is clear that this act is a law.

[3] By the second, the People appoints the chiefs who will be entrusted with the established Government. Now since this appointment is a particular act it is not a second law, but merely a consequence of the first and a function of Government.

[4] The difficulty is to understand how there can be an act of Government before the Government exists, and how the People, which is only either Sovereign or subject, can become Prince or Magistrate in certain circumstances.

[5] Here again is revealed one of those astonishing properties of the body politic by which it reconciles apparently contradictory operations. For this reconciliation is accomplished by a sudden

conversion of Sovereignty into Democracy; so that without any perceptible change, and simply by a new relation of all to [*434*] all, the Citizens having become Magistrates pass from general to particular acts, and from the law to its execution.

[6] This change of relation is not some speculative subtlety without example in practice: It takes place every day in the Parliament of England where the lower House on certain occasions turns itself into a Committee of the whole, the better to discuss business, and thus becomes a simple commission rather than the Sovereign Court it had been an instant before; so that it subsequently reports to itself in its capacity as the House of Commons on what it had just settled as a Committee of the whole, and deliberates anew under one name about what it had already decided under another.

[7] It is the distinctive advantage of Democratic Government that it can be established in fact by a simple act of the general will. After which this provisional Government either remains in office if such is the form that is adopted, or it establishes in the name of the Sovereign the Government prescribed by law, and everything is thus in order. It is not possible to establish Government in any other legitimate manner without renouncing the principles established above.

CHAPTER EIGHTEEN
MEANS OF PREVENTING THE USURPATIONS BY THE
GOVERNMENT

[1] From these clarifications it follows, in confirmation of chapter 16, that the act which institutes Government is not a contract but a Law, that the trustees of the executive power are not the people's masters but its officers, that it can establish or remove them whenever it pleases, that there is no question of their contracting, but of obeying, and that in assuming the charges which the State imposes on them they are only fulfilling their duty as Citizens without in any way having the right to challenge the conditions.

[2] Thus when it happens that the People institutes a hereditary Government, either monarchical in one [*435*] family, or aristocratic in one order of Citizens, this is not an engagement it enters into;

it is a provisional form it gives to the administration, until such time as it pleases to order it differently.

[3] It is true that such changes are always dangerous, and that one should never touch an established Government unless it becomes incompatible with the public good; but this circumspection is a maxim of politics and not a rule of right, and the State is no more bound to leave the civil authority to its [current] chiefs, than it is to leave the military authority to its [current] generals.

[4] It is further true that in such a case one cannot be too careful about observing all the formalities required to distinguish a regular and legitimate act from a seditious tumult, and the will of an entire people from the clamors of a faction. It is above all in such cases that no more should be conceded to the *cas odieux* than what cannot be refused it by right in all its rigor, and it is also from this obligation that the Prince derives a great advantage in preserving its power in spite of the people, without its being possible to say that the Prince has usurped that power: For in appearing to use only its rights, the Prince can very easily expand them and, on the pretext of public calm, prevent assemblies intended to restore good order; so that it takes advantage either of a silence which it prevents from being broken, or of the irregularities which it causes to be committed, to presume that the assent of those whom fear has silenced favors it, and to punish those who dare to speak. That is how the Decemvirs, after first having been elected for one year, and then continued for another year, tried to hold on to their power in perpetuity, by no longer permitting the comitia to meet; and it is by this simple means that all governments of the world, once they are invested with the public force, sooner or later usurp the Sovereign authority.

[5] The periodic assemblies of which I have spoken above are suited to forestall or to postpone this misfortune, above all if they do not require formal convocation: for then the Prince could not prevent them without openly declaring itself a violator of the laws and an enemy of the State.

[6] These assemblies, which have no other object than to maintain the social treaty, ought always to open with two motions which it should be impossible ever to omit, and which ought to be voted on separately:

[436][7] The first; *whether it please the Sovereign to retain the present form of Government.*

[8] The second; *whether it please the People to leave its administration to those who are currently charged with it.*

[9] I assume here what I believe I have demonstrated, namely that in the State there is no fundamental law which could not be revoked, not even the social pact; for if all the Citizens were to assemble to break this pact by a common accord, there can be no doubt that it would be most legitimately broken. Grotius even thinks that everyone can renounce the State of which he is a member, and recover his natural freedom and his goods on leaving the country.* Now it would be absurd if all the Citizens united could not do what each one of them separately can do.

---

* It being understood that one does not leave in order to evade one's duty or to avoid serving the fatherland when it needs us. In such cases flight would be criminal and punishable; it would no longer be withdrawal but desertion.

BOOK IV

CHAPTER ONE
THAT THE GENERAL WILL IS INDESTRUCTIBLE

[1] So long as several men united consider themselves a single body, they have but a single will, which is concerned with their common preservation, and the general welfare. Then all of the springs of the State are vigorous and simple, its maxims are clear and perspicuous, it has no confused, contradictory interests, the common good is everywhere fully evident and requires only good sense to be perceived. Peace, union, equality are enemies of political subtleties. Upright and simple men are difficult to deceive because of their simplicity, they are not taken in by sham and special pleading; they are not even clever enough to be dupes. When, among the happiest people in the world, troops of peasants are seen attending to affairs of State under an oak tree and always acting wisely, can one avoid despising the refinements of other nations which make themselves illustrious and miserable with so much art and mystification?

[2] A State thus governed needs very few Laws, and as it becomes necessary to promulgate new ones, this necessity is universally seen. The first one to propose them only states what all have already sensed, and there is no need for intrigues or eloquence to secure passage into law of what each has already resolved to do as soon as he is sure that the others will do so as well.

[3] What misleads ratiocinators is that since they only see States which are badly constituted from their origin, they are struck [*438*] by the impossibility of maintaining such an administration in them. They laugh as they imagine all the nonsense of which a clever knave or an insinuating talker could persuade the people of Paris or London. They do not know that Cromwell would have been condemned to hard labor by the people of Berne, and the Duc de Beaufort to reformatory by the Genevans.

[4] But when the social knot begins to loosen and the State to weaken; when particular interests begin to make themselves felt,jyand small societies to influence the larger society, the common interest diminishes and meets with opposition, votes are no longer

unanimous, the general will is no longer the will of all, contradictions and disagreements arise, and the best opinion no longer carries the day unchallenged.

[5] Finally, when the State close to ruin subsists only in an illusory and vain form, when the social bond is broken in all hearts, when the basest interest brazenly assumes the sacred name of public good; then the general will grows mute, everyone, prompted by secret motives, no more states opinions as a Citizen than if the State had never existed, and iniquitous decrees with no other goal than particular interest are falsely passed under the name of Laws.

[6] Does it follow that the general will is annihilated or corrupted? No, it remains constant, unalterable, and pure; but it is subordinated to others that prevail over it. Each person, in detaching his interest from the common interest, sees clearly enough that he cannot separate them entirely, but his share of the public evil seems to him as nothing compared to the exclusive good which he seeks to make his own. Except for this particular good, he wills the public good in his own interest just as forcefully as anyone else. Even in selling his vote for money he does not extinguish the general will within himself, he evades it. The mistake he commits is to change the state of the question, and to answer something other than what he is asked: So that instead of saying with his vote, *it is advantageous to the State*, he says, *it is advantageous to this man or to this party that this or that opinion pass.* Thus the law of public order in assemblies consists not so much in upholding the general will in them, as in seeing to it that the general will is always consulted and that it always replies.

[7] I could offer quite a few reflections here on the simple [*439*] right to vote in every act of sovereignty; a right of which nothing can deprive Citizens; and on the right of voicing opinions, proposing, dividing, discussing [motions], which the Government always takes great care to allow only to its own members; but this important matter would require a separate treatise, and I cannot say everything in this one.

CHAPTER TWO
OF SUFFRAGE

[1] From the preceding chapter it is evident that the way in which general business is conducted provides a fairly reliable indication

of the current state of the morals and the health of the body politic. The more concord reigns in assemblies, that is to say the closer opinions come to unanimity, the more the general will also predominates; whereas long debates, dissensions, disturbances, signal the ascendancy of particular interests and the decline of the State.

[2] This seems less obvious when two or more orders enter into its constitution, as did in Rome the Patricians and the Plebeians, whose quarrels often disturbed the comitia even in the finest times of the Republic; but this exception is more apparent than real; for by the vice inherent to the body politic there are then, so to speak, two States in one; [and] what is not true of the two together is true of each separately. And indeed even in the stormiest times the people's plebiscites were always carried quietly and by a large majority, when the Senate did not interfere: The Citizens having but a single interest, the people had but a single will.

[3] At the other end of the cycle, unanimity returns. That is when the citizens, fallen into servitude, no longer have freedom or will. Then fear and flattery turn voting into acclamations; they no longer deliberate, they worship or they curse. Such was the vile manner in which the Senate expressed opinions under the Emperors. Sometimes it did so with ridiculous precautions: Tacitus notes that under Otho, the Senators heaping execration on Vitellius took care at the same time to make a frightful noise, [*440*] so that, if by chance he were to become master, he could not tell what they each had said.

[4] From these various considerations arise the maxims that should regulate the manner in which votes are counted and opinions compared, taking account of whether the general will is more or less easy to know, and the State more or less in decline.

[5] There is only one law which by its nature requires unanimous consent. That is the social pact: for the civil association is the most voluntary act in the world; every man being born free and master of himself, no one may on any pretext whatsoever subject him without his consent. To decide that the son of a slave is born a slave is to decide that he is not born a man.

[6] If, then, at the time of the social pact there are some who oppose it, their opposition does not invalidate the contract, it only keeps them from being included in it; they are foreigners among the Citizens. Once the State is instituted, consent consists

in residence; to dwell in the territory is to submit to the sovereignty.*

[7] Except for this primitive contract, the vote of the majority always obligates all the rest; this is a consequence of the contract itself. Yet the question is raised how a man can be both free and forced to conform to wills which are not his own. How are the opponents both free and subject to laws to which they have not consented?

[8] I answer that the question is badly framed. The Citizen consents to all the laws, even to those passed in spite of him, and even to those that punish him when he dares to violate any one of them. The constant will of all the members of the State is the general will; it is through it that they are citizens and free.* When a law is proposed [*441*] in the People's assembly, what they are being asked is not exactly whether they approve the proposal or reject it, but whether it does or does not conform to the general will, which is theirs; everyone states his opinion about this by casting his ballot, and the tally of the votes yields the declaration of the general will. Therefore when the opinion contrary to my own prevails, it proves nothing more than that I made a mistake and that what I took to be the general will was not. If my particular opinion had prevailed, I would have done something other than what I had willed, and it is then that I would not have been free.

[9] This presupposes, it is true, that all the characteristics of the general will are still in the majority: once they no longer are, then regardless of which side one takes there no longer is any freedom.

[10] When earlier I showed how particular wills were substituted for the general will in public deliberations, I indicated clearly enough the practicable ways to prevent this abuse; I shall have more to say on this subject later. As for the proportional number of votes needed to declare the general will, I have also provided the prin-

---

* This should always be understood with regard to a free State; for elsewhere family, goods, the lack of asylum, necessity, violence, may keep an inhabitant in the country in spite of himself, and then his mere residence no longer implies his consent to the contract or to its violation.

* In Genoa the word *Libertas* can be read on the front of prisons and on the chains of galley-slaves. This use of the motto is fine and just. Indeed it is only the evildoers from every estate who keep the Citizens from being free. In a country where all such folk were in the Galleys, the most perfect freedom would be enjoyed.

ciples by which it can be ascertained. A difference of a single vote breaks a tie, a single opponent destroys unanimity; but between unanimity and a tie there are various uneven divisions, at any one of which this proportion can be fixed, taking the state and the needs of the body politic into account.

[11] Two general maxims can help to regulate these ratios: one, that the more important and serious the deliberations are, the more nearly unanimous should be the opinion that prevails; the other, that the more rapidly the business at hand has to be resolved, the narrower should be the prescribed difference in weighting opinions; in deliberations which have to be concluded straightaway a majority of one should suffice. The first of these maxims appears better suited to Laws, the second to business. Be that as it may, it is by a combination of these two maxims that the best ratios for a deciding majority are determined.

[*442*]

CHAPTER THREE
OF ELECTIONS

[1] With regard to the elections of the Prince and the Magistrates, which are, as I have said, complex acts, there are two ways to proceed; namely, by choice or by lot. Both have been used in various Republics, and a very complicated mixture of the two can still be found at present in the election of the Doge of Venice.

[2] *Voting by lot*, says Montesquieu, *is in the nature of Democracy.* I agree, but why is it? *Drawing lots*, he goes on, *is a way of electing that afflicts no one; it leaves every Citizen a reasonable hope of serving the fatherland.* These are not reasons.

[3] If one keeps in mind that the election of chiefs is a function of Government and not of Sovereignty, one will see why election by lot is more in the nature of Democracy, where the administration is all the better in proportion as its acts are fewer.

[4] In every genuine Democracy, magistracy is not an advantage but a burdensome charge, which one cannot justly impose on one individual rather than another. Only the law can impose this charge on the one to whom the lot falls. For then, since the condition is equal for all and the choice does not depend on a human will, no particular application can distort the universality of the law.

[5] In Aristocracy the Prince chooses the Prince, the Government perpetuates itself by itself, and that is where voting is appropriate.

[6] The example of the election of the Doge of Venice, far from destroying this distinction, confirms it: This composite form suits a mixed Government. For it is an error to take the Government of Venice for a genuine Aristocracy. While the People has no share in the Government, the nobility is itself of the people. A multitude of poor Barnabites never came close to any magistracy, and all they get for being noble is the empty [*443*] title of Excellency and the right to be present at the great Council. Since this great Council is as numerous as our general Council in Geneva, its illustrious members have no more privileges than do our simple Citizens. It is certain that, setting aside the extreme disparity between the two Republics, the bourgeoisie of Geneva corresponds precisely to the Venetian Patriciate, our natives and inhabitants correspond to the Townsmen and the people of Venice, and our peasants correspond to the mainland subjects; in sum, however one considers that Republic, apart from its size, its Government is no more aristocratic than is ours. The entire difference is that since we have no chiefs for life, we have not the same need for election by lot.

[7] Elections by lot would entail few inconveniences in a genuine Democracy where everything is as equal by virtue of morals and talents as maxims and fortune, because choice would make almost no difference. But I have already said that there is no genuine Democracy.

[8] Where election by choice and election by lot are combined, choice should fill the positions that require specific talents, such as military offices; drawing lots is appropriate for the positions for which good sense, justice, integrity suffice, such as judicial responsibilities, because in a well-constituted State these qualities are common to all Citizens.

[9] Neither lot nor voting has any place in a monarchical Government. Since the Monarch is by right the sole Prince and the only Magistrate, the choice of his lieutenants is his alone. When the Abbé de St. Pierre proposed multiplying the Councils of the King of France and electing their members by Ballot, he did not realize he was proposing to change the form of the Government.

[10] It remains for me to speak about the way votes should be cast and collected in the assembly of the people; but perhaps the

historical sketch of Roman administration in this matter will explain more concretely all the maxims which I might establish. It is not unworthy of a judicious reader to consider in some detail how public and particular business was conducted in a Council of two hundred thousand men.

[444]

CHAPTER FOUR
OF THE ROMAN COMITIA

[1] We have no really reliable records of the first times of Rome; there is even every likelihood that most of what is retailed about it are fables;* and in general the most instructive part of the annals of peoples, which is the history of their establishment, is the part we most lack. Experience daily teaches us what causes give rise to the revolutions of empires; but as no more peoples are being formed, we have scarcely anything but conjectures to explain how they were formed.

[2] The practices one finds established at least attest that these practices had an origin. Among the traditions that go back to these origins, the ones which the greatest authorities support and the strongest reasons confirm must pass for the most certain. These are the maxims I have tried to follow in inquiring how the freest and most powerful people on earth exercised its supreme power.

[3] After the founding of Rome the nascent Republic, that is to say the founder's army, composed of Albans, Sabines, and foreigners, was divided into three classes which, from this division, took the name *Tribes*. Each one of these Tribes was subdivided into ten Curiae, and each Curia into Decuriae, at the head of which were placed chiefs called *Curions* and *Decurions*.

[4] In addition a body of one hundred Horsemen or Knights, called a Century, was drawn from each Tribe: which shows that these divisions, which are hardly needed in a small town, were at first entirely military. But it would seem that an instinct for great-

---

* The name *Rome* which purportedly comes from *Romulus* is Greek and means *force*; the name *Numa* is also Greek, and means *Law*. How likely is it that this city's first two Kings would have borne names so appropriately anticipating what they did?

127

ness led the little city of Rome to [*445*] assume in advance an administration suited to the capital of the world.

[5] This initial apportionment soon gave rise to an inconvenience. The Tribes of the Albans* and that of the Sabines** remained forever in the same state, while that of the foreigners*** kept on growing by their continuous influx, so that before long it exceeded the other two. The remedy Servius found for this dangerous abuse was to change the division, and to substitute for the division by race, which he abolished, another division based on the city district which each Tribe occupied. Instead of three Tribes he made four; each of which occupied one of the hills of Rome and bore its name. Thus at the same time as he remedied the existing inequality he forestalled its future recurrence; and so that this might be a division not only of districts but of men, he forbade the inhabitants of one quarter to move to another, which prevented the races from merging.

[6] He also doubled the three ancient centuries of Horsemen and added twelve more to them, but always keeping the ancient names; a simple and judicious means by which he succeeded in distinguishing the body of the Horsemen from that of the People, without causing the latter to grumble.

[7] To these four urban Tribes Servius added fifteen more called rural Tribes, because they were formed of inhabitants of the countryside, apportioned into so many cantons. Later an equal number of new Tribes was created, and the Roman People finally found itself divided into thirty-five Tribes; the number at which they remained fixed until the end of the Republic.

[8] This distinction between the urban and the rural Tribes resulted in an effect worth noting, because there is no other instance of it, and because Rome owed to it both the preservation of its morals, and the growth of its empire. The urban Tribes might have been expected soon to arrogate to themselves the power and honors, and to lose no time debasing the rural Tribes; the very opposite happened. The early Romans' taste for country life is well known. They owed this taste to the wise [*446*] institutor who coupled

---

* *Ramnenses.*
** *Tatienses.*
*** *Luceres.*

freedom with rural and military labors, and so to speak relegated arts, crafts, intrigue, fortune and slavery to the city.

[9] Thus, since all of Rome's illustrious men lived in the country and cultivated the land, it became customary to look only there for the mainstays of the Republic. As it was the state of the worthiest Patricians, it was held in honor by everyone: the Villagers' simple and hardworking life was preferred to the idle and loose life of the Roman Bourgeois, and someone who would have been nothing but a miserable proletarian in the city became a respected Citizen as a farmer in the country. Not without reason, said Varro, did our magnanimous ancestors establish in the Village the nursery of those robust and valiant men who defended them in time of war and fed them in time of peace. Pliny states positively that the rural Tribes were honored because of the men who composed them; whereas cowards whom they wanted to degrade were transferred to the urban Tribes as a disgrace. When the Sabine Appius Claudius came to settle in Rome, he was loaded with honors and enrolled in a rural Tribe which afterwards assumed his family name. Finally, freedmen all entered the urban, never the rural Tribes; and during the whole of the Republic there is not a single instance of any one of these freedmen acceding to any magistracy, even though he had become a Citizen.

[10] This maxim was excellent; but it was pushed so far that it finally resulted in a change and certainly an abuse in the administration.

[11] First, the Censors, after having long arrogated to themselves the right arbitrarily to transfer citizens from one Tribe to another, permitted most of them to enroll in whichever one they pleased; a permission which was certainly not good for anything, and which deprived the censorship of one of its mainsprings. In addition, since the Great and the powerful all had themselves enrolled in rural Tribes, and the freedmen who had become Citizens remained in the urban Tribes along with the populace, the Tribes generally no longer had a district or territory; but all found themselves so intermingled that it became impossible to identify the members of any one of them without consulting the registers, so that the idea of the word *Tribe* thus shifted from the residential to the personal, or rather it became almost a chimera.

[*447*] [12] In addition it happened that the urban Tribes, being more ready to hand, often found themselves the strongest in the comitia, and sold the State to those who deigned to buy the votes of the rabble who composed them.

[13] As for the Curiae, since the institutor had made ten of them in each Tribe, all of the Roman people which was enclosed within the city walls at the time was composed of thirty Curiae, each with its own Temples, its Gods, its officers, its priests, and its festivals called *compitalia*, which were similar to the *Paganalia* later held by the rural Tribes.

[14] At the time of Servius's new apportionment, since this number of thirty could not be evenly distributed among his four Tribes and he did not want to change it, the Curiae independent of the Tribes became another division of the inhabitants of Rome: But neither among the rural Tribes nor among the people who composed them was there any question of Curiae, because the Tribes having become purely civil establishments, and a different administration having been introduced to raise troops, Romulus's military divisions proved superfluous. Thus, although every Citizen was enrolled in a Tribe, far from everyone was enrolled in a Curia.

[15] Servius made yet a third division which bore no relation to the first two, and which by its effects became the most important of all. He distributed the whole Roman people into six classes, which he distinguished neither by district nor by persons, but by goods: So that the first classes were filled with the rich, the last with the poor, and the middle ones with those who enjoyed a moderate fortune. These six classes were subdivided into 193 other bodies called centuries, and these bodies were so distributed that the first Class alone contained more than half of them, and the last formed but a single one. Thus it came about that the Class with the smallest number of men had the largest number of centuries, and that the entire last class counted as only one subdivision although it alone contained more than half the inhabitants of Rome.

[16] In order that the people might less readily discern the consequences of this last form, Servius pretended to give it a military cast: he added two centuries of armor makers to the second class, and two of weapons makers to [*448*] the fourth: In each Class, except the last, he distinguished the young from the old, that is to say those who were obliged to bear arms from those whose age by law exempted them from bearing them; a distinction which more

than the distinction by wealth made it necessary frequently to take a new census or count: Finally he wanted the assembly held in the Campus Martius, and everyone of military age to attend bearing their arms.

[17] The reason why he did not adopt this same division into young and old in the last class is that the populace that composed it was not accorded the honor of bearing arms for the fatherland; one had to have a hearth in order to obtain the right to defend it, and there is perhaps not a single man, among the countless troops of beggars who nowadays sparkle in Kings' armies, who would not have been expelled with contempt from a Roman cohort in the days when soldiers were the defenders of freedom.

[18] A further distinction was, however, drawn in the last class between the *proletarians* and those who were called *capite censi*. The former, not wholly reduced to nothing, at least contributed Citizens to the State, sometimes even soldiers when there was a pressing need for them. As for those who had nothing at all and could be counted only by head, they were regarded as altogether nil, and Marius was the first who deigned to enroll them.

[19] Without deciding here whether this Third count was in itself good or bad, I believe I can safely say that it could only be made to work because of the first Romans' simple morals, their disinterestedness, their taste for agriculture, their contempt for commerce and the ardor for gain. Where is the modern people whose devouring greed, unsettled spirit, intrigue, constant comings and goings, perpetual revolutions of fortune would let such an establishment last twenty years without overthrowing the whole State? Indeed, it has to be stressed that, in Rome, morals and the censorship, stronger than this institution, corrected for its vice, and that some rich men found themselves relegated to the class of the poor for having made an excessive display of their riches.

[20] From all this it is easy to understand why almost never more than five classes are mentioned, although there really were six. The sixth, since it provi[*449*]ded neither soldiers to the army nor votes at the Campus Martius* and was of almost no use in the Republic, was rarely taken into account.

---

* I say at the *campus martius* because that is where the Comitia assembled by centuries; in the other two forms the people assembled in the *forum* or elsewhere, and then the *Capite censi* had as much influence and authority as the first citizens.

[21] Such were the different divisions of the Roman people. Let us now see what effects they produced in the assemblies. These assemblies legitimately convened were called *Comitia*; they were normally held in the Roman forum or in the campus Martius, and were distinguished as Curiate, Centuriate, and Tribal comitia, according to which one of these three forms was their organizing form; the comitia by curiae had been instituted by Romulus, the comitia by Centuries by Servius, the comitia by Tribes by the Tribunes of the people. No law was sanctioned, no magistrate elected except in the Comitia, and since there was not a single Citizen who was not enrolled in a Curia, a Century, or a Tribe, it follows that no Citizen was excluded from the right to vote, and that the Roman People was genuinely Sovereign both by right and in fact.

[22] For the Comitia to be legitimately assembled and for their transactions to have the force of law, three conditions had to be satisfied: first, that the body or the magistrate convening it was vested with the requisite authority to do so; second, that the assembly be held on one of the days permitted by law; third, that the auguries were favorable.

[23] The reason for the first regulation requires no explanation; the second is a matter of administration; thus Comitia were not allowed to be held on feast- or market-days, when country-folk coming to Rome on business had not the time to spend the day in the public square. With the third the Senate held in check a proud and restless people and, when necessary, tempered the ardor of seditious Tribunes; but they found more than one way to rid themselves of this constraint.

[24] The Laws and the election of the chiefs were not the only matters submitted to the judgment of the Comitia: The Roman people having usurped the most important functions of [450] Government, the fate of Europe may be said to have been determined in its assemblies. This variety of objects gave rise to the various forms which these assemblies assumed according to the matters they had to decide.

[25] In order to judge these various forms one need only compare them. Romulus's purpose in instituting the Curiae was to restrain the Senate by the people and the People by the Senate while himself dominating both equally. Hence, by means of this form he gave the people the full authority of numbers to balance the authority of

power and wealth which he left to the Patricians. But in keeping with the spirit of Monarchy he nevertheless gave the Patricians a greater advantage through their Clients' influence on the majority of votes. This admirable institution of Patrons and Clients was a masterpiece of politics and humanity, without which the Patriciate, so contrary to the spirit of the Republic, could not have survived. Rome alone had the honor of setting the world this fine example which never led to any abuse, and yet has never been followed.

[26] Since this same form of Curiae continued under the Kings until the time of Servius, and since the reign of the last Tarquin was not held to be legitimate, the royal laws were generally identified by the name of *leges curiatae*.

[27] Under the Republic the Curiae, still limited to the four urban Tribes and no longer containing anyone but the Roman populace, could suit neither the Senate which was at the head of the Patricians, nor the Tribunes who, although plebeians, were at the head of the well-to-do Citizens. They therefore fell into discredit, and their degradation was such that their thirty Lictors assembled did what the [full] comitia by Curiae should have done.

[28] The division by Centuries favored Aristocracy to such an extent that one is at first left to wonder why the Senate did not always prevail in the Comitia which bore that name and which elected the Consuls, Censors, and other curule Magistrates. Indeed, since of the hundred and ninety-three centuries which formed the six Classes of the entire Roman People, the first Class comprised ninety-eight, and votes were only counted by Centuries, this first Class by itself alone prevailed over all the others by the number of its votes. When all of its Centuries were in agreement, they did not even go on [451] collecting ballots; what the smallest number had decided passed for a decision of the multitude; and in the Comitia by Centuries affairs can be said to have been settled more often by majorities of cash than of votes.

[29] But this extreme authority was tempered in two ways: First, the Tribunes ordinarily, and a large number of the Plebeians always, were in the class of the rich and thus balanced the influence of the Patricians in this first class.

[30] The second way was this, that instead of having the Centuries start voting in order, which would have led to always beginning

with the first, a Century was chosen by lot, and that one* alone proceeded to hold an election; after which all the Centuries having been summoned for another day in the order of their rank repeated the same election and usually confirmed it. In this way the authority of example was withdrawn from rank and given to lot in conformity with the principle of democracy.

[31] This practice had another advantage as well; namely that the Citizens from the countryside had time between the two elections to inform themselves of the merit of the candidate provisionally nominated, so that they might vote only once they could do so knowledgeably. But on the pretext of accelerating the vote they succeeded in abolishing this practice, and both elections were held on the same day.

[32] The Comitia by Tribes were properly the Council of the Roman people. They could only be convened by the Tribunes; they elected the Tribunes and passed their plebiscites. Not only had the Senate no standing in them, it had not even the right to attend them, and the Senators, forced to obey laws on which they could not vote, were in this respect less free than the last of Citizens. This injustice was altogether ill conceived, and it alone was enough to invalidate the decrees of a body to which not all of its members were admitted. Even if all the Patricians had attended these Comitia as, in their capacity as Citizens they had the right to do, they would have been counted as simple particulars, and would therefore have had scarcely any impact on a form of [452] voting which consists in counting heads and in which the least proletarian counts for as much as does the Prince of the Senate.

[33] It is therefore evident that these various divisions [of the population] were not simply forms indifferent in themselves, but that in addition to determining the order in which the votes cast by such a large People were counted, each one of them had effects relative to the opinions that led to its being preferred.

[34] Without going into fuller detail about this, it follows from the preceding clarifications that the Comitia by Tribes were the most favorable to popular Government, and the Comitia by Centu-

---

* The century thus drawn by lot was called *praerogativa* because it was the first to be asked to vote, and this is where the word *prerogative* comes from.

ries to Aristocracy. As regards the Comitia by Curiae where the Roman populace alone formed the majority, since all they were good for was to favor tyranny and evil designs, they inevitably fell into discredit, and seditious parties themselves abstained from using a means which exposed their projects too openly. Certain it is that the whole majesty of the Roman People resided only in the Comitia by Centuries, which alone were complete; for the Comitia by Curiae lacked the rural Tribes, and the Comitia by Tribes lacked the Senate and the Patricians.

[35] As for the manner of collecting the votes, among the first Romans it was as simple as their morals, although still less simple than in Sparta. Everyone called out his vote, a Clerk recorded them in writing, one by one; in each Tribe a majority of votes determined the vote of that Tribe, a majority of votes by the Tribes determined the vote of the People, and the same was done in the Curiae and the Centuries. It was a good practice as long as honesty reigned among the Citizens and each was ashamed to cast his vote publicly for an unjust opinion or an unworthy candidate; but when the people grew corrupt and votes were bought, it agreed to secret balloting so that buyers might be restrained by mistrust, and scoundrels given a way not to be traitors.

[36] I know that Cicero condemns this change and holds it partly responsible for the ruin of the Republic. But although I am sensible of the weight Cicero's authority should carry in this, I cannot share his opinion. I think, on the contrary, that the loss of the State was hastened because not enough such changes were made. Just as the regimen of healthy people is not suited to the sick, one must not try to go[453]vern a corrupt people by the same Laws as those that suit a good people. Nothing proves these maxims better than the long life of the Republic of Venice, which still retains a simulacrum of existence, solely because its laws are suited only to wicked men.

[37] Hence tablets were distributed to the Citizens allowing everyone to vote without anyone else's knowing his opinion. New procedures were also established for collecting these tablets, tallying votes, comparing numbers, etc. None of this prevented the integrity of the officers in charge of these functions* from frequently coming

---

* Custodes, Diribitores, Rogatores suffragiorum.

under suspicion. In the end, to prevent intrigue and the buying and selling of votes, Edicts were issued, the large number of which proves their uselessness.

[38] Toward the final times [of the Republic], they were often compelled to resort to extraordinary expedients in order to make up for the inadequacy of the laws. Sometimes prodigies were alleged; but this means, which could impose on the people, could not impose on those who governed it; sometimes an assembly was convened all of a sudden before the candidates had time to engage in their intrigues; sometimes, when the people was found to have been won over and ready to make a bad choice, an entire session was taken up with talk: but finally ambition eluded everything; and what is incredible is that thanks to its ancient regulations this immense people, in the midst of so many abuses, did not cease to elect Magistrates, pass laws, try cases, dispatch private and public business almost as readily as the Senate itself might have done.

CHAPTER FIVE
OF THE TRIBUNATE

[1] When it is not possible to establish an exact proportion between the constitutive parts of the State, or when indestructible forces consistently upset the relations between them, then a particular magistracy is instituted which is not [454] incorporated with the others, which restores each term to its true relation, and which provides a tie or middle term either between the Prince and the People, or between the Prince and the Sovereign, or between both sides at once if that is necessary.

[2] This body, which I shall call *Tribunate*, is the preserver of the laws and of the legislative power. It serves sometimes to protect the Sovereign against the Government, as the Tribunes of the people did in Rome, sometimes to uphold the Government against the People, as the Council of Ten now does in Venice, and sometimes to maintain the balance between the two, as the Ephors did in Sparta.

[3] The Tribunate is not a constitutive part of the City, and it ought to have no share of either the legislative or the executive

power, but precisely because of this its own power is all the greater: for while it can do nothing, it can prevent everything. It is more sacred and revered as the defender of the Laws than is the Prince which executes them and than the Sovereign which promulgates them. This was seen very clearly in Rome when those proud Patricians, who always despised the entire people, were forced to yield before a plain officer of the people wielding neither patronage nor jurisdiction.

[4] A wisely tempered Tribunate is the firmest bulwark of a good constitution; but if it has even a little too much force it overthrows everything: As for being weak, that is not in its nature, and if it is anything at all, it is never less than it has to be.

[5] It degenerates into tyranny when it usurps the executive power of which it is but the moderator, and tries to administer the laws which it ought only to protect. The enormous power of the Ephors which was without danger so long as Sparta preserved its morals hastened its corruption once corruption had set in. The blood of Agis murdered by these tyrants was avenged by his successor: both the crime and the punishment of the Ephors hastened the fall of the Republic, and after Cleomenes Sparta ceased to be anything. Rome again perished in the same way, and in the end the excessive power the Tribunes had gradually usurped served, with the help of laws that had been made for the sake of freedom, as a safeguard to the Emperors who destroyed freedom. As for the Council of Ten in Venice; it is a Tribunal of blood, equally abhorrent to the Patricians and to the People and which, far from loftily protecting the laws, no longer serves any other purpose [*455*] now that the laws have been debased, than under cover of darkness to strike blows one dare not notice.

[6] The Tribunate, like the Government, is weakened by the multiplication of its members. When the Tribunes of the Roman people, at first two, then five in number, wanted to double this number, the Senate let them do so, confident that it could check some by means of the others; which is just what did happen.

[7] The best means to prevent usurpations by so formidable a body, a means that has so far not occurred to any Government, would be not to make this body permanent, but to stipulate intervals during which it would be suspended. These intervals, which should not be long enough to allow abuses sufficient time to consolidate,

can be fixed by law, so that if need be they could easily be shortened by extraordinary commissions.

[8] This means seems to me free of inconveniences because the Tribunate, since, as I have said, it is not part of the constitution, can be removed without harming it; and it seems to me efficacious because a newly installed magistrate starts out not with the power his predecessors had but with the power which the law grants him.

CHAPTER SIX
OF THE DICTATORSHIP

[1] The inflexibility of the laws, which keeps them from bending to events, can in some cases render them pernicious, and through them cause the ruin of a State in crisis. The orderliness and deliberateness of formalities requires a space of time which circumstances sometimes deny one. A thousand cases can arise for which the Lawgiver did not provide, and it is a very necessary foresight to sense that one cannot foresee everything.

[2] One should therefore not try to consolidate political institutions to the point of depriving oneself of the power to suspend their effect. Even Sparta let its laws lie dormant.

[3] But only the greatest dangers can [456] counterbalance the danger of disturbing the public order, and one should never suspend the sacred power of the laws except when the salvation of the fatherland is at stake. In these rare and manifest cases a special act provides for the public safety, which entrusts it to the worthiest person. This commission can be given in either of two ways according to the kind of danger.

[4] If in order to counteract it, it suffices to increase the activity of the government, then it gets concentrated in one or two of its members; this way it is not the authority of the laws that is disturbed, but only the form of their administration. If however the peril is such that the laws as an instrumentality are an obstacle to guarding against it, then a supreme chief is named who silences all the laws and provisionally suspends the Sovereign authority; in such a case the general will is not in doubt, it is obvious that the people's foremost intention is that the State not perish. This way the suspension of the legislative authority does not abolish it; the magistrate

who silences it cannot make it speak, he dominates it without being able to represent it; he can do everything, except make laws.

[5] The first means was used by the Roman Senate when it charged the Consuls by means of a consecrated formula with providing for the salvation of the Republic; the second took place when one of the two Consuls appointed a Dictator;* a practice for which Alba had set the precedent in Rome.

[6] In the beginnings of the Republic they frequently had recourse to the Dictatorship, because the State was not yet sufficiently firmly settled to sustain itself by the force of its constitution. Since at that time morals made superfluous a good many precautions which would have been necessary at other times, there was no fear that a Dictator would abuse his authority or that he would attempt to keep it beyond his term. It seemed, on the contrary, that so great a power was a burden to the one in whom it was vested, such was his haste to be rid of it; as if taking the place of the laws had been too painful and too perilous a station!

[7] That is why it is not the danger that it might be abused but the danger that it might be debased which prompts me to object to the indiscriminate use of this [457] supreme magistracy in the earliest times. For while it was being lavished on Elections, Dedications, pure formalities, there was reason to fear that it would prove less formidable in times of need, and that people would come to regard as vain a title used only in vain ceremonies.

[8] Towards the end of the Republic, the Romans, having grown more circumspect, were sparing in their use of the Dictatorship with as little reason as they had formerly been lavish in their use of it. It was easy to see that their fear was ill-founded, that by then the weakness of the capital guaranteed its safety against the magistrates in its midst, that a Dictator could in some cases defend the public freedom without ever being in a position to threaten it, and that Rome's chains would be forged not in Rome itself, but in its armies: the feeble resistance which Marius offered Sulla and Pompey offered Caesar showed clearly enough what could be expected from internal authority opposing external force.

[9] This error caused them to commit great mistakes. As, for example, was their failure to appoint a Dictator in the Catiline

---

* This appointment was made at night and in secret, as if they had been ashamed of placing a man above the laws.

affair; for since all that was at issue was internal to the city, and at the very most, to some province in Italy, a Dictator, with the unlimited authority the laws gave him, would easily have crushed the conspiracy, which was only smothered by a concatenation of happy contingencies on which human prudence should never have counted.

[10] Instead, the Senate contented itself with transferring all of its power to the Consuls; which is how it happened that Cicero, in order to act effectively, was constrained to exceed this power on a crucial point, and that, while the first transports of joy led to his conduct being approved, he was later justly called to account for the blood of Citizens shed in violation of the laws; a charge that could not have been levelled at a Dictator. But the Consul's eloquence swept all before him; and since he himself, though a Roman, loved his glory more than his fatherland, he sought not so much the most legitimate and certain way to save the State as the way to get all the honor in this affair.* He was therefore [458] justly honored as the liberator of Rome, and justly punished as a transgressor of the laws. However brilliant his recall, it is certain that it was a pardon.

[11] In any case, whatever may be the manner in which this important commission is conferred, it is important that its duration be fixed to a very brief term which can never be extended; in the crises that lead to its being established the State is soon destroyed or saved, and, the pressing need once passed, the Dictatorship becomes tyrannical or vain. Since in Rome Dictators were Dictators for only six months, most of them abdicated before this term. If the term had been longer, they might perhaps have been tempted to extend it still further, as did the Decemvirs their one-year term. The Dictator had only time enough to attend to the need that had got him elected, he had no time to dream of other projects.

---

* This is what he could not be confident of if he had suggested a Dictator, since he did not dare to appoint himself and he could not be sure that his colleague would appoint him.

CHAPTER SEVEN
OF CENSORSHIP

[1] Just as the general will is declared by law, the public judgment is declared by the censorship; public opinion is the kind of law of which the Censor is the Minister, and which, on the model of the Prince, he does no more than apply to particular cases.

[2] So that, far from being the arbiter of the people's opinion, the censorial tribunal does no more than declare it, and as soon as it departs from it, its decisions are vain and without effect.

[3] It is useless to draw a distinction between a nation's morals and the objects of its esteem; for all this follows from the same principle and necessarily converges. Among all peoples of the world, not nature but opinion determines the choice of their pleasures. Reform men's opinions and their morals will be purified of themselves. One always loves what is fine or what one finds to be so, but it is in this judgment that one is mistaken; hence it is this judgment that has to be regulated. Whoever judges morals judges honor, and whoever judges honor takes opinion as his law.

[*459*] [4] A people's opinions arise from its constitution; although law does not regulate morals, legislation does give rise to them; when legislation weakens, morals degenerate; but by then the Censor's judgment will fail to do what the force of the laws will have failed to do.

[5] It follows that the Censorship can be useful in preserving morals, never in restoring them. Establish Censors while the Laws are in their vigor; once they have lost it, all is hopeless; nothing legitimate any longer has force when the laws no longer have any.

[6] The Censorship maintains morals by preventing opinions from becoming corrupt, by preserving their uprightness through wise applications, sometimes even by fixing them when they are still indeterminate. The use of seconds in duels, which was carried to extravagant extremes in the Kingdom of France, was abolished in it by the following few words in an Edict of the King; *as for those who are so cowardly as to name Seconds*. This judgment, by anticipating that of the public, straightway determined it. But when the same Edicts sought to proclaim that it was also an act of cowardice to fight a duel, which is very true, but contrary to common

opinion, the public scorned this decision about which it already had a settled judgment.

[7] I have said elsewhere* that since public opinion is not subject to constraint there should be no vestige of constraint in the tribunal established to represent it. One cannot too much admire the skill with which this spring, which has been entirely lost among the moderns, was brought into play among the Romans and still better among the Lacedaemonians.

[8] A man of bad morals having offered a good suggestion in the council of Sparta, the Ephors, without taking any notice of him, had the same suggestion brought forward by a good Citizen. What an honor for the one, what a disgrace for the other, without either of them having been praised or blamed! Some drunkards from Samos* defiled the Tribunal of the Ephors: the next day the Samians were permitted by public Edict to be filthy. A true punishment would have been less severe than such impunity. When Sparta has pronounced on what is and what is not honest, Greece does not appeal its judgments.

[460]

Chapter Eight
Of Civil Religion

[1] Men at first had no other Kings than the Gods, nor any other Government than the Theocratic one. They reasoned as had Caligula, and at the time they reasoned correctly. It takes a long degradation of sentiments and ideas before one can bring oneself to accept a being like oneself as master, and flatter oneself [into believing] that one will be well off as a result.

[2] From this alone, that God was placed at the head of every political society, it followed that there were as many Gods as there were peoples. Two peoples alien to one another and almost always enemies could not long recognize the same master: Two armies engaged in battle with one another could not obey the same chief.

---

* In this chapter I merely indicate what I have treated at greater length in the Letter to M. d'Alembert.
* They came from another Island which the delicacy of our language does not permit to be named in this context. [1782 edn.]

Thus from national divisions resulted polytheism, and from it theological and civil intolerance which is naturally the same, as will be stated below.

[3] The Greeks' fancy of rediscovering their Gods among barbarian peoples came from their fancy of also regarding themselves as these peoples' natural Sovereigns. But in our day erudition revolving around the identity of various nations' Gods is quite ridiculous; as if Moloch, Saturn, and Chronos could be the same God; as if the Baal of the Phoenicians, the Zeus of the Greeks and the Jupiter of the Romans could be the same; as if chimerical Beings bearing different names could have anything in common!

[4] It may be asked why under paganism, where every State had its cult and its Gods, there were no wars of Religion? I answer that it was precisely because every State, since it had its own cult as well as its Government, drew no distinction between its Gods and its laws. Political war was also Theological: the departments of the Gods were, so to speak, fixed by the boundaries of Nations. The God of one people had no right over the other peoples. The Gods of the Pagans [461] were not jealous Gods; they divided the empire of the world among themselves: even Moses and the Hebrew People sometimes countenanced this idea in speaking of the God of Israel. They did, it is true, regard as naught the Gods of the Canaanites, proscribed peoples, doomed to destruction, and whose stronghold they were to occupy. But note how they spoke about the divinities of the peoples they were forbidden to attack! *The possession of what belongs to Chamos your God,* Jephthah said to the Ammonites, *is it not legitimately your due? By the same title we possess the lands our victorious God has acquired.** That, it seems to me, indicates a well-recognized parity between the rights of Chamos and those of the God of Israel.

[5] But when the Jews, subject to the Kings of Babylon and subsequently to the Kings of Syria, obstinately sought to recognize no other God than their own, this refusal, regarded as a rebellion

---

* *Nonne ea quae possidet Chamos deus tuus tibi jure debentur?* This is the text of the Vulgate. Fr. de Carrières has translated it: *Do you not believe you have the right to possess what belongs to Chamos your God?* I do not know the force of the Hebrew text; but I see that in the Vulgate Jephthah positively recognizes the right of the God Chamos, and that the French translator weakens this recognition with his *according to you* which is not in the Latin.

against the victor, brought down upon themselves the persecutions we read about in their history, and of which there is no other known example prior to Christianity.*

[6] Since, then, every Religion was tied exclusively to the laws of the State which prescribed it, there was no other way to convert a people than to enslave it, nor were there any other missionaries than conquerors, and since the obligation to change their cult was the law of the vanquished, it was necessary to be victorious before talking about such a change. Far from men fighting for the Gods, it was, as in Homer, the Gods who fought for men; each asked his own for victory, and paid for it with new altars. The Romans, before taking a stronghold, called upon its Gods to abandon it, and when they let the people of Tarentum keep their irate Gods [*462*] they did so because by then they regarded those Gods as subject to their own and forced to pay them homage. They left the vanquished their Gods as they left them their laws. A crown dedicated to Capitoline Jupiter was often the only tribute they exacted.

[7] In the end the Romans having extended their cult and their Gods along with their empire, and often having themselves adopted those of the vanquished by granting them as well as their Gods freedom of the City, the peoples of this vast empire insensibly found that they had multitudes of Gods and of cults, more or less the same everywhere; and this is how paganism eventually became but one and the same Religion throughout the known world.

[8] It was in these circumstances that Jesus came to establish a Spiritual Kingdom on earth; which, by separating the theological from the political system, led to the State's ceasing to be one, and caused the intestine divisions which have never ceased to convulse Christian peoples. Now since this new idea of a Kingdom of the other world could never enter the pagans' head, they always looked upon Christians as true rebels who, under [cover of] a hypocritical submission, were only looking for the opportunity to become independent and the masters, and craftily to usurp the authority which they pretended to respect as long as they were weak. This was the cause of the persecutions.

---

* It is perfectly evident that the war against the Phocaeans called the holy war was not a war of Religion. Its object was to punish sacrilege not to subjugate nonbelievers.

[9] What the pagans had feared came to pass; everything then changed in appearance, the humble Christians changed their language, and before long this supposedly other-worldly kingdom was seen to become under a visible chief the most violent despotism in this world.

[10] However, since there has always been a Prince and civil laws, this dual power has resulted in a perpetual conflict of jurisdiction which has made any good polity impossible in Christian States, and no one has ever succeeded in settling the question of which of the two, the master or the priest, one is obliged to obey.

[11] Yet several peoples, even in Europe or near it, have tried to preserve or to restore the ancient system, but without success; the spirit of christianity has come to pervade everything. Holy worship always remained or reverted to being independent of the Sovereign, and without necessary tie to the body of the State. Muhammad had very sound views, he tied his political system together well, and as long as the form of his [463] Government endured under the Caliphs who succeeded him this Government was strictly unitary, and in this respect good. But once the Arabs had become prosperous, lettered, polished, soft and cowardly, they were subjugated by barbarians; whereupon the division between the two powers began anew; although it is less apparent among Muslims than among Christians, it is nevertheless there, especially in the sect of Ali, and there are States, such as Persia, where it never ceases to make itself felt.

[12] Among us, the Kings of England have established themselves as heads of the Church, and the Tsars have done the same; but with this title they have made themselves not so much its masters as its Ministers; they have acquired not so much the right to change it as the power to preserve it; they are not its lawgivers, they are merely its Princes. Wherever the Clergy constitutes a body* it is the master and lawgiver in its realm. There are therefore two powers, two Sovereigns, in England and in Russia, just as everywhere else.

* It should especially be noted that it is not so much formal assemblies, like those in France, which bind the clergy into a single body, as it is the communion of Churches. Communion and excommunication are the clergy's social pact, a pact by which it will always be the master of peoples and Kings. All priests who are in communication with one another are fellow-citizens, though they may be from opposite ends of the earth. This invention is a masterpiece of politics. There was nothing like it among the pagan Priests; which is why they never constituted a Clergy as a body.

[13] Of all Christian Authors the philosopher Hobbes is the only one who clearly saw the evil and the remedy, who dared to propose reuniting the two heads of the eagle, and to return everything to political unity, without which no State or Government will ever be well constituted. But he must have seen that the domineering spirit of Christianity was inconsistent with his system, and that the interest of the Priest would always be stronger than that of the State. It is not so much what is horrible and false as what is just and true in his politics that has made it odious.*

[14] I believe that by examining the historical facts from this point of view [*464*] it would be easy to refute the opposing sentiments of Bayle and Warburton, one of whom contends that no religion is useful to the body politic, and the other of whom maintains to the contrary that Christianity is its strongest support. One would prove to the first that no State has ever been founded without Religion serving as its base, and to the second that the Christian law is at bottom more harmful than useful to a strong constitution of the State. To make myself fully understood only requires making a little more precise the excessively vague ideas about Religion which bear on my subject.

[15] Religion considered in relation to society, which is either general or particular, can also be divided into two kinds, namely the Religion of man and that of the Citizen. The first, without Temples, without altars, without rites, limited to the purely internal cult of the Supreme God and the eternal duties of morality, is the pure and simple Religion of the Gospel, true Theism, and what may be called divine natural right. The other, inscribed in a single country, gives it its Gods, its own titular Patrons: it has its dogmas, its rites, its external cult prescribed by laws: it regards everything outside the single Nation which adheres to it as infidel, alien, barbarous; it extends the rights and duties of man only as far as its altars. Such were all the Religions of the first peoples, to which one may give the name of divine civil or positive right.

[16] There is a third, more bizarre sort of Religion which, by giving men two legislations, two chiefs, two fatherlands, subjects

---

* See, among other things, in a Letter of Grotius to his brother of 11 April 1643, what that learned man approves and what he disapproves of in the book *De cive*. It is true that, being inclined to be indulgent, he seems to forgive the author the good for the sake of the bad; but not everyone is so lenient.

them to contradictory duties and prevents their being at once devout and Citizens. Such is the Religion of the Lamas, such is that of the Japanese, such is Roman christianity. One may call it the religion of the Priest. It results in a sort of mixed and unsociable right which has no name.

[17] Considering these three sorts of religion politically, all of them have defects. The Third is so manifestly bad that it is a waste of time to amuse oneself demonstrating that it is. Everything which destroys social unity is worthless: All institutions which put man in contradiction with himself are worthless.

[18] The second is good in that it combines divine worship and love of the laws, and in making the fatherland [*465*] the object of the Citizens' worship it teaches them that to serve the State is to serve its tutelary God. It is a kind of Theocracy, in which there ought to be no other pontiff than the Prince, nor other priests than the magistrates. Then to die for one's country is to be a martyr, to break the laws is to be impious, and to subject the guilty to public execration is to deliver him to the wrath of the Gods; *sacer estod.*

[19] But it is bad in that being founded on error and lies it deceives men, makes them credulous, superstitious, and drowns the true cult of the divinity in a vain ceremonial. It is furthermore bad when, becoming exclusive and tyrannical, it makes a people bloodthirsty and intolerant; so that it breathes only murder and massacre, and believes it performs a holy deed in killing whoever does not accept its Gods. This places such a people in a natural state of war with all others, which is most prejudicial to its own security.

[20] There remains, then, the Religion of man or Christianity, not that of today, but that of the Gospel, which is altogether different. Through this saintly, sublime, genuine Religion, men, as children of the same God, all recognize one another as brothers, and the society that unites them does not dissolve even at death.

[21] But this Religion, since it has no particular relation to the body politic, leaves the laws with only the force they derive from themselves without adding any other force to them, and hence one of the great bonds of particular societies remains without effect. What is more; far from attaching the Citizens' hearts to the State, it detaches them from it as from all earthly things. I know of nothing more contrary to the social spirit.

[22] We are told that a people of true Christians would form the most perfect society imaginable. I see only one major difficulty with this supposition; which is that a society of true christians would no longer be a society of men.

[23] I even say that, for all its perfection, this assumed society would be neither the strongest nor the most lasting: By dint of being perfect, it would lack cohesion; its very perfection would be its fatal vice.

[24] Everyone would fulfill his duty; the people would obey the laws, the chiefs would be just and moderate, the magistrates [*466*] would be honest and incorruptible, the soldiers would despise death, there would be neither vanity nor luxury; all this is very well, but let us look further.

[25] Christianity is a wholly spiritual religion, exclusively concerned with the things of Heaven: the Christian's fatherland is not of this world. He does his duty, it is true, but he does it with profound indifference to the success or failure of his efforts. Provided he has nothing to reproach himself for, it does not much matter to him whether all goes well or ill down here on earth. If the State prospers, he hardly dares to enjoy the public felicity, he fears taking pride in his country's glory; if the State declines, he blesses the hand of God that weighs down on his people.

[26] For society to be peaceful and harmony preserved, all Citizens without exception would have to be equally good Christians: But if unhappily there is a single ambitious man among them, a single hypocrite, a Catiline, for example, a Cromwell, that man will most certainly very easily get the better of his pious compatriots. Christian charity does not allow one readily to think ill of one's neighbor. Once he has discovered by some cunning the art of imposing on them and of seizing a part of the public authority, there behold a man vested in dignity; God wills that he be respected; soon behold a power; God wills that he be obeyed; does the repository of this power abuse it? he is the scourge with which God punishes his children. Driving out the usurper would trouble one's conscience; it would require disturbing the public repose, resorting to violence, shedding blood; all this accords ill with a Christian's mildness; and after all what does it matter in this vale of tears whether one is free or a serf? the essential thing is to get to paradise, and resignation is but one more means to that end.

[27] Does a foreign war break out? Citizens march to battle without hesitation; not one of them thinks of fleeing; they do their duty, but without passion for victory; they know better how to die than to win. What matter whether they are victors or vanquished? Does not providence know better than they what they need? Imagine how a proud, impetuous, passionate enemy can take advantage of this stoicism! Pit against them those generous peoples who were consumed by an ardent love of glory and of fatherland, suppose your christian republic [*467*] confronting Sparta or Rome; the pious christians will be beaten, crushed, destroyed before they have time to realize what is happening to them, or they will owe their salvation solely to the contempt their enemy will conceive for them. In my view the oath the soldiers of Fabius took was a fine oath; they did not swear to die or to win, they swore to return victorious, and they kept their word: Christians would never have taken such an oath; they would have believed they were tempting God.

[28] But I am mistaken in speaking of a Christian Republic; each one of these two terms excludes the other. Christianity preaches nothing but servitude and dependence. Its spirit is too favorable to tyranny for tyranny not always to profit from it. True Christians are made to be slaves; they know it and are hardly moved by it; this brief life has too little value in their eyes.

[29] We are told that christian troops are excellent. I deny it. Let me be shown some that are. As for myself, I know of no christian Troops. I will be referred to the Crusades. Without discussing the Crusaders' valor, I will point out that far from being Christians, they were soldiers of the priest, they were Citizens of the Church; they were fighting for its spiritual country, which it had made temporal, one knows not how. Strictly speaking, this belongs under the heading of paganism; since the Gospel does not establish a national Religion, a holy war among Christians is impossible.

[30] Christian soldiers were brave under the pagan Emperors; all Christian Authors say so, and I believe it: it was in emulation for honor with the pagan Troops. As soon as the Emperors were christians this emulation ceased, and once the cross had driven out the eagle, all Roman valor ceased.

[31] But leaving aside political considerations, let us return to right, and let us fix the principles on this important point. The right which the social pact gives the Sovereign over the subjects

does not, as I have said, exceed the bounds of public utility.* Subjects therefore only owe the Sovereign an account [*468*] of their opinions insofar as those opinions matter to the community. Now it certainly matters to the State that each Citizen have a Religion which makes him love his duties; but the dogmas of this Religion are only of concern to the State or to its members insofar as the dogmas bear on morality, and on the duties which anyone who professes it is bound to fulfill toward others. Beyond this everyone may hold whatever opinions he pleases, without its being up to the Sovereign to know them: For since the Sovereign has no competence in the other world, whatever the subjects' fate may be in the life to come is none of its business, provided they are good citizens in this life.

[32] There is therefore a purely civil profession of faith the articles of which it is up to the Sovereign to fix, not precisely as dogmas of Religion but as sentiments of sociability, without which it is impossible to be either a good Citizen or a loyal subject.* Without being able to oblige anyone to believe them, the Sovereign may banish from the State anyone who does not believe them; it may banish him, not as impious but as unsociable, as incapable of sincerely loving the laws, justice, and, if need be of sacrificing his life to his duty. If anyone, after having publicly acknowledged these same dogmas, behaves as if he did not believe them, let him be punished with death; he has committed the greatest of crimes, he has lied before the laws.

[33] The dogmas of the civil Religion ought to be simple, few in number, stated with precision, without explanations or commentary. The existence of the powerful, intelligent, beneficent, prescient, and provident Divinity, the life to come, the happiness of

---

* *In the Republic*, says M. d'A[rgenson], *everyone is perfectly free with respect to what does not harm others.* That is the invariable boundary; it cannot be drawn more accurately. I could not deny myself the pleasure of sometimes quoting this ms. although it is not known to the public, that I might do [*468*] honor to the memory of an honorable and illustrious man, who even in the [royal] Ministry retained the heart of a true citizen, and upright and sane views about the government of his country.

* Caesar pleading for Catiline tried to establish the dogma of the mortality of the soul; to refute it, Cato and Cicero did not waste time philosophizing: they contented themselves with showing that Caesar was speaking like a bad Citizen and advancing a doctrine pernicious to the State. This, indeed, is what the Roman Senate had to pass judgment on, and not on a question of theology.

the just, the punishment of the wicked, the sanctity of the social
Contract and the Laws; these are the positive dogmas. As for the
negative dogmas, [*469*] I restrict them to a single one; namely intolerance: it is a feature of the cult we have rejected.

[34] Those who distinguish between civil and theological intolerance are mistaken, in my opinion. The two intolerances are inseparable. It is impossible to live in peace with people one believes to
be damned; to love them would be to hate God who punishes them;
one must absolutely bring them back [to the fold] or torment them.
Wherever theological intolerance is allowed, it is impossible for it
not to have some civil effect;* and as soon as it does, the Sovereign
is no longer Sovereign, even in the temporal sphere: from then on
Priests are the true masters; Kings are but their officers.

[35] Now that there no longer is and no longer can be an exclusive national Religion, one must tolerate all those which tolerate the
others insofar as their dogmas contain nothing contrary to the duties
of the Citizen. But whoever dares to say, *no Salvation outside the
Church*, has to be driven out of the State; unless the State is the
Church, and the Prince the Pontiff. Such a dogma is good only in
a Theocratic Government, in any other it is pernicious. The reason
for which Henry IV is said to have embraced the Roman Religion
should make any honest man and especially any Prince capable of
reasoning leave it.

---

* Marriage, for example, being a civil contract, has civil effects without which it
would be impossible for society even to subsist. Let us suppose, then, that a Clergy
succeeded in arrogating to itself alone the right to pass on this act; a right which
it is bound to usurp in any intolerant Religion. Then is it not clear that by exercising the authority of the Church in this matter, it will render ineffectual the authority of the Prince who will have no other subjects left but those the Clergy will
be willing to give it? As the master of whether to marry or not to marry people
according to whether they will or will not adhere to this or that doctrine, according
to whether they will accept or reject this or that formulary, according to whether
they will be more or less devoted to it, is it not clear that by behaving prudently
and holding firm, it alone will dispose of inheritances, of offices, of the Citizens,
of the State itself, which could not subsist once it is composed of nothing but
bastards? But, it will be said, abuses will be appealed, summonses issued, warrants
served, temporal holdings seized. What a pity! The Clergy, if it only has, I do
not say courage, but good sense, will not interfere and go its own way; it will
tranquilly allow appeals, summonses, warrants, seizures, and end up being the
master. It is not, it seems to me, a great sacrifice to give up a part when one is
sure to get hold of the whole.

[*470*]

CHAPTER NINE
CONCLUSION

[1] After setting down the true principles of political right and trying to found the State on its basis, it would remain to buttress the State by its external relations; which would include the right of nations, commerce, the right of war and conquests, public right, leagues, negotiations, treaties, etc. But all this forms a new object too vast for my short sight; I should always have fixed it nearer to myself.

From OF THE SOCIAL CONTRACT *or* ESSAY ABOUT THE FORM OF THE REPUBLIC

(Known as the Geneva Manuscript)

BOOK I, CHAPTER TWO

OF THE GENERAL SOCIETY OF MANKIND

[1] Let us begin by inquiring whence the need for political institutions arises.

[2] Man's natural force is so well proportioned to his natural needs and his primitive state that as soon as his state changes and his needs increase ever so slightly [*282*] he needs his fellows' assistance, and when eventually his desires embrace the whole of nature, the assistance of the whole of mankind barely suffices to satisfy them. That is how the same causes that make us wicked also make us slaves, and subjugate us by depraving us; the sentiment of our weakness comes less from our nature than from our cupidity: our needs unite us in proportion as our passions divide us, and the more we become our fellows' enemies, the less can we do without them. Such are the first bonds of general society; such are the foundations of that universal benevolence the sentiment of which seems to get stifled by the recognition that it is necessary, and the fruits of which everyone would like to enjoy, without being obliged to cultivate it: for as to the identity of nature, its effect in this [respect] is nil, because it is as much a subject of quarrel as of union among men, and it introduces competition and jealousy among them as frequently as it does mutual understanding and agreement.

[3] From this new order of things arise multitudes of relations without [common] measure, without rule, without consistency, which men constantly worsen and change, a hundred working to destroy them for every one who works to stabilize them; and as a man's relative existence in the state of nature depends on a thousand other constantly changing relations, he can never make sure of being the same for two instants of his life; peace and happiness are for him but a flash; nothing is permanent but the misery that results from all these vicissitudes; even if his sentiments and his ideas could

rise to the love of order and to the sublime notions of virtue, he would find it impossible ever confidently to apply his principles in a state of things which would prevent him from discerning good or evil, the honest man or the wicked.

[4] The general society which our mutual needs might engender thus offers no effective help to man become miserable, or rather it provides new forces only to the one who already has too many, while the weak, lost, stifled, crushed in the multitude, finds no refuge to which he might flee, no support in his weakness, and in the end he perishes a victim of this deceptive union from which he expected his happiness.

[*283*] [5] ⟨Once one is convinced that among the motives which lead men to unite with one another by voluntary ties there is nothing which relates to the point of union; that far from seeking a goal of common felicity from which each one might derive his own, one man's happiness makes for another's misery; once, finally, one sees that instead of all tending towards the general good, they come together only because they are all moving away from it; one must also sense that although such a state could subsist it would only be a source of crimes and of miseries for men each one of whom would see only his interest, follow only his inclinations and heed only his passions.⟩

[6] Thus the gentle voice of nature is no longer an infallible guide for us, nor is the independence we received from it any longer a desirable state; peace and innocence escaped us forever before we tasted their delights; unsensed by the stupid men of the first times, having escaped the enlightened men of later times, the happy life of the golden age was always a state foreign to the human race, either for its having failed to recognize it when it could enjoy it, or for its having lost it when it could have recognized it.

[7] What is more; this perfect independence and this unregulated freedom, even if it had remained associated with ancient innocence, would always have had one essential vice, and been harmful to the progress of our most excellent faculties, namely the lack of that connectedness of the parts which constitutes a whole. The earth would be covered with men amongst whom there would be almost no communication; we would make contact at some points without being united by a single one; everyone would remain isolated amongst the rest, everyone would think only of himself; our under-

standing could not develop; we would live without sensing anything, we would die without having lived; our entire happiness
would consist in not knowing our misery; there would be neither
goodness in our hearts, nor morality in our actions, and we would
never have tasted the most delicious sentiment of the soul, which
is the love of virtue.

[8] ⟨Certain it is that the word *mankind* offers the mind only a
purely collective idea which does not assume any real unity among the
individuals who constitute it: If you wish, let us add to it the following
Assumption; let us conceive of mankind as a moral person [*284*]
having both a sentiment of common existence which endows it with
individuality and constitutes it as one, and a universal motivation
which makes every part act for the sake of an end related to the whole.
Let us conceive of this common sentiment as that of humanity, and of
the natural law as the active principle of the entire machine. Let us
then attend to what happens to man's constitution in his relation with
his fellows, and, altogether to the contrary of what we have assumed,
we will find that the progress of society stifles humanity in men's
hearts by arousing personal interest, and that the notions of natural
Law, which should rather be called the law of reason, begin to develop
only once the development of the passions which precedes [that of
the notions of natural law] renders all of its precepts powerless.
Which shows that this supposed social treaty dictated by nature is
a veritable chimera; because its terms come together only because
they are always either unknown or impracticable, and one must
necessarily either be ignorant of them or violate them.

[9] If the general society existed anywhere other than in the systems of the Philosophers, it would, as I have said, be a moral Being
with qualities of its own and distinct from those of the particular
Beings constituting it, more or less as chemical compounds have
properties which they owe to none of the components that make them
up: There would be a universal language which nature would teach
all men, and which would be the first instrument of their mutual
communication: there would be a sort of common sensorium which
would make for the concert of all the parts; the public good or evil
would not only be the sum of particular goods or evils as in a mere
aggregate, but would reside in the connectedness between them, it
would be greater than that sum, and the public felicity, far from being
based on the happiness of individuals, would be its source.⟩

[10] It is false that in the state of independence, reason, perceiving our self-interest, inclines us to contribute to the common good; far from there being an alliance between particular interest and the general good, they exclude one another in the natural order of things, and social laws are a yoke which everyone is willing to impose on others, but not to assume himself. "I feel I bring mankind terror and trouble," says [285] the independent man whom the wise man stifles, "but the alternative is that either I am miserable, or I make others miserable, and no one is dearer to me than I myself am." "It is in vain," he might add, "that I would endeavor to reconcile my own interest with that of others; everything you tell me about the advantages of the social law might be fine, if while I scrupulously observed it toward the rest, I were sure that they would all observe it toward me; but what assurance can you give me on this score, and could I be in a worse situation than to find myself exposed to all the evils which the stronger might choose to visit upon me, without my daring to make up for it at the expense of the weak? Either give me guarantees against every unjust undertaking, or give up hope of my refraining from them in turn. It makes no difference that you tell me that by repudiating the duties which natural law imposes on me, I simultaneously deprive myself of its rights, and that my acts of violence will authorize all those which others might choose to commit against me. I accept it all the more readily as I do not see how my moderation might guarantee me against them. Besides it will be up to me to get the strong to side with my interests by sharing with them the spoils of the weak; that will do more for my advantage and my security than will justice." The proof that this is how the enlightened and independent man would have reasoned is that this is how every sovereign society accountable for its conduct solely to itself reasons.

[11] What solid answer can be made to such speeches if one does not want to bring Religion to the assistance of morality, and have the will of God intervene immediately to tie together the society of men. But the sublime notions of the God of the wise, the gentle laws of brotherhood which he imposes on us, the social virtues of pure souls, which are the true cult he wants from us, will always escape the multitude. It will always get made for it Gods as senseless as itself, to whom it will sacrifice minor conveniences for the sake of indulging a thousand horrible and destructive passions in their honor. The whole earth would overflow with blood and mankind would soon

perish if Philosophy and the laws did not restrain the furies of fanaticism, and if the voice of men were not stronger than the Gods'.

[12] Indeed, if the notions of the great Being and of the natural law were innate in all hearts, it was [*286*] quite a superfluous effort explicitly to teach them: It was to teach us what we already knew, and the way it was done would have been better suited to make us forget it. If they were not innate, then all those to whom God did not impart them are exempted from knowing them: Once it required special instruction, each People has its own notions which are proven to it to be the only good ones, and from which Carnage and murder ensure more often than do concord and peace.

[13] Let us therefore leave aside the sacred precepts of the various Religions whose abuse causes as many crimes as their use may prevent, and let us restore to the Philosopher the examination of a question which the Theologian has never dealt with except to the prejudice of mankind.

[14] But the first will send me back to mankind itself up to which alone it is to decide, because the greatest good of all is its only passion. It is, he will tell me, the general will that the individual ought to consult in order to ascertain up to what point he ought to be man, Citizen, subject, Father, child, and when he should live and when die. "I admit that I do, indeed, see that this is the rule which I can consult; but I still do not see," our independent man will say, "the reason for subjecting myself to this rule. It is not a matter of teaching me what justice is; it is a matter of showing me what interest I have in being just." Indeed no one will deny that the general will is in each individual a pure act of the understanding reasoning in the silence of the passions about what man may demand of his fellow man, and about what his fellow man may rightfully demand of him: But where is the man who can thus separate himself from himself and, if care for one's self-preservation is the first precept of nature, can he be forced thus to consider the species in general in order to impose on himself duties whose connection with his own constitution he completely fails to see? Do the previous objections not continue to apply, and does it not still remain to be seen how his personal interest demands that he subordinate himself to the general will?

[15] Moreover; since the art of thus generalizing one's ideas is one of the most difficult and belated exercises of the human understanding, will most men [*287*] ever be in a position to derive the

rules of their conduct from this way of reasoning[;] and if the general will had to be consulted regarding a particular act, how often will a well-intentioned man not make a mistake about the rule or about its application and follow only his inclination while thinking that he is obeying the law? What then will he do to guarantee himself against the error? Will he heed the internal voice? But this voice, it is said, is only formed by the habit of judging and feeling within society and in conformity with its laws, so that it cannot serve to establish them[,] and besides there should never have arisen in his heart any of those passions which speak louder than conscience, overwhelm its timid voice, and lead the philosophers to maintain that that voice does not exist. Will he consult the principles of written right, the social actions of all peoples, the tacit conventions even of the enemies of mankind? The initial difficulty keeps recurring, and it is only from the social order established among us that we derive the ideas of the one we imagine. We conceive of the general society in terms of our particular societies, the establishment of small Republics leads us to think of the large one, and we do not properly begin to become men until after having been Citizens. Which shows what one should think about those supposed Cosmopolites who, justifying their love of fatherland by their love of mankind, boast of loving everyone so that they might have the right to love no one.

[16] What reasoning proves to us on this score is fully confirmed by the facts, and if one but looks back to very ancient times, one easily sees that the healthy ideas of natural right and of the common brotherhood [*fraternité*] of all men spread rather late and made such slow progress in the world that it was only Christianity which generalized them sufficiently. Yet the older [kinds of] violence, not only against declared enemies, but against anyone who was not a subject of the Empire, are found to be authorized in a number of respects even in the Laws of Justinian; so that the humanity of the Romans extended no farther than their dominion.

[17] Indeed, it was long believed, as Grotius notes, that it was permissible to rob, plunder, mistreat foreigners and above all barbarians, to the point of reducing them to slavery. [*288*] This is why strangers used to be asked whether they were Brigands or Pirates, without their taking offense; for this trade, far from being ignominious, was then regarded as honorable. The first Heroes like Hercules

and Theseus who waged war on Brigands nonetheless themselves practiced brigandage and the Greeks often called the treaties made between peoples which were not at war peace treaties. The words for foreigners and for enemies were long synonymous among several ancient peoples, even among the Latins: For our ancestors, says Cicero, called "enemies" what we now should call a "foreigner." Hobbes's error is therefore not to have established the state of war among men who are independent and have become sociable but to have assumed this state to be natural to the species, and to have given it as the cause of the vices of which it is the effect.

[18] But although there is no natural and general society among men, although they become unhappy and wicked on becoming sociable, although the laws of justice and of equality are as naught to those who live at the same time in the freedom of the state of nature and subject to the needs of the social state; far from thinking that there is neither virtue nor happiness for us, and that heaven has abandoned us without resource to the corruption of the species; let us endeavor to derive from the evil itself the remedy which will cure it. By means of new associations, let us correct, if possible, the lack of a general association. Let our violent interlocutor himself be the judge of our success. Let us show him in perfected art the redress of the evils which beginning art caused to nature: Let us show him all the misery of the state which he believed happy, all that is false in the reasoning which he believed solid. Let him behold in a better constitution of things the worth of good deeds, the punishment of bad ones, the endearing harmony of justice and happiness. Let us enlighten his reason with new knowledge, fire his heart with new sentiments, and let him learn to increase his being and his felicity by sharing them with his fellows. If my zeal does not blind me in this enterprise, let us not doubt that if he has fortitude of soul and upright sense, this enemy of mankind will in the end abjure his hatred along with his errors, that the reason which led him astray will bring him back to humanity, that he will learn to prefer to his apparent interest his [*289*] interest rightly understood; that he will become good, virtuous, sensitive, and in sum, finally, instead of the ferocious brigand he wanted to be, the most solid bulwark of a well-ordered society.

[*OC* iii, *328*]

Book ii, Chapter Four

Of the Nature of the Laws, and of the Principle of Civil Justice

[12] The greatest advantage that results from this notion [of the law] is to show us clearly the true foundations of justice and of natural right. Indeed the first law, the only genuine fundamental law that flows immediately from the social pact, is that each man in all things prefer the greatest good of all.

[13] Now, the specification, by various particular laws, of the actions that contribute to this greatest good, constitutes right narrowly so called or positive right. Everything that is seen to contribute to this greatest good, but the laws did not specify, constitutes acts of civility,* of beneficence, and the habit that inclines us to perform these [*329*] acts even to our prejudice is what is called force or virtue.

[14] Extend this maxim to the general society of which the State gives us the idea, protected by the society of which we are members, or by that in which we live, the natural revulsion to do evil no longer being offset by the fear of having evil done to us, we are inclined at once by nature, by habit, by reason, to deal with other men more or less as [we do] with our fellow-citizens, and this disposition reduced to actions gives rise to the rules of reasoned natural right, different from natural right properly so called, which is founded on nothing but a true but very vague sentiment often stifled by the love of ourselves.

[15] This is how the first distinct notions of the just and the unjust are formed in us; for the law precedes justice, not justice the law; and if the law cannot be unjust, it is not because it has justice as its basis, which might not always be true; but because it is against nature to want to injure oneself; which is [true] without exception.

[16] It is a beautiful and sublime precept to do unto others as we would wish to be done unto; but is it not evident, that far from

---

* I need not warn, I believe, that this word should not here be taken in its French usage.

serving as the foundation of justice, it is itself in need of foundation; for what is the clear and solid reason for my behaving, being myself, according to the will I would have if I were someone else? It is also clear that this precept is subject to a thousand exceptions which have never been given any but sophistical explanations. Would not a judge who condemns a criminal wish to be absolved if he himself were a criminal? where is the man who would not wish never to have anything refused him? does it follow that we must grant everything that is asked of us? This other axiom, *cuique suum* [to each his own] which serves as the basis of the whole right of property, what is it founded on, but on the right of property itself? And if I do not say with Hobbes, everything is mine, why should I not at least recognize as mine in the state of nature everything that is useful to me and that I can seize?

[17] It is therefore in the fundamental and universal Law of the greatest good of all and not in the particular relations of man to man that one has to look for the true principles of the just and the unjust, and there is not a single [*330*] particular rule of justice which cannot easily be deduced from this first law. Thus *cuique suum* [to each his own] because private property and civil freedom are the foundations of the community: Thus *love thy neighbor as thyself*, because the particular self spread over the whole is the strongest bond of the general society, and the State has the highest degree of force and of life it can have when all of our particular passions come together in it. In a word, there are a thousand cases where it is an Act of justice to hurt one's neighbor, whereas every just Action necessarily has as its rule the greatest common utility; this is without exception.

THE STATE OF WAR

[1] I open the books on right and on ethics, I listen to the scholars and jurisconsults and, moved by their ingratiating discourses [609], I deplore the miseries of nature, I admire the peace and justice established by the civil order, I bless the wisdom of public institutions, and console myself for being a man by seeing that I am a citizen. Fully instructed about my duties and happiness, I close the book, leave the class-room, and look around me; I see unfortunate peoples groaning under an iron yoke, mankind crushed by a handful of oppressors, starving masses overwhelmed by pain and hunger, whose blood and tears the rich drink in peace, and everywhere the strong armed against the weak with the frightful power of the laws.

[2] All this happens peacefully and without resistance; it is the tranquility of the companions of Ulysses shut up in the Cyclops' cave until they get devoured. All one can do is to groan and not say anything. Let us draw an eternal veil over these objects of horror. I raise my eyes and look afar. I see fires and flames, countrysides deserted, towns sacked. Fierce men, where are you dragging these wretches? I hear a frightful noise; what confusion! what cries! I draw near; I see a scene of murders, ten thousand men slaughtered, the dead piled up in heaps, the dying trampled underfoot by horses, everywhere the image of death and dying. So this is the fruit of these peaceful institutions! Pity, indignation swell up in the depths of my heart. Ah barbarous philosopher! read us your book on a battlefield!

[3] What human bowels would not be moved by these sad objects? but being human and pleading the cause of humanity is no longer permitted. Justice and trust have to be bent to the interest of the most powerful: such is the rule. The People grants neither pensions, nor positions, nor [University] chairs, nor memberships in Academies; why should it be protected? Magnanimous princes, I speak in the name of the literary establishment; oppress the people with a clear conscience; we expect everything from you alone; the people is no good to us.

[4] How can so weak a voice make itself heard above such a self-serving din? Alas! I may not say anything; but could not my heart's voice break through this sad silence? No; without entering into repulsive details which would be mistaken for a satire just

because they are true, I shall confine myself, as I always have done, [*610*] to examining human institutions in terms of their principles, to correcting, if possible, the false ideas about them which self-interested authors give us; and at least to seeing to it that injustice and violence not shamelessly assume the name of right and equity.

[5] When I consider the situation of mankind, the first thing I notice is a manifest contradiction in its constitution, which makes it forever unstable. Man to man we live in the civil state and subject to laws; people to people, each enjoys natural freedom: which at bottom makes our situation worse than if these distinctions were unknown. For by living both in the social order and in the state of nature, we are subject to the inconveniences of both without finding security in either. It is true that the perfection of the social order consists in the union of force and law; but for this to be so, law must guide force; whereas according to the ideas of princes about their absolute independence, force alone, speaking to citizens in the guise of law and to foreigners in the guise of reason of state, deprives the latter of the power and the former of the will to resist, so that everywhere the vain name of justice only serves as a shield for violence.

[6] As for what is commonly called the right of nations, it is certain that, for want of sanction, its laws are nothing but chimeras even weaker than the law of nature. This latter at least speaks to the heart of individuals, whereas the right of nations, having no other guarantee than its utility to the one who submits to it, its decisions are respected only as long as self-interest confirms them. In the mixed condition in which we find ourselves, regardless of which one of the two systems one favors, by doing either too much or too little we have done nothing, and we have placed ourselves in the worst state possible. This, it seems to me, is the genuine origin of public calamities.

[7] Let us briefly contrast these ideas with the horrible system of Hobbes; and we will find that, altogether contrary to his absurd doctrine, the state of war, far from being natural to man, is born of peace, or at least of the precautions men have taken to secure a lasting peace. But before entering into this discussion, let us try to explain what it . . .

[*611*] [8] ⟨Who could have imagined without shuddering the mad system of natural war of each against all? What a strange animal it must be that would believe its good to depend on the destruction

of its entire species! and how can one conceive that this species, so monstrous and so detestable, could last even two generations? Yet this is how far the desire or rather the fury to establish despotism and passive obedience has led one of the finest geniuses that ever lived. So ferocious a principle was worthy of its purpose.

[9] The state of society which constrains all our natural inclinations can, however, not annihilate them; in spite of our prejudices and in spite of ourselves they continue to speak to us in the depths of our heart and often bring us back to the true which we abandon for the sake of chimeras. If this mutual and destructive enmity were part and parcel of our constitution, it would therefore continue to make itself felt and set us against one another in spite of ourselves, past all social chains. The dreadful hatred of humanity would gnaw at man's heart. The birth of his own children would distress him; he would rejoice at the death of his brothers; and upon finding someone asleep, his first movement would be to kill him.

[10] The benevolence that makes us participate in the happiness of our fellows, the compassion that identifies us with the one who suffers and distresses us at his pain, would be sentiments unknown and directly contrary to nature. A sensitive and pitying human being would be a monster; and we would be naturally what we have considerable difficulty becoming amidst the depravation that pursues us.

[11] In vain would the sophist say that this mutual enmity is not innate and immediate, but based on the competition that inevitably follows from everyone's right to all. For the sentiment of this supposed right is no more natural to man than the war which he has arise from it.⟩

[12] I have said before and I cannot repeat too often that the error of Hobbes and of the philosophers is to confuse natural man with the men they have before their eyes, and to move into one system a being that can thrive only in another. Man wants his well-being and everything that can contribute to it, that is incontrovertible. But naturally this well-being of man is limited to the physically necessary; [*612*] for when his soul is healthy and his body does not suffer, what is lacking for him to be happy conformably to his constitution? He who has nothing desires little; he who commands no one has little ambition. But superfluity arouses greed; the more one gets, the more one desires. He who has much wants to have

all; and the madness for universal monarchy never tormented any but a great king's heart. Such is the march of nature, such is the development of the passions. A superficial philosopher observes souls kneaded and risen a thousand times over in the leaven of society and believes he has observed man. But in order to know him well, one has to know how to disentangle the natural gradation of his sentiments, and it is not among people who live in large cities that one should look for the first feature of nature imprinted on the human heart.

[13] Thus this analytical method only leads to abysses and mysteries, where the wisest understands the least. Ask why morals are corrupted in proportion as minds are enlightened; unable to discover the cause, they will have the audacity to deny the fact. Ask why the savages transplanted among us share neither our passions nor our pleasures, and do not care for what we so fervently desire. They will never succeed in explaining it, or they will only explain it on my principles. They only know what they see, and they have never seen nature. They know well enough what a Londoner or a Parisian is; but they will never know what a man is.

[*601*] [14] But even if it were true that this unbounded and uncontrollable greed were as developed in all men as our Sophist assumes, it would still not bring about the universal state of war of each against all of which Hobbes dares to sketch the odious image. This unbridled desire to appropriate everything is incompatible with that of destroying all of one's fellows; and the victor who, having killed everyone, had the misfortune to remain alone in the world, would enjoy nothing in it precisely because he would have everything. What good are even riches if not to be spent; of what use would the possession of the entire universe be to him if he were its sole inhabitant? What? Will his stomach devour all of the earth's fruit? Who will gather for him the produce from the four corners of the earth; who will carry the evidence of his empire to the vast wastes he will never inhabit? What will he do with his treasures, who will consume his provisions, before whose eyes will he display his power? I understand. Instead of massacring them all, he will put them all in chains, in order at least to have Slaves. This immediately changes the state of the question; and since it is no longer a question of destroying, the state of war is abolished. Let the reader suspend judgment for the present. I will not fail to come back to this point.

[15] Man is naturally peaceable and timorous, at the slightest danger his first movement is to flee; he becomes warlike only by dint of habit and experience. Honor, interest, prejudices, vengeance, all the passions that might make him brave perils and death, are far from him in the state of nature. It is only after he has entered into society with another human being that he decides to attack someone else; and he becomes a soldier [*602*] only after having been a citizen. That does not evince strong inclinations to war with all of one's fellows. But I am devoting too much time to a system as revolting as it is absurd, that has already been refuted a hundred times.

[16] There is, then, no general war between man and man; and the human species was not formed solely to destroy itself. It remains to consider the accidental and particular war that can arise between two or more individuals.

[17] If natural law were inscribed only in human reason, it would have little capacity to guide most of our actions, but it is also engraved in the human heart in indelible characters, and it is from the heart that it speaks to him more forcefully than do all the precepts of the Philosophers; it is from the heart that it cries out to him that he is not allowed to sacrifice the life of his fellow except to preserve his own, and causes him to feel horror at spilling human blood not in anger, even when he finds himself obliged to do so.

[18] It is conceivable that in the quarrels without [common] judges that may arise in the state of nature, an irritated man might sometimes kill another, openly or surreptitiously. But if this were genuine war, imagine the strange position this same man would have to be in if he could preserve his own life only at the expense of someone else's, and if by virtue of some relation established between them one had to die so that the other might live. War is a permanent state which presupposes lasting relations, and such relations rarely obtain between man and man, where everything between one individual and another is in continual flux which constantly changes relations and interests. So that the subject of a dispute arises and disappears almost instantaneously, a quarrel begins and ends in a single day, and there may be fights and murders, but never or very rarely extended enmities and wars.

[19] In the civil state, where the life of all citizens is within the power of the sovereign and no one has the right to dispose of his

own or of another's life, the state of war can also not obtain among individuals; and as for Duels, challenges, cartels, calls to single combat, quite aside from the fact that they were illegitimate and barbarous excesses of an entirely military constitution, they led not to a genuine state of war, but to a private affair that was so clearly settled in [*603*] a finite time and place that a second bout required a renewed call [to combat]. The one exception to this are the private wars suspended by daily truces that were called peace of God and sanctioned by Saint Louis's institutions. But this is a case unique in history.

[20] One might raise the further question whether Kings who are *de facto* independent of human power could engage with one another in particular and personal wars independent of those of the state. The question is surely an idle one, for as everyone knows, Princes are not in the habit of sparing others in order to face danger themselves. Moreover, this question is dependent upon another question which I am not the one to settle: to wit whether or not the Prince is himself subject to the laws of the state; for if he is subject to them, his person is tied to the state and his life belongs to it like that of the least citizen. But if the Prince is above the laws, he lives in the pure state of nature and owes neither his subjects nor anyone [else] an account of any of his actions.

Of the Social State

[21] We now enter a new order of things. We shall see men united by an artificial concord, assemble to slaughter one another, and all the horrors of war arise from the efforts made to prevent them. But it is important to begin by forming more exact notions about the essence of the body politic than has been done so far. Let the reader only keep in mind that what is at issue here is not so much history and facts as right and justice, and that I examine things in terms of their nature rather than of our prejudices.

[22] With the first society formed, the formation of all the others necessarily follows. One must either belong to it or unite to resist it. One must either imitate it or let oneself be swallowed by it.

[23] Thus the whole face of the earth is changed; everywhere nature has disappeared; everywhere human art has taken its place[;] independence and natural liberty have given way to laws and

slavery[;] there is no free being anymore; the philo[*604*]sopher looks for a man and no longer finds one. But it is vain to think that nature can be annihilated, it arises anew and appears where it was least expected. The independence that is taken away from men finds refuge in societies, and these great bodies, subject to their own impulsions, produce shocks more terrible in proportion as their mass exceeds that of individuals.

[24] But, it will be said, since each one of these bodies is so solidly set, how can they possibly ever collide? Should not their own constitution preserve eternal peace between them? Do they, like men, have to go look outside for the wherewithal to provide for their needs? Have they not within themselves everything needed for their preservation? Are competition and exchange an inevitable source of discord, and is not the fact that the inhabitants of all the countries in the world supported themselves before there was commerce proof conclusive that they could subsist without it?

[25] "End of the chapter: there is no war between men; there is war only between States."

[26] To this, I could leave it at answering with facts, and I would have no rebuttal to fear, but I have not forgotten that I am here reasoning about the nature of things and not about events that can have a thousand particular causes independent of the common principle. But let us carefully consider the constitution of bodies politic, and although each one could, if necessary, provide for its own preservation, we will find that their mutual relations are nevertheless far closer than those among individuals. For basically man has no necessary relation with those like himself[;] he can subsist in all his vigor without their assistance; he needs not so much the attentions of man as he needs the fruits of the earth; and the earth produces more than enough to feed all those who dwell on it. Add to this that there is a limit to man's force and size, fixed by nature and which he cannot exceed. From whatever angle he looks at himself, he finds all of his faculties limited. His life is short, his years are numbered. His stomach does not grow with his wealth, regardless of how much his passions increase, his pleasures have their measure, his heart has bounds [*605*] like everything else, his capacity for enjoyment is always the same. He may well aggrandize himself in idea, he remains ever small.

[27] The State, by contrast, being an artificial body, has no determinate measure, it is without definite proper size, it can always increase it, it feels weak so long as some are stronger than it. Its security, its preservation demand that it make itself more powerful than all of its neighbors. It can only enlarge, feed, exercise its forces at their expense, and while it may not need to look for its subsistence outside itself, it does constantly look outside itself for new members who might give it greater stability. For the hands of nature set bounds to the inequality among men, but the inequality among societies can grow endlessly, until one absorbs all the others.

[28] Thus, since the size of the body politic is purely relative, it is forced constantly to compare itself in order to know itself; it depends on everything around it, and has to take an interest in everything happening around it, for regardless of how much it might wish to remain within itself without gain or loss, it becomes small or large, weak or strong, according to whether its neighbor expands or contracts and grows stronger or weaker. Finally, its very stability, by steadying its relations, secures a more dependable outcome to all of its actions, and makes all of its quarrels more dangerous.

[29] People seem to have set themselves the goal of overthrowing all true ideas of things. Everything inclines natural man to repose; to eat and to sleep are the only needs he knows; and only hunger rouses him from his laziness. He is made out to be a fierce being, ever ready to torment his kind because of passions of which he knows nothing; on the other hand, these same passions, [which are] excited within society by everything that can inflame them, are said not to exist in it. A thousand writers have dared to assert that the Body politic is without passions and that there is no other reason of state than reason itself. As if it were not evident that, on the contrary, the essence of society consists in the activities of its members, and that a State without movement would be nothing but a dead body. As if all of the world's histories did not show us the best constituted societies also to be the most active, and the continual internal as well as external action and reaction of all [606] their members did not bear witness to the entire body's vigor.

[30] The difference between human art and the works of nature makes itself felt in its effects; even though citizens call themselves members of the state, they cannot join it as true members are joined to the body; it is impossible so to arrange things that each one of

them not have an individual and separate existence which enables him to attend to his preservation by himself; the nerves are less sensitive, the muscles less vigorous, all the ties more slack, the least accident can disjoin everything.

[31] Considering how inferior the public force in the aggregate of the body politic is to the sum of private forces, how much friction there is so to speak in the working of the entire machine, then, all other things being equal, the frailest man will be found to have more force for his self-preservation than the sturdiest State has for its own.

[32] For this state to endure, the liveliness of its passion must therefore make up for the lack of liveliness of its movements, and its will must quicken by as much as its power grows slack. Such is the law of conservation which nature itself establishes among the species and which maintains them all in spite of their inequality. This, incidentally, is also the reason why small states are proportionately more vigorous than large ones, for public sensitivity does not increase with territory, the more it expands, the more the will cools, the movements weaken, and this large body, overwhelmed by its own weight, collapses, languishes, and withers away.

[*OC* III, *1899*] [33] After seeing the earth covered with new States, after discovering a general relation between them which tends to their mutual destruction, it remains for us to see [*1900*] what, precisely, constitutes their existence, their well-being and their life; in order, then, to find out by what kinds of hostilities they can attack and harm one another.

[34] The body politic gets unity and a common self from the social pact; its government and its laws make its constitution more or less sturdy, its life is in the citizens' hearts, their courage and morals make it more or less long-lasting, the only actions which it performs freely and which can be imputed to it are dictated by the general will, and it is by the nature of these actions that one may judge whether the being that produces them is well or badly constituted.

[35] Thus so long as there is a common will to observe the social pact and the laws, this pact continues to subsist, and so long as this will manifests itself in outward acts, the State is not annihilated. But without ceasing to exist, it can find itself at a stage of vigor or of decline from which – weak, healthy or ill, and tending either

to destroy or to strengthen itself – its well-being may improve or deteriorate in an infinite number of ways, almost all of which depend on it [alone]. The full account of all these particulars is beyond my [present] subject; but here is the summary of those that do bear on it.

The General Idea of War between One State and Another

[36] The principle of life of the body politic and, so to speak, the heart of the State, is the social pact which, as soon as it is injured, causes the State instantly to die, collapse and dissolve[;] but this pact is not a charter on parchment which can be destroyed simply by being torn up[;] it is inscribed in the general will, and that is where it is not easily annulled.

[37] Hence, since one cannot begin by dividing the whole, one gets at it through its parts[;] if the body is invulnerable, one injures the members in order to weaken it, if one cannot deprive it of existence, one at least reduces its well-being, if one cannot reach the seat of life, one destroys what preserves it, one attacks the government, the laws, [*1901*] morals, goods, possessions, men. The State will, after all, have to perish when everything that sustains it is annihilated.

[38] All these means are or can be used in a war between one power and another, and they are also frequently the conditions imposed by the victors in order to go on harming the vanquished once he has been disarmed.

[39] For the object of all the harm one does one's enemy by war is to force him to put up with having even greater harm done him by the peace. There is not a single one of these kinds of hostilities of which history does not provide examples. I need not say anything about the financial contributions in [the form of] manufactured goods or foodstuffs[,] or about seized territory, or about resettled populations. A yearly tribute of men is not even uncommon. Without going as far back as Minos and the Athenians, it is well known that the Emperors of Mexico attacked their neighbors solely so that they might have prisoners to sacrifice[,] and in our own day the wars between the Kings of Guinea and their treaties with the peoples of Europe have no other object than tribute and traffic in slaves. Nor

is it difficult to make sense of the fact that sometimes the only aim and effect of war is to weaken the constitution of the enemy State.

[40] The republics of Greece attacked one another less in order to deprive one another of freedom than to change the form of their government, and they changed the government of the conquered only in order to make them more dependent. The Macedonians and all the conquerors of Sparta always attached great importance to abolishing the laws of Lycurgus, and the Romans believed that they could show no greater sign of clemency toward a subject people than to leave it its own laws. It was also a well known maxim of their policy to foster among their enemies and to banish from among themselves the effeminate and sedentary arts that enervate and soften men. Leave their angry Gods to the Tarentines, Fabius said when he was invited to carry off to Rome the statues and paintings that adorned Tarentum[;] and the earliest decadence in Roman morals is rightly imputed to Marcellus for not having followed the same policy in Syracuse. [*1902*] So true is it that a clever conqueror sometimes harms the vanquished more by what he leaves them than by what he takes from them[,] and that, by contrast, a covetous usurper often harms himself more than his enemy by the evil he does him indirectly. Truly enlightened princes have always regarded this influence of morals as most important. The only penalty Cyrus imposed on the rebellious Lydians was a soft and effeminate life[,] and the way the tyrant Aristodemus went about keeping the inhabitants of Cumae dependent on him is too curious not to be related.

What the State of War Is

[41] Although these two words *war* and *peace* appear to be strictly correlative, the second has a much broader meaning, since it is possible to interrupt and to disturb peace in various ways without going as far as war. Repose, unity, concord, all the ideas of benevolence and mutual affection seem contained in this sweet word *peace*. It conveys to the soul a fullness of sentiment that makes us love at once our own and other people's existence, it represents the bond among the beings that unites them in the universal system, it has its full breadth only in the mind of God whom nothing that is

can harm and who wants the preservation of all the beings he has created.

[42] The constitution of this universe does not allow for all the sentient beings that make it up to concur all at once in their mutual happiness[;] but since one sentient being's well-being makes for the other's evil, each, by the law of nature, gives preference to itself, regardless of whether it is working to its own advantage or to another's prejudice; straightaway peace is disturbed as regards the one who suffers, [and] not only is it natural then to repel the evil that pursues us, but when an intelligent being perceives that this evil is due to another's ill-will, he gets irritated at it and tries to repel it. Whence arise discord, quarrels, sometimes fights, but not yet war.

[*1903*] [43] Finally, once things have reached a point where a being endowed with reason is convinced that his preservation is inconsistent not only with another's well-being but with his very existence, he takes up arms against the other's life and tries to destroy him as eagerly as he tries to preserve himself, and for the same reason. The attacked party[,] sensing that the safety of his existence is incompatible with the aggressor's existence, in turn attacks with all his force the life of the one who threatens his own life. This manifest will to destroy one another and all the actions that result from it produce between the two enemies a relation that is called *war*.

[44] From this it follows that war consists not in one or several unpremeditated fights, not even in homicide or murder committed in an outburst of anger, but in the steady, considered and manifest will to destroy one's enemy[;] because to judge that this enemy's existence is incompatible with our well-being requires self-possession and reason, which produce a lasting resolve; and for this relation to be mutual requires that the enemy, in his turn, knowing that his life is threatened, be intent on defending it at the expense of ours. All these ideas are contained in the word *war*.

[45] The public consequences of this ill-will reduced to actions are called hostilities: but regardless of whether there are hostilities or not, the relation of war once established can end only with a formal peace. Otherwise, each of the two enemies, having no evidence that the other has ceased to threaten his life, could not or should not cease defending it at the expense of the other's life.

[46] These differences call for a certain distinction in terminology. When parties keep one another on the alert by continual hostilities, they are properly engaged in what is called waging war. On the other hand, when two declared enemies remain quiet and do not engage in any offensive action toward one another, their relation does not thereby change, but so long as it is without actual consequence, it is called only a *state of war*. [*1904*] Protracted wars of which one wearies and [yet] cannot end commonly produce this state. Sometimes the animosity, far from being lulled into inaction, is merely waiting for an opportune moment to surprise the enemy, and often the state of war that produces the reduction in tension is more dangerous than war itself.

[47] There has been disagreement about whether a truce, an armistice, the peace of God are states of war or of peace. In light of the preceding notions it is clear that all this is nothing but a modified state of war in which the two enemies tie up their hands without losing or disguising the will to harm one another. They make preparations, accumulate weapons, materials for a siege, all military operations not specified [in the truce, armistice, or peace of God] continue [unabated]. This is to indicate clearly enough that intentions have not changed. This is also so when two enemies meet on neutral territory without attacking one another.

[*OC* III, *606*] [48] These examples suffice to give an idea of the various means by which a State can be weakened[,] as well as of those which war seems to allow being used to harm one's enemy; as for the treaties which stipulate one or another of these means as conditions, what else are such [kinds of] peace basically, than war continued all the more cruelly as the defeated enemy no longer has the right to defend himself. I will come back to this in another place.

[49] Add to all this the overt manifestations of ill-will which signal the intention to harm[,] such as denying a power the titles that are its due, ignoring its rights, rejecting its claims, depriving its subjects of the freedom to trade, stirring up enemies against it; [*607*] in short infringing on the right of nations toward it on any pretext whatsoever.

[50] Not all of these different ways of hurting a body politic are equally practicable or equally useful to the one who resorts to them; and those which redound both to our own advantage and to the

enemy's prejudice are naturally preferred. Land, money, men, all the spoils one can appropriate, thus become the principal objects of mutual hostilities. As this base greed insensibly changes [men's] ideas of things, war finally degenerates into brigandage, and having begun as enemies and warriors, they gradually become tyrants and thieves.

[51] Lest we unwittingly adopt these changes in ideas, let us begin by fixing our own ideas with a definition, and try to make it so simple that it is impossible to misuse it.

[52] I call war between one power and another, then, the effect of a mutual, steady and manifest disposition to destroy the enemy State, or at least to weaken it, by all means possible. This disposition reduced to actions is war properly so called; so long as it remains without consequences, it remains nothing but the state of war.

[53] I foresee an objection: since according to me the state of war is natural between powers, why need the disposition from which war results be manifest? To this I answer that previously I spoke of the natural state, that here I speak of the legitimate state, and that in the sequel I will show how, in order to make it legitimate, war requires a declaration.

Fundamental Distinctions

[54] I ask my readers not to forget that I am not inquiring into what makes war advantageous to the one who wages it, but what makes it legitimate. Being just almost always costs something. Is one therefore exempted from being so?

[55] If there never was and never could be a genuine war between individuals, who then are those between whom it takes place and who can truly call themselves [*608*] enemies? I answer that they are public persons. And what is a public person? I answer that it is a moral being called *sovereign*, endowed with existence by the social pact, and all of whose wills bear the name *laws*. Let us here apply the above distinctions; with regard to the effects of war, the sovereign may be said to be the one doing the damage and the State the one suffering it.

[56] If there is war only between moral beings, then it is not directed at [individual] men, and it can be waged without depriving anyone of his life. But this requires an explanation.

[57] Considering things solely in the light of the strict terms of the social pact, land, money, men, and everything included within the confines of the state belongs to it without reservation. But since the rights of society, founded upon those of nature, cannot abrogate them, all these things have to be considered in a two-fold relation: namely, the soil as both public territory and the patrimony of private individuals; goods as belonging in one sense to the sovereign and in another to the owners; the inhabitants as citizens and as men. Basically, the body politic, since it is only a moral person, is only a being of reason. Remove the public convention, straightway the state is destroyed without the least change for the worse in anything which makes it up; and not all of men's conventions could ever change anything in the physical [constitution] of things. What, then, is it to wage war on a sovereign? It is to attack the public convention and all that results from it; for that is all the essence of the State consists in. If the social pact could be severed with a single stroke, straightway there would be no more war; and with that single stroke the State would be killed, without a single man dying. Aristotle says that in order to authorize the cruel treatment to which the Helots were subjected in Sparta, the Ephors, upon assuming office, solemnly declared war on them. This declaration was as superfluous as it was barbarous. They were necessarily in a state of war with one another, simply because they were the masters and the others the slaves. There is no doubt that since the Lacedaemonians killed the Helots, the Helots had the right to kill the Lacedaemonians.

CONSIDERATIONS ON THE GOVERNMENT OF POLAND AND ON ITS PROJECTED REFORMATION

[*953*]

[1] THE STATE OF THE QUESTION

[1] Count Wielhorski's description of the government of Poland, together with the reflections he has appended to it, are instructive documents for anyone trying to form a coherent plan for the recasting of this government. I know of no one in a better position to draw up this plan than himself, who combines the general knowledge required for this work with full knowledge of local conditions and particular details which are impossible to convey in writing and which one nevertheless needs to know in order to conform an institution to the people for whom it is intended. Unless one knows the Nation for which one is working thoroughly, one's labor on its behalf, regardless of how excellent it may be in itself, will invariably fall short in application, and even more so in the case of an already fully instituted nation, whose tastes, morals, prejudices and vices are too deeply rooted to be easily stifled by new seeds. A good institution for Poland can only be the work of the Poles or of someone who has studied the Polish nation and its neighbors at first hand. A foreigner can contribute scarcely any but general views, which might enlighten the institutor, not guide him. Even when my mind was at its most vigorous I would not have been up to grasping these broad relations in their entirety. Now that I am barely left the faculty to combine ideas, I must confine myself, if I am to obey Count Wielhorski and give proof of my zeal for his fatherland, to giving him an account of the impressions which reading his work has made on me, and of the reflections it has suggested to me.

[2] In reading the history of the government of Poland, it is hard to understand how so oddly constituted a State could have survived so long. A great body made up of a large number of dead, and a small number of disjointed limbs, with all of its move[*954*]ments, almost independent of one another, far from having a common end, cancel each other, which tosses about a great deal without getting

anything done, which can offer no resistance to anyone trying to encroach on it, which falls into dissolution five or six times a century, which gets paralyzed with every effort it tries to make, with every need it tries to meet, and which in spite of all this lives and remains vigorous; this, it seems to me, is one of the most singular spectacles that can strike a thinking being. I see all the other States of Europe rushing to their ruin. Monarchies, Republics, all these ever so wonderfully instituted nations, all these fine, ever so wisely balanced governments, have grown decrepit and threaten soon to die; while Poland, this depopulated, devastated, and oppressed region, wide open to its aggressors, at the height of its misfortunes and its anarchy, still displays all the fire of youth; and it dares to call for a government and laws, as if it had only just been born. It is in chains, and debates the ways to remain free! It feels in itself the kind of force which the force of tyranny cannot subjugate. I seem to see Rome beleaguered, tranquilly ruling the territories where its enemies had just pitched camp. Brave Poles, beware; beware lest for wanting to be too well, you only make your situation worse. In thinking about what you want to acquire, do not forget what you might lose. Correct the abuses of your constitution, if it is possible to do so; but do not despise the constitution that made you what you are.

[3] You love freedom, you are worthy of it; you have defended it against a powerful and cunning aggressor who, under pretense of offering you the bonds of friendship, shackled you with chains of servitude. Now, weary of your fatherland's troubles, you sigh for tranquility. I believe it very easy to attain; but to preserve it together with freedom, that seems to me difficult. The patriotic souls that protected you against the yoke were formed in the midst of the anarchy you find so hateful. They fell into a lethargic sleep; the storm awoke them. Having broken the chains intended for them, they are weighed down with weariness. They would like to combine the peace of despotism with the sweetness of freedom. I am afraid that they want things that are [955] contradictory. Repose and freedom seem to me incompatible; one has to choose.

[4] I do not say that things have to be left in the state they are in; but I do say that nothing should be done to them except with the utmost caution. At present the abuses are more striking than the advantages; I fear the time will come when these advantages

will be appreciated more keenly, and unfortunately it will be when they will have been lost.

[5] Granted that it is easy to make better laws. It is impossible to make laws which men's passions do not abuse, as they have abused the earlier ones. To anticipate and to weigh all these future abuses is something which perhaps even the most consummate Statesman may find it impossible to do. Putting the law above man is a problem in politics which I liken to that of squaring the circle in geometry. Solve this problem satisfactorily, and the government based on this solution will be good and free of abuses. But until then, you may be sure that wherever you believe you have made the laws rule, it will be men who will be ruling.

[6] No constitution will ever be good and solid unless the law rules the citizens' hearts. So long as the legislative force does not reach that deep, the laws will invariably be evaded. But how can men's hearts be reached? This is something to which our founders, who never see anything but force and punishments, scarcely give a thought, and which material rewards would perhaps achieve no better; justice, even of the utmost integrity, does not achieve it, because justice, like health, is a good which one enjoys without feeling it, which inspires no enthusiasm, and the value of which one feels only once it has been lost.

[7] How, then, can one move hearts, and get the fatherland and its laws loved? Dare I say it? with children's games; with institutions which appear trivial in the eyes of superficial men, but which form cherished habits and invincible attachments. If I am being extravagant on this point, at least I am being thoroughly so, for I admit that I see my folly exhibiting all the features of reason.

[956]

[2] SPIRIT OF THE ANCIENT INSTITUTIONS

[1] When reading ancient history, one believes oneself transported into another universe and among other beings. What have Frenchmen, Englishmen, Russians, in common with the Romans and the Greeks? Almost nothing but their shape. The strong souls of the Romans and the Greeks appear to them to be exaggerations of

history. How can they, who feel so small, think there ever were such great men? Yet they did exist, and they were humans like ourselves; what keeps us from being men like them? Our prejudices, our base philosophy, and the passions of petty self-interest, concentrated together with egoism in all hearts by inept institutions in which genius never had any share.

[2] I look at modern nations: I see many lawmakers among them but not a single lawgiver. Among the ancients I see three principal ones who deserve particular attention: Moses, Lycurgus, and Numa. All three devoted their principal cares to objects which our learned men would consider laughable. All three achieved successes which would be thought impossible if they were not so well attested.

[3] The first formed and executed the astonishing enterprise of instituting as a national body a swarm of wretched fugitives who had no arts, no weapons, no talents, no virtues, no courage, and who, since they had not an inch of territory of their own, were a troop of strangers upon the face of the earth. Moses dared to make out of this wandering and servile troop a body politic, a free people, and while it wandered in the wilderness without so much as a stone on which to rest its head, he gave it the lasting institution, proof against time, fortune and conquerors which five thousand years have not been able to destroy or even to weaken, and which still subsists today in all its force even though the body of the nation no longer does.

[4] To keep his people from being absorbed by foreign peoples, he gave it morals and practices [957] which could not be blended with those of the other nations; he weighed it down with distinctive rites and ceremonies; he constrained it in a thousand ways in order to keep it constantly alert and to make it forever a stranger among other men, and all the bonds of fraternity he introduced among the members of his republic were as many barriers which kept it separated from its neighbors and prevented it from mingling with them. That is how this singular nation, so often subjugated, so often scattered and apparently destroyed, yet ever idolizing its rule, has nevertheless maintained itself down to our days, scattered among the other nations without ever merging with them, and how its morals, its laws, its rites subsist and will endure as long as the world itself does, in spite of the hatred and persecution by the rest of mankind.

[5] Lycurgus undertook to institute a people already degraded by slavery and the vices which are its effect. He imposed on it an iron yoke the like of which no other people has ever borne; but he attached it to this yoke, he, so to speak, identified it with it, by always keeping it occupied with it. He constantly showed it the fatherland, in its laws, in its games, in its home, in its loves, in its feasts. He did not leave it a moment's respite to be by itself, and from this constant constraint, ennobled by its object, arose in it that ardent love of fatherland which was always the Spartans' strongest or rather their sole passion, and made of them beings above humanity. Sparta was but a city, it is true; but by the sheer force of its institution this city gave laws to the whole of Greece, became its capital, and made the Persian Empire tremble. Sparta was the center from which the effects of its legislation spread in all directions.

[6] Those who have seen Numa as nothing but someone who instituted religious rites and ceremonies have badly misjudged this great man. Numa was the true founder of Rome. If all Romulus had done was to assemble some brigands whom a reversal could scatter, his imperfect work could not have withstood the test of time. It was Numa who made it solid and lasting by uniting these brigands into an indissoluble body, by transforming them into Citizens, not so much by means of laws, for which in their rustic poverty they had as yet little need, as by means of mild institutions which attached them one to another and all of them to their soil so that they eventually sanctified their city with these apparently frivolous and superstitious rites, [958] the force and effects of which so few people appreciate, and yet the first foundations of which Romulus, fierce Romulus himself, had laid.

[7] The same spirit guided all ancient Lawgivers and their institutions. All of them sought bonds that might attach the Citizens to the fatherland and to one another, and they found them in distinctive practices, in religious ceremonies which by their very nature were always exclusive and national (see the end of the *Social Contract*), in games which kept the Citizens frequently assembled, in exercises which increased their pride and self-esteem together with their vigor and strength, in spectacles which by reminding them of the history of their ancestors, their misfortunes, their virtues, their victories, stirred their hearts, fired them with a lively

spirit of emulation, and strongly attached them to the fatherland with which they were being kept constantly occupied. It is the poems of Homer recited before the Greeks solemnly assembled, not in stalls, on stages and cash in hand, but in the open and before the national body, it is the tragedies of Aeschylus, Sophocles and Euripides often performed before them, it is the prizes with which, to the acclaim of all Greece, the victors in their games were crowned, which, by constantly kindling in them emulation and glory, brought their courage and their virtues to that pitch of energy of which nothing now gives us any idea and which the moderns are not even capable of believing. If the moderns have laws it is solely in order to teach them to obey their masters well, not to pick pockets, and to give public scoundrels a great deal of money. If they have manners it is in order to know how to divert the idleness of women of easy virtue, or gracefully to parade their own. If they assemble it is in Temples for a cult which is in no way national, which in no way reminds them of the fatherland, and has been turned almost into ridicule; it is in completely shut-in halls and for money, in order to see, in effeminate, dissolute theaters where all they can talk about is love, thespians declaim and prostitutes simper, and to get lessons in corruption, the only ones of all the lessons their theater pretends to teach that have a lasting effect; it is in festivals where the people, invariably despised, is invariably without influence, where [959] public blame or approval make no difference; it is in licentious crowds in order there to enter into secret liaisons, in order to seek out the pleasures that most divide and isolate men, and most weaken hearts. Are these stimulants to patriotism? Is it surprising that such different ways of life produce such different effects, and that the moderns no longer find within themselves anything of that vigor of soul which everything instilled in the ancients? Forgive these digressions and attribute them to a remnant of warmth you have rekindled. I return with pleasure to the one among all contemporary peoples which separates me least from those about whom I have just been speaking.

[3] APPLICATION

[1] Poland is a large State surrounded by even larger States which, because of their despotism and military discipline, possess great offensive force. It, by contrast, being weak because of its anarchy, is, in spite of Polish valor, the butt of all their offenses. It has no fortifications to stop their incursions. Its depopulation renders it almost completely incapable of defending itself. No economic organization, few troops or none at all, no military discipline, no order, no subordination; ever divided within; ever threatened from without, it is without stability of its own, and dependent on its neighbors' whim. In the present state of things I see only one way of giving it the stability it lacks: to infuse, so to speak, the soul of its confederates into the entire nation, to establish the Republic in the hearts of the Poles so thoroughly that it endures there in spite of all of its oppressors' efforts. That, it seems to me, is the only refuge where force can neither reach nor destroy it. We have just witnessed a forever memorable proof of this. Poland was in the Russian's chains, but the Poles remained free. A great example which shows you how you can defy your neighbors' power and ambitions. You may not be able to keep [*960*] them from swallowing you, do at least see to it that they cannot digest you. No matter what is done, Poland will have been overwhelmed by its enemies a hundred times before it can be given everything it needs in order to be in a position to resist them. The virtue of Citizens, their patriotic zeal, the distinctive form which its national institutions may give their soul, this is the only rampart that will stand ever ready to defend it, and which no army could subdue by force. If you see to it that a Pole can never become a Russian, I assure you that Russia will never subjugate Poland.

[2] It is national institutions which form the genius, the character, the tastes, and the morals of a people, which make it be itself and not another, which inspire in it that ardent love of fatherland founded on habits impossible to uproot, which cause it to die of boredom among other peoples in the midst of delights of which it is deprived in its own. Remember the Spartan, gorged with the voluptuous pleasures at the Court of the Great King, who was chided for missing his black broth. Ah! he said, sighing, to the satrap, I know your pleasures, but you do not know ours.

[3] There are no more Frenchmen, Germans, Spaniards, even Englishmen, nowadays, regardless of what people may say; there are only Europeans. All have the same tastes, the same passions, the same morals, because none has been given a national form by a distinctive institution. All will do the same things under the same circumstances; all will declare themselves disinterested and be cheats; all will speak of the public good and think only of themselves; all will praise moderation and wish to be Croesuses; they have no other ambition than for luxury, no other passion than for gold. Confident that with it they will have whatever tempts them, all will sell themselves to the first man willing to pay them. What do they care what master they obey, the laws of what State they follow? Provided they find money to steal and women to corrupt, they are at home in any country.

[4] Give a different bent to the Poles' passions, and you will give their souls a national physiognomy which will set them apart from all other peoples, which will keep them from merging, from feeling at ease, from inter-marrying with them, [*961*] you will give them a vigor which will take the place of deceptive appeals to empty precepts, which will make them do by preference and passion the things one never does well enough when one does them only by duty or interest. It is upon souls such as these that an appropriate legislation will take hold. They will obey the laws and not elude them because they will suit them and will have the inward assent of their wills. Loving their fatherland, they will serve it out of zeal and with all their heart. With this sentiment alone, legislation, even if it were bad, would make good Citizens; and only good Citizens ever make for the force and prosperity of the State.

[5] I shall discuss below the administrative regime which, while leaving the foundation of your laws virtually untouched, seems to me suited to raise patriotism and the virtues inseparable from it to their highest possible pitch. But whether or not you adopt this regime, always begin by giving the Poles a great opinion of themselves and their fatherland: in view of the account they have just given of themselves, it will not be a false opinion. You must seize the occasion of the latest event to raise their souls to the level of the souls of the ancients. Certain it is that the Confederation of Bar saved the dying fatherland. You must engrave this great epoch in sacred characters in every Polish heart. I should wish to see a monu-

ment erected to its memory, and the names of all the Confederates inscribed on it, even of those who may subsequently have betrayed the common cause; so great a deed ought to erase the faults of an entire lifetime; I should wish to have a regular solemn occasion to celebrate it every ten years with a pomp not brilliant and frivolous, but plain, proud, and republican; to have the worthy Citizens who had the honor of suffering for the fatherland in the enemy's chains be eulogized with dignity, but without ostentation, even to have their families granted some honorific privilege which would forever recall this fair memory to the eyes of the public. However, I should not wish anyone to take the liberty of inveighing against the Russians or even of mentioning them. It would be doing them too much honor. This silence, the memory of their barbarity, and the eulogy of those who resisted them, will say all that needs to be said about them: you ought to despise them too much to hate them. [962]

[6] I should wish all the patriotic virtues to be given luster by attaching to them honors and public rewards, the Citizens to be kept constantly occupied with the fatherland, for it to be made their principal business, for it to be continuously kept before their eyes. I admit that this way they would have less opportunity and time to grow rich, but they would also have less desire or need to do so: their hearts would get to know a happiness other than fortune, and therein lies the art of ennobling souls and turning them into an instrument more powerful than gold.

[7] The brief account of Polish morals which M. de Wielhorski kindly conveyed to me is not sufficient to instruct me of their civil and domestic practices. Yet a great nation which has never mingled much with its neighbors must have many practices that are distinctively its own, and are perhaps being daily bastardized by the general European tendency to adopt the tastes and morals of the French. These ancient practices ought to be preserved, restored, and suitable new ones introduced that are distinctively the Poles' own. These practices, even if they are indifferent, even if they are in some respects bad, provided they are not essentially so, will still have the advantage of making the Poles fond of their country and give them a natural revulsion to mingling with foreigners. I deem it fortunate that they have a distinctive mode of dress. Preserve this asset. Take care to do precisely the opposite of what this widely praised Tsar did. Let not the King, nor the Senators, nor any public

figure ever wear any but the national dress, and let no Pole dare show himself at Court dressed in the French fashion.

[8] [Let there be] many public games where the good mother country delights in seeing her children at play. Let her frequently attend to them so that they always attend to her. The usual courtly entertainments must be eliminated, even at Court, because of the example it sets: gambling, theaters, comedies, opera; all that makes men effeminate, all that distracts them, isolates them, makes them forget their fatherland and their duty; all that makes them be comfortable anywhere at all so long as they are entertained; games must be devised, festivals, solemn occasions so distinctive of this particular Court [*963*] that they are found at none other. People should feel entertained in Poland more than in other countries, but not in the same way. In a word, the execrable proverb must be reversed, and every Pole be made to say in his inmost heart: *Ubi patria, ibi bene.*

[9] Nothing, if possible, exclusively for the Great and the rich. Many spectacles in the open, where ranks are carefully distinguished but the entire people participates equally, as among the ancients, and where, on certain occasions, young nobles display force and skill. The contribution of bullfights in maintaining a certain vigor in the Spanish nation is not negligible. The amphitheaters in which the youth of Poland used formerly to exercise should be carefully restored; they should be turned into theaters of honor and emulation for these youths. Nothing could be easier than to replace the fights that formerly took place in these amphitheaters by exercises less cruel but nevertheless requiring force and skill, and with honors and rewards for the victors as in the past. Horsemanship, for example, is an exercise well suited to Poles and it readily makes for dazzling spectacle.

[10] Homer's heroes all distinguished themselves by their force and skill, and in this way demonstrated in the eyes of the people that they were made to command it. The Knights' tournaments trained men who were not only stout and courageous, but also eager for honor and glory, and fit for all the virtues. The use of firearms, by making these bodily faculties less useful in war, has caused them to fall into discredit. Hence, besides qualities of mind, which are often ambiguous, misplaced, about which one can be mistaken in a

thousand ways, and of which the people is a poor judge, nothing about a man who enjoys the advantage of good birth may set him apart from anyone else, justifying good fortune, demonstrate in his person a natural right to superiority, and the more these external signs are neglected, the more do those who govern us enjoy impunity when they grow effeminate and corrupt. Yet it matters, even more than one might think, that those who are some day to command others should from youth on prove themselves their superiors in every respect, or at least that they try to do so. It is furthermore good that the people often be together with its chiefs on pleasant occasions [*964*], that it know them, that it grow accustomed to seeing them, that it share its pleasures with them. Provided subordination is always maintained, and people and chiefs do not intermingle, this is the way it grows fond of them and combines attachment for them with respect. Finally, a taste for physical exercise diverts from dangerous idleness, from the effeminate pleasures, and from luxuries of the mind. It is above all for the sake of the soul that one must exercise the body, and this is what our small-minded sages are far from realizing.

[11] Do not neglect a certain amount of public display; let it be noble, imposing, and convey magnificence with men rather than with things. It is hard to exaggerate the extent to which the people's heart follows its eyes and how impressed it is with the majesty of ceremonials. Majesty of ceremonials endows authority with a confidence-inspiring air of order and regularity, and dispels the ideas of caprice and fancy associated with the idea of arbitrary power. In the pomp of solemnities, one should, however, avoid the clatter, the glitter, and the luxurious decorations that are common at courts. A free people's festivals should always breathe an air of decorum and gravity, and they should hold up for the people's admiration only objects worthy of its esteem. The Romans displayed enormous luxury in their triumphs; but it was the luxury of the vanquished; the more brilliant it was, the less it was seductive. Its very sparkle was a great lesson for the Romans. The captive Kings were shackled with chains of gold and precious stones. There you have luxury correctly understood. Often one can reach the same goal in one of two opposite ways. In my view the two woolsacks by the seat of the Lord Chancellor in the British House of Lords form a touching

and sublime decoration. Two sheaves of wheat similarly placed in the Polish Senate would make for an effect no less pleasing to my taste.

[12] The enormous disparity of fortune which separates the high and the lower nobility is a major obstacle to the reforms required to make love of fatherland the dominant passion. As long as luxury reigns among the Great, cupidity will reign in all hearts. The object of public admiration will invariably be the object of the wishes of individuals, and if one has to be rich in order to shine then being rich will always be the dominant passion. This is a major means of corruption which has to be weakened as much as [*965*] possible. If other attractive objects, if signs of rank were the distinctions of men in high places, then those who are only rich would be deprived of them, and secret wishes would naturally take the road leading to these honorable distinctions, that is to say to distinctions of merit and of virtue, if that were the only road to success. The Consuls of Rome were often very poor, but they had their lictors, the people of Rome coveted the trappings of these lictors, and plebeians attained the Consulship.

[13] Eliminating all luxury where inequality reigns does, I admit, strike me as an extremely difficult undertaking. But might there not be some way to change the objects of this luxury, and so render its example less pernicious? For example, formerly impoverished Polish nobles attached themselves to the Great who provided them with education and subsistence as their retainers. There you have a truly grand and noble luxury, to the inconvenience of which I am fully sensible, but which at least elevates souls instead of debasing them, gives them sentiments, resilience, and which was not abused among the Romans as long as the Republic endured. I have read that the Duc d'Epergnon, on meeting the Duc de Sulli one day, wanted to pick a quarrel with him; but that since he had only six hundred gentlemen in his retinue, he did not dare attack Sulli, who had eight hundred. I doubt that this kind of luxury leaves much room for a luxury of tinsel; and at least it does not set an example that will seduce the poor. If you get the Great of Poland to go back to indulging no other kind of luxury, it may lead to divisions, factions, quarrels, but it will not corrupt the nation. Next in order, let us tolerate military luxury, the luxury of weapons and horses, but let all effeminate finery be held in contempt, and if women

cannot be made to give it up, let them at least be taught to disapprove and disdain it in men.

[14] Besides, luxury does not get rooted out with sumptuary laws. It has to be extirpated from the depth of men's hearts by impressing healthier and nobler tastes on them. Prohibiting the things people ought not to do is a clumsy and vain thing to do unless one begins by making these things hated and scorned, and the law's disapproval is only effective when it confirms one's own judgment. Whoever goes about instituting a people has to be able to rule men's opinions and through them to go[966]vern their passions. This is true above all regarding the issue about which I am speaking. Sumptuary laws, by restraining desire, stimulate it instead of extinguishing it with punishment. Simplicity of morals and of attire is less the fruit of law than of education.

[4] Education

[1] This is the important subject. It is education that must give souls the national form, and so direct their tastes and opinions that they will be patriotic by inclination, passion, necessity. Upon opening its eyes, a child should see the fatherland, and see only it until his dying day. Every true republican drank love of fatherland, that is to say love of the laws and of freedom, with his mother's milk. This love makes up his whole existence; he sees only his fatherland, he lives only for it; when he is alone, he is nothing: when he no longer has a fatherland, he no longer is, and if he is not dead, he is worse than dead.

[2] National education is suitable only for free men; only they enjoy a common existence and are truly bound together by Law. A Frenchman, an Englishman, a Spaniard, an Italian, a Russian, are all more or less the same man: they all leave school already molded for a higher degree, that is to say for servitude. At twenty a Pole should not be just another man; he should be a Pole. I want that on learning to read, he read about his country, that at ten he know all of its products, at twelve all of its provinces, roads, towns, that at fifteen he know its entire history, at sixteen all of its laws, that in all of Poland there not be a single great deed or illustrious person of which his memory and heart are not full, and of which

he could not then and there give an account. It should be clear from this that I would not want to have children pursue the usual course of studies under the direction of foreigners and priests. The law should regulate the matter, the order and the form of their studies. They should have only Poles for teachers, [967] all of them married, if possible, all distinguished for their morals, their probity, their good sense, their lights, and all destined, when after a number of years they will have fulfilled this employment well, for employment that is no more important or honorable, for that is impossible, but less strenuous and more resplendent. Above all beware of turning the state of being a teacher into a profession. A public person in Poland ought to have no other permanent state than that of Citizen. Each position he fills, and above all a position as important as this one, should be regarded as nothing but a testing ground and a stage from which to rise still higher once he merits it. I urge the Poles to heed this maxim, which I shall stress often: I believe it to be the key to one of the mainsprings of the State. The reader will see below how, in my opinion, it can be made to work without exception.

[3] I do not at all like the distinctions between schools and academies which result in the rich nobility being educated differently and separately from the poor nobility. Since all are equal by the constitution of the State, all ought to be educated together and in the same fashion, and if it is impossible to establish a completely free public education, it must at least be set at a cost the poor can afford. Would it not be possible to set up in each school a certain number of entirely free places, that is to say at the State's expense, and which in France are called scholarships? These places, awarded to the children of the poor gentry who have deserved well of the fatherland, not as an act of charity, but as a reward for the fathers' valuable services, would, on this basis, become places of honor, and could produce a twofold benefit which would not be negligible. To this end, appointments to these places would have to be not arbitrary, but made by a kind of judgment about which I shall speak below. Those filling these places would be called children of the State, and distinguished by some badge of honor that would give them precedence over other children of their age including even the children of the Great.

[4] In every School a gymnasium or place for physical exercise should be established for the children. This much neglected issue is, in my view, the most important part of education, not only because it forms sturdy and healthy temperaments [*968*], but even more because of its moral objective, which either gets neglected or is met only by a lot of pedantic and vain precepts that are so much empty talk. I cannot repeat often enough that good education has to be negative. Prevent vices from arising, you will have done enough for virtue. The way to do this in a good public education is simplicity itself. It consists in keeping children always alert, not by boring studies of which they understand nothing and which they come to hate simply because they are forced to stay put; but by exercises they like, because they satisfy their growing bodies' need for movement, and which they will find enjoyable in other ways as well.

[5] They should not be allowed to play by themselves as they please, but all together and in public, so that there is always a common goal to which all aspire and which excites competition and emulation. Parents who prefer domestic education, and have their children brought up under their own supervision, must nevertheless send them to these exercises. Their instruction may be domestic and individual, but their games ought always to be public and common to all; for the point here is not only to keep them busy, to give them a robust constitution, to make them agile and limber, but to accustom them from early on to rule, to equality, to fraternity, to competitions, to living under the eyes of their fellow-citizens and to seeking public approbation. To this end, the winners' prizes and rewards should be distributed not arbitrarily by the coaches or school principals, but by acclamation and the judgment of the spectators; and these judgments can be trusted always to be just especially if care is taken to make these games attractive to the public by organizing them with some pomp and so that they become a spectacle. In which case it is a fair assumption that all honest folk and good patriots will regard it a duty and a pleasure to attend them.

[6] In Berne, they have a rather unusual exercise for young Patricians graduating from school. It is called the *moot State [l'État extérieur]*. It is a copy on a small scale of everything that makes

up the government of the Republic: a Senate, Chief Magistrates, Counselors, Officers, Bailiffs, Advocates, lawsuits, judgments, solemnities. [*969*] The moot State even has a small government and some revenues, and this institution, authorized and protected by the sovereign, is the nursery of the Statesmen who will one day direct public affairs in the same capacity which they first exercise only in play.

[7] Regardless of the form given to public education, about which I do not here enter into detail, it is important to establish a College of Magistrates of the first rank charged with its supreme administration, and which appoints, dismisses and transfers at will not only the Principals and heads of schools who, as I have already said, will themselves be candidates for the higher magistracies, but also the coaches whose zeal and alertness will also have to be aroused by higher positions which will be open or closed to them depending on how they will have filled their present positions. Since it is on these institutions that the hope of the Republic, the glory and fate of the nation depend, I must admit that I attach to them an importance I am rather surprised it has not occurred to anyone anywhere else to attribute to them. I am distressed for the sake of humanity that so many ideas which seem to me good and useful are, although eminently practical, always so wide of what is done.

[8] Besides, I do no more than to point the way here; but that is enough for those I am addressing. These inadequately developed ideas show from afar the paths unknown to the moderns by which the ancients led men to that vigor of soul, to that patriotic zeal, to that esteem for the truly personal qualities and without regard for merely external trappings which are without example among us, but the leaven for which is in all men's hearts ready to ferment just as soon as it is activated by suitable institutions. Direct the Poles' education, practices, customs, morals in this spirit, you will develop in them the share of this leaven which has not yet been dissipated by corrupt maxims, outworn institutions, an egoistical philosophy whose preaching is deadly. The nation will date its second birth from the terrible crisis from which it is emerging and when it sees what its as yet undisciplined members accomplished, it will expect much and obtain even more from a carefully considered institution; it will cherish, [*970*] it will respect laws which flatter its noble pride, which will make and keep it happy and free; extirpating from its

breast the passions that elude the laws, it will foster those that cause them to be loved; finally, renewing itself so to speak by itself, it will resume at this new stage of its life all the vigor of a nascent nation. But without these precautions expect nothing from your laws. However wise they may be, however much they may anticipate, they will be eluded and remain vain, and you will have corrected some abuses that wound you, while introducing others you will not have anticipated. So much for the preliminaries I thought indispensable. Let us now look at the constitution.

[5] THE RADICAL VICE

[1] Let us avoid, if possible, rushing from the very outset into chimerical projects. What, Gentlemen, is the enterprise you are about just now? Reforming the Government of Poland, that is to say, giving to the constitution of a large kingdom the solidity and vigor of that of a small Republic. Before working on the execution of this project, one should first inquire whether it can succeed. Greatness of Nations! Size of States! the first and principal source of the miseries of humankind, and above all of the countless calamities that sap and destroy politically organized peoples. Almost all small States, republics as well as monarchies, prosper simply because they are small, because all their citizens know and watch one another, because the chiefs can see for themselves the evil being done, the good they have to do; and because their orders are carried out within their sight. All great peoples crushed by their own mass groan either in anarchy as do you, or under subordinate oppressors which a necessary devolution forces Kings to set over them. Only God can govern the world, and it would take more than human faculties to govern [971] great nations. It is astonishing, it is wondrous that the vast expanse of Poland has not already a hundred times converted its government into a despotism, bastardized the Poles' souls, and corrupted the mass of the nation. The case is unique in history of such a State being, after many centuries, still only at [the stage of] anarchy. This progression has been so slow because of advantages inseparable from the inconveniences of which you wish to get rid. Ah! I cannot repeat it too often; think carefully before you lay hands on your laws, and above all on those that made

you what you are. The first reform you need is a reform in the size of your country. Your vast provinces will never tolerate the severe administration of small Republics. Begin by contracting your boundaries, if you wish to reform your government. Perhaps your neighbors are thinking of performing this service for you. It would no doubt be a great evil for the dismembered parts; but it would be a great good for the body of the Nation.

[2] If these reductions do not take place, I see only one means of possibly making up for them and, happily, this means is already in the spirit of your institution. Let the separation between the two Polands be as pronounced as that between them and Lithuania: have three States united into one. If possible, I would wish you to have as many as you now have Palatinates; form within each one of them an equal number of individual administrations. Perfect the form of the Dietines, extend their authority within their respective Palatinates; but carefully fix their limits, and make sure that nothing can break the bond of common legislation between them or break the bond of subordination between them and the body of the Republic. In a word, seek to extend and to perfect the system of federative Governments, the only system which combines the advantages of large and of small States, and hence the only one that can suit you. If you ignore this advice, I doubt that you can ever do a good job.

[972]
[6] THE QUESTION OF THE THREE ORDERS

[1] I hardly ever hear people speak of government without finding that they go back to principles which seem to me either false or suspect. The Republic of Poland, it has often been said and repeated, is composed of three orders: the Knightly Order, the Senate, and the King. I would prefer to say that the Polish nation is composed of three orders: the nobles, who are everything, the bourgeois, who are nothing, and the peasants, who are less than nothing. If the Senate is counted as an order within the State, why not also count the Chamber of Deputies as one, which is no less distinct and has no less authority? What is more, this distinction,

even in the sense in which it is offered, is manifestly incomplete; because to it should have been added the Ministers, who are neither Kings, nor Senators, nor Deputies, and who, while enjoying the utmost independence, are nevertheless the trustees of all executive power. How will anyone ever get me to understand that the part which exists only by virtue of the whole nevertheless forms in relation to the whole an order independent of it? In England the Peerage, being hereditary, does form, I admit, an order existing by itself. But in Poland, eliminate the knightly order, and there is no more Senate, since no one can be a Senator who is not first a Polish nobleman. There is also no more King; since it is the knightly order that elects him, and the King can do nothing without it: but eliminate the Senate and the King, and the knightly order and through it the State and the Sovereign remain entire and the very next day, if it so pleases, it will have a Senate and a King as before.

[2] But from its not being an order in the State, it does not follow that the Senate counts for nothing in it; and even if it were not, as a body, the trustee of the laws, its members, independently of the authority of the body, would nonetheless be the trustees of the legislative power, and to prevent them from voting in the Senate in plenary sessions of the Diet whenever it [*973*] is a matter of enacting or repealing laws would be to deprive them of the right they have by birth; but in that case they would no longer be voting as Senators but simply as Citizens. As soon as the legislative power speaks, all revert to equality; every other authority is silent in its presence; its voice is the voice of God on earth. The King himself, although he presides over the Diet, has not then, I maintain, the right to vote in it unless he is a Polish nobleman.

[3] I will probably be told at this point that I am proving too much, and that if the Senators have no vote in the Diet in their capacity as Senators, they ought not to have it in their capacity as citizens either, since the members of the knightly order do not vote in the Diet in person but only through their representatives, which the Senators are not. And why should they vote in the Diet as individuals, since no other nobleman may vote in it unless he is a deputy? The objection seems to me solid in the current state of things; but it will no longer be so once the proposed changes will have been made; for then the Senators themselves will be perpetual

representatives of the nation, who, however, in matters of legislation will be able to act only with the concurrence of their colleagues.

[4] It should therefore not be said that the concurrence of the King, the Senate, and the knightly order is necessary to draft a law. This right appertains exclusively to the knightly order, of which the Senators as well as the deputies are members, but in which the Senate as a body has no role. Such is or must be the law of the State in Poland; but the law of nature, this sacred, imprescriptible law, which speaks to man's heart and to his reason, does not permit legislative authority to be thus restricted, nor laws to obligate anyone who has not voted on them as the deputies have done, or at least anyone who has not voted on them through his representatives as the nobles have done as a body. This sacred law cannot be violated with impunity, and the state of weakness to which so great a nation finds itself reduced is the product of that feudal barbarism which leads to cutting off from the State its most numerous and sometimes its most wholesome part.

[5] God forbid that I should think it necessary to prove here what everyone with a modicum of good sense and stomach senses! And where does Poland propose to get the power and forces which it wantonly stifles [*974*] in its own bosom? Nobles of Poland, be something more, be men. Only then will you be happy and free, but never flatter yourselves that you are so, as long as you keep your brothers in chains.

[6] I am sensible to the difficulty of the project of emancipating your peoples. What I fear is not only the masters' wrongly understood [self-]interest, amour propre and prejudices. This hurdle once cleared, I would still fear the serfs' vices and cowardice. Freedom is hearty fare, but hard to digest; it takes very healthy stomachs to tolerate it. I laugh at those degraded peoples who, letting plotters rouse them to riot, dare to speak of freedom without so much as an idea of it, and, their hearts full of all the vices of slaves, imagine that all it takes to be free is to be unruly. Proud and holy freedom! if these poor people only knew you, if they only realized at what price you are won and preserved, if they were only sensible to how much your laws are more austere than the tyrants' yoke is hard; their weak souls, the slaves of passions that should be stifled, would fear you a hundred times more than servitude; they would flee you in terror as a burden about to crush them.

[7] To emancipate the peoples of Poland is a grand and fine undertaking, but bold, dangerous, and not to be attempted thoughtlessly. Among the precautions to be taken, there is one that is indispensable and that requires time. It is, before everything else, to make the serfs who are to be emancipated worthy of freedom and capable of tolerating it. I shall present below one of the means that might be used to this end. It would be rash of me to guarantee its success, although I do not doubt it. If there is some better means, let it be adopted. But regardless of what it may be, recognize that your serfs are men like yourselves, that they have in them the stuff to become all that you are: work, first of all, at activating it, and emancipate their bodies only once you have emancipated their souls. Without this preliminary, be prepared for your operation to turn out badly.

[975]
[7] MEANS OF MAINTAINING THE CONSTITUTION

[1] Poland's legislation was made successively by bits and pieces, like all legislations in Europe. When an abuse was noticed, a law was made to remedy it. That law gave rise to other abuses which had to be corrected in turn. This way of going about it is endless, and it leads to the most terrible abuse of all, which is to debilitate all the laws by dint of multiplying their number.

[2] In Poland the weakening of legislation happened in a rather singular and possibly unique way. Indeed, it lost its force without having been subjugated by the executive power. Even now the legislative power still retains its full authority; it is inactive, but sees nothing above it. The Diet is as sovereign as it was when it was first established. Yet it is without force; nothing dominates it, but nothing obeys it. This state of affairs is remarkable and deserves reflection.

[3] What has preserved the legislative authority up to the present? It is the continuous presence of the lawgiver. It is the frequency of the Diets, the frequent renewal [of the mandates] of the Deputies that have maintained the Republic. England, which enjoys the first of these advantages, lost its freedom for having neglected the other. One and the same Parliament sits for so long, that the Court, which

would exhaust its resources buying it every year, finds it profitable to buy it for seven years, and does not fail to do so. Your first lesson.

[4] A second means by which the legislative power has been preserved iǹ Poland is, in the first place, the division of the executive power, which has prevented its trustees from acting in concert to oppress it, and in the second place the frequent passing of this same executive power through diffcrent hands: which has checked every sustained system[atic policy] of usurpation. Each King took some steps in the direction of arbitrary power in the course of his reign. [976] But his successor, since he is elected, was forced to move backward instead of forward; and at the beginning of each reign your Kings were all constrained by the *pacta conventa* to start out at the same point. So that in spite of the habitual slope toward despotism, there was no real progress made [in that direction].

[5] The same was true of the ministers and the high officials. All of them, since they are independent of the Senate as well as of one another, enjoyed boundless authority in their respective departments: but these offices, since they balanced one another and were not perpetuated in the same families, did not concentrate absolute force in them; and all power, even when usurped, always returned to its source. Things would not have been the same if the entire executive power had resided either in a single Body such as the Senate, or in a single family through inheritance of the crown. This family or this body would probably sooner or later have oppressed the legislative power and thus placed the Poles under the yoke which all nations bear, and of which the Poles alone are still free: for I have already ceased to count Sweden. Your second lesson.

[6] This is the advantage; it is unquestionably great, but here is the inconvenience, which is scarcely lesser. The executive power divided among several individuals lacks harmony between its parts, and causes a continual tug-of-war which is incompatible with good order. Each trustee of a portion of this power, by virtue of this one portion, sets himself above the magistrates and the laws in all respects. It is true that he recognizes the authority of the Diet; but since it is the only authority he recognizes, when the Diet is dissolved he no longer recognizes any authority at all; he despises the courts and defies their judgments. They are so many petty Despots who, without exactly usurping the sovereign authority, nevertheless

oppress the Citizens piecemeal, and set the fatal and all too frequently followed example of violating without scruple or fear the rights and the freedom of individuals.

[7] I believe that this is the first and principal cause of the anarchy that reigns in the State. I see but one way to eliminate it. It is not to arm individual tribunals with the public force against these petty tyrants; for this force, sometimes because it is badly administered and sometimes because it is overwhelmed by a superior force, might [977] stir up troubles and disorders which could gradually lead to civil wars: but, [instead], to arm with the full executive force some respectable and permanent body, such as the Senate, capable by its solidity and authority to hold to their duty Magnates tempted to stray from it. This seems to me an effective way, and it would certainly be so; but its attendant danger would be terrible and extremely difficult to avoid. For as can be seen in the *Social Contract*, every body entrusted with the executive power has a strong and steady tendency to subjugate the legislative power, and sooner or later succeeds in doing so.

[8] To guard against this inconvenience, you have been advised to divide the Senate into several councils or departments, each presided over by the Minister in charge of that department; which Minister together with the members of each Council would change at the end of a fixed time and rotate with those of the other departments. The idea might be good; it was that of the Abbé de Saint-Pierre, and he developed it at length in his *Polysynodie*. The executive power thus divided and temporary will be more subordinate to the legislative, and the various parts of the administration will be dealt with more thoroughly and better for being dealt with separately. However, do not rely on this means too much: if the various parts of the administration are always separated, they will fail to act in concert, and soon, working at cross-purposes, they will use up almost all their forces against one another, until one of them gains ascendancy and dominates them all: or else, if they do agree and act in concert, they will really constitute but a single body and be of one mind, like the houses of a Parliament; and in any event, I regard it impossible for independence and balance to be maintained so well between them that their division does not invariably result in a center of administration in which all particular forces will invariably unite to oppress the sovereign. In almost all of our

republics, the Councils are divided in this fashion into departments which originally were independent of one another, and soon ceased to be so.

[9] The invention of this division by chambers or departments is modern. The ancients who knew better how to maintain freedom than do we were not acquainted [*978*] with this expedient. The Roman Senate ruled half the known world, and had not so much as the idea of these divisions. Yet this Senate never succeeded in oppressing the legislative power, although the Senators held office for life. But the laws had Censors, the People had Tribunes, and the Senate did not elect the Consuls.

[10] For the administration to be strong, good and efficient in the pursuit of its aims, the entire executive power has to be in the same hands: but it is not enough that these hands change; if possible they should act only under the eyes of the Lawgiver and that it be he who guides them. This is the true secret of keeping them from usurping his authority.

[11] So long as the Estates meet and the Deputies change frequently, it will be difficult to have the Senate or the King oppress or usurp the legislative authority. It is striking that the Kings have so far not attempted to make the Diets less frequent, although they are not forced, as are the Kings of England, to convene them frequently on pain of running out of money. Things must either always have been in a state of crisis which rendered the royal authority inadequate to attend to them, or the Kings had made sure by their intrigues in the Dietines of always having the majority of Deputies at their disposal, or, because of the *liberum veto*, they were sure of always being able to put an end to deliberations that might displease them and to dissolve the Diets at will. Once all these motives no longer obtain, the King, or the Senate, or both together, may be expected to make great efforts to rid themselves of the Diets and to make them as infrequent as possible. It is this, above all, that has to be forestalled and prevented. The means which I propose is the only one, it is simple, and it cannot fail to be effective. It is rather odd that prior to the *Social Contract*, where I present it, it had not occurred to anyone.

[12] One of the greatest inconveniences of large States, the one which more than any other makes it most difficult to preserve freedom in them, is that in them the legislative power cannot show

itself as such, and can act only by delegation. This has both bad and good aspects, but the bad aspects predominate. The Lawgiver as a body is impossible to corrupt, but easy to deceive. [*979*] Its representatives are difficult to deceive, but easily corrupted, and it rarely happens that they are not corrupted. You have before your eyes the example of the English Parliament and, because of the *liberum veto*, that of your own nation. Now someone who errs can be enlightened, but how can someone who is for sale be restrained? Without being well informed about Polish affairs, I would wager anything that there is more enlightenment in the Diet and more virtue in the Dietines.

[13] I see two means of preventing this terrible evil of corruption, which turns the organ of freedom into the instrument of servitude.

[14] The first, as I have already said, is frequent Diets, which by often changing representatives makes it more costly and more difficult to seduce them. On this point your constitution is better than that of Great Britain, and once the *liberum veto* has been abolished or modified, I see no other change that needs to be made, lest it be to add a few obstacles to returning the same representatives to two consecutive Diets, and to prevent their being elected a great many times. I shall return to this topic below.

[15] The second means is to require the representatives to adhere exactly to their instructions, and to render a strict account of their conduct in the Diet to their constituents. As regards this, I can only marvel at the negligence, the carelessness, and I dare say the stupidity of the English Nation which, after arming its deputies with the supreme power, adds not a single restraint to regulate the use they might make of it during the entire seven years of their mandate.

[16] I see that the Poles are not sufficiently sensible of the importance of their Dietines, neither of all they owe them nor of all they can obtain from them by expanding their authority and by giving them a more regular form. For my own part, I am convinced that while the Confederations saved the fatherland, the Dietines preserved it, and that they are the true Palladium of freedom.

[17] The Deputies' instructions should be drawn up with great care, with respect to the topics announced in the agenda, as well as to the other current needs of the State and the Province, and this should be done by a commission presided over, if necessary,

by the Marshal of the Dietine, [*980*] but for the rest made up of members chosen by majority vote; and the nobility should not disband until these instructions have been read, discussed and approved in plenary session. In addition to the original copy of these instructions, handed to the Deputies together with their credentials, a copy signed by them should be deposited in the records of the Dietine. It is on the basis of these instructions that they ought upon their return to give an account of their conduct to the report-session of the Dietine which should absolutely be restored, and it is on the basis of this accounting that they should either be excluded from ever again being deputies, or be declared eligible again if they have followed their instructions to their constituents' satisfaction. This scrutiny is of the utmost importance. It cannot be conducted too attentively, nor can its results be recorded too carefully. The Deputy must, with every word he speaks in the Diet, with every action he takes, anticipate himself under the scrutiny of his constituents, and sense the influence their judgment will have on his projects for advancement as well as on the esteem of his fellow citizens, which is indispensable for the realization of these projects of his: for after all the Nation sends Deputies to the Diet not in order to have them state their private sentiment but to declare the wills of the Nation. This restraint is absolutely necessary to hold them to their duty and to prevent all corruption, from whatever quarter it might come. Regardless of what might be said on this subject, I see no inconvenience in this constraint, for the chamber of Deputies, since it has or should have no part in the detail of administration, cannot ever have to deal with an unforeseen matter: besides, so long as a deputy does nothing contrary to the express will of his constituents, they would not hold it against him that he voted like a good Citizen on a matter they had not anticipated, and on which they had reached no decision. I add, finally, that even if it did entail some inconvenience to keep the Deputies thus subordinated to their instructions, there would still be no comparison between it and the immense advantage of never having the law be anything but the real expression of the nation's wills.

[18] But then, once these precautions have been taken, no conflict of jurisdiction should ever arise between the Diet and the Dietines, and when a law has been carried in the plenary Diet I do not even concede to the Dietines the right to protest. Let them [*981*] punish

their deputies, if necessary let them even cut off their heads if they have prevaricated: but let them obey fully, always, without exception, without protest, let them bear, as it is just that they should, the penalty of their bad choice; while allowing them to make as lively representations as they please at the next Diet, if they think it appropriate.

[19] Since the Diets are frequent, there is less need that they be long, and six weeks' duration seems to me quite sufficient for the ordinary needs of the State. But it is self-contradictory for the sovereign authority to place restrictions on itself, especially when it is immediately in the hands of the nation. Let the duration of ordinary diets continue to be fixed at six weeks, by all means; but it will always remain up to the assembly to prolong this term by an express decision when business requires it. For, after all, when the Diet, which by its nature is above the law, says *I want to stay*, who is there to tell it, *I do not want you to stay*. Only in case a Diet would wish to last more than two years, it could not do so: its powers would then end and those of another Diet begin in the third year. The Diet, since it can do anything, can unquestionably prescribe a longer interval between Diets: but this new law could only apply to subsequent Diets, and the Diet which passes it cannot take advantage of it. The principles from which these rules can be deduced are established in the *Social Contract*.

[20] As regards extraordinary Diets, orderly procedure requires that they indeed be infrequent, and called only in situations of urgent necessity. When the King judges that such a situation exists, I admit that he must be believed: but such situations might exist without his conceding that that they do; should the Senate then judge? In a free State, everything that might threaten freedom has to be anticipated. If the Confederations are retained, they can in some cases take the place of extra-ordinary Diets: but if you abolish the Confederations, provisions will necessarily have to be made for such Diets.

[21] It seems to me impossible for the law reasonably to fix the duration of the extraordinary Diets, since they are absolutely dependent on the nature of the business for which they are called. Ordinarily such business requires dispatch [*982*]; but since dispatch is here relative to the matters requiring attention which are not integral to the regular routine of business, nothing can be legislated

about them in advance, and a state of affairs might arise which made it important for the Diet to remain in session until this state has changed, or until the [next regular] term of the ordinary Diets causes the powers of this [extraordinary] one to expire.

[22] In order to husband the Diets' precious time, one should try to rid these assemblies of idle discussions which only make for a waste of time. To be sure, Diets have to have not only rule and order, but also ceremony and majesty. I should even like this topic attended to with particular care and, for example, to have people sensitized to the barbarity and awful indecency of seeing the sanctuary of the laws profaned by the bearing of arms. Poles, are you more warlike than the Romans? yet never in the times of greatest trouble in their Republic did the sight of a sword defile the assemblies or the Senate. But I should also wish that by concentrating on important and necessary things, one avoid [attending in the Diet to] anything that can equally well get done elsewhere. For example, the Rugi, that is to say the review of the Deputies' legitimacy, is a waste of time in the Diet: not that this review is not in itself important, but because it can be conducted as well and better in the very place where the Deputies were elected, where they are best known and where they have all their rivals. It is in their own Palatinate, it is in the Dietine which delegates them that the validity of their election can be verified better and in less time, as is the practice regarding the commissioners of Radom and the Deputies to the Tribunal. This done, the Diet should admit them without discussion on the basis of the Laudum they present, in order to avoid not only the obstacles that might delay the election of the Marshal, but above all the intrigues by which the Senate or the King might interfere with the elections and challenge subjects who might not be to their liking. What recently took place in London is a lesson for the Poles. I know well enough that this Wilkes is just a troublemaker; but disqualifying him establishes the precedent, and from now on only subjects acceptable to the Court will be admitted to the House of Commons.

[*983*] [23] One should begin by paying more attention to the choice of members with a vote in the Dietines. This would make it easier to identify those who are eligible to be deputies. The Golden Book of Venice is a model that should be followed because of its simplicity. It would be convenient and very easy to maintain

in each Grod a precise register of all the nobles who meet the qualifications required to attend and vote in the Dietines. They would
be entered in the register of their district as they reach the age
specified by the laws, and remove those who should be excluded
from it as soon as that is called for, recording the reason for their
exclusion. By means of these registers, which would have to be
authenticated in some form, the legitimate members of the Dietines
as well as the subjects eligible to be deputies could easily be identified, and this would greatly reduce the length of the debates on
this topic.

[24] Improved administration of the Diets and Dietines would
certainly be most useful; but, I cannot repeat it too often, one
should not will two contradictory things at once. Administration is
good, but freedom is better, and the more you cramp freedom with
formalities, the more means of usurpation will these formalities furnish. All the means you adopt to prevent license in the legislative
order, good though they may be in themselves, will sooner or later
be used to oppress it. Long and empty harangues which waste such
precious time are a great evil, but it is a much greater evil for a
good Citizen not to dare to speak when he has useful things to say.
As soon as only certain people open their mouths in the Diets, and
even they are forbidden to say everything, they will no longer say
anything but what might please the powerful.

[25] Once the indispensable changes in appointments to office
and in the distribution of favors have been made, fewer empty harangues and fawning flatteries are likely to be addressed to the King
in this form. Still, in order to cut down on the rambling and gibber-
ish somewhat, every haranguer might be required to state at the
beginning of his speech the proposition he wants to advance, and,
after he has spelled out his argument, to give a summary of his
conclusions, as the King's men do in the law-courts. Even if this
did not shorten [*984*] speeches, it would at least restrain those who
only want to talk for the sake of talking, and to take up time doing
nothing.

[26] I do not fully know the Diets' established form for sanc-
tioning laws; but I do know that for reasons stated above, it should
not be the same form as that in the Parliament of Great Britain;
that the Senate of Poland should have administrative, not legislative
authority, that in all legislative matters the Senators should vote

solely as members of the Diet, not as members of the Senate, and that the votes should be tallied by counting heads in both chambers alike. The use of the *liberum veto* may have stood in the way of drawing this distinction, but it will be very necessary once the *liberum veto* has been abolished, and it will be all the more necessary as abolishing the *liberum veto* will deprive the chamber of Deputies of an immense advantage, for I do not suppose that the Senators, let alone the Ministers, ever shared in this right. The *veto* of the Polish Deputies corresponds to that of the Tribunes of the people in Rome. Now the Tribunes did not exercise this right as Citizens, but as Representatives of the Roman People. The loss of the *liberum veto* is therefore a loss only for the chamber of Deputies, and the body of the Senate, since it loses nothing by it, consequently gains by it.

[27] This being so, I see one defect in the Diet which calls for correction; namely that since the number of Senators almost equals the number of Deputies, the Senate has too much influence in the deliberations [of the Diet], and by its prestige in the knightly order it can easily win the small number of voices it needs in order always to prevail.

[28] I say that this is a defect; for the Senate, being a particular body in the State, necessarily has corporate interests different from those of the nation, and which may even in certain respects be contrary to them. Now the law, which is but the expression of the general will, is indeed the resultant of all the particular interests combined and in balance by virtue of their large number. But corporate interests, because of their excessive weight, would upset the balance, and should not be included in it collectively. Each individual should have his vote, no [corporate] body whatsoever should have one. Now if the Senate carried too much weight in the Diet, it would not only bring its own interest to bear on it, but make it prevail.

[*985*] [29] A natural remedy for this defect suggests itself; it is to increase the number of Deputies; but I would be afraid that this might make for too much agitation in the State and come too close to Democratic tumult. If it should prove absolutely necessary to change the proportion, then instead of increasing the number of Deputies, I would prefer to decrease the number of Senators. And basically, I do not quite see why, since there already is one Palatin at the head of each province, there is still need for great Castellans. But let us never lose sight of the important maxim not

to change anything unnecessarily, neither by subtracting nor by adding.

[30] It is preferable, in my opinion, to have a less numerous Council and to leave those who make it up more freedom, than to increase their number and cramp their freedom of deliberation, as one is invariably forced to do when this number grows too large: to which I will add, if I may be permitted to anticipate the good as well as the bad, that one should avoid making the Diet as large as it can be in order not to deprive oneself of the means of some day admitting to it new Deputies without [thereby creating] confusion, if ever it comes to ennobling the Cities and emancipating the serfs, as is to be desired for the sake of the nation's force and happiness.

[31] Let us therefore look for a means to remedy this defect in some other way and with the least change possible.

[32] All Senators are appointed by the King, and hence are his creatures. Moreover, they are appointed for life, and on this basis they form a body independent both of the King and of the knightly order which, as I have said, has its own separate interest and must tend to usurpation. And I should not here be accused of contradicting myself because I recognize the Senate as a distinct body in the Republic, although I do not recognize it as a component order of the Republic; for the two are very different.

[33] First, the King ought to be deprived of [the right of] appointing the Senate, not so much because of the power he thereby retains over the Senators, which may not be great, as because of the power he has over all those who aspire to be Senators, and through them over the entire body of the Nation. In addition to the effect of this change on the constitution, it will have the inestimable advantage of moderating the courtier spirit among the nobility, [986] and substituting the patriotic spirit for it. I see no inconvenience in having the Senators appointed by the Diet, and I see in it many benefits too obvious to require detailed description. Such an appointment could be made either all at once in the Diet, or, initially, in the Dietines, by nominating a certain number of subjects for each vacancy in their respective Palatinates. Of these, the Diet would [then] choose or elect a smaller number, among whom the king might still be left the right to choose. But to go straightway to the simplest [solution], why should not each Palatin be elected directly by the Dietine of his province? What inconvenience has

arisen from this way of electing the Paladins of Polock and of Witebsk, or the Starost of Samogitia, and what would be the harm if the privilege of these three provinces became a right common to all provinces? Let us not lose sight of how important it is for Poland to turn its constitution in the direction of the federative form, in order to set aside as much as possible the evils that attach to the greatness or rather to the size of the State.

[34] In the second place, if you see to it that Senators are no longer for life you will substantially weaken the corporate interest which tends to usurpation. But this operation is attended by difficulties of its own: first, because it is hard for men accustomed to manage public affairs to find themselves suddenly reduced to the private state without any failing on their part; second, because the positions of Senators are tied to the titles of Palatin and of Castellan together with the local authority that attaches to them, and the constant transfer of these titles and this authority from one individual to another would lead to disorder and discontents. Finally, such term limits cannot be extended to Bishops, and perhaps they ought not to be extended to [cabinet] Ministers whose positions call for special talents and are therefore not always easy to fill well. However, if only Bishops held office for life, then the authority of the clergy, which is already excessive, would substantially increase, and it is important that this authority be counterbalanced by Senators who, like the Bishops, hold office for life and no more fear being removed than they do.

[35] Here is what I would imagine as a remedy for these various inconveniences. I should like the positions of the Senators of [*987*] the first rank to continue to be for life. This, including besides the Bishops and the Paladins, all the Castellans of the first rank, would amount to eighty-nine Senators without term limits.

[36] As for the Castellans of the second rank, I should like all of them to serve for a fixed term, either for two years, with new elections for each Diet, or for longer if that is what is judged to be indicated; but always leaving office at the end of each term, if only to have re-elected those whom the Diet would like to retain, something I would permit only a limited number of times, according to the project that will be found below.

[37] Titles would be a weak obstacle, for since these titles confer

almost no other function than sitting in the Senate, they could be abolished without inconvenience, and instead of the title senatorial Castellans they would simply bear that of Senator-deputies. Since, with the reform [just outlined], the Senate, vested with the executive power, would have a certain number of its members permanently assembled, a proportion of Senator-deputies would be required also always to attend it on a rotating basis. But this is not the place for such details.

[38] With this scarcely sensible change, these Castellans or Senator-deputies would really become so many representatives of the Diet who would act as a counterweight to the body of the Senate and reinforce the knightly order in the assemblies of the Nation; so that the Senators for life, although they will have become more powerful by the abolition of the *veto* as much as by the reduction of the royal and the Ministers' power which has been partly merged into their own body, could nevertheless not dominate the spirit of the Senate, and this body, thus composed half of members for a term and half of members for life, would be constituted in the best way possible to act as an intermediate power between the chamber of Deputies and the King, since it would be sufficiently solid to regulate the administration, and at the same time sufficiently dependent to be subject to the laws. The operation strikes me as good, because it is simple and yet far-reaching in its effects.

[39] I do not pause here to consider how votes are to be tallied. It is not difficult to regulate in an assembly composed of about three hundred members. They manage it in London, in a much larger Parliament; in Geneva, where the General Council is still larger, and everyone lives in suspicion of everyone else; and even in Venice in the Great Council composed of some twelve hundred nobles, where vice and knavery are enthroned. Besides, I have discussed this matter in the *Social Contract*, and anyone prepared to take account of my opinion may look for it there.

[40] It has been suggested, as a means of mitigating the abuses of the *veto*, that the Deputies' votes no longer be counted by the head but by Palatinates. Such a change should be considered with the utmost care before being adopted, in spite of [*988*] its advantages and of its being favorable to the federative form. Aggregated and collective votes always point less directly to the common

interest than do separate votes, individual by individual. Very often among the Deputies of a Palatinate there is one who, in their private deliberations, will assume ascendancy over the others, and sway to his opinion a majority which would not have sided with him if each vote had remained independent. Corruptors will thus have less to do and know better whom to approach; moreover, it is preferable to have each Deputy answerable for himself alone in his Dietine, so that no one can invoke the others as an excuse, the innocent and the guilty not be confused, and distributive justice be better observed. Many reasons come to mind against this collective form of voting which would greatly loosen the common bond, and could threaten the State with division in every Diet. By making the Deputies more dependent on their instructions and their constituents one achieves more or less the same advantage without any inconvenience. This assumes, it is true, that votes are cast not by ballot but by voice, so that the conduct and opinion of each Deputy to the Diet may be known, and that he may answer for them in his own and personal name. But since this matter of voting is among those I discussed with the greatest care in the *Social Contract*, it is superfluous to repeat it here.

[41] As for elections, it may perhaps at first prove somewhat difficult to appoint so many Senator-deputies all at once in each Diet, and in general to elect a large number from an even larger number as the project I propose will periodically require: but on this point, recourse to the ballot, distributing to the electorate on the eve of the election printed and numbered cards listing the names of all the candidates, would easily eliminate this difficulty. The following day the electors would come in a file and drop all their cards in a basket, having marked, each one on his own card, those for and those against whom he votes, according to the instructions at the top of the card. These cards would be read off right away in the presence of the assembly by the secretary of the Diet assisted by two additional [989] secretaries *ad actum* named then and there by the Marshal from among the Deputies present. Following this method the operation would take so little time and be so simple that without any argument or noise the entire Senate would easily be filled in a single session. It is true that a rule would still be needed to draw up the list of candidates; but that topic will have its proper place and will not be forgotten.

[42] It remains to speak of the King, who presides over the Diet, and who by virtue of his office ought to be the supreme administrator of the Laws.

[8] OF THE KING

[1] It is a great evil for the Chief of a nation to be the born enemy of the freedom whose defender he should be. This evil is not, in my view, so intrinsic to the office that it cannot be separated from it, or at least considerably reduced. Where there is no hope there is no temptation. Make usurpation impossible for your Kings, you will keep them from fantasizing about it; and they will devote to governing you well and defending you all the efforts they now bend on enslaving you. The Founders of Poland did, as Count Wielhorski has observed, give thought to depriving Kings of the means of doing harm but not of the means of corrupting, and the favors at their disposal give them ample means to do so. The difficulty is that to deprive them of the granting of favors would seem to deprive them of everything: yet this is precisely what one ought not to do; for it would be tantamount to not having a King at all, and I believe it impossible for so large a State as Poland to do without one; that is to say of a supreme chief who holds office for life. Now unless the chief of a nation is a complete non-entity, and hence useless, he has to be in a position to do something, and however little he does do, it must necessarily be either good or evil.

[2] At present the King appoints the entire Senate: that is too much. If he has no share in appointing it, that is not enough. Although the Peerage in England is also appointed by the King, it is much less dependent on him because the Peerage, once granted, is heredi[990]tary, whereas Bishoprics, Palatinates and Castellanships, being for life only, revert to the King for his appointment on the death of each incumbent.

[3] I have said how it seems to me that these appointments should be made, namely the Palatins and grand Castellans for life by their respective Dietines; the Castellans of the second rank for a [specific] term and by the Diet. With regard to the Bishops, it seems to me difficult to deprive the King of their appointment, unless it be to have them elected by their chapters, and I believe that their

appointment may be left to him, except, however, that of the Archbishop of Gniezno, which naturally appertains to the Diet, unless the Archbishopric is separated from the office of Primate which should be solely at the disposal of the Diet. As for the Ministers, above all the ranking Generals and the heads of the Treasury, although their power, which acts as a counterweight to the King's, should be reduced in proportion to his, it does not seem to me prudent to leave to the King the right to fill these positions with his creatures, and I should at least wish that he be restricted to choosing from a small number of subjects submitted by the Diet. I admit that since he can no longer withdraw these offices once he has granted them, he can no longer absolutely count on those who fill them: but the power they give him over candidates is sufficient, if not to put him in a position to change the face of the government, at least to leave him the hope of doing so, and it is above all of this hope that it matters to deprive him at all cost.

[4] As for the Grand Chancellor, he should, in my view, be appointed by the King. Kings are the born judges of their people; this is the function for which they were established in the first place, although they have all given it up: they cannot be deprived of it; and when they choose not to perform it themselves, it is within their right to appoint their substitutes to this position, since it is always they who must answer for judgments handed down in their name. The nation can, it is true, give them associate justices, and it must do so when they themselves do not act as judges: thus the Crown's Court which is presided over not by the King, but by the Grand Chancellor, is under the supervision of the nation, and it is right that the Dietines should appoint its other members. If the King gave justice in person, I hold that he would have the right to be sole judge. In any case, it would always be in his interest to be just, and unjust judgments [991] have never proven to be a good way to achieve usurpation.

[5] With respect to the other dignities, the Crown's as well as the Palatinates', which are merely honorific titles and confer more glitter than credit, one cannot do better than to leave them fully at the King's disposal: let him honor merit and flatter vanity, but let him not be in a position to confer power.

[6] The majesty of the throne should be maintained with splendor, but it is important that of all the outlay required to that

end, as little as possible be left up to the King. It would be desirable for all of the King's officials to be on the Republic's payroll rather than on his own, and for all royal revenues to be reduced proportionately, so as to minimize as far as possible the flow of cash through the King's hands.

[7] It has been suggested that the Crown be made hereditary. Be assured that the moment this law is enacted, Poland can bid farewell forever to its freedom. They think that freedom can be sufficiently provided for by limiting the royal power. They fail to see that in the course of time these bounds set by the laws will be transgressed by gradual usurpations, and that a system adopted and uninterruptedly followed by a royal family is bound in the long run to win out over a law which by its nature constantly tends to slacken. If the King cannot corrupt the Great by favors, he can always corrupt them with promises to be redeemed by his successors, and since the plans formed by the royal family are perpetuated together with the family itself, people will trust its commitments and count on their being fulfilled much more than when the elective crown plainly shows that the monarch's projects end with his life. Poland is free because every reign is preceded by an interval during which the nation, restored to all its rights and resuming renewed vigor, makes a sharp break with the progress of abuses and usurpations, during which legislation rewinds itself and resumes its initial resilience. What will become of the *pacta conventa*, the aegis of Poland, when a family established on the throne in perpetuity will occupy it without interruption and leaves the nation, between the death of the father and the crowning of the son, nothing but an empty, ineffectual shadow of freedom which will soon be destroyed by the pretense of the oath sworn by [992] all Kings upon their coronation, and by all of them forever forgotten the next moment? You have seen Denmark, you see England, and you shall see Sweden. Profit from these examples to learn once and for all that regardless of how many precautions one might pile one on top of the other, heredity in the throne and freedom in the nation will forever be incompatible.

[8] The Poles have always had a tendency to transmit the Crown from Father to son, or to those next in the line of succession, though always according to the right of election. This inclination, if they continue to follow it, will sooner or later lead them to the misfortune of rendering the crown hereditary, and once it is they cannot

hope to struggle against royal power as the members of the Holy Roman Empire have struggled against the Emperor's power, because Poland has not within it a counter-weight sufficient to keep a hereditary King subordinate to the laws. In spite of the power of several members of the Empire, if it had not been for the chance election of Charles VII, the imperial capitulations would by now be an empty formula, as they were at the beginning of the century; and the *Pacta Conventa* will become emptier still, once the royal family will have had the time to establish itself more solidly and to put down all the others. To state my sentiment on this subject in a word, I think that an elective Crown even with the most absolute power would still be preferable for Poland to a hereditary Crown with almost no power.

[9] In place of this fateful law which would make the Crown hereditary I would suggest one to the opposite effect which, if adopted, would preserve Poland's freedom. Namely to establish by a fundamental law that the Crown never pass from father to son, and that every son of a King of Poland be forever excluded from the throne. I say that I would suggest this law if it were necessary: but as I have a project in mind which would achieve the same effect without it, I defer the explanation of this project to its proper place, and on the assumption that it has the effect of excluding sons, at least immediately, from their fathers' throne, I believe that a well secured freedom will not be the only advantage resulting from this exclusion. It will give rise to [993] this further very considerable advantage: that by depriving Kings of all hope of usurping arbitrary power and passing it on to their children, it will bend all their energies upon glory and the prosperity of the State, the only prospect left open to their ambition. This is how the Nation's Chief will no longer be its born enemy, but become its foremost Citizen. This is how he will make it his guiding concern to render his reign illustrious by useful institutions which will endear him to his people, earn him his neighbors' respect, cause his memory to be blessed after him, and this, not with the means to harm and to seduce which must never be left in his hands, is how his power should be increased in all matters that might contribute to the public good. He will have little immediate and direct force to act on his own, but he will have much authority to supervise and to inspect, to hold everyone to his duty and to point the Government

to its true end. To preside over the Diet, the Senate and all corporate groups, to keep a strict watch over all office-holders, to exercise great care to maintain justice and integrity in all law-courts, to preserve order and tranquility within the State, to secure it a good position with the outside, commanding its armies in time of war, attending to useful projects in time of peace, these are duties particularly related to his office of king, and which will keep him sufficiently occupied if he tries to perform them on his own; for since the details of administration are entrusted to Ministers appointed for this purpose, it should be a crime for a King of Poland to entrust any part of his own [administrative functions] to favorites. Let him do his job in person, or else give it up. An important point on which the nation ought never to yield.

[10] It is on such principles that the balance and equipoise of the powers that make up legislation and administration should be established. These powers, in the hands of their trustees and in the best ratio possible, should vary directly with the number of those who hold them, and inversely with how long they hold them. The parts making up the Diet will approximate this optimum relation quite closely. The chamber of Deputies, being the more numerous, will also be the more powerful, but its entire membership will change frequently. The Senate, being the less numerous, will have a lesser share in legislation, but [994] a greater share in the executive power, and its members, since they participate in the constitution at both extremes will, some of them, be for limited terms, and some of them for life, as befits an intermediary body. The King, who presides over everything, will continue to be so for life, and his power, which remains very great as regards inspection, will be limited by the chamber of Deputies as regards legislation, and by the Senate as regards administration. But in order to maintain equality, the principle of the constitution, nothing should be hereditary in it save the nobility. If the Crown were hereditary, then, in order to maintain the balance, the Peerage or the Senatorial order would have to be so as well, as it is in England. In which case the diminished knightly order would lose its power because the Chamber of deputies, unlike the House of Commons, has not the power annually to open and to close the public purse, and the Polish constitution would be completely overthrown.

[9] SPECIFIC CAUSES OF ANARCHY

[1] The Diet, well balanced and equipoised in this fashion in all its parts, will be the source of good legislation and good government. But this requires that its orders be respected and followed. The contempt for laws and the anarchy in which Poland has lived up to now are due to causes that are easy to see. I have already pointed out the principal one above, and indicated the remedy. The other contributing causes are, (1) the *liberum veto*, (2) the confederations, and (3) the abuse by private individuals of the right they have been left to keep armed men in their service.

[2] This last abuse is such that, if it is not eliminated from the outset, all other reforms will prove useless. So long as private individuals have the power to resist the executive force, they will believe they have the right to do so, and so long as they engage in small wars with one another, how can the State be at peace? I admit that strongholds require garrisons; but what is the need for strongholds that are strong only against Citizens and [995] weak against the enemy? I am afraid that this reform will meet with difficulties; however, I do not believe that they are insuperable, and provided a powerful Citizen is but reasonable, he will readily consent no longer to keep armed men of his own once no one else has any.

[3] I intend to speak about military establishments in the sequel; I therefore refer to that section what I might have to say [about it] in this one.

[4] The *liberum veto* is not in itself a vicious right, but as soon as it exceeds its bounds it becomes the most dangerous of abuses: it used to be the guarantor of public freedom; now it is nothing but the instrument of oppression. The only way to eliminate this fatal abuse is to destroy its cause entirely. But the human heart is such that it clings to personal privilege more than to greater and more general advantages. Only a patriotism enlightened by experience can learn to sacrifice for the sake of greater goods a brilliant right grown pernicious through abuse, and henceforth inseparable from that abuse. All Poles must feel keenly the evils which this wretched right has made them suffer. If they love order and peace, they have no way to establish either in their midst as long as they allow this right to remain in effect among them, a right that is good during the formation of the body politic or when it is in its full

perfection, but that is absurd and fatal so long as changes remain to be made, and it is impossible that there not always remain some changes to be made, above all in a great State surrounded by powerful and ambitious neighbors.

[5] The *liberum veto* would be less unreasonable if it applied exclusively to the fundamental points of the constitution: but its being available indiscriminately in all deliberations of the Diets, that is altogether inadmissible. One of the vices of the Polish constitution is that it fails to distinguish sufficiently clearly between legislation and administration, and that in the course of exercising legislative power, the Diet mixes in bits of administration, performing indifferently acts of sovereignty and acts of government, often even mixed acts in which its members are simultaneously magistrates and legislators.

[6] The proposed changes tend to distinguish more clearly between these two powers and thus to mark the limits of the *liberum veto* more clearly. For I do not believe that [996] it ever entered anyone's mind to extend it to matters of pure administration, which would amount to annihilating civil authority and all government.

[7] By the natural right of societies unanimity was required for the formation of the body politic and for the fundamental laws that bear on its existence, such as, for example, the first one as corrected, the fifth, the ninth, and the eleventh, enacted by the pseudo-Diet of 1768. Now the unanimity required to establish these laws should equally be required for their abrogation. These, then, are points with regard to which the *liberum veto* may continue to apply, and since it is not a question of doing away with it entirely, the Poles who, without much grumbling, saw this right restricted by the illegal Diet of 1768 should not be troubled to see it reduced and limited by a freer and more legitimate Diet.

[8] The principal points to be established as fundamental laws must be carefully weighed and considered, and they are the only points on which the force of the *liberum veto* will be brought to bear. This way the constitution will be made as solid and these laws as irrevocable as they can be: for it is contrary to the nature of the body politic to impose upon itself laws which it cannot revoke; but it is not contrary to nature or to reason that it should be able to revoke these laws only with as much formality as it took to establish them. That is the only chain it can impose on itself for the future.

It suffices to consolidate the Constitution and to satisfy the Poles' love for the *liberum veto*, without later exposing them to the abuses to which it has given rise.

[9] As for the innumerable articles which have foolishly been included among the fundamental laws, and which merely make up the body of laws, as well as for all the articles classified under the heading "matters of State," they are, given the variable course of things, subject to unavoidable changes which preclude requiring unanimity for them. Furthermore it is absurd that on any question whatsoever a single member of the Diet should be able to bring its operation to a halt, and that the retirement or the protests of one or several Deputies should be able to dissolve the assembly and thus to break up the sovereign authority. This barbarous right must be abolished and the death penalty imposed on anyone who might be tempted to exercise it. If there were occasions for protest against the Diet, which cannot happen so long as [997] it is free and plenary, then this right might be conferred on the Palatinates and the Dietines, but never on Deputies who, as members of the Diet, should not have the slightest authority over it nor challenge its decisions.

[10] Between the *veto* which is the greatest individual force the members of the sovereign power can have and which should only be exercised with respect to genuinely fundamental laws, and a bare majority, which is the least force they can have and which applies to simple administrative matters, there are any number of proportions at which the required majority can be set, depending on the importance of the matters [under consideration]. For example, when it comes to legislation, one might require at least a three quarters majority, two thirds in matters of State, no more than a bare majority for elections and other business of routine and immediate interest. This is merely an example to explain my idea and not a proportion I am laying down.

[11] In a State like Poland where souls still have great resilience, it might have been possible to preserve this fine right of *liberum veto* in its entirety without much risk, and perhaps even with some benefit, provided it had been made dangerous to exercise it, and severe consequences attached to it for anyone availing himself of it. For, I dare say, it is outrageous that anyone who thus breaks up the operation of the Diet and leaves the State without recourse

should go home to enjoy tranquilly and with impunity the public havoc he has wrought.

[12] If, then, in the event of an almost unanimous resolution, a single opponent retained the right to annul it, I would wish him to be answerable for his opposition with his head, not only to his constituents in the post-session Dietine, but also subsequently to the entire nation whose misfortune he brought on. I should like it to be required by law that six months after his opposition he be solemnly tried by an extraordinary tribunal established solely to this end, made up of all the nation's wisest, most illustrious and most respected persons, which could not simply acquit him, but would either have to condemn him to death without possible pardon, or to bestow upon him a reward and public honors for life, without ever being able to adopt a middle course between these two alternatives.

[998] [13] Institutions of this kind, so favorable to energizing courage and the love of freedom, are too remote from the modern spirit to allow the hope that they might be adopted or appreciated, but they were not unknown to the ancients, and by means of them their founders were able to uplift souls and, when necessary, fire them with truly heroic zeal. In Republics with even harsher laws, generous Citizens have been known, at times when the fatherland was in danger, to dedicate themselves to death in order to get an opinion adopted that might save it. A *veto* entailing the same danger may on occasion save the State, and need never cause it fear.

[14] Dare I speak here of confederations without sharing the opinion of the learned? They see only the evil which confederations do; the evil which they prevent has to be seen as well. Confederation is, without question, a violent state in the Republic; but there are extreme evils which render violent remedies necessary, and which one must try to cure at any price. Confederation is in Poland what the Dictatorship was among the Romans: both silence the laws in times of pressing peril, but with this great difference that the Dictatorship, being directly contrary to the laws of Rome and to the spirit of its government, ended by destroying it, whereas Confederations, on the contrary, being but a means of consolidating and restoring a constitution under great strain, can tighten and reinforce the slackened spring of the State without ever being able to break it. This federative form, which may originally be due to a fortuitous

cause, strikes me as a masterpiece of politics. Wherever freedom reigns it is forever under attack and very often in danger. Every free state in which great crises have not been anticipated is in danger of perishing with every storm. The Poles are the only ones who have succeeded in extracting from these very crises a new way of preserving the Constitution. Without the Confederations, the Republic of Poland would long ago have ceased to exist, and I greatly fear that it will not long survive them if it were decided to abolish them. Look at what has just happened. Without the Confederations the State would have been subjugated; freedom would have been destroyed forever. Do you want to deprive the Republic of the resource that has just saved it?

[15] And let no one think that, once the *liberum veto* is [999] abolished and majority rule restored, confederations will become useless, as if their only advantage consisted in this majority rule. The two are not the same. The executive power associated with the confederations will invariably give them in times of extreme need a degree of vigor, of activity, of speed unavailable to the Diet, which is forced to proceed by slower steps, with more formalities, and which cannot make a single irregular move without overthrowing the constitution.

[16] No, the Confederations are the shield, the refuge, the sanctuary of this constitution. So long as they endure it seems to me impossible for it to destroy itself. They must be kept, but they must be regulated. If all abuses were eliminated, the confederations would become almost useless. The reform of your Government should achieve this result. Only violent undertakings will still make it necessary to resort to them; but such undertakings are in the order of the things that have to be anticipated. Hence instead of abolishing the confederations, determine the situations in which they may legitimately take place, and then carefully regulate their form and function, so as to give them legal sanction as far as it is possible to do so without interfering with their formation or their activity. There are even situations the very occurrence of which should lead to an immediate confederation of the whole of Poland; as for example the moment when, on whatever pretext and short of outright war, foreign troops set foot in the State; for, after all, regardless of what may be the occasion of their entering, and even if the government consented to it, confederation at home is not hostility

toward others. Whenever, owing to any obstacle whatsoever, the Diet is prevented from meeting at the time stipulated by law, whenever, at regardless whose instigation, men at arms are found at the time and place of its meeting, or its form is changed, or its activity suspended, or its freedom interfered with in any way; in all such situations the general Confederation ought to be in being by virtue of their very occurrence; private meetings and signatures are nothing but its offshoots, and all its Marshals should be subordinate to the one who shall have been named first.

[*1000*]

[10] ADMINISTRATION

[1] Without entering into details of administration about which I am equally lacking in knowledge and opinions, I shall only venture some ideas about the two areas of finance and of war, ideas which I must state because I believe them good, although I am almost certain that they will not be appreciated: but first of all I shall say something about the administration of justice which departs somewhat less from the spirit of the Polish Government.

[2] The two estates of men of the sword and men of the robe were unknown to the ancients. Citizens were neither soldiers, nor judges, nor priests by profession; they were all [of these] by duty. That is the true secret of having everything proceed to the common goal, of keeping the spirit of [loyalty to one's] estate from taking root in the corporations at the expense of patriotism, and the hydra of chicanery from devouring a nation. The function of judge, in the highest as well as in the local courts, should be a transitional, testing state by which the Nation might assess a Citizen's merit and probity, so that it might then elevate him to the positions of greater eminence he is found capable of fulfilling. This way of viewing themselves cannot fail to make judges particularly careful to place themselves beyond all reproach and generally to instill in them all the attentiveness and integrity which their position demands. This is how in the fair days of Rome men rose through the Praetorship to reach the Consulate. This is the way to see to it that with few clear and simple laws, even with few judges, justice is well administered, by leaving judges with the power to interpret and,

when necessary, to amplify the laws by the natural lights of uprightness and good sense. Nothing could be more puerile than the precautions the English take on this point. In order to avoid arbitrary
judgments, they have subjected themselves to a thousand iniquitous
and even outrageous judgments: swarms of lawyers devour them,
endless lawsuits consume them, and with the mad idea of trying to
anticipate everything, they have turned their laws into an immense
labyrinth in which memory and reason alike get lost.

[*1001*] [3] You must have three codes. One political, another civil,
the third criminal. All three as clear, short and precise as possible.
These codes will be taught not only in the universities, but in all
secondary schools, and there is no need of any other body of right.
All the rules of natural right are better graven in the hearts of men
than in all the jumble of Justinian. Just make them honest and
virtuous and I assure you they will know enough [about] right.
But all Citizens and especially public figures must be taught their
country's positive laws and the particular rules by which they are
governed. They will find them in the codes they have to study, and
all noblemen, before being entered in the golden book which grants
them admission to a Dietine, have to pass about the subject of these
codes, and especially on the first, an exam which is not a mere
formality, and about which, if they do not know it sufficiently well,
they will be sent back until they know it better. As regards Roman
and customary right, all this, if it exists at all, has to be eliminated
from the schools and the law courts. They should recognize no
other authority than the Laws of the State; these should be uniform
throughout the provinces in order to dry up one source of litigation,
and the questions not settled by the laws will have to be settled by
the good sense and the integrity of the judges. You may assume
that once the magistracy is for its incumbents but a testing stage
for higher office, they will not abuse its authority as much as one
might fear, or that if such abuse does take place, there will always
be less of it than there will be arising from the often contradictory
masses of laws which, because of their number, drag out lawsuits
endlessly, and because of the conflicts between them, make for
equally arbitrary judgments.

[4] What I am here saying about judges applies with even greater
force to Lawyers. This estate, so respectable in itself, is cheapened
and debased as soon as it becomes a profession. The lawyer ought

to be his client's first and most severe judge. His work should be as it was in Rome and still is in Geneva, the first step on the way to magistracies; and indeed, in Geneva lawyers are highly regarded and deserve to be so. They are candidates for the Council, very attentive not to do anything that might bring them public disapproval. I should like for every [*1002*] public function thus to lead from the one to the next: so that no one could arrange to stay in the one he is in, turn it into a profitable profession, and place himself above men's judgment. This would perfectly satisfy the wish to have the children of wealthy citizens spend some time as lawyers, a state which will this way have been made both honorable and temporary. I shall develop this idea more fully in a moment.

[5] I must note in passing at this point, since it crosses my mind, that entails and Primogeniture are contrary to the system of equality within the knightly order. Legislation should always tend to lessen the great inequality of fortune and power which places too great a distance between Magnates and simple noblemen, and which a natural progression invariably tends to increase. As regards the Property Qualification that would fix the amount of land a nobleman has to possess in order to be admitted to the Dietines, since I can see in it both good and evil, and since I do not know the country well enough to weigh the consequences, I simply dare not pronounce on the question. It would undeniably be desirable that every Citizen with a vote in a Palatinate own some land in it, but I would not much like its quantity to be fixed: in letting possessions count for much, are men then to count for nothing at all? What then! does a Gentleman cease to be noble and free for having little or no land, and is his poverty a sufficiently serious crime to cause him to lose his right as a Citizen?

[6] Furthermore, no law should ever be allowed to fall into disuse. Be it indifferent, be it bad, it should either be formally repealed or vigorously enforced. This maxim, which is fundamental, will require reviewing all ancient laws, repealing many of them, and attaching the most severe sanctions to those that are to be kept. In France it is an accepted maxim of State to turn a blind eye on many things; that is what despotism always obliges one to do: but in a free Government it is a sure way to weaken the legislation and upset the constitution. Few laws, but well assimilated and above all well observed. All abuses that are not prohibited remain without

consequence. But whoever, in a free State, invokes law, invokes that before which every Citizen trembles, and the King [*1003*] the first of all. In a word, tolerate anything rather than to wear out the spring of the laws; for once that spring is worn out, the State is lost without recourse.

[11] THE ECONOMIC SYSTEM

[1] The choice of economic system Poland should adopt depends on the end it sets itself in correcting its constitution. If your only wish is to become noisy, brilliant, fearsome, and to influence the other peoples of Europe, you have their example, seek to follow it. Cultivate the sciences, the arts, commerce, industry, maintain regular troops, fortifications, Academies, above all a good financial system which makes money circulate well, which thereby multiplies it, which provides you with a lot of it; strive to make it very necessary, in order to keep the people in great dependence, and to that end foster material luxury as well as the mental luxury which is inseparable from it. This way you will form a people that is scheming, intense, greedy, servile and knavish like the others, forever at one of the two extremes of misery or opulence, of license or slavery, without any middle ground: but you will be reckoned among the great powers of Europe, you will be a party to all political systems, you will be sought out as an ally in all negotiations, you will be tied by treaties: there will not be a single war in Europe into which you will not have the honor of being dragged; if happiness has it in for you, you will be able to recover your ancient possessions, perhaps conquer new ones, and then say like Pyrrhus or like the Russians, that is to say like children: "Once the whole world is mine I'll get to eat candy."

[2] But if by chance you preferred to form a free, peaceful and wise nation which neither fears nor needs anyone, is self-sufficient and is happy; then you must adopt an altogether different method, preserve, restore among you simple morals, wholesome tastes, a warlike spirit free of ambition; form [*1004*] courageous and disinterested souls; involve your peoples in agriculture and the arts necessary for life, make money contemptible and, if possible, useless, seek, find more powerful and more reliable springs to achieve

great things. I grant that in following this path you will not fill newspapers with the noise of your festivities, your negotiations, your exploits, that the philosophers will not sing your praises, that the poets will not celebrate you, that you will not be much talked about in Europe: perhaps they will even pretend to hold you in contempt; but you will live in genuine abundance, in justice, in freedom; but no one will pick quarrels with you, you will be feared without pretense, and I answer for it that neither the Russians nor anyone else will come again to lord it over you, or that, if to their misfortune they do come, they will be in an even greater hurry to leave. Above all, do not try to combine these two projects; they are too contradictory, and to try to reach both by going in opposite directions is to want to miss both. Choose then, and if you prefer the first alternative, stop reading me here; for everything I have left to propose pertains solely to the second.

[3] The papers I have been sent unquestionably contain sound economic views. The flaw I see in them is that they are more partial to wealth than to prosperity. As regards new institutions, one should not leave it at looking to their immediate effects; one also has to anticipate carefully their remote but necessary consequences. For example the proposal to sell the starosties and for the use of the proceeds seems to me well conceived and easily carried out in the system prevalent throughout Europe of doing everything with money. But is this system good in itself and does it achieve its goal? Is it certain that money is the sinews of war? Rich peoples have always been beaten and conquered by poor peoples. Is it certain that money is the mainspring of good government? Financial systems are modern. I see nothing good or great come from them. The ancient Governments did not even know the word *finance*, and yet what they accomplished with men is prodigious. Money is at best the supplement to men, and the supplement [*1005*] will never be worth the thing itself. Poles, leave be all this money to others, or be content with as much of it as they will have to give you since they need your wheat more than you do their gold. Believe me, it is better to live in plenty than in opulence; be more than pecunious, be prosperous. Cultivate your fields well, without worrying about the rest, soon you will harvest gold and more than you need to provide yourselves with the oil and wine you lack, since but for them Poland abounds or can abound in everything. If you want to

stay happy and free, heads, what you need are hearts and arms: they are what make up the force of a State and the prosperity of a people. Financial systems make venal souls, and as soon as all one wants is to profit, one invariably profits more by being a knave than by being an honest man. Money is used in misleading and secretive ways; it is intended for one thing and used for another. Those who handle it soon learn to divert it, and what are all the supervisors who are set over them if not more knaves sent to go shares with them? If all riches were public and visible, if transfers of gold left a discernible mark and could not hide, there would be no instrument better suited for buying services, courage, loyalty, virtues; but in view of its secret circulation, it is even better suited for making plunderers and traitors, and putting the public good and freedom on the auction block. In a word, money is at once the weakest and the most ineffectual spring I know to get the political machine to move to its end, and the strongest and most certain to deflect it from it.

[4] Men can be moved to act only by their interest, I know; but pecuniary interest is the worst of all, the vilest, the most liable to corruption, and even, I confidently repeat and will always maintain, the least and weakest in the eyes of anyone who knows the human heart well. In all hearts there is naturally a reserve of great passions; when the only one left is the passion for money, it is because all the others, which should have been stimulated and encouraged, have been enervated and stifled. The miser has properly speaking no dominant passion; he aspires to money only by anticipation, in order to satisfy the passions he might some day experience. Learn how to foment and [*1006*] satisfy them directly without this resource; it will soon lose all of its value.

[5] Public expenditures are unavoidable; again, I grant it. Make them with anything other than money. In Switzerland one sees even today officers, magistrates and others on public salaries being paid in kind. They receive tithes, wine, wood, useful as well as honorific rights. All public service is discharged by corvées, there is almost nothing the State pays for with money. Money, it will be said, is needed to pay troops. This issue will be taken up in its place, shortly. This method of payment is not without inconveniences; there is loss, waste: administering this kind of goods is more cumbersome; the people in charge of it dislike it especially, because

there is less profit in it for them. All this is true; but how small
that evil is by comparison to the evils it avoids! If a man wished
to engage in malfeasance, he could not do so, at least not without
it being obvious. The Bailiffs of the Canton of Berne will be cited
in objection to me; but what are their vexations due to? to the
money fines they impose. These arbitrary fines are a sufficiently
great evil in themselves. Yet if they could exact them only in kind,
it would be of almost no consequence. The money they extort is
easily hidden, stores could not be hidden as readily. Ten times more
money changes hands in the Canton of Berne alone than in all the
rest of Switzerland; and its administration is correspondingly
iniquitous. Look in any country, any government and all over the
earth. Nowhere will you find a great moral or political evil in which
money is not involved.

[6] I will be told that the equality of fortunes that reigns in
Switzerland makes parsimoniousness in the administration easy:
whereas in Poland the many powerful families and Magnates
require large expenditures for their upkeep and the financial
resources to meet them. Not at all. These Magnates have great
inherited wealth, and once luxury ceases to be honored in the State,
their expenses will be smaller, without distinguishing them any the
less from lesser fortunes which will diminish proportionately. Pay
for their services with authority, honors, high places. In Poland
ine[*1007*]quality of rank is made up for by the advantage of nobility
which makes those who occupy the various ranks more jealous of
honors than of profit. By grading and judiciously distributing these
purely honorific awards, the Republic accumulates a treasury that
will not ruin it, and that will give it heroes for Citizens. This treasury of honors is an inexhaustible resource for a people with a sense
of honor; and would to God that Poland could hope to exhaust it.
Happy the nation that can find in its breast no further possible
distinctions for virtue!

[7] In addition to not being worthy of it, monetary rewards have
the drawback of not being sufficiently public, of not constantly
speaking to men's eyes and hearts, of disappearing as soon as they
have been conferred, and of leaving no visible trace which might
arouse emulation by perpetuating the honor that should attach to
them. I should like that all grades, all employments, all honorific
awards be marked by external signs, that no public figure be allowed

ever to move about incognito, that the marks of his rank or dignity follow him everywhere, so that the people at all times show him respect, and that he himself at all times have self-respect; that he might thus always keep the upper hand over opulence; that a rich man who is nothing but rich, feeling forever eclipsed by Citizens who are titled and poor, find neither deference nor approval in his fatherland; that he be forced to serve it if he wishes to shine in it, to have integrity out of ambition, and to aspire, in spite of his riches, to ranks that can be reached only through public approbation, and from which disapprobation can at all times cause one to fall. This is how to drain the force of riches, and how to make men who are not for sale. I strongly stress this point, persuaded as I am that your neighbors and above all the Russians will spare no effort to corrupt your officials, and that the major business of your Government is to endeavor to make them incorruptible.

[8] If I am told that I am trying to turn Poland into a people of Capuchins, I answer first of all that that is nothing but an argument in the French fashion, and that jesting is not reasoning. I answer further that my maxims should not be stretched beyond my intentions and reason; that my object is not to abolish the circulation of [*1008*] specie, but only to slow it down, and above all to prove how important it is that a good economic system not be a system of finance and money. Lycurgus, in order to uproot cupidity in Sparta, did not abolish money, but made it of iron. As for myself, I do not propose to ban silver and gold but to make them less necessary, and to see to it that a man who has no gold or silver might be poor without being destitute. At bottom, money is not wealth, it is only a sign of it; it is not the sign that should be multiplied, but the thing represented. I have seen, in spite of the travelers' fables, that the English in the midst of all their gold were, man for man, no less needy than the other peoples. And, after all, what does it matter to me to have a hundred guineas instead of ten, if these hundred do not yield me a more commodious living. Monetary wealth is only relative, and, because of relations that can change for a thousand causes, one can find oneself successively rich and poor with the same sum; but not so with goods in kind, for since they are immediately useful to man they always have their absolute value which in no way depends on a commercial transaction. I will grant that the English people is richer than the other peoples, but it does

not follow that a bourgeois of London lives more commodiously than a bourgeois of Paris. Between one people and another, the one with more money enjoys an advantage; but this in no way affects the fate of individuals, and that is not where the prosperity of a nation lies.

[9] Encourage agriculture and the useful arts, not by enriching farmers, which would only incite them to give up farming, but by making it honorable and pleasant for them. Establish manufactures of the primary necessities; constantly multiply your wheat and your men without worrying about the rest. The surplus produce of your soil, which will be in short supply in the rest of Europe because of growing monopolies, will necessarily bring you more money than you will need. Beyond this necessary and certain produce, you will be poor as long as you want more; as soon as you are able to do without it, you will be rich. This is the spirit I should like to see prevail in your economic system. To give little thought to other countries, to be little concerned with commerce; but at home to increase as much as [*1009*] possible both the food supply and consumers. The infallible and natural effect of a free and just Government is population. Hence the more you perfect your Government, the more you increase your people without even thinking about it. This way you will have neither beggars nor millionaires. Luxury and indigence will insensibly disappear together, and the Citizens, cured of the frivolous tastes opulence fosters, and of the vices associated with poverty, will place their cares and their glory in serving the fatherland well, and find their happiness in their duties.

[10] I should like always to have more taxes borne by men's arms than by their purse; to have roads, Bridges, public buildings, the service of Prince and of State performed by corvées and not paid for by money. This sort of tax is basically the least burdensome and above all the one least liable to be abused: for money disappears in leaving the hands that pay it, but everyone sees what men do, and they cannot be overburdened at a pure loss. I know that this method is impracticable where luxury, commerce and the arts reign: but nothing is as easy among a simple people with good morals, and nothing is more useful for keeping them so: that is another reason to prefer it.

[11] I return, then, to the starosties, and I once again agree that the project of selling them in order to use the proceeds to the benefit

of the public treasury is good and sound in terms of its economic objective; but as to its political and moral objective, this project is so little to my liking that if the starosties were sold, I should wish them to be bought back and used as the fund for the salaries and rewards of those who might serve the fatherland or deserve well of it. In a word, I should like that, if it were possible, there be no public treasury, and the taxing authority not even know about payments in money. I am sensible to the fact that this is not strictly possible; but the spirit of the government should always tend to making it possible, and nothing is more contrary to this spirit than the sale in question. The Republic would be richer for it, it is true; but the mainspring of government would be correspondingly weaker for it.

[12] I recognize that managers would find the management of public goods more difficult and above all less agreeable [*1010*] once all these goods are in kind rather than in money: but this management and its supervision must then be made into so many tests of good sense, of vigilance, and above all of integrity for reaching more eminent positions. One would, in this respect, simply be imitating the municipal administration of Lyon, where one has to begin by being the Administrator of the Municipal Charity Hospital before proceeding to civic office, and the judgment as to whether one is worthy of the other offices is based on how well one acquits oneself of the first. The Quaestors of the Roman army were models of integrity because the Quaestorship was the first step on the way to curule office. In the positions that might tempt covetousness, one has to see to it that ambition repress it. The greatest good to result from this is not what is saved from embezzlements; but making disinterestedness honorable, and rendering respectable a poverty due to integrity.

[13] The revenues of the Republic do not meet its expenses; I should think not; Citizens do not want to pay anything at all. But men who want to be free ought not to be slaves to their purse, and where is the State where freedom does not have to be paid for, and even very dear? I will be told about Switzerland; but as I have already said, in Switzerland the Citizens themselves perform the functions for which everywhere else they prefer to pay so that others perform them. They are soldiers, officers, magistrates, laborers: they are everything in the service of the State, and as they are ever

ready to pay with their person, they need not also pay with their purse. When the Poles are ready to do the same, they will no more need money than do the Swiss: but if a large State refuses to act on the maxims of small Republics, it should not look for their advantages, nor should it seek the effect while rejecting the means to achieve it. If Poland were what I would wish it to be, a confederation of thirty-three small States, it would combine the force of great Monarchies with the freedom of small Republics; but this would require renouncing ostentation, and I am afraid that this is the most difficult issue.

[14] Of all the bases for a tax, the most convenient and the least costly is, without [*1011*] question, capitation; but it is also the most forced, the most arbitrary, and that is undoubtedly why Montesquieu finds it servile, although it was the only one practiced by the Romans and it still continues in existence at the present time in several Republics, under other names, it is true, as in Geneva, where it is called *paying the Guards* and only Citizens and Bourgeois pay it, while residents and natives pay other taxes; which is precisely the opposite of Montesquieu's idea.

[15] But since it is unjust and unreasonable to tax people who have nothing, taxes on property are always preferable to taxes on persons. Except that one has to avoid those that are difficult and costly to collect, and especially those that can be evaded by contraband, which is unproductive [of revenue], fills the State with cheats and brigands, and corrupts the Citizens' loyalty. Taxation has to be so nicely proportioned that fraud is more troublesome than profitable. Hence never a tax on what is easily hidden, like lace and jewelry; it is better to prohibit wearing them than to prohibit importing them. In France the temptation for contraband is freely encouraged, and this leads me to believe that the Revenue Service finds it in its interest that there be people involved in contraband. This system is abominable and in every way contrary to good sense. Experience teaches that tax stamps are particularly burdensome to the poor, interfere with trade, greatly increase chicanery, and make the people complain a great deal wherever they are established; I would not advise considering them. A tax on livestock seems to me much better, provided fraud is avoided, for every possible fraud is always a source of evils. But it might be burdensome to the taxpayers because it has to be paid in money, and the proceeds of

contributions of this kind are too subject to being diverted from their destination.

[16] The best tax, in my opinion, the most natural and the one which is in no way subject to fraud, is a proportional tax on land, and on all land without exception, as proposed by Marshal de Vauban and the Abbé de Saint-Pierre; for after all what produces is what ought to pay. All lands, the King's, the Nobles', the Church's, the Commons must pay equally, that is to say in pro-[*1012*]portion to size and productivity, regardless of who may be the proprietor. Such a charge would seem to call for an extensive and costly preliminary operation, namely a general land registry. But this expense can be avoided easily, and even to good advantage, by assessing the tax not directly, on the land, but on its produce, which would be even more just; that is to say by establishing a tithe of whatever proportion is deemed appropriate, which would be levied in kind on the harvest, like the ecclesiastical tithe, and, in order to avoid the bother of management and storage, these Tithes would be leased by auction, as they are by the priests. Thus private individuals would be required to pay the Tithe only on their harvest, and they would pay out of their purse only if that is what they prefer to do, at a rate fixed by the government. These leases, pooled, could be made an item of trade through the sale of the foodstuffs they produce, and which could be sent abroad by way of Danzig or of Riga. This way one would also avoid all the costs of collection and administration, all those swarms of clerks and functionaries whom the people find so odious and the public so bothersome and, most important of all, the republic would have money without the citizens having to give it any: for I cannot repeat often enough that what makes the poll-tax and all taxes burdensome to the tiller of the soil is that they are monetary, and that he must begin by selling in order to be able to pay.

[12] The Military System

[1] Of all of the Republic's expenses, the upkeep of the Crown's army is the most considerable, and surely the services this army renders are not commensurate to what its costs. Yet, it will immediately be said, troops are needed to protect the State. I would grant

it if these troops did indeed protect it: but I do not see that this army ever guaranteed against any invasion, and I am rather afraid it will no more do so in the future.

[2] Poland is surrounded by warlike powers [*1013*] with large, perfectly disciplined, permanently standing armies, to which Poland could not, even with the utmost efforts, ever oppose similar forces without soon exhausting itself, especially given the deplorable state in which the brigands who are ravaging it will leave it. Besides, its neighbors would never let it do so, and if, with the means of the most vigorous administration, it tried to put its army on a respectable footing, its neighbors, intent on preventing it from doing so, would promptly crush it before it could carry out its project. No, if it wants only to imitate them, it will never resist them.

[3] The Polish nation is different in nature, in government, in morals, in language, not only from its neighbors, but from all the rest of Europe. I should wish it also to differ in its military constitution, its tactics, its discipline, always being itself and not another. Only then will it be all it is capable of being, and draw forth from its bosom all the resources it can muster. The most inviolable law of nature is the law of the stronger. No legislation, no constitution can exempt from this law. To look for the means of guaranteeing yourselves against the invasions of a neighbor stronger than you is to look for a chimera. It would be an even greater one to try to make conquests and to acquire offensive force; it is incompatible with the form of your government. Whoever wants to be free ought not to want to be a conqueror. The Romans were so by necessity and, so to speak, in spite of themselves. War was a necessary remedy for the vice of their constitution. Always attacked and always victorious, they were the only disciplined people among barbarians, and became the masters of the world by always defending themselves. Your situation is so different that you could not even defend yourselves against whoever might attack you. You will never have offensive force; it will be a long time before you have defensive force; but soon you will have or, more precisely, you already have the force to preserve yourselves, which will secure you, even if subjugated, against destruction, and preserve your government and your freedom in its one and true sanctuary, the heart of the Poles.

[4] Regular troops, the scourge and depopulators of Europe, [*1014*] are good for only two purposes: to attack and conquer

neighbors, or to shackle and enslave Citizens. Both are equally foreign to you: therefore renounce the means to attain them. The State must not be left without defenders, I know; but its true defenders are its members. Each citizen ought to be a soldier by duty, none by profession. Such was the military system of the Romans; such is that of the Swiss now; such ought to be that of every free State, especially of Poland. Since it is not in a position to hire an army sufficient to defend it, it must, when it needs an army, find it among its inhabitants. Only a good militia, a genuine, well-trained militia is capable of achieving this end. This militia will cost the Republic little, it will always be ready to serve it, and will serve it well, because after all one always defends one's own goods better than another's.

[5] Count Wielhorski proposes raising one Regiment per Palatinate, and always keeping it on active footing. This assumes that the Crown's army or at least the infantry gets disbanded: for I believe that maintaining these thirty-three Regiments would overburden the republic excessively if, in addition, it had to pay for the crown's army. This change would have its advantages, and it seems to me easy to make, but it can also become burdensome and its abuses will be difficult to prevent. I would not favor scattering the soldiers to maintain order in towns and villages; it would be bad discipline for them. Soldiers, above all professional ones, should never be left in charge of their own conduct, and they should even less be entrusted with any oversight of citizens. They should always march and live together in a body: always subordinated and supervised, they should be nothing but blind instruments in the hands of their officers. However small a supervisory role they might be assigned, it would lead to acts of violence, irritations, abuses without number; the soldiers and the population would become enemies: a misfortune that accompanies regular troops everywhere: the [proposed] standing regiments would take on their spirit, and that spirit is never favorable to freedom. The Roman republic was destroyed by its legions when the remoteness of its conquests forced it [*1015*] always to have some on active footing. Once again, the Poles should not look about them with a view to imitating even the good that is done elsewhere. Such a good relative to entirely different constitutions would be an evil in theirs. They should exclusively do what suits them and not what others do.

[6] Why not, then, instead of regular troops which are a hundred times more burdensome than useful to any people not animated by a spirit of conquest, establish in Poland a genuine militia exactly as it is established in Switzerland where every inhabitant is a soldier, but only when he has to be one? I admit that the instituted serfdom in Poland precludes arming the peasants right away: arms in servile hands will always be more dangerous than useful to the State; but pending the happy moment of emancipating them, Poland abounds in cities, and their inhabitants organized into regiments could, in times of need, furnish numerous troops whose upkeep, except in these times of need, would cost the State nothing. Most of these inhabitants, since they have no land, would in this way pay their taxes in service, and this service could easily be so distributed as not to be burdensome to them, even though they were being kept sufficiently trained.

[7] In Switzerland every individual who marries must be provided with a uniform which becomes his holiday dress, with a rifle and the full equipment of a foot-soldier, and he is enrolled in the company of his precinct. In summer, on Sundays and holidays, these militias are drilled in the order of their enlistment, first by small squads, then by companies, then by regiments; until their turn has come and they assemble in the field and one after the other set up small encampments where they are drilled in all appropriate infantry maneuvers. So long as they do not leave their place of residence, they are subject to little or no interference in their work, and therefore receive no pay, but as soon as they are in the field they draw rations and are paid by the State, and no one is allowed to send another in his place so that each may be trained, and all see service. In a State like Poland enough people can be drawn from its vast provinces to replace the Crown's army easily [*1016*] with a militia of adequate size and ever on the ready, and in which individuals would not find it particularly burdensome to serve because its membership would change at least once a year and be drawn by small detachments from all the corps, so that their turn would come hardly more than once every twelve to fifteen years. This way the entire nation would be trained, a fine and numerous army would always be ready in times of need, and it would cost much less, especially in peace-time, than the Crown's army costs now.

[8] But in order to succeed in this operation, one would have to

begin by changing public opinion about an estate which will indeed be entirely changed, and see to it that in Poland a soldier is no longer looked upon as a bandit who sells himself for a few pennies a day in order to live, but as a Citizen who serves the fatherland and does his duty. This estate has to be restored to the honor which it formerly enjoyed, and which it still enjoys in Switzerland and in Geneva where the best Bourgeois are as proud in their corps and under arms as they are in the town hall and in the Sovereign Council. To achieve this, it is important, in the selection of officers, not to take account of birth, position and wealth but only of experience and talent. Nothing is easier than to make skill in the handling of arms a point of honor for the sake of which everyone drills zealously for service to the fatherland in the sight of his family and of those close to him; a zeal impossible to arouse in the same way in a rabble recruited at random, sensitive only to how troublesome training is. I remember the time when the Bourgeois of Geneva performed maneuvers much better than did regular troops; but the Magistrates, finding that this instilled a martial spirit in the Bourgeoisie which did not suit their views, took pains to stifle this emulation, and succeeded only too well.

[9] In the execution of this project one could without any danger restore to the King the military authority that naturally attaches to his position; for it is not conceivable that the Nation could be used to oppress itself, at least not when all those who make it up will have a share in freedom. Only with regular and standing troops can the executive power ever enslave the State. The great Roman armies were not misused so long as they changed with each Consul, and until [*1017*] Marius it never so much as occurred to any Consul that he might turn them into a means to enslave the Republic. It was only when the great remoteness of their conquests forced the Romans to keep the same armies on active footing for long periods of time, to induct vagabonds into them, to extend command over them indefinitely to Proconsuls, that these Proconsuls began to sense their independence and to try to use it to establish their own power. The armies of Sulla, Pompey, and Caesar became genuine regular troops, which substituted the spirit of military government for the spirit of republican government, so much so that Caesar's soldiers regarded themselves as greatly offended when on the occasion of some mutual dissatisfaction he called them Citizens,

Quirites. In the plan I imagine and shall soon finish outlining, the whole of Poland will become warlike as much for the defense of its freedom against undertakings by the Prince, as against those by its neighbors, and I dare say that once this project has been properly implemented, the office of Commander-in-chief could be eliminated and reunited with the Crown without its causing the least threat to freedom, unless the Nation allows itself to be lured by projects of conquests, in which case I would no longer answer for anything. Whoever dares to deprive others of their freedom almost always ends up by losing his own; this is true even of kings, and even truer of peoples.

[10] Why should not the knightly order, in which the republic genuinely resides, follow a plan like the one I am here proposing for the infantry? Establish in all the Palatinates cavalry corps in which the entire nobility would be enrolled, with its own officers, its own general Staff, its own standard, its own assigned emergency barracks, its set times for their yearly call-up: and let these brave noblemen practice close drill, marching, counter-marching, slow-marching, all sorts of formations, evolutions, being orderly and pre-cise in their maneuvers, acknowledging military hierarchy. I should not like it slavishly to imitate the tactics of other nations. I should like it to devise its own distinctive tactics, which would develop and perfect its natural and national dispositions, to train primarily for speed and lightness, to break formation, disperse, and regroup without strain or confusion; to excel in what is known as guerilla warfare, all the maneuvers appropriate to light troops, the art of sweeping over a country like a torrent, to strike [*1018*] everywhere without ever being struck, always to act in concert even though separated, to cut communications, to intercept convoys, to attack rearguards, to capture vanguards, to ambush detachments, to harass large contingents marching and camping in a body; that it adopt the manner of the ancient Parthians, whose valor it has, and learn like them to defeat and destroy the best disciplined armies without ever joining battle and without leaving them a moment's respite. In a word, have infantry since it is necessary, but rely only on your cavalry, and omit nothing in inventing a system that will place the entire fate of the war in its hands.

[11] A free people is ill advised to have fortifications; they are not in the least suited to the Polish genius, and sooner or later they

become nests of tyrants anywhere. You will invariably be fortifying for the Russians the places which you think you are fortifying against them, and they will become constraints of which you will never rid yourselves. Ignore even the advantages of outposts, and do not bankrupt yourselves with artillery: none of that is what you need. A sudden invasion is a great misfortune, no doubt, but permanent chains are a far greater one. You will never succeed in making it difficult for your neighbors to enter your territory; but you can succeed in making it difficult for them to leave it with impunity, and that should be the object of all your cares. Anthony and Crassus entered the Parthians' territory easily, but to their misfortune. A country as vast as yours always offers its inhabitants places of refuge and great opportunities to escape its aggressors. All of man's art cannot prevent the sudden onslaught of the strong on the weak, but it can devise ways to respond, and when experience will have taught [your neighbors] how difficult it is to leave your country, they will be in less of a hurry to enter it. Hence, leave your country wide open as did Sparta; but, like Sparta, build good citadels in the Citizens' hearts, and just as Themistocles carried away Athens aboard its fleet, carry away your cities on your horses if need be. The spirit of imitation produces few good things and never anything great. Each country has advantages which are distinctively its own and which its insti[*1019*]tution ought to enlarge and to foster. Husband and cultivate those of Poland, it will have few other nations to envy.

[12] A single thing is enough to make Poland impossible to subjugate; the love of fatherland and of freedom animated by the virtues inseparable from that love. You have just given a forever memorable example of it. This love, so long as it burns in your hearts, may not secure you against a temporary yoke; but sooner or later it will burst forth, shake off the yoke, and make you free. Work, then, without relief, without respite, to carry patriotism to the highest pitch in all Polish hearts. I indicated above some of the means best suited to this end: it remains for me to detail here the means I believe to be the strongest, the most powerful, and even infallibly successful, if well implemented. It is to see to it that all Citizens constantly feel under the public's eyes, that no one advance or succeed save by public favor, that no position, no office be filled save by the nation's wish, and finally, that everyone, from the least

nobleman, even the least peasant up to the King, if possible, be so dependent on public esteem, that no one can do anything, acquire anything, achieve anything without it. Out of the enthusiasm aroused by this shared emulation will arise that patriotic intoxication which alone is capable of raising men above themselves, without which freedom is but an empty word and legislation but a chimera.

[13] In the knightly order this system is easy to establish, if care is exercised always to proceed gradually, and not to admit anyone to the honors and dignities of State who has not first passed through the lower grades, which will serve as the gateway and the test for further promotion. Since equality among noblemen is a fundamental law of Poland, a career in public affairs in Poland should invariably begin with the subordinate positions; that is the spirit of the constitution. These positions ought to be open to any Citizen sufficiently eager to apply for them and confident he can fill them successfully: but they should be the indispensable first step for anyone, great or small, who wishes to advance in this career. Each is free not to apply for it; but once someone has entered upon it, he must, [*1020*] short of withdrawing voluntarily, either advance or be rejected with disapprobation. He has to know that, in every aspect of his conduct, he is being seen and judged by his fellow-citizens, that his every step is being observed, that all of his actions are being weighed, and that a faithful account is being kept of the good and the evil [he does], which will influence the whole of the rest of his life.

[13] PROJECT FOR SUBJECTING ALL MEMBERS OF THE GOVERNMENT TO GRADUATED PROMOTIONS

[1] Here is a project for graduating these promotions which I have tried to adapt as closely as possible to the form of the established government, reformed only with respect to the appointment of Senators in the manner and for the reasons set forth above.

[2] All active members of the Republic, I mean all those who will take part in the administration, will be divided into three classes identified by as many distinctive insignia which those who will make up these classes will wear on their persons. The orders of knight-

hood which formerly were proofs of virtue are now nothing more than signs of the Kings' favor. The ribbons and jewels that are their badge have about them an air of baubles and feminine finery which must be avoided in our institution. I would wish the badges of the three orders I am proposing to be plaques of different metals, the material value of which would be inversely proportional to the rank of those wearing them.

[3] Before their first step in public affairs, young people shall be tested in positions as Lawyers, Assessors, even as lower court judges; as managers of some portion of the public monies, and in general in all the lower posts which provide those who occupy them with the opportunity to exhibit their merit, their ability, their accuracy, and above all their integrity. This probationary state should last at least three years, at the end of which, furnished with the certificates from their superiors, and the testimony of the public voice, they shall ap[*1021*]ply to the Dietine of their province where, after strict scrutiny of their conduct, those who are judged worthy shall be honored with a gold plaque bearing their name, the name of their province, their date of admission, and underneath this inscription in larger characters: *Spes Patriae*. Recipients of this plaque shall wear it at all times either attached to their right arm or over their heart; they shall assume the title of *Servants of the State*, and from the knightly order none but Servants of the State will ever qualify for election as Deputies to the Diet, Associate Justices, Commissioners of the chamber of accounts, or be entrusted with any public function which appertains to the Sovereignty.

[4] To attain the second grade one will have to have been a Deputy to the Diet three times, and each time to have obtained his constituents' approval in the report-session of the Dietines, and no one may be elected Deputy a second or a third time unless he has such a record regarding his previous deputyship. Service as Associate Justice or as a commissioner or a deputy at Radom shall be equivalent to a deputyship, and it will suffice to have sat three terms in any one of these assemblies, but always with approval, to qualify for the right to the second grade. So that, upon presentation of the three certificates to the Diet, the Servant of the State who has obtained them shall be honored with the second plaque together with the title of which it is the badge.

[5] This plaque shall be of silver of the same shape and size as the preceding one, it shall bear the same inscriptions, except that

in place of the two words *Spes Patriae* will be found the following two, *Civis electus*. Those who wear this plaque shall be called *Citizens elect* or simply *Elect*, and may no longer be simple Deputies, Associate Justices, or Commissioners of the Chamber [of accounts]: but shall be so many candidates for positions as Senators. No one will be admitted to the Senate until he has passed into this second grade and worn its badge, and all Senator Deputies who, according to this project, will be drawn immediately from among them will continue to wear it until they reach the third grade.

[6] It is from among those who have reached the second grade that I should like to choose the Principals of secondary schools and the inspectors of primary education. They might be obliged to fill this position for a certain period of time before [*1022*] being admitted to the Senate, and would be expected to present to the Diet the formal approbation of the College of the administrators of education: without forgetting that this approbation, like all the others, always has to be endorsed by the public voice, which there are a thousand ways of consulting.

[7] The election of the Senator Deputies will take place in the chamber of Deputies at each regular session of the Diet, so that they will hold office for only two years; but they can be continued in office or be re-elected two more times, provided that, each time they leave office, they first obtain from that Chamber a certificate of approbation similar to the one that has to be obtained from the Dietines in order to be elected Deputy a second and a third time: for without such a certificate received after each term of service one can no longer get anywhere, and one's only recourse to avoid being shut out of government would be to start anew in the lower grades, which ought to be allowed in order not to deprive a zealous citizen, regardless of the fault he may have committed, of all hope of eradicating it and of succeeding. Furthermore, it should never be made the responsibility of some specific committee to issue or to deny these certificates or approbations; these judgments should always be made by the chamber as a whole, which will be done without difficulty or loss of time if the same method of balloting by Cards is followed in judging outgoing Senator Deputies as I suggested for their election.

[8] It may perhaps be objected at this point that all these acts of approbation given first by specific bodies, then by the Dietines and finally by the Diet will not so much be awarded to merit, justice

and truth, as they will be extorted by intrigue and credit. To this I have but one reply. I believed myself to be speaking to a people which, while not free of vices, still had some resilience and virtues, and on that assumption my project is a good one. But if Poland is already at the point where everything is venal and rotten to the core, then it is in vain that it seeks to reform its laws and to preserve its freedom, it has to renounce doing so and bow its head to the yoke. But let us return.

[9] Every Deputy Senator who will have been in that office three times with approbation shall by right pass to the third grade, the highest in the State, and its badge will be conferred upon him by the King upon his being nominated by the Diet. This badge will be a plaque of blue steel similar to the preceding ones and [*1023*] shall bear the following inscription *Custos legum*. Those who have received it shall wear it the rest of their lives regardless of how eminent a position they may attain, and even on the throne if they should happen to ascend it.

[10] The Palatins and great Castellans will be drawn only from the body of the Guardians of the laws, in the same manner as these were drawn from the Citizens-elect, that is to say by the choice of the Diet, and since these Palatins occupy the most eminent positions in the republic and occupy them for life, in order to keep their spirit of emulation from going to sleep when they are in positions where all they see above themselves is the Throne, access to it shall be open to them, but in such a way that they can again reach it only through the public voice and by dint of virtue.

[11] Let us note, before proceeding further, that the course I set out for the citizens to traverse in order gradually to get to the head of the Republic seems to conform well enough to the rhythm of human life so that those who hold the reins of Government, having the impetuosity of youth behind them, may nevertheless still be in the prime of life, and so that after fifteen or twenty years of being continuously tested under the eyes of the public they still have sufficiently many years left during which the fatherland may enjoy their talents, their experience and their virtues, and during which they themselves may enjoy in the foremost positions of the State the respect and the honor they will have so well deserved. Assuming a man begins his public career at twenty, it is possible that he already is a Palatin at thirty-five; but since it is rather difficult and

not even indicated for this gradual progression to proceed this rapidly, one is not likely to reach this eminent position before one's
forties, and in my opinion that is the age best suited to bring
together all the qualities one should look for in a statesman. Let us
here add that this progression seems as appropriate as possible to
the needs of the government. Calculating the probabilities, I esti-
mate that every two years there will be at least fifty new citizens-
elect and twenty guardians of the laws: numbers that are more than
sufficient to recruit the two parts of the Senate to which these two
grades respectively lead. For it is easy to see that although the first
rank of the Senate is the more numerous, since it is for life it will
less frequently have vacancies to [*1024*] be filled than the second
which, according to my project, is renewed at each regular session
of the Diet.

[12] It has already been shown and it will shortly be shown again
that I do not leave the supernumerary *elect* idle until they enter the
Senate as deputies; in order also not to leave the Guardians of the
laws idle until they return [to the Senate] as Palatins or Castellans,
I would draw on this body to form the college of the Administrators
of education about which I have spoken above. The Presidency of
this college might be reserved for the Primate or some other Bishop,
on condition of stipulating further that no other Ecclesiastic, even
if he should be both Bishop and Senator, may be admitted to it.

[13] There you have, it seems to me, a rather well graduated
progression for the essential and intermediate part of the whole,
namely, the nobility and the magistrates; but we are still lacking
the two extremes, namely, the people and the King. Let us begin
with the first, which until now has counted for nothing but which
it is important finally to count for something if one wants to give
Poland a certain force, a certain stability. Nothing could be more
delicate than the operation in question, for although everyone is
sensible to how great an evil it is for the Republic that the nation
should as it were be confined to the knightly order, and that all
the rest, Peasants and Bourgeois, should count for nothing both in
Government and legislation, such, after all, is the ancient Constitution. Right now it would be neither prudent nor possible to
change it all at once; but it might be prudent and possible to bring
about this change gradually, to see to it that, without perceptible
revolution, the most numerous part of the nation grow attached by

ties of affection to the Fatherland and even to the Government. This will be achieved in two ways: the first, scrupulously to observe justice, so that serf and commoner, never having to fear being unjustly harassed by nobles, get cured of the aversion they must naturally feel toward them. This requires a massive reform of the law-courts and special attention to the formation of the corps of lawyers.

[14] The second way, without which the first is nothing, is to open a door to the serfs to attain freedom and to the Bourgeois to attain nobility. Even if this should not be practicable as a matter of fact, it should at least be perceived to be so as a possibility; but more can be done, it [*1025*] seems to me, and without running any risk. Here, for example, is a way which seems to me to lead in just this fashion to the proposed end.

[15] Every other year, in the interval between one Diet and the next, a convenient time and place would be set aside in each province at which the *Elect* of that province who are not yet Senator Deputies assemble, under the presidency of a *Custos legum* who is not yet a Senator for life, in a Censorial or welfare committee, to which would be invited not all Priests, but only those judged most worthy of that honor: I even believe that this preference, inasmuch as it represents a tacit judgment in the people's eyes, might also introduce a measure of emulation among Village Priests, and protect a great many of them from the vile morals to which they are all too prone.

[16] This assembly, to which elders and notables of all the estates might also be invited, would review proposals for projects useful to the province; it would receive reports from the Priests about the state of their own and neighboring parishes, and from the notables about the state of agriculture and of the families in their canton; these reports would be carefully checked; each member of the Committee would add his own observations to them, and a faithful record would be kept of all this, succinct summaries of which would be drawn up for the Dietines.

[17] It would review in detail the needs of overburdened families, invalids, widows, orphans, and provide for them proportionately from a fund formed by the voluntary contributions of the well-to-do of the province. These contributions would be all the less burdensome as they would become the only charitable contribution, since

neither beggars nor poor-houses should be tolerated anywhere in Poland. The Priests will, no doubt, set up a great hue and cry in favor of preserving the poor-houses, and this outcry is just one more reason for destroying them.

[18] In this same committee, which would never concern itself with punishments and reprimands, but only with benefits, praise and encouragements, accurate lists would be drawn up, based on reliable information, of per[*1026*]sons of all stations whose conduct was deserving of honor and reward.* These lists would be forwarded to the Senate and to the King to take into account as the occasion arises and always to select and to promote well, and it is on the basis of the information provided by these same assemblies that the Administrators of education would award the free places [in the secondary schools] about which I spoke above.

[19] But the principal and most important function of this committee would be to draw up, on the basis of trustworthy accounts and the carefully checked reports of the public voice, a roster of the Peasants who distinguished themselves by good conduct, good husbandry, good morals, the good care of their family, fulfilling well all the duties of their station. This roster would then be submitted to the Dietine which would choose from it a number fixed by law to be emancipated, and provide in agreed-upon ways for the Owners' compensation, by granting them exemptions, prerogatives, in short advantages proportionate to the number of their peasants found worthy of freedom. For it must absolutely be seen to that the emancipation of serfs brings the master honor and advantage instead of being a burden to him. Of course in order to avoid abuse these emancipations would be made not by the masters, but in the Dietines by [formal] judgment and only up to as many as the number fixed by law.

---

* In such assessments, one has to take persons into account much more than some few isolated actions. True good is done with little show. A man can earn honors by his steady and sustained conduct, by private and domestic virtues, by fulfilling well all the duties of his station, and, finally, by actions that derive from his character and his principles, rather than by a few spectacular feats which find sufficient reward in public admiration. Philosophical ostentation is particularly fond of showy actions; but there are those who with five or six actions of this kind, brilliant, noisy and widely touted, have no other purpose than to mislead about themselves and to be harsh and unjust with impunity all life long. "*Give us the small change of great deeds.*" This woman's sally is most judicious.

[20] Once a number of families in a canton had been successively emancipated, entire villages could be emancipated, communes could little by little be formed in the canton [*1027*], they could be assigned some real property, some communal land-holdings as in Switzerland, have some communal officers established, and once things had gradually been brought to the point where the operation can be brought to completion on a large scale without perceptible revolution, they could finally be restored to the right nature gave them to participate in the administration of their country by sending deputies to the Dietines.

[21] All this having been done, one would arm all these peasants become free men and Citizens, register them in the army, train them, and end up with a truly excellent militia, one more than sufficient for the defense of the State.

[22] One might adopt a similar method to ennoble a certain number of Bourgeois, and even without ennobling them reserve for them certain conspicuous positions which they alone would fill, to the exclusion of the nobility, and this would be done in imitation of the Venetians who, jealous as they are of their nobility, nevertheless always allocate to a commoner, among other subordinate positions, the second position in the State, namely that of grand Chancellor, to which no Patrician may ever lay claim. This way, by opening to the Bourgeoisie the door to nobility and honors, one would attach it by ties of affection to the Fatherland and to preserving the constitution. Alternatively, one also might ennoble certain cities collectively, without ennobling individuals, giving preference to the cities where commerce, industry and the arts were most flourishing, and where therefore the municipal administration was the best. These ennobled cities could, like the imperial cities, send Deputies to the Diet, and their example would not fail to arouse in all the others a keen desire to secure the same honor.

[23] The Censorial Committees responsible for this branch of beneficence – a branch which, to the shame of Kings and of peoples, has never existed anywhere – would be composed, though not by election, in the manner best suited to perform their functions with zeal and integrity; for their members are candidates for the Senatorial positions open to their respective grades, and they would therefore try hard to deserve, by public approbation, the votes of the Diet; and they would provide enough work to keep these candi-

dates alert and in the public eye [*1028*] during the intervals that might occur between their successive elections. Note, however, that this would be done without changing their status during these intervals from that of plain Citizens of a given rank, because this kind of tribunal, so useful and so respectable, with no other function than to do good, would not be vested with any coercive power: so that I am not here multiplying magistracies, but only availing myself, along the way, of the transition from one magistracy to another, by making use of those who are to fill these magistracies.

[24] Under this plan, graduated in its implementation into successive steps that could be speeded up, slowed down, or even halted, depending on its success or failure, one would proceed only at will, guided by experience, one would kindle in all the inferior ranks an ardent zeal to contribute to the public good, one would finally succeed in instilling life in all the parts of Poland, and in tying them together so as to make but a single body whose vigor and strengths would be at least ten times greater than they can be today, and this with the inestimable advantage of having avoided all sharp and abrupt change and the danger of revolutions.

[25] You have a fine opportunity to begin this operation in a splendid and noble fashion which should produce the greatest effect. During the misfortunes Poland has just suffered, the confederates must surely have received help and tokens of attachment from some of the bourgeois and even some of the peasants. Imitate the magnanimity of the Romans who were so scrupulous, after the great calamities of their republic, to heap proofs of their gratitude on strangers, subjects, slaves, and even animals who had rendered them some signal service during their misfortunes. Oh what a fine beginning it would be, in my view, solemnly to ennoble these bourgeois and emancipate these peasants, and to do so with all the pomp and circumstance necessary to make the ceremony august, moving and memorable! And do not stop with this beginning. The men thus distinguished should ever remain the favorite children of the fatherland. They should be watched over, protected, helped, sustained, even if they should be a bad lot. They must at all cost be made to prosper their whole life long, so that, with this example placed before the eyes of the public, Poland might show to [*1029*] all of Europe what anyone who dared to assist it in its distress might expect from it in its prosperity.

[26] This is a rough idea and only by way of example of how one might go about having everyone see the road before him open to attain anything, having everything that serves the fatherland well gradually tend to the most honorable ranks, and having virtue open all the doors which fortune sees fit to close.

[27] But not everything has as yet been done, and the part of this project which it remains for me to detail is without a doubt the most awkward and the most difficult; it seeks to overcome obstacles which have invariably defeated the prudence and the experience of the most consummate politicians. Yet it seems to me that, assuming my project is adopted, the very simple measure I am about to propose removes all difficulties, prevents all abuses, and in its implementation turns what seemed to be yet another obstacle into an advantage.

[14] ELECTION OF THE KINGS

[1] All these difficulties come down to the single one of giving the State a chief whose selection causes no troubles and who does not attempt against freedom. What increases the difficulty is that this chief has to be endowed with the great qualities needed in anyone who dares to govern free men. A hereditary Crown prevents trouble, but brings on slavery; election preserves freedom, but shakes the State with each new reign. This alternative is unfortunate, but before I speak about the means to avoid it, permit me to reflect for a moment on how the Poles ordinarily dispose of their Crown.

[2] First, I ask, why must they give themselves foreign Kings? What singular blindness led them thus to adopt the surest means of enslaving their nation, abolishing their practices, making themselves the playthings of the other courts, and gratuitously magnifying the storm of the interregnums? What an injustice toward themselves, what [*1030*] an affront to their fatherland, as if, despairing of finding among their own a man worthy to command them, they were forced to go seek him afar. How could they have failed to sense, how could they have failed to see that the very opposite is the case? Open the annals of your Nation, you will never see it illustrious and triumphant save under Polish Kings; you will see it

almost always oppressed and debased under foreigners. May experience finally come to the assistance of reason; see what evils you visit upon yourselves, and what goods you deny yourselves.

[3] For, I further ask, how is it that it did not occur to the Polish Nation, after having gone so far as to make its crown elective, to take advantage of this law to instill in the members of the administration a spirit of emulation in zeal and glory, which by itself alone would have done more for the good of the fatherland than all the other laws together? What a powerful spring for great and ambitious souls this crown destined for the worthiest, and held up as a prospect before the eyes of every citizen capable of deserving public esteem! What virtues, what noble efforts must not the hope of acquiring its highest prize be expected to excite in the nation, what a ferment of patriotism in all hearts, if all knew that this is the only way to win this post which has become every individual's secret desire, once it depended on themselves alone to come ever closer to it by dint of effort and services, and, if fortune favors, finally to reach it outright. Let us look for the best way to activate this great spring, so powerful in the republic and hitherto so neglected. I will be told that restricting the Crown to Poles alone is not enough to remove the difficulties in question: we will see about that shortly, after I have suggested my expedient. It is a simple expedient: but when I shall have said that it consists in introducing the drawing of lots into the election of Kings, it will at first appear to stray wide of the aim which I myself have just set. I ask please to be allowed the time to explain myself, or at least to be re-read attentively.

[4] For if someone said: how can one be sure that a King chosen by lot has the required qualities to fill his position worthily, he would be raising an objection I have already met; since it is sufficient for this purpose that the King can be drawn only from [*1031*] Senators for life; for since they themselves will have been drawn from the order of *Guardians of the laws*, and will have passed with honor through all the grades of the Republic, their having been tested their whole life long and earned public approbation in all the positions they will have filled will be sufficient guarantee of the merit and the virtues of each one of them.

[5] Nevertheless I do not mean the preference even between Senators for life to be decided solely by drawing of lots: to do so would partly miss the larger goal at which one ought always to aim.

The drawing of lots should do something, and choice should do much, in order on the one hand to check the intrigues and plots of foreign powers and, on the other, so intensely to involve all Palatins' self-interest that they will not relax in their conduct, but will continue to serve the fatherland zealously, so that they might merit the preference over their competitors.

[6] I admit that the class of these competitors seems to me quite large if one includes in it the great Castellans who, under the present constitution, are almost equal in rank with the Palatins; but I do not see what the inconvenience would be in restricting immediate access to the Throne to the Palatins alone. This would introduce a new rank into the same order, through which the great Castellans would still have to pass in order to become Palatins, and hence an additional means of keeping the Senate dependent on the lawgiver. I have already indicated that these great Castellans seem to me superfluous in the Constitution. If, for the sake of avoiding massive changes, they are nevertheless left their place and rank in the Senate, I approve of it. But in the gradation I propose nothing requires placing them on the same level as the Palatins, and since nothing prevents it either, there is no inconvenience in opting for whichever alternative is judged to be the best. My assumption here is that this preferred alternative will be to open immediate access to the throne only to the Palatins.

[7] Directly after the death of the King, then, that is to say after the briefest interval possible and fixed by law, the electoral Diet shall be solemnly convened; the names of all the Palatins shall be placed in competition and of these three shall be drawn by lot with all due precautions to make sure no fraud adulterates the process. These three names shall be announced out loud to the assembly which, at the same session and by [*1032*] majority vote, shall choose the one it prefers, and he shall be proclaimed King that same day.

[8] I admit that this form of election will be found to have one great inconvenience: that the nation cannot freely choose among the Palatins the one whom it most honors and cherishes, and judges worthiest of the kingship. But this inconvenience is not new in Poland where in several elections, and especially in the last, we have seen the Nation forced to choose without regard for those it favors someone it would have rejected: but in exchange for this advantage which it no longer had [anyway] and which it [would now formally]

sacrifice, how many other more important ones it gains from this form of election!

[9] First of all, the drawing of lots at once checks the factions and plots of foreign Nations which cannot influence this election, being too uncertain of success to invest much effort in it, since even fraud would be insufficient on behalf of a subject whom the nation can always reject. This advantage alone is so great that it insures calm for Poland, stifles venality in the republic, and makes election almost as tranquil as hereditary succession.

[10] The same advantage obtains against the intrigues of the candidates themselves. For who among them would go to the trouble of securing for himself a preference that does not depend on men, and sacrifice his fortune for the sake of an outcome with so many odds of failing for one of succeeding? Let us add that those whom the lottery has favored will not have the time to buy voters, since the election has to take place at the same session.

[11] The Nation's freely choosing among three candidates protects it against the inconveniences of the lot, in case it picks an unworthy subject; for in that case the Nation will take care not to choose him, and it is not possible that of thirty-three illustrious men, the elite of the Nation, among whom it is not even conceivable how there can be a single unworthy subject, all three of the men chosen in the draw should be unworthy.

[12] Thus, and this observation carries great weight, with this form we combine all the advantages of election with those of hereditary succession.

[13] For in the first place, since the crown does not pass from [*1033*] father to son there will never be continuity of any system[atic policy] to enslave the republic. In the second place, in this form the drawing of lots itself is the instrument of an enlightened and voluntary election. From the respectable body of the Guardians of the laws, and of the Palatins who are elected from among them, drawing of lots, whatever may be its outcome, cannot result in a choice that had not already been made by the nation.

[14] But consider what a spirit of emulation this prospect must introduce into the body of Palatins and great Castellans who, since they hold their offices for life, might relax in the certain knowledge that they can no longer be removed from them. They can no longer be restrained by fear; but the hope of occupying the throne which

each one of them sees so close at hand is a fresh spur that keeps them constantly watching themselves. They know that being favored in the draw would have been in vain if they are going to be rejected at the election, and that the only way to be chosen is to merit it. This advantage is too great, too obvious, to require elaboration.

[15] Let us for a moment assume, to take the worst possibility, that fraud cannot be avoided in the operation of the lottery and that one of the competitors has succeeded in eluding the vigilance of all the others who have such a lively interest in this operation. Such a fraud would be a misfortune for the excluded candidates; but the effect on the republic would be the same as if the outcome had been fair: for there would nevertheless be the advantage of election; the troubles of interregna and the dangers of hereditary succession would have been prevented nevertheless; the candidate whom ambition would have seduced to the point of resorting to this fraud would, in other respects, nevertheless be a man of merit, capable, in the judgment of the nation, of wearing the crown with honor, and, finally, in order to take advantage of it, he would, even after this fraud, be nevertheless dependent on the subsequent and formal choice of the Republic.

[16] With this project adopted in its entirety everything is linked in the State, and no one, from the least individual to the foremost Palatin, sees any way of advancing but on the road of duty and of public approbation. Only the King, once elected, no longer seeing anything but the laws above himself, has no other curb restraining him, and since he no longer needs public approbation, he can dispense with it without risk if his projects require it. To this I see only one remedy about which one should not even think. It is that the Crown were in some [*1034*] way revocable and Kings had to be re-confirmed at regular intervals. But, once again, this is not a practicable expedient: by keeping throne and State in constant turmoil, it would never leave the administration on a sufficiently firm footing to allow it to concentrate exclusively and usefully on the public good.

[17] There was an ancient practice which has never been put to use save by a single people, but it is astonishing that its success should never have tempted any other people to imitate it. It is true that it is scarcely suited to any but an elective kingdom, although

it was invented and put in use in a hereditary kingdom. I am referring to the judgment passed on the Kings of Egypt after their death,
and to the verdict which granted or refused them royal burial and
honors according to whether they had governed the state well or
ill during their lives. The moderns' indifference to all moral concerns and to everything capable of endowing souls with resilience
will undoubtedly make them look upon the idea of restoring this
practice for the kings of Poland as sheer folly, and it would not
occur to me to try to have Frenchmen and above all philosophers
adopt it, but I believe that it can be suggested to Poles. I even
venture to submit that instituting this practice would bring them
great advantages impossible to provide in any other way, and not
a single inconvenience. As regards the point at issue, it is not possible that, short of having a vile soul insensitive to whether his
memory is held in honor, the King should remain unaffected by
the integrity of an inevitable verdict and that this not impose on
his passions a brake, more or less forceful, I admit, but always capable of restraining them to a certain extent; especially if to this one
adds the interest of his children whose fate will be decided by the
verdict passed on the memory of the father.

[18] I should like, then, that after the death of each King his
body be kept in a suitable place until judgment has been passed on
his memory; that the tribunal charged with making this judgment
and decreeing about his burial be convened as promptly as possible;
that it review his life and reign strictly; and that, after hearings in
the course of which every citizen would be allowed to accuse and
to defend him, the completed trial be followed by a verdict proclaimed with the greatest possible solemnity.

[19] As a consequence of this verdict, if it should prove to be
favorable, the [*1035*] late King would be declared a good and just
Prince, his name inscribed with honor in the roll of the Kings of
Poland, his body ceremoniously entombed in their burial-ground,
the epithet *of glorious memory* added to his name in all public documents and speeches, a dower settled on his widow, and his children,
created royal Princes, would be honored throughout their lives with
all of the privileges attendant upon that title.

[20] If, on the contrary, he were found guilty of injustice, violence, malversation, and above all of having attempted against the
public freedom, his memory would be condemned and dishonored,

his body, denied royal burial, would be interred without honors like
that of a private individual, his name eradicated from the public
roll of kings; and his children, deprived of the title royal Princes
and of the prerogatives attendant upon it, would return to the class
of simple citizens, without any distinction, honorable or
dishonorable.

[21] I should like this judgment to be conducted with the utmost
formality, but, if possible, prior to the election of his successor, so
that this successor's good reputation not affect a sentence the severity of which it would be in his self-interest to soften. I know that
it would be desirable to have more time to uncover a good many
hidden truths and to conduct a more exhaustive trial. But I would
be afraid that if this trial were delayed until after the election, this
important action would soon turn into nothing more than a vain
ceremonial and, as would inevitably be the case in a hereditary kingdom, a funeral oration for the dead King rather than a just and strict
judgment of his conduct. Under the circumstances it is preferable to
concede more to the public voice and forego some minor information for the sake of preserving the integrity and austerity of a
judgment which would otherwise become useless.

[22] As regards the tribunal delivering this sentence, I should
like it to be neither the Senate, nor the Diet, nor any body vested
with any governmental authority, but an order made up entirely of
Citizens, which cannot easily be deceived or corrupted. It seems to
me that the *cives electi*, better educated, more experienced than the
Servants of the State, and less self-interested than the *Guardians of
the laws* who are already too close to the throne, would be just the
intermediary body in which to find both the most enlightenment
and the most integrity, the most apt to reach only reliable judgments, and hence preferable to the two others [*1036*] under the
circumstances. Even if this body should happen not to be sufficiently numerous to render a judgment of this importance, I would
prefer that it be given adjuncts drawn from the Servants of the
State rather than from the Guardians of the laws. Finally, I should
like this tribunal to be presided over not by an office-holder, but
by a Marshal drawn from among this body and elected by it, as are
the Marshals of the Diets and of the Confederations: so important
is it to avoid having any particular interest influence these proceed-

ings, which can become either very exalted or very ridiculous, depending on how they are conducted.

[23] In concluding this section on the election and the judgment of the Kings, I must say that one thing in your practices seemed to me quite shocking and quite contrary to the spirit of your constitution; namely, to see it overthrown and almost annihilated at the death of the King, to the point of suspending and shutting down all courts of law, as if this constitution were so dependent on this Prince that the death of the one is the destruction of the other. My god! it should be precisely the other way around. With the King dead, everything should proceed as if he were still alive; the absence of one piece of the machine should go almost unnoticed, so unessential to its stability was this piece. Fortunately this incoherence is unrelated to anything else. One need only announce that it shall be no more, and nothing further need be changed: but this strange contradiction should not be left standing: for if it already is one in the present constitution, it would be a much greater one still after the reform.

[15] CONCLUSION

[1] My plan is now sufficiently outlined: I stop. Regardless of which plan is adopted, one should not lose sight of what I said in the *Social Contract* about the state of weakness and anarchy in which a nation finds itself while it establishes or reforms its constitution. In that moment of disorder and excitement it is in no state to offer any resistance and the least shock can topple everything. It is therefore important at all cost to secure for oneself an interval of tranquility during which [*1037*] to work on oneself without risk and to rejuvenate one's constitution. Although the changes that need to be made in yours are not fundamental and do not appear to be very great, they are sufficient to require this precaution, and it necessarily takes a certain amount of time for the effects of the best reforms to make themselves felt and assume the consistency that is to be their fruit. One can only think about the enterprise at hand if one assumes that its success will be commensurate with the Confederates' courage and the justice of their cause. You will never be free

so long as a single Russian soldier remains in Poland, and you will always be under threat of losing your freedom so long as Russia continues to meddle in your affairs. But if you succeed in forcing it to deal with you as one Power with another and no longer as a protector with a protégé, then take advantage of how exhausted the war with Turkey will have left it to complete your task before it is in a position to disturb it. Although I set no store by the external security acquired by treaties, this unique set of circumstances may perhaps force you to lean as much as possible on this support, if only in order to gauge the present disposition of those who will be dealing with you. But except for this one case and, perhaps, at different times, for a few commercial treaties, do not wear yourselves out with vain negotiations, do not bankrupt yourselves with Ambassadors and Ministers at other courts, and do not count on alliances and treaties to be of any consequence. All this is worthless with christian powers. They know no other bonds than those of self-interest; when they find that it consists in fulfilling their commitments, they will fulfill them; when they find that it consists in breaking them, they will break them; one might as well not enter into any. Still, if this interest were always true, knowing what it is appropriate for them to do would permit anticipating what they will do. But it is almost never reason of State that guides them, it is the momentary interest of a Minister, a mistress, a favorite; it is the motive no human wisdom could anticipate that determines them now for, now against their true interests. What can one be sure of with people who have no fixed system[atic policy], and act only on random impulsions? There is nothing more frivolous than the political science of Courts: since it is without a single stable principle, [*1038*] one cannot draw a single certain conclusion from it; and this whole fancy doctrine of the interests of Princes is a child's game which makes sensible men laugh.

[2] Do not, then, confidently rely either on your allies or on your neighbors. You have only one on whom you can count somewhat. It is the Sultan [of Turkey], and you must spare no effort to have him lend you support: not that his maxims of State are much more reliable than those of the other powers. There too everything depends on a Vizir, a Favorite, a Harem intrigue: but the interest of the [Sublime] Porte is clear, simple, it has everything at stake, and generally it proceeds with rather less enlightenment and

finesse, but with greater uprightness and good sense. With it as compared with the christian Powers one at least enjoys the added advantage that it likes to fulfill its commitments, and ordinarily respects treaties. You should try to make a twenty-year treaty with it, as strong and as clear as possible. So long as another power keeps its projects concealed, this treaty will be the best and perhaps the only guarantee you can have, and, given the state in which the present war will probably leave Russia, I expect that it may be sufficient to go about your task in safety; all the more so as the common interest of the powers of Europe, and especially of your other neighbors, is always to keep you as a buffer between themselves and the Russians, and that by dint of switching from one folly to another they cannot help being wise at least sometimes.

[3] One thing leads me to believe that by and large others will look without jealousy upon your working on the reform of your constitution. It is that this labor only tends to consolidate legislation, hence freedom, and that in all courts such freedom is taken to be a mania of visionaries which tends to weaken a State rather than to strengthen it. That is why France has always favored the freedom of the union of German States and of Holland, and that is why Russia at present favors the current government of Sweden, and opposes the prospects of the King with all its strength. All these great Ministers who, judging men in general in terms of themselves and of those around them, believe that they know them, cannot begin to imagine what resilience the love of fatherland and the surge of virtue can impart to [*1039*] free souls. Regardless of how often they are duped by their low opinion of republics which offer to all of their undertakings a resistance they did not expect, they will never abandon a prejudice based on the contempt which they feel they themselves deserve and in terms of which they judge humankind. In spite of the Russians' rather striking recent experience in Poland, nothing will make them change their opinion. They will always look upon free men as they themselves must be looked upon, as non-entities on whom only two instruments have a hold, money and the Knout. When, therefore, they see the Republic of Poland, instead of being bent on filling its coffers, increasing its revenue, raising a large standing army, think, on the contrary, of disbanding its army and dispensing with money, they will believe that it is bent on weakening itself, and persuaded that all they will

have to do in order to conquer it is to appear there whenever they wish, they will let it organize itself undisturbed as they laugh up their sleeve about its work. And it has to be conceded that the state of freedom deprives a people of offensive force, and that in adopting the plan I propose one has to give up all hope of conquest. But let the Russians try to invade you when your work is completed, twenty years from now, and they will find out what soldiers in the defense of their own hearths are these men of peace who are unable to attack other people's hearths and have forgotten the price of money.

[4] What is more, once you are rid of these cruel guests, beware of entering into any compromises regarding the King they wanted to give you. Either have his head cut off as he deserves; or, without regard to his first election which is null and void, have him elected anew with other *Pacta conventa* by which you will make him renounce [the authority of] appointment to high offices. This second alternative is not only the more humane, but also the wiser; I even find in it a certain generous pride which will perhaps mortify the Court of Petersburg quite as much as if you held another election. Poniatowski was undoubtedly very criminal; perhaps today he is no more than miserable; at least in the present situation he seems to me to behave rather as he ought by not meddling in anything at all. Naturally he must in the bottom of his heart [*1040*] fervently desire the expulsion of his harsh masters. Patriotic heroism would perhaps consist in [his] joining the Confederates to chase these masters; but everyone knows that Poniatowski is no hero. Besides, in addition to the fact that he would not be allowed the opportunity to do so and that he is being constantly watched, I must frankly say that, since he owes the Russians everything, if I were in his place I should not like for anything in the world to be capable of that kind of heroism.

[5] I realize that this is not the King you will need when your reform is completed; but perhaps it is the one you need to complete it tranquilly. Even if he lives no more than another eight or ten years, since your machine will by then have started running, and several Palatinates will by then already be filled with *Guardians of the laws*, you will not have to fear that you are giving him a successor who resembles him: whereas I, for my part, fear that if you simply remove him you will not know what to do with him, and will expose yourselves to new troubles.

[6] Still, regardless of the difficulties which his free election might spare you, you should consider it only after having made quite sure of his genuine dispositions, and on the assumption that you will find that he retains some good sense, some sense of honor, some love of country, some knowledge of his true interests, some desire to heed them: for at any time, and above all in the sad circumstances in which its misfortunes will leave Poland, nothing could be more fatal for it than to have a traitor at the head of the Government.

[7] As for how to get the task at hand under way, I have no taste for all the cunning ways being suggested to you of as it were surprising and deceiving the Nation about the changes that have to be made in its laws. I would only advise that, in revealing the full extent of your plan, you not set about putting it into effect brusquely by filling the republic with malcontents, that you leave most of those who hold office where they are, and fill positions according to with the new reform only as they become vacant. Never shake up the machine too brusquely. I have no doubt that a good plan, once adopted, will change the mind of even those who had a part in the Government under another plan. Since it is impossible to create new citizens all at once, one has to begin by making do with those [*1041*] there are; and offering their ambition a new avenue is the way to incline them to follow it.

[8] If, in spite of the courage and constancy of the Confederates and of the justice of their cause, fortune and all the powers forsake them and deliver the fatherland to its oppressors . . . But I have not the honor of being a Pole, and in a situation such as the one you are in, one is not entitled to give one's opinion except by example.

[9] I have now fulfilled to the full measure of my forces the task which Count Wielhorski set for me, and would to God that I have done so with as much success as eagerness. Perhaps all this is just so many chimeras, but these are my ideas; it is not my fault that they are so little like other men's, and it has not been up to me to organize my head some other way. I even admit that however odd others may find these ideas, I myself see in them nothing that is not well adapted to the human heart, good, practicable, especially in Poland, because I have sought in my views to adhere to the spirit of this Republic, and to propose as few changes in it as I could in order to correct its defects. It seems to me that with such springs

a Government should move toward its true goal as directly, as surely, and for as long as possible; without, however, losing sight of the fact that all the works of men are imperfect, transitory and perishable, as they themselves are.

[10] I have purposely omitted many very important topics about which I did not feel sufficiently knowledgeable to judge soundly. I leave it up to more knowledgeable and wiser men than myself to do so; and I bring these long ramblings to an end with apologies to Count Wielhorski for having taken up so much of his time with them. Although I think differently from other men, I do not flatter myself with being wiser than they, nor that he will find in my reveries anything that might prove really useful to his fatherland; but my wishes for its prosperity are too true, too pure, too disinterested that pride at contributing to it could increase my zeal. May it triumph over its enemies, become and remain peaceful, happy and free, set a great example to the universe, and, profiting from the patriotic labors of Count Wielhorski, find and form in its midst many Citizens who resemble him!

SELECTED LETTERS

LETTER TO M. D'OFFREVILLE
Montmorency, 4 October 1761

[1] The question which you put to me in your letter of 15 September, Sir, is important and weighty; knowing whether there is a demonstrable morality or not hinges on how it is resolved.

[2] Your adversary maintains that everyone, no matter what he does, acts only in relation to himself, and that even in the most sublime acts of virtue, even in the purest works of charity, everyone relates everything to himself.

[3] You, Sir, you think that one ought to do good for the sake of good, even without any returns in personal interest; that the good works one relates to oneself are no longer acts of virtue, but of amour propre; you add that our alms are without merit if we give them only out of vanity, or with a view to dismissing from our minds the idea of the miseries of human life, and in this you are right.

[4] But as to the heart of the matter, I must admit to you that I am of your adversary's opinion: for when we act, we have to have a motive for acting, and this motive cannot be extrinsic to ourselves, since it is ourselves it sets to work; it is absurd to imagine that being myself, I will act as if I were another. Is it not true that if you were told that a body is being pushed without anything touching it, you would say that is not conceivable? The same holds regarding morality, when one believes oneself to be acting without any interest.

[5] But the word interest calls for explanation, because you might attach to it a meaning, you and your adversary, such that you agree without knowing it, and [alternatively] he might attach to it a meaning so crude that you would then be the one who is right.

[6] There is a sensible and tangible interest which bears solely on our material well-being, on fortune, on consideration, on the physical goods that may accrue to us from another's good opinion. Whatever one does for the sake of such an interest only produces a good of the same order, as with the good a merchant does by selling his wares on the best terms he can. If I oblige someone with a view to acquiring rights to his gratitude, I am nothing but a

merchant engaged in commerce, and cheating the buyer at that. If I give alms to be esteemed charitable and to enjoy the advantages attending on this esteem, I am again nothing but a merchant buying reputation. More or less the same holds if I give these alms only to rid myself of a beggar's importunacy or of the sight of his misery; all actions of this kind which have some external advantage in view cannot be called good deeds, and one does not say of a merchant who has conducted his business well that he has done so virtuously.

[7] There is another interest, which is entirely unrelated to social advantages, which is relative only to ourselves, to the good of our soul, to our absolute well-being, which therefore I call spiritual or moral interest, by contrast to the first; an interest which, in spite of having no sensible, material objects, is no less true, no less great, no less solid, and, in a word, the only interest which tends toward our genuine happiness, since it is intimately related to our nature. This, Sir, is the interest which virtue pursues and ought to pursue, and which in no way deprives the actions it inspires of merit, purity, or moral goodness.

[8] First of all, in the system of Religion, that is to say of punishments and rewards in the other life, you see that the interest of pleasing the Author of our being and the supreme judge of our actions is so important as to outweigh the greatest evils, as to cause true believers to fly to martyrdom, and at the same time so pure as to be capable of ennobling the most sublime duties. The law to act well is derived from reason itself, and a Christian needs only logic in order to have virtue.

[9] But besides this interest, which might be viewed as in some way extrinsic to the issue, as bearing on it only by the explicit will of God, you might perhaps ask me whether there is some other interest which is, by its nature, tied more intimately, more necessarily to virtue, and which should make us love virtue solely for its own sake. This is related to other questions, the discussion of which exceeds the limits of a letter, and into which I will therefore not attempt to inquire here: such as, whether we have a natural love of order, of the morally beautiful; whether this love can by itself be sufficiently lively to override all our passions; whether conscience is innate to man's heart, or is only the work of prejudices and of education: for in this latter case it is clear that since no one has within himself any interest in acting well, he cannot do good except

for the sake of the profit which he expects in return from others; that therefore only fools believe in virtue and only dupes practice it; such is the new philosophy.

[10] Without here getting involved in this metaphysics which would lead us too far, I will leave it at submitting to you a fact which you may propose for discussion to your adversary, and which, when well discussed, may perhaps tell you more about his true sentiments than you could learn about them if you remained at the level of generality of your thesis.

[11] In England, when a man faces a criminal charge, twelve jurors, locked up in a room in order to deliberate in light of the proceedings whether he is or is not guilty, do not leave that room and do not get anything to eat until they all agree, so that their judgment is always unanimous and conclusive regarding the fate of the accused.

[12] In one of these deliberations, with the proofs appearing to be convincing, eleven jurors condemned him without hesitation; but the twelfth held out so stubbornly for his acquittal without being willing to offer any other reason than that he believed him innocent, that all the others, seeing him prepared to die of hunger rather than to share their opinion, in order not to risk the same fate rallied to his opinion, and the accused was let go, absolved.

[13] Once the case was settled, some of the jurors secretly pressed their colleague to tell them the reason for his stubbornness, and finally learned that it was he himself who had committed the crime of which the other man stood accused, and that he had been less horrified by the prospect of death than by the prospect of causing the death of the innocent man accused of his own crime.

[14] Put this case to your man and do not fail to examine with him this juror's state in all of its aspects. He was not a just man, since he had committed a crime, and in this [particular] affair the enthusiasm of virtue could not have elevated his heart and made him despise life: he had the most real interest in condemning the accused in order to bury with him the imputation of the crime; he must have feared that his invincible stubbornness would rouse suspicions as to its true cause, and be a first clue against him. Prudence and concern for his safety would, so it seems, have required that he do what he did not do, and no discernible sensible interest had to lead him to do what he did; yet only a very powerful interest

could have swayed him, thus, in the secret of his heart, to run all sorts of risks: what, then, was this interest to which he sacrificed his very life?

[15] To deny the fact would be unfairly to evade the issue; for one can always assume it, and inquire what, setting aside all extrinsic interests, any man of sense who is neither virtuous nor a villain would do in such a case out of self-interest.

[16] Stating the two cases in turn, one, that the juror voted to condemn the accused and caused him to perish in order to secure his own safety; the other, that he absolved him, as he did do, at his own risk; then, tracing the rest of the juror's life and his likely fate in either case, press your man to pass a definitive judgment on this conduct, and to state clearly the interests and motives for and against the side he would have chosen; then, if your quarrel is not settled, you will at least know whether you do or do not understand one another.

[17] In case he distinguishes between interest in committing or not committing a crime, and interest in performing or not performing a good deed, you will easily get him to see that, on our hypothesis, the reason for refraining from an advantageous crime one can commit with impunity is of the same kind as the reason for performing a burdensome good deed with no other witness than heaven and yourself; for aside from being no more than just when we do whatever good we might do, one can have no inherent interest in not doing evil without having a similar interest in doing good; both flow from the same source, and cannot be separated.

[18] Above all, Sir, consider that one should never strain things beyond the truth, nor confuse, as the Stoics did, happiness with virtue. It is certain that to do good for the sake of good is to do it for one's own sake, out of self-interest, since it gives the soul an internal satisfaction, a contentment with itself without which there is no true happiness; it is further certain that the wicked are all wretched, regardless of what may be their apparent fate, because external happiness gets poisoned in a corrupt soul just as sensory pleasure does in an unhealthy body; but it is false that the good are all happy in this world; and just as a body's being in good health does not suffice for it to have the food which it requires, so a soul's being healthy does not suffice for it to obtain all the goods which it needs. Although only good people can live content, that is not

to say that every good person lives content. Virtue does not bestow happiness, but it alone teaches one to enjoy it when one has it; virtue does not protect against the evils of this life, and it does not secure its goods; nor does vice for all its cunning do so; but virtue makes us bear the first with greater patience, and savor the others with greater delight. We therefore have, in any case, a genuine interest in cultivating it, and we do well to work on behalf of this interest, although there are cases when it, by itself, without the expectation of a life to come, would not suffice. Such is my sentiment regarding the question you put to me.

[19] In thanking you for thinking well of me, I nevertheless advise you, Sir, no longer to waste your time defending or praising me. All the good and the evil one says about a man one does not know means little. If those who accuse me are wrong, it is up to my conduct to justify me; any other defense is useless or superfluous.

[20] I should have answered you sooner; but the state in which I live, daily struggling with pain and death, must excuse this delay. I do not answer complimentary letters, and I would not have answered yours either if the question which you put to me in it did not make it my duty to tell you my opinion about it.

I greet you wholeheartedly,

LETTER TO USTERI
Motiers, 18 July 1763

[1] You must, my dear Friend, make allowances for the visit I did not pay you: for I set out last month on this wished-for pilgrimage, not with M. Moultou, who is too poor a walker, but with M. de Sauttern; but the deterrent of bad weather which delayed us several days in an inn, my weakness, and the length of the journey, made me give up on it, much as I wished for it, and we retraced our steps after a ten days' absence which took us no farther than Estavayé. I have not given up hope of being more fortunate another time; but my travel companion has left, and I must admit to you that in my state I lack the courage to tackle alone a trip of forty leagues there, and as many back.

[2] However weary I may be of disputes and objections, and however repugnant I find it to take up the precious intercourse of

friendship with such skirmishes, I continue to address the difficulties you raise, since you demand it. I will therefore tell you with my
usual frankness that you do not seem to me to have clearly grasped
the state of the question. The great Society, human Society in general, is founded on humanity, on universal beneficence; I say and
have always said that Christianity is favorable to this Society.

[3] But particular Societies, political and civil Societies, have an
altogether different principle. They are purely human establishments from which true Christianity, consequently, detaches us, as
it does from everything that is merely earthly: nothing but men's
vices make these establishments necessary, and nothing but human
passions preserve them. Take away all vices from your Christians;
they will no longer need magistrates or laws: deprive them of all
human passions, the civil bond straightway loses all of its resilience;
no more emulation, no more glory, no more striving for preferment,
particular interest is destroyed, and for want of appropriate support,
the political State languishes.

[4] Your assumption of a political and vigorous Society of Christians, who may even all of them be perfect, is therefore contradictory. It is also extravagant if you will not allow a single unjust man,
not a single usurper in it. Will it be more perfect than the Apostles'?
And yet in its midst there was a Judas. Will it be more perfect than
the Angels'? And the devil, they say, came from it. My dear friend,
you forget that your Christians will be men, and that the perfection
I assume them to have is such as humanity admits of. My book is
not made for Gods.

[5] Nor is this all: You attribute to your Citizens an exquisitely
delicate moral tact, and why? Because they are good Christians.
What! can one not be a good Christian on your view without being
a La Rochefoucault or a La Bruyère? What then was our Lord
thinking about when he blessed the poor in spirit? In the first place,
this assertion is not reasonable; since delicacy of moral tact is
acquired only by dint of comparisons, and is even infinitely better
developed with the vices one hides than with the virtues one does
not hide. In the second place, the assertion is at odds with all experience, and one consistently sees that it is in the largest Cities, among
the most corrupt people that one learns better to delve into hearts,
better to observe men, better to interpret their speeches by their
sentiments, better to distinguish reality from appearance. Will you

deny that there are infinitely better moral observers in Paris than in Switzerland, or would you conclude from this that one lives more virtuously in Paris than among you?

[6] You say that your Citizens would be infinitely shocked by the first occurrence of injustice. I believe it; but by the time they noticed it, it would be too late to attend to it, and all the more so as they would not readily allow themselves to think ill of their neighbor, nor to place a bad construction on what might admit of a good one; it would be too much at odds with charity. You are not unaware that the artfully ambitious take great care not to start out with acts of injustice. On the contrary, they spare nothing in order initially to gain public trust and esteem by an outward performance of virtue. They cast off the mask and strike their massive blows only once they hold the winning hand, and there is no going back. Cromwell was recognized as a Tyrant only after he had, for fifteen years, been taken to be the avenger of the laws and the defender of Religion.

[7] In order to preserve your Christian Republic, you make its neighbors as just as you make it; well and good; I grant that for all intents and purposes it will defend itself well enough, provided it is not attacked. As regards the courage you attribute to its soldiers by virtue of the mere love of self-preservation, that is a courage no one lacks; I have attributed to it a motive that is even more powerful with Christians, namely the love of duty. About this, I believe that by way of reply I can refer you to my Book where this point is discussed well. How can you fail to see that only great passions do great things, and that whoever has no other passion than that for his Salvation will never do anything great in the temporal realm? If Mucius Scaevola had been no more than a Saint, do you think that he would have succeeded in breaking the siege of Rome? You might perhaps refer me to the great-souled Judith: but our hypothetical Christian women being less barbarously coquettish, will not, I believe, go and seduce their enemies, and then lie with them only to massacre them in their sleep.

[8] My dear friend, I do not propose to convince you. I know that no two heads are organized alike, and that after a good many disputations, a good many objections, a good many clarifications, everyone always ends up adhering to the same sentiment as before. To repeat, I answer you because you wish me to do so; but I will

love you no less for not thinking as I do. I have stated my opinion to the public, and I believed myself in duty bound to state it in matters that are important and relevant to humanity. Besides, I may have been mistaken always, and I have undoubtedly been mistaken often. I have stated my reasons, it is up to the public, it is up to you to weigh them, to judge them, to choose. As for myself, I know no more, and it seems to me perfectly good that those who have other sentiments keep them, so long as they leave me in peace with mine.

[9] M. L. M. D. A. whose name you ask me for is the late M. le Marquis d'Argenson, who had been Minister of foreign affairs, and who, although a Minister, was nevertheless an honest and a well intentioned man.

[10] Congratulate M. and Mme. Hesse on my behalf; the stock of such a worthy couple could not increase too soon or too much: I was looking forward to the pleasure of seeing them again during the visit I wanted to pay you; I would also have had the pleasure of making M. Gessner's acquaintance and of talking a little with him about the kind offer you extended to me on his behalf. When will come the happy time when I will be able to embrace you, and to find myself in the midst of your worthy compatriots? In the meantime, I am to my last breath, yours faithfully.

JJR

LETTER TO MIRABEAU

Trye, 26 July 1767

[1] I should have written you, Sir, upon receiving your latest note, but I preferred to postpone a few days longer making up for my negligence so that I might speak to you at the same time about the book you sent me. Since I could not read it in its entirety, I chose the chapters in which the Author speaks his mind bluntly and which seemed to me to be the most important ones. Reading them satisfied me less than I expected; and I feel that the vestiges of my old ideas, grown calloused in my brain, no longer allow such novel ideas to make strong impressions on it. I have never been able to understand just what the evidence is on which legal despotism is supposed to

be based; and nothing seemed to me less evident than the chapter devoted to all this evidence. This rather resembles the system of the Abbé de Saint-Pierre who claimed that human reason was forever perfecting itself, since every century adds its lights to those of the preceding centuries. He did not realize that the scope of human understanding is always one and the same, and very narrow, that it loses at one end as much as it gains at the other, and that ever recurring prejudices deprive us of as much enlightenment as cultivated reason might replace. It seems to me that the evidence can be in the natural and political laws only when they are considered by abstraction. In any particular government, which is a composite of so many diverse elements, this evidence necessarily disappears. For the science of government is nothing but a science of combinations, applications and exceptions, according to times, places, circumstances. The public will never be able to perceive with evidence the relations and the interplay of all this. And what, pray, will happen? what will happen to all your sacred rights of property in times of great danger, in extraordinary disasters when your available assets no longer suffice, and the [maxim] "Let the salvation of the people be the supreme law" will be pronounced by the despot?

[2] But let us assume this whole theory of natural laws to be always perfectly evident, even in its applications, and of a clarity that adjusts to all eyes. How can philosophers who know the human heart grant so much authority over men's actions to this evidence, as if they did not know that one very rarely acts by one's lights, and very frequently by one's passions? One proves that the despot's most genuine interest is to govern legally; this has been recognized at all times: but who conducts himself according to his truest interests? only the wise man, if he exists. So that, Gentlemen, you are turning your despots into so many wise men. Almost all men know their true interests, and do not follow them any the better for all that. The prodigal who eats his capital knows perfectly well that he is ruining himself, and nevertheless keeps on going ahead; what is the use of reason's enlightening us, when passion leads us?

> I see the better and approve it
> but follow the worse.

[3] This is what your despot, ambitious, prodigal, miserly, amorous, vindictive, jealous, weak, will do; for this is what they all do, and

what we all do. Gentlemen, allow me to say it to you; you attribute too much force to your calculations, and not enough to the inclinations of the human heart and the play of the passions. Your system is very good for the people of Utopia, it is worthless for the children of Adam.

[4] Here, according to my old ideas, is the great problem of Politics, which I compare to that of squaring the circle in Geometry, and of longitudes in Astronomy: *To find a form of Government that might place the law above man.*

[5] If this form can be found, let us look for it and try to establish it. You claim, Gentlemen, to find this dominant law in other people's evidence. You prove too much: for this evidence had to be in all Governments, or it will never be in a single one of them.

[6] If unfortunately this form cannot be found, and I frankly admit that I believe that it cannot be, then I am of the opinion that one has to go to the other extreme and all at once place man as much above the law as he can be, consequently to establish a despotism that is arbitrary and indeed the most arbitrary possible: I would wish the despot could be God. In a word, I see no tolerable mean between the most austere Democracy and the most perfect Hobbesism: for the conflict between men and the laws, which makes for a perpetual intestine war in the State, is the worst of all political States.

[7] But the Caligulas, the Neros, the Tiberiuses! . . . My God! . . . I writhe on the ground, and bewail being a human being.

[8] I did not understand everything you said about laws in your book, and what the new Author says about them in his. I find that he deals somewhat lightly with the different forms of Government, rather lightly above all with voting procedures. What he said about the vices of elective despotism is most true: these vices are terrible. Those of hereditary despotism, about which he said nothing, are even more so.

[9] Here is another problem that has been on my mind for a long time:

[10] *To find in arbitrary despotism a form of succession that is neither elective nor hereditary, or rather which is both at once, and by which one makes sure, as much as it is possible to do so, to have neither Tiberiuses nor Neros.*

[11] If ever I have the misfortune of dealing with this mad idea again, I will blame you for the rest of my life for getting me away from my fodder rack. I hope it will not happen; but whatever happens, Sir, do not ever again speak to me about your *legal despotism*. I could not appreciate or even understand it; and I see in it nothing but two contradictory words, which together signify nothing to me.

[12] I am all the more puzzled by your principle of population as it seems to me inexplicable in itself, in contradiction with the facts, impossible to reconcile with the origin of nations. According to you, Sir, population growth should only have begun when it really ceased. On my long held ideas, as soon as there was a penny's worth of what you call riches or disposable value, as soon as the first exchange took place, population growth must have ceased; and that is what did happen.

[13] Your economic system is admirable. Nothing is more profound, more true, more perceptive, more useful. It is full of great and sublime truths which transport one. It covers everything; the field is vast; but I am afraid that it will lead to countries quite different from those toward which you claim to go.

[14] I wanted to pay you obeisance by showing you that I had at least perused you. Now, illustrious friend of men and mine, I prostrate myself at your feet to implore you to take pity on my state and my misfortunes, to leave my dying head in peace, to refrain from awakening in it ideas that are almost extinct and can arise again only to plunge me into new abysses of suffering. Love me always; but do not send me any more books; do not again ask me to read any; do not even attempt to enlighten me if I stray; this is no longer the time for it. One does not become a sincere convert at my age. I may err, and you may convince me, but you cannot persuade me. Besides, I never engage in disputes; I prefer to yield and remain silent: accept my adhering to this resolve. I embrace you with the most tender friendship and most true respect.

[*OC* iv, *1133*]
LETTER TO M. DE FRANQUIÈRES

Here it is, Sir, this wretched chatter for which my humbled amour propre made you wait such a long time, because I failed to sense that a much nobler amour propre should have taught me to overcome the first. It does not much matter that my rambling might strike you as wretched, so long as I am satisfied with the sentiment which dictated it to me. As soon as my improved state restored some of my strength, I took the occasion to re-read and send it to you. If you have the courage to go on to the end, I ask you to be so kind and return it to me, without telling me anything of what you may have thought about it, and which I understand in any event. I greet you, Sir, and embrace you wholeheartedly.

Renou

Monquin, 25 March 1769

Bourgoin, 15 January 1769

[1] I feel, Sir, how useless it is for me to fulfill the duty of answering your latest letter: but after all it is a duty you impose on me, and I fulfill it readily though poorly, given the distractions of my present state.

[2] My aim in here telling you my opinion about the principal points raised by your letter is to tell it to you plainly, and without trying to make you adopt it. To try to make you do so would be at odds with my principles and even my taste. For I am just, and I no more try to subjugate others than I like to have anyone try to subjugate me. I know that the common reason is very restricted, [*1134*] that as soon as one goes beyond its narrow limits everyone has his own which suits only himself, that opinions are propagated by opinions [and] not by reason, and that anyone who yields to another's reasoning, which is already rare enough, yields by prejudice, by authority, by affection, by laziness; rarely, perhaps never, by his own judgment.

[3] You inform me, Sir, that the outcome of your inquiries about the author of things is a state of doubt. I cannot judge of this state, because it has never been mine. I believed in childhood by

authority, in youth by sentiment, in my mature years by reason; now I believe because I always believed. While my faded memory no longer puts me back on the track of my reasonings, while my weakened judgment keeps me from beginning them all over again, the opinions to which they led stay with me in all their force, and although I have neither the will nor the courage to re-examine them, I continue to hold to them in confidence and in conscience, certain that I devoted to their discussion all the attention and good faith of which I was capable [at a time] when my judgment was at its most vigorous. If I erred it is not my fault, it is the fault of nature, which did not grant my head a greater share of intelligence and reason. I have no more of them now, I have much less. On what basis, then, would I begin to deliberate all over again? Time grows short; departure draws near. I would never have time or strength enough to complete the great labor of a recasting. Allow me in any event to leave with the consistency and steadiness of a man, not the discouraging and timid doubts of a dotty driveller.

[4] From what I can recall of my old ideas, from what I can tell about how yours proceed, I can see that since we did not follow the same road in our inquiries, it is not surprising that we should not have reached the same conclusion. In balancing the proofs of the existence of God against the difficulties, you have not found either side outweighing the other sufficiently to reach a decision, and have remained in doubt. That is not how I went about it. I examined all the systems about the formation of the universe about which I could find out, I meditated about those I could imagine. I compared them all as [*1135*] best I could: and decided, not in favor of the one that presented me with no difficulties, for they all presented me with some; but in favor of the one that seemed to me to have the fewest. I told myself that these difficulties were in the nature of the thing, that the contemplation of the infinite would always exceed the limits of my understanding, that since I should never hope fully to conceive the system of nature, all I could do was to consider it from the sides I could grasp, that one had to know how to leave all the rest in peace, and I admit that in these inquiries I was thinking like the people about whom you speak, who do not reject a clear or sufficiently demonstrated proof because of the attendant unsolvable difficulties. I admit that at the time I was so rashly confident, or at least so strongly persuaded, that I would

have dared any philosopher to propose any other intelligible system about nature, to which I could not have opposed more forceful, more irresistible objections than those he could have opposed to mine, and I therefore had to resolve to be left not believing anything as you do, which did not depend on myself, or to reason badly, or to believe as I did.

[5] An idea that came to me thirty years ago contributed perhaps more than any other to make me unshakable. Let us assume, I said to myself, mankind having grown old until now in the most complete materialism, without ever any idea of divinity or of souls ever having entered a single human mind. Let us assume that philosophical atheism had exhausted all of its systems [in the effort] to explain the formation and the working of the universe exclusively by the interplay of matter and of necessary motion, an expression of which, by the way, I have never made any sense. I further assumed, excuse my candor, Sir, that what I have always seen would obtain in this state: that the restless partisans of these systems, instead of remaining quietly satisfied in them as in the lap of truth, constantly wanted to talk about their doctrine, to elucidate it, to expand it, to explain it, to moderate it, to correct it and, like someone who feels his house shaking under his feet, to bolster it with new arguments. Let us finally put an end to these assumptions with the assumption of a Plato, a Clarke, suddenly arising among them and telling them: my friends, if you had begun the analysis of this [*1136*] universe with the analysis of yourselves, you would have found in the nature of your being the key to the constitution of this very universe, which otherwise you seek in vain. That thereupon explaining the distinction between the two substances to them, he would have proven to them by the very properties of matter that, regardless of what Locke may say on the subject, the assumption of thinking matter is a genuine absurdity. That he would have shown them the nature of the truly active and thinking being, and that once this judging being had been established, he would finally have risen from it to the confused but certain notions of the supreme being: who can doubt that, struck by the brilliance, the simplicity, the truth, the beauty of this ravishing idea, mortals, who had been blind up to then, illumined by the first rays of the divinity, would have offered it their first homage by acclamation, and that above all the thinkers and the philosophers would have blushed at having contemplated the outside of this immense machine for such

a long time, without finding, without even suspecting the key to its constitution and, forever crudely limited to their senses, at never having been able to see anything but matter where everything showed them that another substance gave the universe life and intelligence to man. Under these circumstances, Sir, it is this new philosophy that would have been fashionable; young people and the wise would have found themselves in agreement; a doctrine so beautiful, so sublime, so sweet and so consoling to any just man would really have aroused all men to virtue, and this fair word *humanity*, nowadays hackneyed by the least humane people in the world to the point of becoming dull, ridiculous, would have been stamped in men's hearts better than in books. So that all it would have taken is a simple shift in time for philosophical fashion to be the very opposite of what it is, with this difference, that the current philosophical fashion, for all of its ostentatious verbiage, does not hold out the promise of a particularly estimable generation [of young people], or of particularly virtuous philosophers.

[6] You object, Sir, that if God had wanted to obligate men to know him, he would have made his existence evident to all eyes. It is up to those who make of faith in God a dogma necessary for salvation to reply to this objection, and they reply to it with revelation. As for myself, who believe in God without believing this faith to be necessary, I do not see why God would have obligated himself [*1137*] to give it to us. I believe that everyone will be judged not by what he believed, but by what he did, and I do not believe that a system of doctrine is necessary for works, because conscience takes its place.

[7] I do believe, it is true, that one has to be in good faith in one's belief, and not turn it into a system favoring our passions. Since we are not all intelligence, we cannot philosophize so disinterestedly that our will does not influence our opinions somewhat; one can often ascertain a man's secret inclinations by his purely speculative sentiments; and, on this assumption, I think that it might well be the case that someone who did not want to believe might be punished for not having believed.

[8] However, I believe that God revealed himself sufficiently to men both in his works and in their hearts, and if there are any who do not know him, it is, in my view, because they do not want to know him, or because they have no need of it.

[9] The latter case is that of man, savage and without culture,

who has not yet made any use of his reason, who, being governed solely by his appetites, needs no other guide, and following only the instinct of nature, always proceeds in an upright fashion. This [savage] man does not know God, but does not offend him. The former case, by contrast, is that of the philosopher who by dint of trying to exalt his intelligence, to refine, to subtilize what has been thought prior to him, ends up undermining all the axioms of simple and original reason, and who, because he is forever trying to know more and better than everyone else, succeeds in not knowing anything at all. The man who is both reasonable and modest, whose developed but restricted understanding feels its limits and confines itself to them, finds within these limits the notion of his soul and that of the author of his being without being able to go beyond [them] to clarify these notions and to contemplate each as closely as if he himself were a pure spirit. Whereupon, overcome by respect, he stops, and does not touch the veil, satisfied with knowing that the immense Being is underneath. This is how far it is useful to practice philosophy. The rest is nothing more than idle speculation for which man was not made, from which the moderate reasoner refrains, and in which vulgar man does not engage. This [reasonable and modest] man who is neither brute nor prodigy is man properly so called, the mean between [*1138*] the two extremes, and who makes up the nineteen twentieths of human Kind. It is up to this numerous class to sing the Psalm *Coeli enarrant*; and it is indeed this class which sings it. All peoples on earth know and adore God, and although each dresses him in its fashion, yet under all these different garbs one always finds God. The small elite who have higher doctrinal aspirations, and whose genius is not limited to common sense, want a more transcendent one: for which I do not blame them; but when from this they go on to put themselves in the place of human kind and to say that God has hidden himself from men because the small number no longer see him, I find that they are wrong in this. It can happen, I grant, that the sweep of fashion and the workings of intrigue expand the philosophical sect and for a moment persuade the many that they no longer believe in God: but this passing fashion cannot last, and regardless of how one goes about it, in the long run man will always have to have a God. Finally, if by forcing the nature of things the Divinity became more evident to us, I have no doubt that in the new Lyceum they would become proportionately more subtle in denying it. In the long run reason assumes the bend the heart gives it, and when one wants to think differently from the people about everything, one sooner or later manages to do so.

[10] None of this strikes you, Sir, as particularly philosophic, any more than it does me; but ever in good faith with myself I feel my reasonings, simple though they are, combining with the weight of internal assent. According to you one should be suspicious of it; I cannot share your view on this point, and I find, on the contrary, that this internal judgment is a natural safeguard against the sophisms of my reason. I am even afraid that on this occasion you mistake the secret inclinations of our heart which lead us astray for this still more secret, more internal dictamen, which protests and grumbles against these [self-]interested decisions, and in spite of ourselves sets us back on the road toward truth. This internal sentiment is the sentiment of nature itself, it is a call by it against all the sophisms of reason, and the proof of it is that it never speaks more forcefully than when our will yields most readily to the judgments which the internal sentiment persists in rejecting. Far from believing that whoever judges according to it is liable to [*1139*] err, I believe [rather] that it never misleads us and that it is the light of our feeble understanding, when we try to go beyond what we are capable of conceiving.

[11] And, after all, how often is not philosophy itself, for all its pride, forced to have recourse to this internal judgment which it pretends to despise? Was it not it alone that made Diogenes walk as his only reply to Zeno who denied motion? Was it not with it that the whole of ancient philosophy answered the skeptics? We need not go that far back; while all modern philosophy rejects spirits, suddenly Bishop Berkeley rises and maintains that there are no bodies. How did they succeed in refuting this terrible logician? Do away with the internal sentiment, and I defy all modern philosophers combined to prove to Berkeley that there are bodies. Dear young man, who seem to me to be so well born, be in good faith, I implore you, and allow me here to refer you to an author you will not find suspect, the author of the *Pensées philosophiques*. If someone were to tell you that, having thrown down a great many letters at random, he saw the *Aeneid* fully ordered result from this throw: grant that instead of going out to verify this wonder, you

will answer him coldly: Sir, this is not impossible; but you lie. By virtue of what, I ask you, do you answer him this way?

[12] Ah, who does not know that without the internal sentiment there would soon not be a trace of truth left on earth, that we would all be tossed about successively by the most monstrous opinions, as those propounding them have more genius, skill and wit, and that at last, reduced to blush of our very reason, we would end up at a loss to know what to believe or think.

[13] But the objections . . . No doubt there are some we are incapable of solving, and indeed there are many of them, I know. But, once again, give me a system without any, or tell me how I am to decide. What is more; by the nature of my system, provided my direct proofs are well established, the difficulties should not stop me, in view of the impossibility for me, who am a composite being, to reason with precision about pure spirits, and to observe their nature sufficiently [adequately]. But you materialists who speak to me [*1140*] of a single substance, tangible, and subject by its nature to the inspection of the senses, you are obliged not only to tell me nothing but what is clear, adequately demonstrated, but also to resolve all my difficulties in a fully satisfactory fashion, because both you and I are in possession of all the instruments needed for this solution. And, for example, when you have thought arise from combinations of matter, you must make these combinations and their result perceptible to me by the laws of physics and mechanics alone since you allow for no others. You Epicurean, you make up the soul with subtle atoms. But what, pray, do you call *subtle*? You are aware that we know no absolute dimensions, and that nothing is small or large except relatively to the eye looking at it. I assume I take a sufficiently powerful microscope and look at one of your atoms. I see a big chunk of hooked rock. I am waiting to see thought result from the swirling and linking up with one another of such chunks. You Modernist, you show me an organic molecule: I take my microscope, and I see a dragon as large as half my room; I wait to see such dragons mould and twist themselves until I see resulting from all this a being that is not only organized but intelligent; that is to say a being that is not an aggregate but is strictly one, etc. You told me, Sir, that the world had arranged itself fortuitously, the way the Roman Republic had done. For the analogy not to limp, the Roman Republic would have to have been

made up not of men but of pieces of wood. Show me clearly and in a way perceptible to the senses the purely material generation of the first intelligent being, I ask nothing more of you.

[14] But if everything is the work of an intelligent, powerful, beneficent being, where does the evil on earth come from? I admit to you that this terrible difficulty never greatly struck me, either because I had not understood it adequately, or because it is indeed not as solid as it appears to be. Our philosophers have risen in protest against metaphysical entities, yet I know no one who makes up so many of them. What do they understand by *evil?* what is *evil* in itself? where is *evil* in relation to nature and its author? The universe subsists, order prevails and [*1141*] endures in it; everything in it successively perishes, because such is the law of material and moved beings; but everything in it renews itself and nothing in it degenerates, because such is the order of its author, and this order cannot be denied. I see nothing evil in all this. But when I suffer, is that not an evil? When I die, is that not an evil? Gently: I am subject to death because I received life; there was but one way for me never to die, which was never to have been born. Life is a positive but finite good, whose term is called death. The term of the positive is not the negative, it is zero. Death seems terrible to us, and we call this terror an evil. Pain is another evil for the one who suffers, I grant it. But pain and pleasure were the only means by which to attach a sentient and perishable being to his self-preservation, and these means are managed with a goodness worthy of the supreme Being. At the very moment of writing this, I once again experienced how much the cessation of an acute pain is a lively and delicious pleasure. Would anyone dare tell me that the cessation of the most lively pleasure is an acute pain? The sweet enjoyment of life is permanent; all that is required to savor it is not to be suffering. Pain is but a warning, importunate but necessary, that this good which is so dear to us is in danger. When I examined all this closely, I found, perhaps I proved that the sentiment of death and that of pain are almost nil in the order of nature. It is men who have given it a sharp edge. Without their senseless refinements, without their barbarous institutions, physical evils would hardly reach or affect us, and we would not feel death.

[15] But moral evil! another work of man in which God has no other share than to have made him free and like himself in this

respect. Will God then have to be blamed for men's crimes and the evils which they visit upon them? Will he have to be reproved, at the sight of a battlefield, for having created so many broken legs and arms?

[16] Why, you will say, have made man free, since he was bound to abuse his freedom? Ah! M. de Franquières, if ever a mortal existed who did not abuse it, this mortal alone honors humanity more than all the scoundrels who cover the earth degrade it. My God: give me virtues, and some day place me next to [*1142*] the likes of Fénelon, of Cato, of Socrates. What will the rest of mankind matter to me? I will not blush to have been a man.

[17] I told you, Sir, that what is at issue here is my sentiment, not my proofs, as you all too readily see. I recall formerly meeting up along my way with this question of the origin of evil and touching on it; but you have not read these harpings, and I have forgotten them: we have both done well. All I know is that I found it so easy to resolve them because of the opinion I always held regarding the eternal coexistence of two principles, one active which is God, the other passive, which is matter [and] which the active being has full power to combine and to modify, but did not create and has not the power to annihilate. This opinion has led to my being booed by the philosophers to whom I told it; they decided that it was absurd and contradictory. It may be, but it did not seem to me to be so, and I found that it had the advantage of explaining effortlessly and clearly to my satisfaction so many questions in which they get caught up; among others the one you here presented to me as insoluble.

[18] Besides, I dare believe that while my sentiment may not carry much weight in any other matter, it must carry some in this matter, and once you are better acquainted with my fate, you will perhaps some day say in thinking of me: has anyone else the right to expand the range he found of the evils man suffers here below.

[19] You attribute to the difficulty of this very question – of which fanaticism and superstition have taken advantage – the evils which religions have caused on earth. That may be so, and I even admit to you that all formulae in matters of faith seem to me to be so many chains of iniquity, falsity, hypocrisy and tyranny. But let us beware of being unjust, and not eliminate the good for the sake of magnifying the evil. To wrest all belief in God from men's heart

is to destroy all virtue in it. That is my opinion, Sir, perhaps it is wrong, but so long as it is mine I will not be so cowardly as to hide it from you.

[20] To do good is a well-born man's sweetest occupation. His probity, his beneficence are not the work of his principles, but of his good nature. He yields to his inclinations in practicing justice, as the [*1143*] wicked man yields to his inclination in practicing iniquity. To satisfy the taste that inclines us to do good is goodness, but not virtue.

[21] This word virtue means *force*. There is no virtue without struggle, there is none without victory. Virtue consists not only in being just, but in being so by triumphing over one's passions, by ruling over one's own heart. Titus, making the Roman people happy, everywhere spreading gifts and benefits, might not waste a single day, and yet not be virtuous; he certainly was so in sending back Berenice. Brutus causing his children to be put to death may have been more than just. But Brutus was a tender father; to do his duty he tore up his insides, and Brutus was virtuous.

[22] Here you already see the question brought back to the main point. This divine simulacrum about which you tell me shows itself to me as a not ignoble image, and I believe that I feel the warmth which this image is capable of generating from the impression which it makes on my heart. But in the final analysis this simulacrum is still nothing but one of those metaphysical entities which you do not want men to turn into their Gods. It is a pure object of contemplation. How far do you take the effect of this sublime contemplation? If all you want is to derive from it further encouragement to do the right thing, I agree with you: but that is not the issue. Let us assume your honest heart a prey to the most terrible passions, which you cannot escape because, after all, you are a man. Will this image, which shows itself so ravishing in your heart when it is calm, lose none of its charms and not get tarnished amidst the torrents [of these passions]? Let us set aside the discouraging and terrible assumption of the dangers that might tempt virtue driven to despair. Let us only assume that an overly sensitive heart burns with an involuntary love for his friend's daughter or his wife, that with heaven that sees no part of it on one side, and himself who wants not to tell anyone anything about it on the other, he is free to enjoy her; that her charming figure adorned by all the attractions

of beauty and voluptuousness attracts him; will this abstract image of virtue deny his heart the real object that strikes it at the very moment when his intoxicated senses are ready to yield to their pleasures? will it in that instant appear to him to be the more beautiful, will it wrest him out of his beloved's arms to [*1144*] devote himself to the vain contemplation of a specter he knows to be devoid of reality? Will he end up like Joseph, and leave his coat? No, Sir, he will close his eyes and succumb. The believer, you will say, will succumb as well. Yes, the weak man; the one who is writing to you, for example: but give both of them the same amount of force, and watch the difference which their fulcrum makes.

[23] How is one to resist violent temptations, Sir, when one can yield to them without fear by telling oneself: what is the good of resisting? In order to be virtuous, the philosopher needs to be so in the eyes of men; but the just man is strong enough under the eyes of God. He sets so little stock by this life and its goods and evils and all of its worldly glory! he perceives so much beyond! Invincible force of virtue, none knows you but the one who feels your whole being and who knows that it is not within men's power to dispose of it. Do you sometimes read Plato's *Republic*? Look up with how much energy Socrates's friend, whose name I have forgotten, depicts to him the just beset by the outrages of fortune and the injustices of men, defamed, persecuted, tormented, a prey to all the disgrace of crime while deserving all the rewards of virtue, already seeing death drawing nigh, and certain that the hatred of the wicked will not spare his memory once they no longer have the power to harm his person. What a discouraging scene, if anything can discourage virtue. Socrates himself frightened, calls out, and believes he has to invoke the Gods before answering; but without the hope of another life, he would have answered poorly for this one. However, if everything should end for us with death, which cannot be if God is just and hence if he exists, even the mere idea of this existence would be for man an encouragement to virtue and a consolation in his miseries, which the person who, believing himself isolated in this universe, lacks for not feeling in the depths of his heart a confidant of his thoughts. It is at least one solace in adversity to have a witness to one's not having deserved it; it is a pride truly worthy of virtue to be able to say to God: You who read in my heart, you see that I use the freedom you have given me as a strong

soul and a just man does. The true believer, who everywhere feels under the eternal eye, likes to do himself honor in the face of heaven by having fulfilled his duties on earth.

[*1145*] [24] You see that I have not taken issue with you about this simulacrum which you presented to me as the sole object of the wise man's virtues. But, my dear Sir, return to yourself now, and see how uncombinable, incompatible this object is with your principles. How can you fail to be sensible [to the fact] that this same law of necessity which, according to you, alone regulates how the world and all events proceed, also regulates all the actions of men, all the thoughts of their heads, all the sentiments of their hearts, that nothing is free, that all is forced, necessary, inevitable; that all the movements of man, directed by blind matter, depend on his will only because his will itself depends on necessity: that there are in consequence neither virtues nor vices, neither merit nor demerit, nor [any] morality in human conduct, and that for you the words honest man or scoundrel must be devoid of all sense? Yet they are not so, I am quite certain of it. For all of your arguments, your honest heart protests against your sad philosophy. You are sensible to the sentiment of freedom, to the charm of virtue in spite of yourself, and this is how on all sides this forceful and salutary voice of the internal sentiment recalls everyone whom his misguided reason leads astray to the bosom of truth and of virtue. Bless this holy and beneficent voice, Sir, which returns you to the duties of man and which the fashionable philosophy would end up making you forget. Yield to your arguments only when you feel that they agree with the dictamen of your conscience, and whenever you feel that they contradict it, you may be sure that it is they that deceive you.

[25] Although I do not wish to quibble with you, nor to follow your two letters step by step, I can nevertheless not refrain from saying a word about the parallel between the Hebrew wise man and the Greek wise man. Being an admirer of the one as well as of the other I can scarcely be suspected of prejudice in speaking about them. I do not believe that the same is true of you. I am not greatly surprised that you give every advantage to the second. You have not become sufficiently acquainted with the other, and you have not taken sufficient care to disentangle what is truly his from what is foreign to him and disfigures him in your eyes, as it does in those

of a good many other people who, [*1146*] in my view, have not examined this any more closely than have you. If Jesus had been born in Athens and Socrates in Jerusalem, if Plato and Xenophon had written the life of the first, and Luke and Matthew that of the other, you would speak very differently; and what discredits him in your mind is precisely what makes his loftiness of soul more astonishing and more admirable, namely, his birth in Judaea among perhaps the most abject people at that time, whereas Socrates, born among the most educated and agreeable people, found all the assistance he needed to ascend easily to the tone which he assumed. He rose up against the Sophists as Jesus did against the Priests, with this difference that Socrates often imitated his opponents, and that if his beautiful and fine death had not done honor to his life he would have been taken for a sophist like themselves. As for Jesus, the great flight his great soul took invariably raised him above all mortals, and from the age of twelve to the moment he expired in the most cruel as well as the most ignominious of all deaths he was never untrue to himself. His noble project was to raise up his people anew, once again to make it a free people and worthy of being free; for this is where the beginning had to be made. His profound study of the Law of Moses, his efforts to arouse enthusiasm and love for it in [his people's] hearts exhibited his aim as much as it was possible to do so in order not to frighten the Romans. But instead of heeding him his abject and cowardly compatriots grew to hate him precisely because of his genius and his virtue which were a reproof to them for their worthlessness. In the end, it was only after he had seen how impossible it was to carry out his project that he expanded it in his head and, unable to make a revolution among his People by himself, he sought to make one in the Universe by his disciples. What prevented his succeeding in his first plan, besides the baseness of his people [who were] incapable of all virtue, was the excessive gentleness of his own character; a gentleness more like an angel's and a God's than a human being's, and which did not forsake him for an instant, even on the cross, and causes anyone to weep torrents of tears who is capable of reading his life as one ought to, through all the ado with which these poor folk disfigured it. Fortunately they respected and faithfully transcribed his speeches which they did not understand: discard a few oriental or poorly translated turns, there is not a word in them that is not worthy [*1147*] of him, and it is in this that one recognizes the divine man, who of such paltry disciples nevertheless made men who in their crude but proud enthusiasm were eloquent and courageous.

[26] You raise as an objection against me that he performed miracles. The objection would be terrible if it were just. But you know, Sir, or at least you could know that, according to me, Jesus, so far from having performed miracles, very positively declared that he would not perform any, and showed very great contempt for those who asked for them.

[27] How many things remain to be said! But this letter is enormous; it is time to end. This is the last time I shall return to these matters. I wanted to oblige you, Sir, and I do not repent I did; on the contrary. I thank you for having made me take up a thread of ideas that have almost faded, but the remains of which may be of some use to me in the state I am in.

[28] Adieu, Sir, remember occasionally a man whom, so I flatter myself, you would have loved if you had known him better, and who concerned himself with you at a time when one is scarcely concerned with anyone other than oneself.

Renou

Abbreviations and textual conventions

Buffon, *OP*	Georges-Louis Leclerc, Comte de Buffon, *Oeuvres philosophiques*, edited by Jean Piveteau (PUF, Paris, 1954)
CC	Jean-Jacques Rousseau, *Correspondance complète*, collected, edited, and annotated by R.A. Leigh (Institut et Musée Voltaire, Geneva, and The Voltaire Foundation at the Taylor Institution, Oxford, 1965–1989)
Conf.	*Confessions*
d'Alembert	*Lettre à M. d'Alembert sur les spectacles*, in *OC* V, 1–125, and edited by M. Fuchs (Droz, Geneva, 1948)
tr.	translated by A. Bloom as *Politics and the Arts* (The Free Press, Glencoe, IL, 1960)
Dictionnaire de Musique	in *OC* V, 603–1191
Discourses tr.	Jean-Jacques Rousseau, *"The Discourses" and other early political writings*, translated, with an Introduction and Notes, by Victor Gourevitch (Cambridge Texts in the History of Political Thought, Cambridge, 1997)
Emile	*Emile, ou de l'éducation*, in *OC* IV, 239–868
Emile tr.	translation by A. Bloom (Basic Books, New York, 1979)
First Discourse	*Discourse on the Sciences and Arts*: in *Discourses* tr.

Franquières	*Letter to Franquières*: in *SC* tr.
Geneva ms.	the extensive early draft of the *Social Contract*: portions of which are translated in *SC* tr.
Grotius, *Right*	Grotius, *The Right of War and Peace* (London, 1738)
Hero	*Discourse on the Virtue a Hero Most Needs* or *Discourse on Heroic Virtue*: in *Discourses* tr.
Hobbes, *De cive*	Hobbes, *De cive*, edited by H. Warrander (Clarendon, Oxford, 1983)
Ineq.	*Discourse on the Origin and Foundations of Inequality among Men* (the so-called *Second Discourse*): in *Discourses* tr.
E	Exordium
ED	Epistle Dedicatory
N	Rousseau's Notes, thus: N IX [13] refers to para. 13 of Rousseau's Note IX
P	Preface
Languages	*Essay on the Origin of Languages*: in *Discourses* tr.
LM	*Lettres écrites de la montagne*: in *OC* III, 683–897
Meier, *Diskurs/ Discours*	Heinrich Meier, *Diskurs über die Ungleichheit/ Discours sur l'inégalité, kritische Ausgabe des integralen Textes, mit sämtlichen Fragmenten und ergänzenden Materialien nach den Originalausgaben und den Handschriften neu ediert, übersetzt und kommentiert* (second edition, Schöningh, Munich, 1990)
Method	*Idea of the Method in the Composition of a Book*: in *Discourses* tr.
Montaigne, *OC*	Montaigne, *Oeuvres complètes*, edited by A. Thibaudet and M. Rat (Paris, Pléiade, 1962)
Montaigne tr.	Montaigne, *The Complete Essays*, translated by Donald Frame (Stanford University Press, Stanford, 1958)
Narcissus	*Preface to "Narcissus"*: in *Discourses* tr.
NH	*La Nouvelle Héloïse*
OC	Jean-Jacques Rousseau, *Oeuvres complètes*, edited by B. Gagnebin and M. Raymond

	(Paris, Pléiade, 1959–1995). For example, *OC* III, 202–204 refers to pages 202–204 in volume III; [*202*] in the body of a translation indicates that what follows corresponds to page 202 of the relevant volume of *OC*.
Philopolis	*Letter to Philopolis*: in *Discourses* tr.
Pol. Ec.	*Discourse on Political Economy*: in *SC* tr.
Poland	*Considerations on the Government of Poland*: in *SC* tr.
Pufendorf, *Droit*	Samuel Pufendorf, *Le Droit de la nature et des gens*, translated by Jean Barbeyrac (Amsterdam, 1712)
Pufendorf, *Man and Citizen*	Samuel Pufendorf, *Les Devoirs de l'homme et du citoyen*, English translation by Michael Silverthorne (Cambridge Texts in the History of Political Thought, Cambridge, 1991)
Rêveries	*Rêveries du promeneur solitaire*,
tr.	translated as *Reveries of the Solitary Walker* by Charles E. Butterworth (New York University Press, New York, 1979; reprint, Hackett Publishing, Indianapolis, IN and Cambridge, MA, 1992)
SC	*Of the Social Contract*: in *SC* tr.
SC tr.	Jean-Jacques Rousseau, *"The Social Contract" and other later political writings*, translated, with an Introduction and Notes, by Victor Gourevitch (Cambridge Texts in the History of Political Thought, Cambridge, 1997)
Second Discourse	*Discourse on the Origin and the Foundations of Inequality among Men*: in *Discourses* tr.
Second Letter	*Preface of a Second Letter to Bordes*: in *Discourses* tr.
Vaughan, *Rousseau*	*Jean-Jacques Rousseau: The Political Writings*, edited by C. E. Vaughan, 2 vols. (CUP, Cambridge, 1915; reprinted by Basil Blackwell, Oxford, 1962)
Voltaire	*Letter to Voltaire*: in *Discourses* tr.
War	*The State of War*: in *SC* tr.

[23]	paragraph numbers
[*23*]	*OC* page numbers (see explanation above)
*, **	Rousseau's footnotes, numbered by paragraph in the sequence *, **

Editorial notes

POLITICAL ECONOMY (pages 3–38)

The essay on *Political Economy* was first published in November 1755, in volume V of Diderot's and d'Alembert's *Encyclopedia*, the volume which also contained Diderot's important article "Natural Right." An unauthorized reprint in pamphlet form of the article appeared in 1758 under the title *Discourse on Political Economy*, a title which Rousseau retained in the subsequent, authorized and corrected editions.

Rousseau certainly worked on the *Political Economy* between October 1754 and mid-1755, immediately after the *Second Discourse*, and he may well have worked on it earlier. The differences between the two works are best understood as due to the different perspectives from which they are written: in the *Second Discourse* he digs, as he says, to the roots (*Ineq.* I [47]) or first principles, to what in the title of the *Discourse* he refers to as "the origin and foundations" of political society; in the *Political Economy*, by contrast, he is primarily concerned with the workings of a legitimate political order, and most particularly with its administration, what he here primarily means by its "economy," and what in the language of the *Social Contract* he will call the "government" in contrast to the "sovereign."

The present translation is based on the Pléiade edition text, *OC* III, 239–278, edited by Robert Derathé. This edition records the additions and corrections in the 1782 Moultou-Du Peyrou edition; the more important are flagged in the Editorial Notes to this translation.

The other important recent edition of the *Political Economy* is that by C.E. Vaughan, included in his *Jean-Jacques Rousseau: The Political Writings*, 2 vols. (CUP, Cambridge, 1915; reprinted by Basil Blackwell, Oxford, 1962), vol. I, pp. 237–273; Vaughan also published fragments of drafts of the text, *ib.* pp. 274-280. Michel Launay has published additional drafts and fragments in his edition of Rousseau's *Oeuvres complètes* (Editions du Seuil, Paris, 1971), vol. II, pp. 294–305.

In preparing the present translation, I have consulted the annotated translations into English by Roger D. and Judith R. Masters (St. Martin's Press, New York, 1978), and by Charles Sherover (Harper & Row, New York, 1984); and into German by Dietrich Leube *et al.*, in *Jean-Jacques Rousseau, sozialphilosophische und politische Schriften* (Winkler, Munich, 1981), annotations by Eckhart Koch. Professor William J. Barber helped with some technical tax terminology. I have not had access to the manuscript or to the editions supervised by Rousseau himself, and have therefore followed the Pléiade text to the point of not capitalizing words he normally capitalizes, such as "State" (as used in *SC* I 7 [10]).

So far as I know, this important and difficult text has never been the object of a detailed, critical commentary. Yet it amply repays careful study. It is to be hoped that someone will undertake one before long.

[1] **state** Throughout this text I have adhered to the Pléiade *OC* edition's practice of consistently spelling "state" in both senses of the term with a lower-case "s." In all other major texts, Rousseau reserved the lower-case spelling to "state" in the sense of "condition:" as in "state of affairs" or "state of nature." Both Vaughan and Launay therefore capitalize "State" in the sense of "political society" throughout their editions of the *Discourse on Political Economy*. **general** or **political economy** Rousseau also twice calls it *public economy*: [7], [8]. **see** FATHER OF THE FAMILY I.e. see the *Encyclopedia* article under that heading.

[3] **the magistrate can command others only by virtue of the laws.** The 1782 edition continues: "the power of the father over the children, based on what is to their particular advantage, can, by its nature, not extend to the right of life and death: but the sovereign power, which has no other object than the common good, has no other bounds than public utility properly understood: a distinction I will explain in the appropriate place."

[7] **Sir** Robert **Filmer**, *Patriarcha, or the Natural Power of Kings*, London, 1680; discussed by Barbeyrac in his translation of Pufendorf's *Droit de la nature et des gens*, IV, 2, § x, n. 2; refuted by Locke, *First Treatise of Government* and by Algernon Sidney, *Discourse Concerning Government*; **Aristotle saw fit to combat it . . . in the first book of his** *Politics*: "Those who suppose that the same person is expert in political [rule], kingly [rule], managing the household and being a master [of slaves] do not argue rightly. For they consider that each of these differs in the multitude or fewness [of those ruled] and not in

kind": I, I, 1252a 6–11 (Lord, tr.); cp. I, 12, 1259b; III, 1278b, 1285b, 14, 15; *Nicomachaean Ethics* VIII, 10, 1160b 24–1161a 9.

[10] **The body politic ... can be looked upon as an organized body, ... similar to a man's.** So, too, Hobbes at the beginning of the Introduction to the *Leviathan*; as Rousseau expressly warns, the analogy limps. Rousseau also frequently compares political society to a mechanism moved by springs which have to be re-wound every now and then.

[12] **moral being** Rousseau understands the expression in the technical sense attached to it by Pufendorf: a moral, in contrast to a physical being, is constituted by men's beliefs and practices; for a fuller statement of how he understands this expression, see *Geneva ms.* I 2 [8] *et seq.* **general will** This is the first occurrence of the expression in Rousseau's writings. It occurs in Diderot's article *"Droit naturel"* ("Natural Right"), to which Rousseau refers a few lines below, and which appeared in the same volume of the *Encyclopedia* as this article of Rousseau's; for a history of the term and the conception, see Patrick Riley, *The General Will before Rousseau: The Transformation of the Divine into the Civic* (Princeton, 1986); and see the Introduction above, pp. xiii, xvii, xx–xxii. **the cunning prescribed to Lacedaemonian children to earn their frugal meal** So, too, Hobbes, *De cive* VI, 16 and XIV, 10; discussed and rejected by Pufendorf, *Droit*, VIII, 1, § iii. *See under* RIGHT I.e. Diderot's article on "Natural Right" (translated by Wokler and Mason in their edition of *Diderot's Political Writings* [Cambridge Texts in the History of Political Thought, Cambridge, 1992], pp. 17–21); see also Introduction, p. xiii above.

[17] **even brigands ...** Diderot, *Natural Right*, ix, 4.

[19] **men united by their mutual needs in the great society** Or "general society:" *Geneva ms.* I 2 [2]; this is the stage introduced by the division of labor and hence of mutual dependence that made the institution of political society necessary: *Ineq.* II [19]–[29] and *SC* I 6 [1]; contrast with Locke, *Treatises* II, § 128.

[21] **Plato ... a reasoned preamble which shows their justice and utility** *Laws* IV 719e–724a. **It has always been noted that the countries where punishments are most terrible are also the countries where they are most frequent ...** Rousseau does not go on to say, as did Montesquieu, that frequency and severity of punishments decreases in direct proportion as political freedom increases: *Of the Spirit of the Laws* VI 9.

[23] **lawgiver** The first mention of the figure – or conception – that will be assigned such a prominent place in the *Social Contract* (II 7). **Not that the affair is not subsequently examined ...** Reading *Ce*

n'est pas qu'on n'examine with Vaughan, Launay, and as the sense requires, in place of the Pléiade *OC*'s *Ce n'est pas qu'on examine.*

[24] **form men if you want to command men** We would be more likely to say "train men"; but here and in a number of later passages "form" is preferred because of its associations with the traditional distinction between form and matter, and because the reader would miss Rousseau's allusions when he uses such terms as "malformed" and "transform" [36].

[26] **those who are only waiting for impunity to do evil will scarcely lack** Reading *manquent* as the sense requires, in place of the Pléiade *OC*'s *manque.*

[28] **wicked oneself** The 1782 edition goes on: " 'Sicuti enim est aliquando misericordia puniens, ita est crudelitas parcens.' Aug[ustine], *Epist[olae]*, 54." ["Just as pity can sometimes punish, so can cruelty pardon."]

[30] **Socrates . . . Cato** Socrates (469–399 BC) lived through the Peloponnesian War (431–404 BC), but did not long survive Athens's defeat by Sparta; the Younger Cato (95–46 BC), a Stoic; long opposed Caesar; when all was lost he committed suicide rather than survive the death of the Republic; Rousseau called him "the greatest of men"; on the comparison, see the Introduction, p. xxx above. **Caesar and Pompey** had long competed for the first place in Rome; for a time they had done so as allies, but later became enemies. Caesar defeated Pompey at Pharsalus (48 BC); Pompey thereupon fled to Egypt where, not long afterwards, he was murdered.

[33] **the lex Porcia** or Porciae, named for the Elder Cato, M. Portius Cato, was promulgated probably in 198 BC; it also prohibited the scourging of Roman citizens without appeal.

[35] **tax-farmers** or publicans (*fermiers généraux*), were, by the middle of the eighteenth century, sixty individual financiers or syndicates who bought (at auction) the privilege of collecting taxes in a district (for a period of six years), in exchange for remittal of an agreed upon sum to the State. It is obvious that the system invited gross abuse; but certainly not all tax-farmers abused their powers. The philosopher Helvétius, as well as the chemist Lavoisier, were tax-farmers. For a melancholy account, see Tocqueville, *The Ancien Régime and the Revolution* II, 12.

[36] **anyone who has to govern men should not look for a perfection beyond their nature of which they are not capable** Cp. the opening of the *Social Contract*: "I want to inquire whether in the civil order there can be some legitimate and sure rule of administration, taking men as they are . . ."

[39] **public education in former times; namely, the Cretans, the Lacedaemonians, and the ancient Persians** Plato, *Laws* 671–674, *Alcibiades* 121e–122a, reported by Montaigne, *Essays*, I, 25 and I, 31; also *First Discourse* [22], [51]**.

[43] **Pufendorf has shown, by its nature the right of property does not extend beyond the life of the proprietor** "since the things that can be objects of property are of use to men only as long as they are alive, and the dead have no more part in the affairs of this world; it was not necessary for the institution of Property to extend to the point of giving the Proprietor the power of choosing whomever he likes to inherit the goods he leaves at death": *Droit de la nature et des gens* IIV, 10, § iv.

[45] **If the people governed itself . . . But things cannot possibly work this way . . . civil society is always too numerous to allow it to be governed by all of its members.** This is a constant in Rousseau's analysis of political society; it leads to the rise of what he calls "governments" and the "hypothetical history of governments" in the *Second Discourse* II [36]; and it leads him to reject direct democracy in the *Social Contract*: III 4 [3].

[47] **the integrity of the quaestor Cato**: Plutarch, *Cato the Younger* XVII, I, ii; XVIII, 1–4. **an emperor rewarding a singer's talents.** Galba (3 BC–AD 69), emperor for a year after Nero's murder. Plutarch says it was a flute-player, not a singer, Galba rewarded out of his own pocket: Plutarch, *Galba* XVI, 1–2.

[50] **on sufferance** By which Rousseau appears to mean that a state in debt is a state that is not entirely stable, and hence does not fully enjoy – or deserve – the citizens' trust.

[51] **granaries** A practice sharply criticized by the physiocrat Quesnais in his article "Grain" in the *Encyclopedia* vol. VII (p. 825), in 1757; Rousseau repeats his endorsement of the practice in his *Project for a Constitution for Corsica*, OC III, 923 (Derathé). *It nourishes and enriches: alit et ditat.*

[52] **the policy Joseph followed with the Egyptians** *Genesis* 47:14–26; cp. *ib.* 41:34–36, 47–49.

[55] **courageous citizens who were ready to shed their blood for the fatherland** Rousseau consistently favors citizen armies and consistently criticizes professional or mercenary troops: e.g. *Poland* [12]; it is in this spirit that he goes on: **Marius . . . in the war against Jugurtha, [111–105 BC] dishonored the legions . . .** Because the changes he introduced marked the beginning of a professional army in Rome; Rousseau develops this theme at length in the *Social Contract*

(especially IV 4 [18]); there, as here, he draws a close parallel between the professionalization of the army and the decline of the Republic. This criticism goes hand in hand with his criticism, in the present *Discourse* as well as in the *Considerations on the Government of Poland*, of taxation in the form of money rather than in the form of public service (II [5]) and of his criticism, in the *Social Contract*, of claims to represent the sovereign will (*Social Contract*, III 15 [6]–[8]).

The argument and even the language of the remainder of this paragraph very closely corresponds to the description of the final stage of inequality in the *Second Discourse* II [53]–[57].

[58] ... everyone obligates himself, at least tacitly, to contribute toward the public needs; ... to be legitimate, this contribution has to be voluntary ... by a general will, with a majority vote ... In the margin of the draft version of the *Discourse* Rousseau wrote at this point: "see Locke." The reference would be to the following paragraph: " 'Tis true, Governments cannot be supported without great Charge, and 'tis fit every one who enjoys his share of the Protection, should pay out of his Estate his proportion of the maintenance of it. But still, it must be with his own Consent, *i.e.* the Consent of the Majority, giving it either by themselves, or their Representatives chosen by them. For if anyone shall claim a *Power to lay* and levy *Taxes* on the People, by his own Authority, and without the consent of the People, he thereby invades the *Fundamental Law of Property*, and subverts the end of Government. For what property have I in that which another may by right take, when he pleases to himself?": *Second Treatise of Government* 11, § 140. Rousseau's argument and language very closely correspond to this passage, down to the reference to "fundamental law."

[59] taxes i.e. *impôts*; which, in Rousseau's usage, may mean, as it does here, what we would call "tax" in the most general sense of that term, or, sometimes, "impost"; very occasionally he distinguishes between *taxe* and *impôt*, as he does in the next paragraph. not excepting Bodin, who pointed out that "It was decided at the estates of this Kingdom[,] King Philip de Valois being in attendance[,] in the year 1338[,] that no taxes would be levied of the people, without its consent": *The Six Books on the Republic* (1576) VI, ii (Derathé).

[60] In the book on the *Spirit of the Laws* one finds that the head tax is more in keeping with servitude, and the real tax more conformable with freedom. Rousseau is quoting the opening sentence of Montesquieu's *Of the Spirit of the Laws* XIII, 14. But if reading: *Mais si la* taxe, as the sense requires, in place of *Mais la taxe* as in the Pléiade *OC* edition.

[62] ... **everything the poor man pays is forever lost to him, and remains in the hands of the rich or returns to them** For the argument in support of this conclusion, see [69].

[68] **financier**: the official charged with levying the public revenues; both tax-assessor and tax-collector. **Chardin** ... **Herodotus reports**: "In the reigns of Cyrus and Cambyses there had been no regular and fixed tax, only collection of gifts ... I have not recorded any taxation of Persia, which is the only country not subject to tax. The Persians hold their land free of tax": Herodotus, *Histories* III, 89, 97 (David Grene, tr.). This report follows immediately upon Herodotus's report of the discussion about the best regime by the seven liberators of Persia, and of Otanes's relinquishing any title to rule, which Rousseau discusses in *Ineq.* Note I. **intendants** To a mid-eighteenth-century French reader, this would most particularly have called to mind the *intendants*, of whom there were thirty at the time, and who administered entire provinces in the King's name; very loosely, their powers and responsibilities corresponded to those of what are now known as "prefects."

[77] **I said** in [59] above **that** ... **personal taxes and imposts** ... **are always liable to dangerous consequences, unless** ... **established with the express consent of the people or of its representatives**. Rousseau's explicitly calling attention to this remark clearly indicates that his mention of "representatives" is not accidental; yet in the *Social Contract* he very emphatically rejects the possibility of representing the general will or sovereignty (III 15; cp. II 1 [1]; II 4 [6]; III 14 [1]); it is, of course, possible that he changed his mind on this subject, but there are other, more plausible ways of explaining this difference.

OF THE SOCIAL CONTRACT (pages 39–152)

The present translation is based on the corrected 1979 printing of the Pléiade edition of the text, edited by Robert Derathé: *OC* III, 347–470; departures from it are flagged in the Editorial Notes.

The other authoritative critical editions of the *Social Contract* are: *Du Contrat Social*, edited and annotated by E. Dreyfus-Brisac (Alcan, Paris, 1896); *Du Contrat Social*, edited and annotated by Georges Beaulavon (Société nouvelle de librairie et d'édition, Paris, 1903); *Du Contrat social*, edited and annotated by C. E. Vaughan (Manchester University Press, Manchester, 1918); *Du Contrat Social*, edited and annotated by R. Grimsley (Clarendon, Oxford, 1972).

Title page Rousseau wavered about his title: the manuscript title page of an early draft of the work, known as the *Geneva ms.*, shows "Of the

Social Contract" crossed out and replaced by "Of Civil Society," which is again crossed out and replaced by the original "Of the Social Contract"; the second line reads "or"; and the third line gives as sub-title "Essay on the Constitution of the State"; "Constitution of the State" is then crossed out and replaced by "Formation of the Body Politic"; "Body Politic" is then crossed out and replaced by "the State," which is then also crossed out, to leave the sub-title to read "Essay on the Form of the Republic." In the definitive version, the subtitle became "Principles of Political Right." See the reproduction in Dreyfus-Brisac's edition of *Du Contrat Social*, pp. 244–245, and the account of it, pp. xxi *et seq.* **foederis** . . . **leges** "Let us declare the fair laws of a compact": Virgil, *Aeneid* XI, 321; spoken by the King of Latium, whose army has just been defeated by the invading Trojans under Aeneas's command. In the event his suggestion goes unheeded, and the victorious Trojans proceed to found Rome.

I [1] **taking men as they are** The sentiment goes back to Machiavelli, *Prince* XV [1]. Spinoza, echoing Machiavelli's sentiment, uses the very expression Rousseau here uses, in criticizing the philosophers for conceiving of men not "as they are" but as they would like them to be: *Political Treatise* (1670), I, § 1; so does Vico: *The New Science* (1725, 1730, 1744), II, § 131. It is a matter of debate in the Rousseau literature, especially in the discussions surrounding the *Essay on the Origin of Languages*, whether Rousseau was acquainted with Vico's work, possibly from the time of his stay in Venice. Rousseau acknowledges Machiavelli's point, but refuses to leave it at that: "While it is good to know how to use men as they are, it is much better still to make them what one needs them to be . . .": *Pol. Ec.* [24].

I 2 [4] **Grotius . . . most frequent mode of argument is always to establish right by fact.** Rousseau is here criticizing Grotius, Aristotle and Hobbes for proceeding *a posteriori* or by way of what in *War* [13] and in *Method* [6], [10] he calls the analytic method; see also Editorial Note to *Ineq.* epigraph "What is natural," *Discourses* tr. p. 351.

I 3 [3] **All power comes from God, I admit it** *Romans* 13:1.

I 4 [2] **If, says Grotius, an individual can alienate his freedom, and enslave himself to a master, why could not a whole people alienate its freedom and subject itself to a king?** *Right of War and Peace* I, 3 § viii.

I 4 [7]–[12] summarizes *On War* [34]–[57].

I 4 [7] **Grotius and the rest derive from war another origin of the alleged right of slavery** Grotius, *Right of War and Peace* III, 7 §§ 1–3; Locke, *Treatises* II, ch. 4, § 24.

I 4 [8] **peace of God** or *treuga dei*, suspension of hostilities from Thursday evening until Monday morning as well as on designated religious holidays, introduced in 1033 and promulgated as the law of the land in 1082.

I 4 [9]* **Cato wrote to his son** The episode is told by Cicero in *On Duties* I, xi, 36.

I 5 [2] **A people, says Grotius ... examine the act by which a people is a people.** *Right of War and of Peace* I, 3 § viii, in the context of an argument against popular sovereignty.

I 6 [7] **the union is as perfect as it can be** The Pléiade *OC* reads *qu'elle ne peut l'être*; all other authoritative editions read *qu'elle peut l'être*.

I 6 [10]* **the four orders of men (even five, if simple foreigners are included) there are in our city, and only two of which make up the Republic.** Citizens (*citoyens*), born in the city of citizen parents; Bourgeois (*bourgeois*), born in the city, who purchased "titles of bourgeoisie"; Natives (*natifs*), born in the city of resident parents; Residents (*habitants*), foreigners who had purchased residence rights in the city. Only the first two were members of the *Conseil Général* or Sovereign (Launay, *Jean-Jacques Rousseau écrivain politique*, p. 34).

I 9 [3] **legal titles** The corresponding passage of the *Geneva ms.* speaks of "a man's rights prior to the state of society": I 5 [2], *OC* III, 301.

I 9 [6] **the rights the Sovereign and the proprietor have to the same land** Reading *fonds* for *fond* with Dreyfus-Brisac, Vaughan and all other authoritative editors, and as the sense requires. **as will be seen below:** II 4 [3]; and consider *On War* [57].

II 1 [3] **while it is not impossible that a particular will agree with the general will on some point,** Reading a comma instead of a semi-colon with Dreyfus-Brisac, Vaughan and all other authoritative editors, and as the sense requires. **but it cannot say: what this man ...** Reading a colon instead of a semi-colon with Dreyfus-Brisac, Vaughan and all other authoritative editors, and as the sense requires.

II 2 [2] **But our politicians [*politiques* – see the Note on the Translations, p. li above] ... as if they were putting together man** See Derathé, *Jean-Jacques Rousseau et la science politique de son temps*, pp. 280–294; and *OC* III, 1455, n. 5.

II 2 [5] **If ... [Barbeyrac and Grotius] had adopted the true principles, all their difficulties would have been solved** Grotius begins his discussion of the relation between people and sovereign with a criticism of popular sovereignty: *Right of War and Peace* I 3, § viii.

II 3 [2] **what is left as the sum of the differences is the general will.** I.e. the sum of the remaining wills is the general will.

II 3 [4] **Solon, Numa, Servius** On how this was done by Numa and especially Servius, see the important discussion in IV 4, [1]*, [5]–[9].

II 3 [4]* **In truth, says Machiavelli** *Vera cosa è que alcune divisioni nuocono alle Republiche, e alcune giovano: quelle nuocono che sono dalle sette e da partigiani accompagnate: quelle giovano che senza sette, senza partigiani si mantengono. Non potendo adunque provedere un fundatore d'una Republica que non siano nimicizie in quella, hà da proveder almeno che non vi siano sette.*

II 4 [5] **Which proves ... and hence from the nature of man;** Reading semi-colon with Dreyfus-Brisac, Vaughan and all other authoritative editors, and as the sense requires.

II 6 [2] **a universal justice** universal – as contrasted with particular – justice consists of our duties of friendship, affection, respect and gratitude toward those to whom we owe them; it pertains to all men, in contrast to the various forms of particular justice which pertain to the citizens of the different political societies. Duties of universal justice are duties "of imperfect obligation": they cannot be enforced by law; duties of particular justice are duties of "strict right," and can be enforced: Pufendorf, *Droit de la nature et des gens*, I, 7, §§ vii, viii, xii, xv, cp. III, 4, § i. "Universal justice" so understood corresponds to what on one occasion Rousseau calls "civility" (*Geneva ms.* II 4 [13]). Rousseau also refers to this distinction between universal justice and particular justice or strict right in the *Letter to d'Alembert* (*OC* V, 61; Fuchs, ed. p. 89; Bloom, tr. p. 66); on "strict right" see also *Ineq.* N XIX. Pufendorf traces this understanding of "universal justice" to Aristotle's view of justice as virtue entire in contrast to the specific virtue of justice: *Nicomachean Ethics* V, 1 1129b 26–V, 2 1130a 17; see, also, Aristotle's mention, in the context of forensic rhetoric, of "universal ... unwritten" law which is "according to nature," in contrast to the "particular ... written" laws of any given political society: *Rhetoric* I, 13, 1373b 4–18. **emanating from reason alone** In the corresponding passage of the *Geneva ms.* this reads "emanating from reason alone, and founded on the simple right of humanity" (II, 4 [2], *OC* III, 326).

II 6 [8] In the earlier *Geneva ms.*, Rousseau had gone on at this point with the important discussion that will be found on pp. 160 f. above.

II 7 [2] **The same reasoning ... Plato ... in his book on ruling** *Statesman* 261d–e.

II 7 [5]* **Calvin['s] ... institution** Many editors and translators read this as a reference to Calvin's *Institutes*.

II 7 [9] **persuade without convincing** about this formula, see the Editorial Note to *Voltaire* [30], *Discourses* tr, pp. 289 f.

II 7 [11]* says Machiavelli *E veramente mai non fù alcuno ordinatore di legge straordinarie in un populo, che non ricoresse a Dio, perche altrimenti non sarebbero accettate; perche sono molti beni conosciuti da uno prudente, i quali non hanno in se raggioni evidenti da potergli persuadere ad altrui.*

II 7 [12] Warburton *Divine Legation of Moses* (1738), II, §§ 5f.

II 8 [2] Peoples, like men The 1782 edition reads: Most peoples.

II 8 [4] (main)spring(s), *ressort(s)*, is how Rousseau and many of his contemporaries often refer to the artifices by which institutions and individuals are set and kept in motion.

II 8 [5] For Nations as for men . . . In the 1782 edition, the paragraph begins: "Youth is not childhood. For nations as for man there is a time of youth, or if you prefer of maturity . . ." The Russians will never be truly politically organized [policés] literally "politicized"; about *policé(s)*, see A Note on the Translations, p. li above.

II 10 [3] the enjoyment of prosperity and peace The Pléiade *OC* omits *et*, "and."

II 10 [6] There is one country . . . Corsica In part as a result of this remark, Rousseau was invited, two years after the publication of the *Social Contract*, to draft a Constitution for Corsica. He agreed to try to do so, but never completed more than a partial draft. Many of his most distinctive proposals found their way into his *Considerations on the Government of Poland.*

III 1 [8] It is in the Government that are located the intermediate forces whose relations constitute the relation of the whole to the whole, or of the Sovereign to the State. See II 12 [1] above and III 1 [17] below. the ratio between the extremes of a continued proportion of which the mean proportional is the Government. The Government receives from the Sovereign the orders which it gives the people, and for the State to be well balanced . . . the product or power of the Government . . . [has to] be equal to the product or power of the citizens who are sovereign on the one hand, and subjects on the other. In the continued proportion $A : B = B : C$, A and C are the extremes; and $A \leftrightarrow C = B \leftrightarrow B = B^2$ is the mean proportional. In this example, A represents the sovereign or the citizens as sovereign, C represents the citizens as subjects, and B represents the government with its various "intermediate forces," or branches. For the mathematical language throughout this discussion, see Marcel Françon, "Le Langage mathématique de J.-J. Rousseau," *Isis* (1949), 40:341-344 (reprinted in *Cahiers pour l'analyse* [1970], 8:85-88), and "Le Langage algébrique de Rousseau," *Annales J.-J. Rousseau* (1953–1955), 33:243-246.

III 1 [12] the ratio considered in terms of quantity is measured by the quotient more precisely, the quotient of B divided by A.

III 1 [15] since one of the extremes, namely the people as subjects, is fixed and represented by unity – in the above example, $C = 1$ – every time the doubled ratio – the doubled ratio of the proportion $A : B = C : D$ is the product $A : B \leftrightarrow C : D = AC : BD$; hence, in the continued proportion $A : B = B : C$, the doubled ratio is $AB : BC$; which, since $C = 1$, gives $AB : B = A$ – increases or decreases, the single ratio – $A : B$ or the citizens as sovereign over the government – similarly increases or decreases, and the middle term – that is to say, the government – is correspondingly changed.

III 1 [16] If, in order to reduce this system to ridicule, it were said that, according to me, finding this mean proportional and forming the body of the Government requires no more than taking the square root of the number of the people – if $A \times C = B^2$ and $C = 1$, then $B = \sqrt{A}$ – I would reply that I am here using this number only as an example; that the ratios about which I am speaking are measured not only by numbers of men, but more generally by the amount of activity, which is the combined result of a great many causes; The Pléiade *OC* punctuates "number of the people; . . . an example, . . . many causes, . . ."; all other authoritative editions punctuate ". . . number of the people, . . . an example; . . . many causes; . . ."

III 1 [17] The Government[,] . . . active like the Sovereign, passive like the State, . . . can be analyzed into further, similar relations, from which a new proportion consequently arises, and within it yet another proportion corresponding to the judiciary . . . The over-arching structure described in terms of the continued proportion $A : B = B : C$ can be broken down or analyzed into various other continued proportions of the form $a' : b' = b' : c'$ based on smaller sub-structures. (I am indebted for this formulation to my colleague, Professor Wistar Comfort.) . . . until an indivisible middle term is reached, that is to say a single chief or supreme magistrate, who might be conceived of in the middle of this progression as the unity between the series of fractions and of the series of integers. For one reading of this remark, see H. Gildin, *Rousseau's Social Contract, The Design of the Argument* (University of Chicago Press, Chicago, 1983), pp. 96f.

III 1 [19] Thus the Prince's dominant will is or should be nothing but the general will or the laws; Following the punctuation in Dreyfus-Brisac, Vaughan, and all other authoritative editors, and as the sense requires, in place of the Pléiade *OC*'s comma.

III 4 [2] It is not good . . . to devote it . . . Reading *la* with the Pléiade *OC* and most other modern editions, and as the sense requires; however the authoritative early editions have *les*.

III 4 [4] **Indeed ... as a principle** Reading *principe*, as the sense requires; however all authoritative early editions have *principes*.

III 4 [6] **a famous Author attributed virtue to Republics as their principle** Montesquieu, *Of the Spirit of the Laws* III, 3; Rousseau is here criticizing him for failing to recognize that the same principle has to apply in every well-constituted state.

III 4 [7] **I prefer ...** *Malo periculosam libertatem quam quietum servitium.* Stanislas Leszinski, King of Poland, attributed the remark to his father; see also *Poland* I [3] (Derathé, Fabre).

III 5 [10] **Aristotle contends ... that the rich always be preferred.** Aristotle nowhere contends that aristocracy invariably seeks to give preference to the rich, but he does note that it consistently tends to do so: *Politics* V, 7, i, 1306b 24; V, 7, x, 1307a 35.

III 6 [5] **what Samuel forcefully represented to the Hebrews** I *Samuel*, 11–18.

III 6 [11] **"Ah, the son replied ..."** Plutarch, *Sayings of Kings* 175e.

III 6 [12] **"The most practical ..."** *Nam utilissimus idem ac brevissimus bonarum malarumque rerum delectus, cogitare quid aut nolueris sub alio Principe aut volueris:* Tacitus, *Histories* I, 17.

III 6 [15]* *Statesman* E.g. 397 b–c.

III 8 [11] *We are, says* Jean **Chardin** (1643–1714), *Voyages du Chevalier Chardin en Perse* (Amsterdam, 1735), vol. III, pp. 76, 83–84; *Travels in Persia and the East Indies* (1686).

III 9 [4]* *such was their ignorance ... idque apud imperitos humanitas vocabatur, cum pars, servitutis esset:* Tacitus, *Agricola* XXI. *where they make a desolation ... ubi solitudinem faciunt, pacem appelant:* Tacitus, *Agricola* XXX. **the Cardinal Coadjutor** i.e. the Bishop's appointed assistant; the reference is to Paul de Gondi (1613–1679), a leader of the Fronde, who became the Cardinal de Retz **attended Parliament with a dagger in his pocket** Retz records this episode in his *Mémoires*, Bk. III (Vaughan). **It seemed, says Machiavelli ...** in the Preface to his *History of Florence*; paraphrased by Rousseau.

III 10 [3]* *Serrar di Consiglio* Closing of the Council. *squittinio della libertà veneta* An anonymous writing published in 1611, which sought to establish the Emperors' sovereignty over the republic of Venice (Vaughan).

III 10 [8] **Anarchy** absence of rule; **Democracy** rule by the people; **Ochlocracy** mob-rule, a term introduced by Polybius (204–122 BC), *Histories* VI, 4; **Aristocracy** rule by the best; **Oligarchy** rule by the few.

III 10 [9]* **For all those are called and considered tyrants ...** *Omnes enim et habentur et dicuntur Tyranni qui potestate utuntur perpetua,* *in ea Civitate quae libertate usa est.* **the *Hiero* of Xenophon** Through-out which Hiero, tyrant of Syracuse, freely calls himself "tyrant" and does not object when the poet Simonides calls him "tyrant" to his face. Barbeyrac makes the same point Rousseau is here making, and he also does so with a reference to the *Hiero*, in his French edition of Grotius's *Of the Right of War and Peace* I, I, § viii (2), note 50.

III 15 [9] **... cannot make themselves be heard in the open** see also especially *Languages* 20 [3].

III 18 [4] *cas odieux* The Government's authority temporarily to sus-pend rights the exercise of which it perceives as particularly dangerous under the circumstances (Beaulavon).

IV 1 [3] **Duc de Beaufort** (1616–1696) a leader of the *Fronde des princes*, the armed struggle by a part of the French nobility to reclaim feudal powers from an increasingly absolute monarchy.

IV 2 [3] **Tacitus notes:** *Histories* IV, 17.

IV 3 [2] *Voting by lot*, **says Montesquieu** ... *Spirit of the Laws* II, 11.

IV 3 [6] **poor Barnabites** the impoverished Venetian nobility.

IV 3 [9] **The abbé de St. Pierre proposed** in his *Discours ou Polysnodie.*

IV 4 [19] **... Third count, i.e. the census by head; ... the censorship, stronger than this institution,** again, the census by head, **corrected for its vice,** namely, establishing a class of those who had nothing.

IV 4 [28] **curule Magistrates** see Ed. Note at *Poland* 11[12], p. 315 below.

IV 4 [36] **I know that Cicero condemns** ... in *De legibus* III, 15; mentioned by Montesquieu, *Of the Spirit of the Laws* II, 11.

IV 5 [5] **The blood of Agis** King of Sparta, murdered in 241 BC by the Ephors Leonidas and Amphares for trying to restore the austere order of Lycurgus; **was avenged by his successor** Cleomenes, who eliminated the Ephorate: Plutarch, *Agis*, 20; *Cleomenes*, 8–10.

IV 6 [10] **However brilliant his [Cicero's] recall ... a pardon** Cicero having twice defeated him for the Consulship, Catiline conspired to raise a private army, to murder Cicero as well as some other prominent citizens, and to assume power himself. After the first indications of the conspiracy, the Senate passed the emergency decree by which it transferred all of its power to the Consuls in October 63 BC. Cicero set a trap for the conspirators. They were caught. The Senate voted the death penalty. Cicero had them strangled in the city jail without allowing them due process. Eventually he was, as Rousseau says, "called to account for the blood of Citizens shed in violation of the laws." He was exiled in 58. He was recalled the following year.

IV 7. Although he focuses on the Roman Censorial Tribunal, a number of Rousseau's examples as well as his reference to his fuller discussion of the subject in his *Letter to d'Alembert* (*OC* v, pp. 60–68, Bloom, tr. 65–75) clearly indicate that he is thinking in much broader terms. At the time of this writing, France had a Censorial Office, headed by de Lamoignon de Malesherbes, with whom Rousseau was on good terms.

In Rome, from 444 BC, two Censors were elected to carry out the census of persons and property that took place at five-year intervals, or lustra. This census determined to which Century one was assigned for military service, and in which centuriate assembly one voted. The Censors could exclude from the rolls anyone judged unworthy because of a criminal record or for any other reason. After 312 BC the Censors could also dismiss any Senator who had broken the law or offended against morality; and nominate replacements for vacant Senate seats. Rousseau here again takes account of Machiavelli: *Discourses* I, 40; see also Montesquieu, *Spirit of the Laws* v, 19, near the end.

IV 7 [8] **what a disgrace** Reading *note* for the Pléiade *OC*'s *honte*, as do Dreyfus-Brisac, Vaughan and all other authoritative editors.

IV 8 [1] **Men at first had no other Kings than the Gods, nor any other Government than the Theocratic one.** Cp. "...the religion of the Gentiles was a part of their policy": Hobbes, *Leviathan* ch. XII, 21. **They reasoned as had Caligula** "That kings were Gods": see I 2 [6] above.

IV 8 [4]* *Nonne ea quae possidet Chamos deus tuus tibi jure debentur?* The King James translation reads "Wilt not thou possess what Chemosh thy god giveth thee to possess?" By inserting the "Do you not believe" – Rousseau's **"according to you"** – Carrières' translation weakens Jephthah's challenge to King Sihon of the Ammonites. The Bible has Jephthah base all claim to the land on the god's grant to the stronger; Carrières' translation has him base it on a belief. Locke cites the story of Jephthah to make much the same point as Rousseau: the appeal to heaven is the appeal to the sword: *Second Treatise of Government* § 21; cp. § 109. **the text of the Vulgate** *Judges* 11:24.

IV 8 [5]* ... **called the holy war** called "holy" (*sacrée*) by the Thebans who fought and in 356 BC prevailed against **the Phocaeans** who had conquered Delphi and plundered its treasury a decade earlier.

IV 8 [13] **Of all Christian Authors the philosopher Hobbes**: "Now seeing it is manifest, that the civil power, and the power of the commonwealth is the same thing; and that supremacy, and the power of making cannons, and granting faculties implieth a commonwealth; it followeth, that where one is sovereign, another supreme; where one can make laws, and another make cannons; there must needs be two commonwealths, of one and the same subjects; which is a kingdom divided in itself, and cannot stand": *Leviathan* ch. XXIX [15];

"...whatever power ecclesiastics take upon themselves, (in any place where they are subject to the state), in their own right, though they call it God's right, is but usurpation": *ib.* ch. XLVI [42].

IV 8 [15] **divine natural right ... divine civil or positive right**
The distinctive feature of Rousseau's contrast is that he applies the expression "divine civil or positive right" to the positive religious prescriptions and prohibitions of all earliest peoples; by contrast, other writers restrict the term to the positive prescriptions and prohibitions of the Biblical God: Hobbes, *De cive* (1642), XIV, 4, cp. VIII, 10, as well as *Leviathan* XXVI, 40; see also Locke, *Treatises of Government* (1690), I, § 126, and II §§ 1 and 52; Grotius had spoken of divine positive right in reference to the New Testament: *Of the Right of War and Peace* (1625), I, 3, § iii, and Bayle regards Grotius's remark that natural right would obtain even if there were no divinity (*Right*, Proleg., § xi, cp. I, 1, § x, 5) as referring to what is meant by the expression divine natural right: *Continuation des pensées diverses* (1704), § 152; in this chapter, Bayle discusses the distinction between divine natural and divine civil right, and traces its history to the distinction Socrates draws between what is loved by the gods because it is holy, and what is holy because it is loved by the gods: Plato, *Euthyphro* 10a2; divine natural law, understood in the sense in which "philosophers style laws those general rules of nature according to which everything happens," in other words, divine natural right, is the primary subject of Spinoza, *Tractatus theologico-politicus* (1670), ch. 4 and especially *ib.* ch.16, Gebhardt n. xxxiv: "As for divine natural law ... I have called it law in the sense in which philosophers call law the general rules of nature according to which everything [necessarily] happens." Spinoza contrasts divine natural right with what he refers to by the traditional expression "ceremonial law": *ib.*, ch. 5. See also Leibniz's brief but incisive remarks regarding this distinction between divine natural and divine positive right, or between the moral and the ceremonial laws, in *Theodicy* (1710), II, § 182.

IV 8 [16] **There is a third ... sort of Religion ... the Religion of the Lamas ... of the Japanese ... Roman christianity. One may call it ... "it"**: the original edition reads *celle-ci*, i.e. this "third sort of Religion"; however the 1782 edition reads *celui-ci*, i.e. "Roman christianity."

IV 8 [18] *sacer estod* "be accursed": the ancient Roman formula uttered upon delivering someone to public execration and the wrath of the Gods. "It cannot be sufficiently admired, that among the first Romans the sole punishment provided for by the Laws of the Twelve Tables against the greatest criminals was to be held in horror by everyone, *sacer estod.* There is no better way of understanding how virtuous that people was than to realize that among it public hate or esteem was distributed by Law": *Fragments politiques*, IV, 12, *OC* III, 495.

IV 8 [31] **The right which the social pact gives the Sovereign over the subjects does not, as I have said, exceed the bounds of public utility.** He said so in II 4 [3] and [4] above.

IV 8 [32]* **Caesar pleading for Catiline** see Sallust, *The Catiline Conspiracy*, chs. 51f.

IV 9 **right of nations** I follow Derathé's ordering of Rousseau's list: *Jean-Jacques Rousseau et la science politique de son temps*, p. 396 and *OC* III, pp. 1507f.

GENEVA MS. (pages 153–161)

What has come to be known as the *Geneva ms.* is an earlier version of the *Social Contract*. It is not a working draft, but a finished text, written neatly enough to be handed to a printer. Rousseau most probably worked on it over a period of several years. He incorporated parts of it in the article on *Political Economy*, published in 1755, and much of the rest in the *Social Contract*. The passages selected for inclusion in this volume spell out reflections and arguments not incorporated in either of these writings. For a fuller discussion of them, see the Introduction, especially pp. xii–xv, xxviii–xxx.

Title: The initial title of this chapter read: *That by Nature there is not Any Society Among Men*; in one fragment, the chapter is entitled *Of natural Right and General Society*.

I 2 [5], [8]–[9] These paragraphs are framed by angle brackets to indicate that they were crossed out in the manuscript.

I 2 [10] **"I feel I bring mankind terror and trouble . . . that will do more for my advantage and my security than will justice"** Quoting Diderot's article "Natural Right", pp. 18f. of the Wokler and Mason translation (somewhat modified).

I 2 [12] **Indeed, if the notions of the great Being and of the natural law were innate in all hearts, it was quite a superfluous effort explicitly to teach them:** compare: "those who will see in the intention of giving to human actions from the first a morality which they would not have acquired for a long time, the reason for a precept indifferent in itself and inexplicable in any other System . . .": *Ineq.* N IX [14].

I 2 [14] **But the first . . . when he should live and when die.** The first sentence of this paragraph directly quotes Diderot's article, section vi, and the second sentence quotes section vii.

I 2 [17] **as Grotius notes** in *Of the Right of War and Peace* II, 15, § v (2); Hobbes makes the same point in *De cive* v, 2 and again in Leviathan ch. II, 17 [2]. **even among the Latins** . . . **Cicero** *Hostis enim apud majores nostros dicebatur, quem nunc peregrinum dicimus*: Cicero, *On Duties* I, xii, 37 (see the edition by Griffin and Atkins [Cambridge Texts in the History of Political Thought, Cambridge, 1991], p. 16). In his French translation of Grotius, Barbeyrac footnoted the passage cited in the Editorial Note to Grotius above with a reference to this remark of Cicero's. **Hobbes's error** . . . **of which it is the effect** For Rousseau's full argument, see especially *Ineq.* I [35], together with the Editorial Note, *Discourses* tr., pp. 151 f., 360 f.

II 4 [16] **if I do not say with Hobbes, everything is mine** e.g. ". . . in the state of men without civill society (which state we may properly call the state of nature) . . . all men have equall right to all things": *De cive*, Preface to the Reader [14].

THE STATE OF WAR (pages 162–176)

Rousseau mentioned that he planned a book on the *Principles of the Right of War (Principes du droit de la guerre)* in a letter to his publisher Marc-Michel Rey (9 March 1758), and he concludes the *Social Contract* (IV 9) as well as his summary of Emile's education in the principles of political right with a mention of "the true principles of the right of war" (*OC* IV, 849). However, the following fragment appears to be the only continuous surviving portion of this project. Rousseau did incorporate portions of it in the body of the *Social Contract*. The fragment itself was first published by E. Dreyfus-Brisac in Appendix II to his edition of the *Social Contract* (Paris, Alcan, 1896), pp. 304–316. It was re-edited by J.-L. Windenberger, *Essai sur le système de politique étrangère de J.-J. Rousseau* (Paris, Picard, 1900), pp. 289–301. Rousseau had initially entitled the fragment *That the State of War Arises from the Social State*, but had subsequently crossed out this title. C. E. Vaughan named it *The State of War*, arranged the text in what appeared to him a more logical fashion in his edition of *Jean-Jacques Rousseau: The Political Writings*, pp. 293–307, and translated portions of it in Jean-Jacques Rousseau, *A Lasting Peace through the Federation of Europe and The State of War* (London, Constable & Co., 1917) pp. 120–128 (reprinted with an Introduction by Richard Schmitt for The Graduate Philosophy Club of Yale University by Whitlock's, New Haven, CT, n.d.). Sven Stelling-Michaud follows Vaughan's arrangement of the text in his edition for the Pléiade *OC*, vol. III, pp. 601–612. In 1965 the Public and University Library of Geneva acquired a few Rousseau manuscript pages which are clearly a segment of the present text, and two years later Bernard Gagnebin published them under the title "Un inédit de Rousseau sur l'état de guerre," in *De Ronsard à Breton. Hommage à Marcel Raymond* (Librairie José Corti, Paris, 1967), pp. 103–109. It has been appended to subsequent reprints of *OC* vol. III (pp. 1899–1904). The text, even as re-arranged by Vaughan, was always recognized to lack coherence. In 1985 Grace G. Roosevelt examined the original of this frequently reprinted text, and restored what appears to be its proper order by the simple and ingenious expedient of re-folding the manuscript pages; and she fit the fragment first published by Gagnebin into what appears to be its proper place in the argument. She published her results together with her translation of the text as "A Reconstruction of Rousseau's Fragments on the State of War," *History of Political Thought* (1987), 8:225–244, and again in *Reading Rousseau in the Nuclear Age* (Temple University Press, Philadelphia, 1990), pp. 13-16, 185–198. I have followed her arrangement of the text, but the Pléiade's reading of it.

[6] **As for what is commonly called the right of nations** or, also, law of nations, and, in current usage, international law.

[8]–[11] These paragraphs are framed by angle brackets to indicate that they were crossed out in the manuscript.

[11] **everyone's right to all** "Nature hath given to *every one a right to all*": Hobbes, *De cive* I, x.

[13] **this analytical method** which Rousseau had described and criticized in *Method* [6], [10]; see also Editorial Note to *Ineq.*, epigraph, "What is natural," *Discourses* tr. p. 251.

[14] **even if it were true that this unbounded and uncontrollable greed were as developed in all men as our Sophist assumes** i.e. Hobbes's premise – referred to in [11] above – of everyone's right to all things. **I understand.** Referring to Hobbes's argument in *De cive* I, xiv; Rousseau goes on to elaborate his earlier claim – in [8] above – that one aim of Hobbes's account of the state of nature as a war by all against all is to show that despotism is the lesser evil, and thus to justify it. **I will not fail to come back to this point.** He does so at the end of [57].

[18] **But if this were genuine war**: which, on Rousseau's view, it is not, as he goes on to explain in the next two sentences.

[19] **Saint Louis**, or Louis IX, who ruled France from 1226 to 1270, outlawed private wars in his realm in 1267.

[25] **no war between men** reading *entre les hommes*, with the Pléiade *OC*.

[26] **To this** i.e. to the question at the end of [24]; **events that can have a thousand particular causes independent of the common**

principle Rousseau had originally written: which a thousand particular causes can change (render directly contrary to the most natural effects) (Pléiade *OC* note *ad loc.*).

[33]–[46] is the fragment discovered and first published by Bernard Gagnebin, and reprinted in the second (1979) edition of *OC*, vol. III.

[39] **Minos and the Athenians** According to tradition, King Minos of Crete, having defeated Athens in war, exacted a yearly tribute of seven Athenian youths and seven maidens, to be devoured by the Minotaur. One year, Theseus volunteered to be one of the youths, slew the Minotaur, and thus freed Athens of its tribute.

[40] **Leave their angry Gods to the Tarentines, Fabius** Maximus, surnamed Cunctator ("Procrastinator") for his reluctance to engage Hannibal's armies directly during the Second Punic War, **said, when he was invited to carry off to Rome the statues and paintings that adorned Tarentum** Livy, *Histories* XXVII, 16, 8; Plutarch, *Fabius* XXII, 7; he did, however, carry off the monumental statue of Hercules, had it installed on the Capitoline hill, and next to it a heroic statue of himself **and the earliest decadence in Roman morals is rightly imputed** to Marcus Claudius **Marcellus,** surnamed the Sword of Peace, **for not having followed the same policy in Syracuse** when he conquered the city in 213 BC, and had its treasures of Greek art shipped to Rome; **a covetous usurper often harms himself more than his enemy by the evil he does him indirectly** by depriving his enemies of objects that effeminate or corrupt, and appropriating them for himself. **The only penalty Cyrus imposed on the rebellious Lydians was a soft and effeminate life** Herodotus, *Histories* I, 155 **and the way the tyrant Aristodemus went about keeping the inhabitants of Cumae dependent on him** was, among other things, to force them to bring up their sons in the most effeminate ways and to prepare them only for menial occupations: Dionysius of Halicarnassus, *Antiquities* VII, 9.

[41]–[46] Gagnebin points out that these paragraphs were crossed out in the manuscript: "Un inédit de Rousseau sur l'état de guerre," n. 8.

[44] **war consists not in one or several unpremeditated fights, not even in homicide or murder committed in an outburst of anger, but in the steady, considered and manifest will to destroy one's enemy** Formally, this definition closely corresponds to Hobbes's definition: ". . . WARRE, consisteth not in Battell only, or in the act of fighting; but in a tract of time, wherein the Will to contend by Battell is sufficiently known: and therefore the notion of *Time*, is to be considered in the nature of Warre; as it is in the nature of weather. For as the nature of Foule weather, lyeth not in a shower or two of

rain; but in the inclination thereto of many days together: So the nature of War, consisteth not in actual fighting; but in the known disposition thereto, during all the time there is no assurance to the contrary": *Leviathan* ch. XIII.

[47] **peace of God** see Editorial Note to *SC* 1 4 [8], p. 298 above.

[48] **I will come back to in this another place.** He never does go on to develop this point more fully; he does repeat it in his *Extract from the Abbé de Saint Pierre's Project for Perpetual Peace, OC* III, 568.

[57] **not all of men's conventions could ever change anything in the physical [constitution] of things.** Rousseau had originally written: in the nature of men. **Aristotle says that . . . the Ephors . . . solemnly declared war on . . . [the Helots].** He says so according to Plutarch, *Lycurgus* XXVIII, 7; there is no independent surviving evidence of his saying so.

CONSIDERATIONS ON THE GOVERNMENT OF POLAND
(pages 177–260)

Rousseau wrote the *Considerations* during the half year between October 1770 and March 1771. In the late 1760s Poland was deeply divided between the party of those who sought greater stability by strengthening ties to Russia, and those who strove for greater independence from Russia and political reform. The first met in June 1767 in Radom and formed a Confederation which called on Catherine the Great of Russia to support the status quo; the second, larger, group met in February 1768 in the town of Bar, and formed a rival Confederation. Confederation was a traditional Polish resource by which a portion of the nobility organized in the face of crises. Confederations clearly had a destabilizing effect. The political division between the two Confederations in large measure overlapped with a religious division: the Confederates of Radom were for the most part Greek Orthodox; the Confederates of Bar were for the most part Roman Catholic.

The ruling King, Stanislas-August Poniatowski (1732–1795), was utterly dependent on accommodation with Russia. His opponents charged that he was Catherine the Great's creature and the "usurper" of the Polish crown. Yet he did, at various times, attempt to negotiate with the Confederates of Bar, and Rousseau seems to have gauged his political leanings correctly when, late in these *Considerations*, he suggests that the wisest course might be to seek accommodation with him (15 [4]).

The Confederates of Bar turned to various western political thinkers for advice on how to reform Poland. One of their representatives, Count Wielhorski, enlisted Rousseau's assistance in this project. Count

Wielhorski also asked the Abbé de Mably to draw up a proposal for reform. Voltaire, the great partisan of enlightened despots, and of Peter the Great, Catherine the Great and Frederick the Great, took sides against the Confederates, and wrote pamphlets taxing them with being "fanatics" (Fabre, in the Pléiade *OC*, vol. III, p. 1737).

Rousseau's and Mably's texts were to be private documents, not intended for public dissemination or attribution. Yet each was clearly shown portions of the other's manuscript, and each refers to points the other makes. Specifically, whenever Rousseau explicitly criticizes or rejects suggestions that have been made for the reform of the government of Poland, he is referring to suggestions in the Abbé de Mably's memorandum. Within a very few years, manuscript copies of the *Considerations* began circulating, leading Rousseau to feel that Wielhorski had betrayed his confidence. The full text was first published in the posthumous 1782 edition of Rousseau's works.

Fabre has shown that at the time at which Rousseau was writing these *Considerations*, the fortunes of the Confederates of Bar looked particularly bright: Turkey had declared war on Russia in early 1769; the Confederates had taken some of the King's strongholds; France, in pursuit of its policy of opposing Russia, was lending them support. Before long their fortunes changed. In 1772 Poland was partitioned by Catherine's Russia, Frederick's Prussia, and Marie Thérèse's Austria; twenty years later it was partitioned again; and in 1795 it was partitioned a third and last time. It was not restored until after the First World War.

The *Considerations* take detailed account of Polish conditions and political structures. The informed mid-eighteenth-century European public appears to have been reasonably familiar with the political circumstances of Poland. The contemporary reader may find a brief overview of them helpful.

Poland, the largest nation in Western Europe at the time, was an electoral monarchy. In addition to the King, the country was ruled, at the national level, by a Diet and a Senate. It was divided into thirty-three Palatinates, each with its Palatine or governor, as well as its local so-called Dietine. Delegates to the Dietines were elected locally, by the local nobility. Only the nobility, which in mid-century made up about 10 percent of the population, was fully enfranchised. At the opening session of a Dietine, the Delegates elected a Marshal or presiding officer. The Dietines then decided on an agenda of the local issues to be taken up by the national Diet, and elected Representatives to the Diet charged with implementing this agenda. The Dietines did not legislate for their Palatinates or have administrative authority over them. In

1767, 236 of the Representatives to the Dietines were chosen to be Delegates to the Diet. A number of these were, in turn, appointed by the King as Senators. Senators were appointed for life. In 1768 the Senate numbered 153 members.

The Diet had initially been established in 1493. It met regularly every other year for sessions of up to six weeks. At the end of these sessions, the Delegates reported on them to their Dietines' so-called Report Sessions (which Rousseau mistakenly thought had been abolished: 7 [17]); the Dietines then either ratified or rejected the Diet's actions, i.e. the laws or "constitutions" which it had passed.

The Diet's decisions were reached by consensus, and were regarded as approved unless challenged. Every member of the Diet enjoyed the right of challenge, the notorious *liberum veto*. The effect of the *liberum veto* was especially disruptive because it defeated not just some one motion or proposal, but the entire slate of decisions reached at a given session of the Diet. The *liberum veto* and the Confederations, together, were the main causes of what was widely characterized as Polish "anarchy."

The Senate met regularly while the Diet was in session, and was convened by the King as required at other times. Between sessions of the Diet a core of twenty-eight Senators remained at Court. The head of the Senate was called its Primate, a position held by the Archbishop of Gniezno (7 [3]).

The historical information in these notes is largely based on C. E. Vaughan, *Jean-Jacques Rousseau: Political Writings*, II, pp. 369–409; Jean Fabre, *OC* III, 1733–1804; Eckhart Koch, in *Jean-Jacques Rousseau, Sozial-philosophische und politische Schriften*, pp. 836–872; Bronislaw Baczko, *Lumières de l'utopie* (Payot, Paris, 1978), pp. 67–100. The translation is based on Fabre's edition, *OC* III, 921–1041.

Title **Government** Rousseau first wrote *Constitution and Republic*, which he crossed out and replaced with *Government*; indeed, he is clearly here using the term as it is commonly used, to mean body politic or State, not in the restricted, technical sense he usually attaches to it, i.e. the executive in contrast to the sovereign: *SC* III 1 [5].

[1] THE STATE OF THE QUESTION The section titles are Rousseau's; later editors added the numbering.

[3] **powerful and cunning aggressor** Russia.

1 [5] ... **the law above man ... squaring the circle in geometry.** Cp. *To Mirabeau* [4].

2 [7] **see the end of the *Social Contract*** I.e. IV 8 [1]–[6].

3 [2] **Remember the Spartan:** Brasidas; see also *Ineq.* II [38].

3 [5] **You must seize the occasion of the latest event** a military victory by the Confederates on 10 September 1770; see Rousseau's letter to Count Wielhorski, in *CC*, vol. XXVIII, pp. 116–118 (Fabre).

3 [7] **this widely praised Tsar** Peter the Great, who tried to Westernize the Russians; on Peter's exclusively "imitative" genius, *SC* II 8 [5].

3 [8] **mother country** *mère patrie*; see also p. xlvi above. *ubi patria, ibi bene* "Where my fatherland is, there is my good"; whereas the traditional, cosmopolitan, and hence, in the present context, "execrable" saying holds "Wherever my good is, there is my fatherland."

3 [10] **trained,** literally "formed"; see Editorial Note to *Pol. Ec.* [24].

3 [13] **formerly impoverished Polish nobles . . . among the Romans as long as the Republic endured** On Roman patronage, *SC* IV 4 [25].

4 [1] **give to souls the national form** Reading *forme* with Vaughan, and as the sense requires, in place of the Pléiade *OC*'s *force*.

4 [2] **(main)spring(s),** *ressort(s)*, is how Rousseau and many of his contemporaries often refer to the artifices by which institutions and individuals are set and kept in motion.

5 [2] **Let the separation between the two Polands be as pronounced as that between them and Lithuania** which, at the time, was a province of Poland. **Perfect the form of the Dietines** A Dietine was the Diet of a Palatinate or province which, in turn, elected deputies to the national Diet.

6 [6] **Freedom is hearty fare** Cp. *Ineq.* ED [6].

6 [7] **I shall present below** in 13 [14]–[20].

7 [3] **the continuous presence of the lawgiver** may simply refer to the legislative; but, more plausibly, Rousseau is here indicating that the lawgiver need not be a founder or even a single individual, but may be the public-spirited citizenry; cp. 7 [10] and 7 [12]: "the Lawgiver as a body"; see Introduction above, pp. xxiif.

7 [4] *pacta conventa* the set of fundamental laws which, upon assuming the throne, Kings of Poland swore to uphold; see also 8 [7] and [8] below, and what Rousseau there calls "imperial capitulations"; and contrast with the discussions of the contract of government in *Ineq.* II [44]–[46], and *SC* III 1 [6], and III 16 [3]–[7].

7 [5] **I have already ceased to count Sweden** King Adolphe-Frederic of Sweden died in 1771; Rousseau anticipated that his son and heir, Gustav III, whom he had met, would reject the restrictions Parliement had imposed on the Crown; his expectations were confirmed in 1772.

7 [6] **The executive power divided among several individuals**
... For the argument of this paragraph, see *SC* III 10 [7].

7 [8] **you have been advised** Here and throughout the *Considerations*
this formula refers to some proposal by the Abbé de Mably.

7 [11] *liberum veto* every Deputy's right to veto acts of the Diet; as
Rousseau here indicates, the *liberum veto* favored the King, since he
could reasonably expect always to find at least one Deputy to block
any Diet action he wanted to see defeated; **the means which I propose** ... *Social Contract*: III 12, 13.

7 [12] **the Lawgiver as a body** see Editorial Note to 7 [3] above.

7 [16] **Palladium** guardian.

7 [17] **Marshal of the Dietine** The Presiding Officer, elected at the
Dietine's opening session.

7 [19] **The principles from which these rules can be deduced are
established in the** *Social Contract*: They are found in *SC* III 13.

7 [22] **the commissioners of Radom** The body charged with supervising the Crown's and the army's finances; **Deputies to the Tribunal**
i.e. to the Appeals Courts; **the Laudum they present** specifically,
the local confirmation of the election of deputies to the Dietines; more
generally any decision of a Dietine; John **Wilkes** (1727–1797), publicist
and politician, critic of the British Crown, repeatedly elected to the
House of Commons, and repeatedly denied accreditation because of
pressure from the Crown. Rousseau compares his own treatment at the
hands of Geneva with Wilkes's treatment at the hands of Parliament
in the ninth of his *Letters from the Mountain* [33] *et seq.* (*OC* III, 876f.).

7 [23] **The Golden Book of Venice** The register in which the
descendants of noble families have to be inscribed in order to qualify
for public office; **Grod** Electoral District.

7 [29] **I do not quite see why ... there is still need for great
Castellans** At the time there were thirty-four Great Castellans, whom
Rousseau suggests depriving of their Senatorial seats; **Palatin** Elder
or Prefect.

7 [32] **... Senators ... as I have said ... must tend to usurpation**:
He said so in 7 [28].

7 [33] **Starost** Elder or Prefect.

7 [36] **will be found below** in 13 [7]–[9].

7 [39] This paragraph is inserted at this point in the manuscript of the
Neuchâtel library. **I have discussed this matter in the** *Social Contract* IV 3 and 4; see also section 14 of the present *Considerations*.

7 [40] **... voting ... in the** *Social Contract* He did so in Bk. IV,
chs. 2–4.

7 [41] *ad actum* for the purposes at hand.

8 [3] **I have said how ... these appointments should be made** He said so in 7 [35], [36] above; **the Archbishop of Gniezno** was, as Rousseau indicates in the immediate sequel, the Primate of Poland.

8 [7] **Denmark ... England ... Sweden** In 1770 the Queen of Denmark's favorite, J. F. Struensee, succeeded in assuming unlimited powers; **England** see, on Wilkes, 7 [22] above with the Editorial Note; **Sweden** see the Editorial Note to 7 [5] above.

9 [1] **I have already pointed out the principal one above** Namely the size of the country: [5] The Radical Vice, pp. 193 f.

9 [7] **unanimity was required for the formation of the body politic and for the fundamental laws that bear on its existence, such as, for example, the first one as corrected, the fifth, the ninth, and the eleventh, enacted by the pseudo-Diet of 1768.** The first fundamental law to which Rousseau here refers states that the Polish Republic is made up of three orders: the King, the Senate, and the Knightly order; Rousseau spelled out his reasons for taking issue with this claim in section 6 above; the fifth states that the King must be elected unanimously, and that the Kingship is not hereditary; the ninth affirms the indissoluble union of the Crown and the Grand-Duchy of Lithuania; the eleventh guarantees the equality and the prerogatives of the political body of the nation, the *szlachta* (Fabre).

9 [10] **any number of proportions** Reading *proportions* with Vaughan, and as the sense requires, in place of the Pléiade *OC*'s *propositions*.

9 [14] **Confederations . . . this federative form** see the Editorial Note ad 15 [3], p. 317 below.

10 [4] **I shall develop this idea more fully in a moment** in section 13, especially [3].

10 [6] **attach the most severe sanctions to those** Reading *celles* instead of the *OC*'s *celle*.

11 [3] **the sale of the starosties** lands belonging to the Crown; see also 11 [11] below.

11 [5] **corvée** or "statute labor": obligatory unpaid or partly paid work on public projects. **This issue . . . in its place** i.e. in section 12, especially [6]–[11].

11 [8] **a people of Capuchins** an order of mendicant friars.

11 [12] **The Quaestors of the Roman army . . . curule office.** The quaestors supervised public finances; the office was, as Rousseau says, the first rung on the ladder to high office; the curule office or chair was reserved for Consuls, Praetors or Dictators.

11 [14] **capitation** Taxes on individuals or households; hence also on nobles and clergymen; Rousseau discusses capitation and Montesquieu's objection to it more fully in *Pol. Ec.* [60].

11 [15] **Revenue Service** or *La Ferme*: the administrative structure coordinating and overseeing the tax farmers; see Editorial Note to *Pol. Ec.* [36]. **tax stamps** or *Papiers timbrés*: official forms for contracts and similar legal instruments which require the payment of a tax to acquire legal force.

11 [16] Sébastien le Prestre **Marshal de Vauban** (1633–1707), Louis XIV's chief military architect, and author of a project for tax reform; **Abbé de Saint-Pierre** (1648–1743) published an influential *Project for Perpetual Peace in Europe* (1713), and a *Polysynodie* (1718) advocating that rulers rely on the advice of Councils of Experts; Rousseau at one time undertook to edit the Abbé's papers, and he eventually published an *Extract from the Project for Perpetual Peace* and a *Judgment on the Project for Perpetual Peace*, *OC* III, 563–589, 591–600. **All lands, the King's, the Nobles', the Church's, the Commons should pay equally, that is to say in proportion to size and productivity, regardless of who may be the proprietor.** The Pléiade *OC* note correctly points out how very revolutionary this proposal is.

12 [9] **it is not conceivable that the Nation could be used to oppress itself** Reading *concevable* with Vaughan and as the sense requires, in place of the *OC*'s *convenable*; **he called them Citizens, Quirites** According to Tacitus, *Annals* I, 42, his doing so quelled their mutiny. **Whoever dares … even truer of peoples.** This sentence is found in only one of the manuscripts.

12 [10] **to excel in … guerilla warfare** Reading *excellât* with Vaughan, in place of the *OC*'s *s'exerseât pour*.

12 [12] **You have just given a forever memorable example** see Editorial Note to 3 [5] above.

13 [1] **for the reasons set forth above:** 7 [33] *et seq.*

13 [3] *Spes Patriae* i.e. Hope of the Fatherland.

13 [4] **the report-session of the Dietines** or *Diétines de relation*; at 7 [17] Rousseau says these *Diétines de relation* should absolutely be restored; in fact they were never suspended; **a deputy at Radom** or at the office or Commission supervising governmental finances, primarily its expenditures; apparently the same as the *Chambre des comptes*

13 [5] *Civis electus* Elected Citizen.

13 [7] **the same method … in judging outgoing Senator Deputies as I suggested for their election.** He did so in 7 [41] above.

13 [9] *Custos legum* Guardian of the laws.

13 [12] **the college of the Administrators of education about which I have spoken above.** He did so in 4 [7] and 13 [6].

13 [18] **the free places [in the secondary schools] about which I spoke above.** He did so in 4 [3].

14 [19] *of glorious memory* reading *de glorieuse mémoire*, with Vaughan and as the sense requires; *OC* reads: de *glorieuse mémoire*.

15 [1] **not lose sight of what I said in the** *Social Contract*, i.e. at II 10 [3] *et seq.*

15 [2] **the Sultan** The French, *le grand Seigneur* or "the great Lord," can give the reader pause; **the [Sublime] Porte** is the government of the Ottoman Empire.

15 [3] **the freedom of the union of German States ... Holland ... current government of Sweden** Three forms of what Rousseau calls "confederation" or "confederative State." Confederation, ". . . by uniting Peoples with ties similar to those that unite individuals, subjects each [i.e. the Peoples in question, as well as the individuals that make them up] equally to the authority of the Laws. Such a government seems preferable, besides, because it combines at the same time the advantages of large and of small States, that it is formidable to the outside because of this power, that the Laws are in full vigor within it, and that it alone is able to contain Subjects, Chiefs and Foreigners alike": *Extract from the Abbé de Saint Pierre's Project for Perpetual Peace, OC* III, 564. Rousseau indicates some of his reservations about this project in his *Jugement sur le projet de paix perpétuelle, OC* IV, 848f (tr., 466f). See also Montesquieu, *Spirit of the Laws*, IX 1–3.

LETTER TO D'OFFREVILLE (pages 261–265)

This letter has been edited most recently and fully by R. A. Leigh in his edition of Rousseau's *Correspondance complète*, vol. IX, pp. 143–148.

The addressee of this letter, Grimprel d'Offreville, had written to Rousseau on 15 September 1761 (*CC* IX, 127–129), expressing his great admiration, and raising the question which Rousseau goes on to discuss, whether or in what sense moral conduct is self-interested; he acknowledged Rousseau's reply in a somewhat ponderous letter dated 17 October 1761 (*CC* IX, 178–182). He subsequently published the entire correspondence, after slightly revising his own letters.

Rousseau himself evidently regarded his letter as a public statement. The original has not been found, but two manuscript copies are known, one of them in Rousseau's hand, apparently intended for inclusion in an edition of his complete works. Leigh's critical edition of the letter flags the few, essentially stylistic differences between these two copies. The present translation is based on the text in Rousseau's hand.

[9] **no one has within himself any interest in acting well, he cannot do good** Rousseau is allowing a pun to imply that acting well

is to do good: *bien faire* means "to act well"; with the order of the terms reversed, *bien* becomes a noun instead of an adverb, and the expression *faire (du) bien* means "to do good."

LETTER TO USTERI (pages 265–268)

This letter has been edited most recently and fully by R. A. Leigh in his edition of Rousseau's *Correspondance complète*, vol. XVII, pp. 62–65.

The addressee, Leonhard Usteri (1741–1789), was a Protestant minister in Zurich. The present letter speaks most specifically to questions Usteri had raised about Rousseau's views regarding the relations between Christianity and political society in letters to Rousseau dated 16 April 1763, 30 April 1763, and especially in one dated 23 June 1763.

[1] Paul-Claude **Moultou** (1731–1787), Protestant minister in Geneva, one of Rousseau's closest and steadiest friends. **Sauttern** is Jean-Ignace Sauttermeister de Sautersheim (1738–1767), a young Hungarian Baron or pseudo-Baron whom Rousseau befriended: *Confessions* XII, *OC* I, 615–618.

[5] **our Lord ... blessed the poor in spirit** *Matthew* 5:3.

[7] **I can refer you to my Book** *SC* IV 8 [22]–[30]. **Mucius Scaevola ... breaking the siege of Rome** By the Etruscan king Lars Porsena who was trying to restore the Tarquins to power in Rome (in 507 BC); Livy, *Histories* II, 13; Seneca, *On Providence* III, 5; and see Editorial Note to *First Discourse* [53]; **great-souled Judith** saved her people by seducing and beheading Halophorness, the Assyrian general who was besieging the Jewish city of Bethulia; her story is told in the *Book of Judith* of the *Apocrypha*.

[8] **everyone always ends up adhering to the same sentiment as before.** One of the ms. drafts of this letter goes on at this point: "Besides, however much you may be a philosopher, I feel that one always has to be somewhat attached to the state." [*D'ailleurs quelque philosophe que vous puissiez être, je sens qu'il faut toujours un peu tenir à l'état.*]

[10] **M. Gessner's ... kind offer** Salomon Gessner (1730–1788), a poet living in Zurich, had had the idea of having Rousseau's works printed in Zurich.

LETTER TO MIRABEAU (pages 268–271)

Recent editions of this *Letter* are C. E. Vaughan, *Jean Jacques Rousseau: Political Writings*, vol. II, pp. 159–162; R. A. Leigh, *CC* XXXIII, 238–246.

Victor Riquetti, Marquis de Mirabeau (1715–1789), the physiocrat known ever since the publication of his first work, *L'Ami des hommes ou Traité de la population [The Friend of Men or Treatise on Population]* (1756–1758), as "The friend of men"; which is how Rousseau refers to him at one point in this *Letter*.

This is Rousseau's only properly speaking political letter to Mirabeau. Their correspondence began with a most remarkable, highly personal letter from Mirabeau, generously offering Rousseau, who at that time was a refugee in England, hospitality in one of his properties (27 October 1776). Rousseau was clearly touched, and answered in an equally personal vein.

Mirabeau replied to the present letter extraordinarily promptly, on 30 July 1767, with a lengthy, detailed and characteristically personal summary of the physiocratic principles of his master François Quenais – to whom he refers as "the venerable Confucius of Europe." He subsequently published both this letter of Rousseau's and his reply to it: see Rousseau's letter to Moultou, 14 February 1769.

[1] **the book you sent me** *L'Ordre naturel et essentiel des Sociétés politiques [The Natural and Essential Order of Political Societies]* by Mercier de la Rivière (London, 1767); **what the evidence is on which legal despotism is supposed to be based; and nothing seemed to me less evident than the chapter devoted to all this evidence.** de la Rivière calls rule according to necessary laws "legal despotism"; Euclid ruling all enlightened people with his geometrical truths exercises legal despotism: ch. 25, p. 185. **what will happen to all your sacred rights of property in times of great danger** de la Rivière bases all society on the right to property and, like Locke, he bases the right to property on everyone's exclusive property in his own person: ch. 2. **"Let the salvation of the people be the supreme law"**: the maxim of Roman public right, *salus populi suprema lex esto*.
[2] **"I see the better and approve it/but follow the worse"**: *Video meliora proboque,/deteriora sequor*: Ovid, *Metamorphoses* VII, 20–21.
[4] **the great problem of Politics, which I compare to that of squaring the circle in Geometry** Cp. *Poland* 1 [5] **and of longitudes in Astronomy** i.e. of how, in an age of less than fully reliable timepieces, to ascertain one's longitude, especially on the high seas.

[13] **I am afraid that it will lead to rather different countries than those toward which you claim to go.** The first draft of the letter goes on at this point: "Therefore I regret to tell you that as long as monarchy endures in france [sic] it will never be adopted there": Vaughan, *Rousseau: Political Writings*, vol. II, p. 162, n. 3; Leigh, *CC*, vol. XXXIII Letter 5991 *bis*, n. 56.

LETTER TO M. DE FRANQUIÈRES (pages 272–285)

This letter has been edited by P.-M. Masson in his classical *La "Profession de foi du Vicaire savoyard"* (Librairie de l'Université, Fribourg, 1914), pp. 513–536; Henri Gouhier edited it for the Pléiade *Oeuvres complètes*, vol. IV, pp. 1133–1147; Ralph Leigh's edition in his *Correspondance complète*, vol. XXXVII, pp. 13–24, faithfully reproduces Rousseau's orthography and punctuation. Leigh has identified the addressee as one Laurent Aymon de Franquières.

Renou The warrant issued for Rousseau's arrest by the Parliament of Paris in 1762 was still in effect, and Rousseau had therefore been advised to go under an assumed name upon his return to France from England in 1768.

[5] **necessary motion, an expression of which . . . I have never made any sense.** It is a premise of the materialists, in contrast to the deists' premise which Rousseau adopts in [17] of this *Letter*, that God is required to impart motion to matter; Diderot speaks of "essential" motion in his *Pensées philosophiques* XVIII and XXI; the latter being the *pensée* which Rousseau repeatedly singles out as particularly important: see [11] below, with the editorial note. **a Clarke** Samuel Clarke (1675–1729), disciple and friend of Newton's, he attacked materialism in the name of what he called the mathematical principles of philosophy, and in this connection he criticized Locke's speculation about thinking matter; in his *Discourses Concerning the Being and Attributes of God* (1706) he endeavored to prove the existence of God in as mathematical a manner "as the subject matter allows." **regardless of what Locke may say on the subject, the assumption of thinking matter is a genuine absurdity.** see *Letter to Voltaire* [8] and the Editorial Note; Rousseau returns to the problem of thinking matter in [13] below.

[8] **because they have no need of it.** i.e. of knowing God. The French is equivocal: it can equally well be read as saying "because they have no need of him" i.e. of God.

[9] ***Coeli enarrant*** "The heavens declare" the glory of God: *Psalm* 19.1

[10] **the dictamen of your conscience** Rousseau regularly refers to the dictate of conscience as its dictamen.

[11] **Diogenes walk as his only reply to Zeno who denied motion** Rousseau considers this episode from a different point of view in *Languages* 1 [7]. **Bishop Berkeley ... maintains that there are no bodies** Rousseau had made the same point in *First Discourse* [57]. **the author of the *Pensées philosophiques*** Rousseau does not name the author because Diderot had published the *Pensées* anonymously; he also discusses Diderot's materialist argument in *Voltaire* [30].

[13] **You Epicurean, you make up the soul with subtle atoms** Specifically, Lucretius, *On the Nature of Things* III, 179, 206f., 209; Lucretius recognizes the difficulty to which Rousseau here calls attention: *ib.* III 176–257. **You Modernist, you show me an organic molecule** The challenge is directed specifically at Buffon, who had formulated the theory of organic molecules to account for the generation of living beings in his *Histoire naturelle générale et particulière* (1749), especially chs. 2–4, Buffon *OP*, pp. 238b–256a; Rousseau's wording echoes Buffon's formulations.

[14] **When I examined all this closely** In *Ineq.* I [19] and *Voltaire* [8].

[16] **the likes of Fénelon, of Cato, of Socrates** Fénelon (1651–1715) wrote on education, politics and religion. His *Adventures of Telemachus* served as one of the models for Rousseau's *Emile*. Although his defense of religious "quietism" brought him into conflict with the ecclesiastical authorities, he remained Archbishop of Cambrai. In his *Traité de l'existence et des attributs de Dieu* (I, 1) he discusses and rejects the Epicurean arguments about the origin of the visible universe which Rousseau mentions in the *Letter to Voltaire* [30], and again in the present *Letter* [11]. Rousseau consistently expressed great admiration for Fénelon. On Cato and Socrates, see especially *Pol. Ec.* [30] and the Introduction, p. xxx.

[17] **I recall ... meeting up ... with this question of the origin of evil ...** see especially the *Letter to Voltaire*.

[21] **Titus** (39–81), Emperor of Rome (79–81), **making the Roman people happy ... might not waste a single day, and yet not be virtuous; he certainly was so in sending back Berenice.** He would say he had wasted his day if it went by without his doing some good; see also *Last Reply* [57]*. Titus wanted to marry Berenice, the niece and widow of Herod, but did not lest his doing so offend the Roman people; an action about which Racine and Corneille each wrote a tragedy. Rousseau discusses Racine's play in his *Letter to d'Alembert*, *OC* V, 48–50. **Brutus causing his children to be put to death may**

have been more than just. But Brutus was a tender father See *Last Reply* [54]–[56] with the Editorial Note.

[22] Will he end up like Joseph, and leave his coat? When he fled the attempts by Potiphar's wife to seduce him: *Genesis* 39:12-20.

[23] Do you sometimes read Plato's *Republic*? . . . Socrates's friend, whose name I have forgotten, Glaucon, depicts to him the just beset by the outrages of fortune and the injustices of men . . . *Republic* II, 359b–362c Socrates . . . believes he has to invoke the Gods before answering; he says it would be impious of him not come to the assistance of justice: *Republic* II, 368b but without the hope of another life – with which the *Republic* begins (328e–331b) and ends (608d–621d).

[25] you give every advantage to the second. Rousseau wrote "to the first"; all editors agree this was a slip of the pen.

[26] according to me, Jesus . . . very positively declared that he would not perform any [miracles] Rousseau discusses and documents this claim most fully in *LM* III (*OC* III, 735–736); on miracles in general, see especially *SC* II 7 [11].

Index of editors, translators, and annotators

Italic page numbers refer to the Editorial Notes

323

General index

This index lists most occurrences of significant terms, concepts or names. Occasionally the indexed term occurs more than once on the listed page. **Bold** type indicates more important occurrences of the indexed term. As a rule Rousseau's first use of a significant term, concept or name is accompanied by an Editorial Note identifying it. The reader is urged to consult the Editorial Notes alongside the text, as index entries do not always refer to them. Page references to the Editorial Notes are in *italics*. An asterisk (*) indicates a footnote of Rousseau's. Whenever necessary, such a footnote is further identified by paragraph: 150[31]* refers to Rousseau's first footnote in the paragraph marked [31] on page 150.

active principle 280
 see also God
Adam 43
 the children of Adam 270
aerarium see public treasury
Aeschylus 182
aggregation/association 48, 49, 50
Agis, King of Sparta 137
agriculture 224f
aim of the political association *see* end of
 the political association
Alembert, Jean Le Rond d' 51*
alienate, alienation
 oneself or one's freedom 44–46
 oneself and all one's rights to the
  community 50, 56, **61**, **63**
 not to a superior or master 116
 see also inalienable
America, savages of northern 92

amour propre xvi, 196
 and reciprocity xviii
 and patriotism xxif
 and doing what one ought 261, 272
analytic method **163**, *297*, *308*
anarchy 83, 108, 255
 of Poland 178, 183, 193, 199, 216–220
 its causes 198f, 216–221
ancient
 virtues 16, 219
 fiscal parsimoniousness 27
 governments 13
  did not even know the word
   "finance" 225
  /modern governments' use of
   public opinion 142
 /modern men and lawgivers 180–182
 citizens/modern estates 221
 skeptics 272

illegitimate
  forced taxation 25, 30
  profits 36
  consequences of irrational conduct 45
  alleged right of slavery 48
  see also legitimate
imperial capitulations 214
  see also pacta conventa
imposteurs 37
imprescriptible, the law of nature 196
inalienable
  one's children or their freedom 45
  sovereignty 57, **116**
inconvenience(s) 5, **26**, 33, 34, 97, 100,
    110, 114, **115**, 128, 163, 200,
    202, 208, 250, 253
  the advantages inseparable from them
    193
indignation 162
inequality
  physical or natural 56
  of fortunes 19, 94
  natural/instituted 92
  earned 186f, 188
  see also equality
interest(s) xvi, xvii, 14
  private/public 19, 25, 48, 57, 60[2]*,
    121, 180, 250
  private /general good **155f**
  apparent/rightly understood 159, 269
  common 16, 57, 121, 122
  /duty 8, 15, 52
  /right 41
  /justice 62
  whether moral conduct is
    (self)interested or not 261–265,
    269
  forms of (self)interest 226, **261f**, 263f
intermediate orders 96
internal voice, assent, judgment,
    sentiment 158, 277f, 283
  /proof 280
  see also dictamen
intolerance, theological and civil are the
    same 143, 151

James II, King of England 59
Jephtha 143, *304*
Jesus xxvf, xxx, 144
  his project to establish a spiritual
    kingdom on earth 144, 284

which became the most violent
    despotism on earth 144
  separated the theological from the
    political system 144
  and has divided the sovereignty ever
    since 144f
  kings have tried to reassert their
    sovereignty, but failed 145
  performed no miracles 285
  /Socrates 283–285
  see also Christianity
Jews 143f
Joseph
  economic policies 28
  leaving his coat behind 282
Judas 266
judges 221f
Judith 267, *318*
juries 263f
just/unjust
  rule of what is just and what unjust is
    the general will 6
  how the notions of it are acquired
    160f
  its true principles based on the
    fundamental and universal law of
    the greatest good of all 161
justice xiiif
  universal *299*
  from God or reason xiiif, 66, *399*
  notion of, based on reciprocity xviif,
    10, **61f**
  general will, rule of justice for
    domestic relations 7
  general will, rule of what is just and
    what unjust 6
  and law 10, **160**
  requires severity 15
  /pity xxviii
  law of nature, rule of justice in
    foreign relations 7
  /utility xvi
  distributive 210
  the maxim of **190**
  see also merit; promotions
Justinian 158

Kant, Immanuel xxxviiif, xliv, xlvi
king(s)
  large States cannot do without them
    211

Cambridge Texts in the History of Political Thought

Titles published in the series thus far

Aristotle *The Politics* and *The Constitution of Athens* (edited by Stephen Everson)

Arnold *Culture and Anarchy and other Writings* (edited by Stefan Collini)

Astell *Political Writings* (edited by Patricia Springborg)

Austin *The Province of Jurisprudence Determined* (edited by Wilfrid E. Rumble)

Bakunin *Statism and Anarchy* (edited by Marshall Shatz)

Baxter *A Holy Commonwealth* (edited by William Lamont)

Beccaria *On Crimes and Punishments and other Writings* (edited by Richard Bellamy)

Bentham *A Fragment on Government* (introduction by Ross Harrison)

Bernstein *The Preconditions of Socialism* (edited by Henry Tudor)

Bodin *On Sovereignty* (edited by Julian H. Franklin)

Bolingbroke *Political Writings* (edited by David Armitage)

Bossuet *Politics Drawn from the Very Words of Holy Scripture* (edited by Patrick Riley)

The British Idealists (edited by David Boucher)

Burke *Pre-Revolutionary Writings* (edited by Ian Harris)

Christine de Pizan *The Book of the Body Politic* (edited by Kate Langdon Forhan)

Cicero *On Duties* (edited by M. T. Griffin and E. M. Atkins)

Constant *Political Writings* (edited by Biancamaria Fontana)

Dante *Monarchy* (edited by Prue Shaw)

Diderot *Political Writings* (edited by John Hope Mason and Robert Wokler)

The Dutch Revolt (edited by Martin van Gelderen)

Early Greek Political Thought from Homer to the Sophists (edited by Michael Gagarin and Paul Woodruff)

The Early Political Writings of the German Romantic (edited by Frederick C. Beiser)

Ferguson *An Essay on the History of Civil Society* (edited by Fania Oz-Salzberger)

Filmer *Patriarcha and other Writings* (edited by Johann P. Sommerville)

Sir John Fortescue *On the Laws and Governance of England* (edited by Shelley Lockwood)

I

Fourier *The Theory of the Four Movements* (edited by Gareth Stedman Jones and Ian Patterson)

Gramsci *Pre-Prison Writings* (edited by Richard Bellamy)

Guicciardini *Dialogue on the Government of Florence* (edited by Alison Brown)

Harrington *A Commonwealth of Oceana* and *A System of Politics* (edited by J. G. A. Pocock)

Hegel *Elements of the Philosophy of Right* (edited by Allen W. Wood and H. B. Nisbet)

Hobbes *Leviathan* (edited by Richard Tuck)

Hobhouse *Liberalism and other Writings* (edited by James Meadowcroft)

Hooker *Of the Laws of Ecclesiastical Polity* (edited by A. S. McGrade)

Hume *Political Essays* (edited by Knud Haakonssen)

King James VI and I *Political Writings* (edited by Johann P. Sommerville)

John of Salisbury *Policraticus* (edited by Cary Nederman)

Kant *Political Writings* (edited by H. S. Reiss and H. B. Nisbet)

Knox *On Rebellion* (edited by Roger A. Mason)

Kropotkin *The Conquest of Bread and other Writings* (edited by Marshall Shatz)

Lawson *Politica sacra et civilis* (edited by Conal Condren)

Leibniz *Political Writings* (edited by Patrick Riley)

Locke *Political Essays* (edited by Mark Goldie)

Locke *Two Treatises of Government* (edited by Peter Laslett)

Loyseau *A Treatise of Orders and Plain Dignities* (edited by Howell A. Lloyd)

Luther and Calvin on Secular Authority (edited by Harro Höpfl)

Machiavelli *The Prince* (edited by Quentin Skinner and Russell Price)

de Maistre *Considerations on France* (edited by Isaiah Berlin and Richard Lebrun)

Malthus *An Essay on the Principle of Population* (edited by Donald Winch)

Marsiglio of Padua *Defensor minor* and *De translatione Imperii* (edited by Cary Nederman)

Marx *Early Political Writings* (edited by Joseph O'Malley)

Marx *Later Political Writings* (edited by Terence Carver)

James Mill *Political Writings* (edited by Terence Ball)

J. S. Mill *On Liberty*, with *The Subjection of Women* and *Chapters on Socialism* (edited by Stefan Collini)

Milton *Political Writings* (edited by Martin Dzelzainis)

Montesquieu *The Spirit of the Laws* (edited by Anne M. Cohler, Basia Carolyn Miller and Harold Samuel Stone)

More *Utopia* (edited by George M. Logan and Robert M. Adams)

Morris *News from Nowhere* (edited by Krishan Kumar)

Nicholas of Cusa *The Catholic Concordance* (edited by Paul E. Sigmund)

Nietzsche *On the Genealogy of Morality* (edited by Keith Ansell-Pearson)

Paine *Political Writings* (edited by Bruce Kuklick)

Plato *Statesman* (edited by Julia Annas and Robin Waterfield)

Price *Political Writings* (edited by D. O. Thomas)

Priestley *Political Writings* (edited by Peter Miller)

Proudhon *What is Property?* (edited by Donald R. Kelley and Bonnie G. Smith)

Pufendorf *On the Duty of Man and Citizen According to Natural Law* (edited by James Tully)

The Radical Reformation (edited by Michael G. Baylor)

Rousseau *"The Discourses" and other early political writings* (edited by Victor Gourevitch)

Rousseau *"The Social Contract" and other later political writings* (edited by Victor Gourevitch)

Seneca *Moral and Political Essays* (edited by John Cooper and John Procope)

Sidney *Court Maxims* (edited by Hans W. Blom, Eco Haitsma Mulier and Ronald Janse)

Spencer *Man versus the State* and *The Proper Sphere of Government* (edited by John Offer)

Stirner *The Ego and its Own* (edited by David Leopold)

Thoreau *Political Writings* (edited by Nancy Rosenblum)

Utopias of the British Enlightenment (edited by Gregory Claeys)

Vitoria *Political Writings* (edited by Anthony Pagden and Jeremy Lawrance)

Voltaire *Political Writings* (edited by David Williams)

Weber *Political Writings* (edited by Peter Lassman and Ronald Speirs)

William of Ockham *A Short Discourse on Tyrannical Government* (edited by A. S. McGrade and John Kilcullen)

William of Ockham *A Letter to the Friars Minor and Other Writings* (edited by A. S. McGrade and John Kilcullen)

Wollstonecraft *A Vindication of the Rights of Men* and *A Vindication of the Rights of Woman* (edited by Sylvana Tomaselli)